Microeconomics:
A Contemporary Introduction
Sixth Edition

William A. McEachern

University of Connecticut

Prepared by

John Lunn

Hope College

THOMSON

SOUTH-WESTERN

Australia · Canada · Mexico · Singapore · Spain · United Kingdom · United States

SOUTH-WESTERN ™
THOMSON LEARNING

Study Guide to accompany Microeconomics: A Contemporary Introduction, 6e

William A. McEachern

Editor-in-Chief:
Jack Calhoun

VP, Team Director:
Michael P. Roche

Acquisitions Editor:
Michael W. Worls

Sr. Developmental Editor:
Susanna C. Smart

Sr. Production Editor:
Elizabeth A. Shipp

Exec. Marketing Manager:
Lisa L. Lysne

Media Technology Editor:
Vicky True

Media Developmental Editor:
Peggy Buskey

Media Production Editor:
Pam Wallace

Manufacturing Coordinator:
Sandee Milewski

Design Project Manager:
Michael H. Stratton

Cover Design:
Tin Box Studio/Cincinnati, Ohio

Cover Image:
Digital Vision

Production House:
DPS Associates, Inc.

Printer:
Patterson Printing

CONTENTS

PREFACE

The purpose of this *Study Guide* is to provide a review of the materials in the textbook, exercises for you to practice using the analytical tools presented in the text, and an opportunity for you to check your understanding of the material. Each chapter in the *Study Guide* contains an introduction; an outline of the text chapter; a discussion of the chapter's topics; some extensions or examples of materials in the text in a section entitled "Lagniappe" (which is a French term used in Louisiana—it means "a little extra," something added for good measure); a list of key terms; review questions; and answers to all the questions.

You should always read the text before using the *Study Guide*. The discussion section presented in the *Study Guide* is not a substitute for the textbook. In fact, you will be unable to answer some of the questions in the *Study Guide* if you have not read the text. Work through the questions and answers carefully, making sure that you understand why the correct answers are correct. Note, too, that the answers to the discussion questions are suggestive rather than full and complete.

Thanks to my wife Sheryl and my children—Robert, David, and Shelley—for putting up with my grumbling when I had trouble coming up with just one more multiple-choice question. Thanks also to Elizabeth Husa for help in preparing the manuscript for publication.

John Lunn

CHAPTER 1

The Art and Science of Economic Analysis

I. INTRODUCTION

This chapter presents an overview of economics and explains how economic analysis is performed. In particular, it introduces the concept of the economic problem and an important type of economic analysis: marginal analysis. There is also an appendix that discusses how graphs are used. Other tools of economic analysis are presented in the next chapter.

II. OUTLINE

1. The Economic Problem. Because resources are scarce and human wants are unlimited, people cannot have everything they want. Economics is the study of how individuals choose to use their scarce resources in an attempt to satisfy their unlimited wants.

    1.1   Resources
        a.   Labor (physical and mental effort). Payments to labor are called *wages*.
        b.   Capital. Payments to capital are called *interest*.
            (1)   Physical capital (manufactured items used in the production of goods)
            (2)   Human capital (knowledge and skills people acquire to enhance their ability to produce)
        c.   Land (includes all natural resources). Payments to land are called *rent*.
        d.   Entrepreneurial ability (the talent of a person who tries to discover and exploit profitable activities). Payments for entrepreneurial ability are called *profit*.

    1.2   Goods and Services
        a.   Goods and services are produced to satisfy human wants.
        b.   Goods are tangible; services are intangible.
        c.   Both goods and services require scarce resources and are therefore themselves scarce.
        d.   Without scarcity there would be no economic problem.

    1.3   Economic Decision Makers
        a.   There are four types of decision makers in the economy: households, firms, governments, and the rest of the world.
        b.   Markets are the means by which buyers and sellers carry out exchanges.

    1.4   Simple Circular-Flow Model
        a.   The circular-flow model describes the flow of resources, products, income, and revenue among households, firms, government, and the rest of the world.
        b.   The flows of resources in one direction are offset by flows of money in the other direction.

2.　The Art of Economic Analysis

    2.1　Rational Self-Interest
        a.　Economists assume that individuals act in their own best interests.
        b.　Economists also assume that individuals are rational, which means that people try to make the best choices possible under the circumstances.

    2.2　Choice Requires Time and Information

    2.3　Economic Analysis Is Marginal Analysis
        a.　Marginal means "incremental" or "extra."
        b.　An individual changes his or her behavior whenever the expected marginal benefit from doing so is greater than the expected marginal cost.

    2.4　Microeconomics and Macroeconomics
        a.　Microeconomics is the study of how individual economic agents make decisions and how the choices of various decision makers are coordinated.
        b.　Macroeconomics is the study of the economy as a whole.

3.　The Science of Economic Analysis

    3.1　The Role of Theory
        a.　A theory, or model, is a simplification of reality that focuses on the most important features of a relationship.
        b.　Theory is needed to determine which facts are relevant in a relationship.
        c.　Theory is also used to make predictions about the real world.

    3.2　The Scientific Method
        a.　Step One: Identify the question and define the relevant variables. (A variable is a quantity that can take on different possible values.)
        b.　Step Two: State the assumptions that specify the conditions under which the theory is to apply.
            (1)　*Ceteris paribus*: other things are held constant
            (2)　Behavioral assumption: a notion concerning individual behavior that is taken to be true; for example, rational self-interest
        c.　Step Three: Formulate hypotheses about relations among the key variables.
        d.　Step Four: Test the theory.

    3.3　Normative Versus Positive Analysis
        a.　A positive statement is one that can be verified by referring to the facts.
        b.　A normative statement is a statement representing someone's opinion or values; it cannot be proved or disproved.

    3.4　Economists Tell Stories

    3.5　*CASE STUDY:* A Yen for Vending Machines

    3.6　Predicting Average Behavior
        a.　Economic theories do not permit an economist to predict the behavior of individuals because any individual may behave in unpredictable ways.
        b.　The random behaviors of individuals tend to cancel each other, so the average behavior of a large group can be predicted.

3.7 Some Pitfalls of Faulty Economic Analysis
    a. Fallacy That Association Is Causation. It is a mistake in analysis to think that one event caused another simply because the first event preceded the second.
    b. Fallacy of Composition. It is erroneous to believe that what is true for the individual is true for the group.
    c. Mistake of Ignoring the Secondary Effects. Economic analysis should not ignore secondary effects, which develop slowly over time as people react to events.

3.8 If Economists Are So Smart, Why Aren't They Rich? The economics profession thrives because its models usually do a better job of explaining the real world than do alternative approaches.

3.9 *CASE STUDY:* College Major and Career Earnings

4. Appendix: Understanding Graphs. Graphs are a way of compressing information.

4.1 Drawing Graphs. Graphs can express three types of relations between two variables:
    a. Positive (direct) relation: as one variable increases, the other variable increases.
    b. Negative (inverse) relation: as one variable increases, the other variable decreases.
    c. Independent relation: as one variable increases, the other remains constant; the variables are unrelated.

4.2 The Slopes of Straight Lines. Slope is the change in the vertical distance between two points divided by the corresponding change in the horizontal distance between the points.

4.3 The Slope, Units of Measurement, and Marginal Analysis
    a. The mathematical value of the slope depends on the units of measurement on the graph; e.g., the slope of a line relating price and output will be different if output is measured in feet than if it is measured in yards.
    b. The slope measures the marginal effects, so it is important in economic analysis.

4.4 The Slopes of Curved Lines
    a. Slope of a curved line is different for each point on the curve.
    b. Slope of a curved line at a point is found by measuring the slope of a straight line tangent to the curve at the point.

4.5 Curve Shifts. A curve can shift when a variable not measured on the horizontal or vertical axis changes.

III. DISCUSSION

The Economic Problem

Two facts of life create the economic problem: scarce resources and unlimited human wants. Resources are combined to produce *goods* and *services*. Since resources are scarce, not all goods and services that people desire can be produced; that is, goods and services are also scarce. Consequently, individuals must make choices. Even though we cannot have everything we want, we can have some of the things we want.

Households, firms, governments, and the rest of the world are the four economic actors in the economy. Households act both as consumers who demand the goods and services produced and as resource owners who supply resources to firms and government. Everybody owns at least one productive resource: his or her own labor. Firms supply goods and services to consumers by hiring resources to produce them. The government provides some goods and services, such as national defense, that tend not to be produced by private firms. The government also makes and enforces rules to be followed by other economic actors. The rest of the world includes foreign households, firms, and governments. The circular-flow model shows the flow of resources, products, incomes, and revenues among the economic actors—households, firms, government, and the rest of the world.

Buyers and sellers come together to carry out exchange in *markets*. Some markets—farmers' markets, for example—are physical places with specific geographic locations. Other markets are less concrete and consist of communications by individuals thousands of miles apart. For example, people can order books from a book club through the mail.

The Art of Economic Analysis

Economists assume that people are motivated by self-interest. This means that they not only act selfishly, but that they also make choices that will make them better off, as they themselves define "better off." Religious or political zealots who risk their lives for a cause presumably do so because they believe they will be better off for doing so. Self-interest, by itself, does not allow us to make predictions or to explain human behavior adequately. However, when the assumption of rationality is added, we can begin to analyze and explain human behavior. By "rational" we mean consistent and reasonable. If we assume that people behave consistently, then we can predict how they will change their behavior when they face different economic environments.

Rational choice takes time and information. A choice can be a poor one if a decision maker lacks good information. The collection and assimilation of information take time and use up resources. Rational individuals collect information from a variety of sources as long as the expected marginal benefit of doing so exceeds the expected marginal cost.

It is very rare for people to have to make all-or-nothing decisions. Instead, decisions usually involve choices between the status quo and something else. One chooses among having apple pie for dessert, cake for dessert, or no dessert at all. A decision is made on the basis of a comparison of the extra (marginal) benefits and the extra (marginal) costs of the contemplated change. When marginal benefits exceed marginal costs, the individual makes the change.

Economics is broken down into two parts: *microeconomics* and *macroeconomics*. Microeconomics concerns the economic behavior of individual decision makers, such as the consumer, the worker, and the manager of a firm. Macroeconomics examines the economic system as a whole and tries to explain unemployment, inflation, and economic growth.

The Science of Economic Analysis

An economy as large, diverse, and interrelated as the U.S. economy is too complex for any individual to understand. There is so much economic data that people cannot understand the reason for every transaction. A *theory* is used to reduce the complexity of an economic system to manageable limits. Consequently, a theory does not contain all relevant details and facts. A theory attempts to simplify economic reality by capturing the essential features of economic relations.

Economic analysis follows the scientific method, which can be broken down into four steps. First, the specific economic question must be identified and the relevant *variables* must be defined. Second, the assumptions that specify the conditions under which the theory applies must be identified. In economics, it is common to employ the assumption of *ceteris paribus*, which means "other things held constant." For example, when we say that a higher price for a good causes fewer units of the good to be sold, we hold income and tastes, among other things, constant. Third, hypotheses about the relations among variables are stated. These generally take the form of if-then statements. Fourth, the hypotheses are tested.

Economists distinguish between positive economic statements and normative economic statements. *Positive economic statements* are associated with economic theory and involve facts or predictions that are testable. *Normative economic statements* involve value judgments and opinions. The statement "Tariffs on imported steel will increase employment in the U.S. steel industry" is an example of a positive statement. "Higher tariffs should be placed on imported steel" is an example of a normative statement.

Economics is a social science that attempts to explain economic behavior. But human beings are complex and individuals are unique in many ways. Economists try to explain and predict the average behavior of people. Specific individuals may not behave as expected even though the average behavior of people is predicted well.

It is easy to fall into several traps that lead to incorrect economic thinking. The *association-causation fallacy* is common. It is especially easy to fall into this trap when one event precedes another in time. It can even be the case that the second event caused the first event. For example, if one observed that many people at the race track were betting on a particular horse and then observed that that particular horse won the race, it would be erroneous to conclude that the horse won because many people bet on it. Rather, people expected the horse to win so they bet on the horse. Another common error is the *fallacy of composition*, which is the mistaken belief that what is true for the individual is also true for the group. One person can see a football game better by standing up, but if everyone stands nobody has a better view. Mistakes are also made when people ignore the *secondary effects* of an economic activity or policy.

Appendix: Understanding Graphs

If this is your first course in economics, read the appendix to this chapter in the textbook carefully. Economists often use *graphs* to represent relations. Graphs generally reflect a relation between two variables, such as price and quantity, money supply and interest rates, or wages and hours worked. An *independent variable* is one that has a causal effect on another variable. The other variable is called the *dependent variable* because its value depends on the value of the first variable.

A question that is often of interest in economics is whether one variable has a *positive*, or *direct*, effect on another variable or an *inverse*, or *negative*, effect. Exhibit 1 shows a line that represents a consumption function. The independent variable is income and the dependent variable is consumption expenditures. The graph represents the assumption that as a family's income increases, its consumption spending also increases. Hence, there is a direct, or positive, relation between a family's income and the amount the family spends.

Exhibit 1

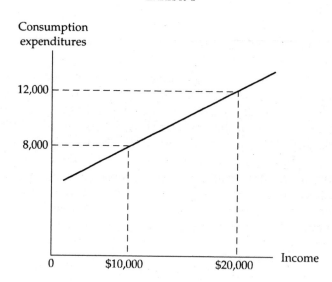

A negative, or inverse, relation is illustrated in Exhibit 2. Here the independent variable is hours of practice and the dependent variable is one's golf score. The more one practices, the lower the golf score will be.

Exhibit 2

The *slope* of a line is the amount the vertical variable changes for a given increase in the horizontal variable. The slope of an upward-sloping line is positive; the slope of a downward-sloping line is negative. The slope of a straight line is constant, but the slope of a curved line changes at every point. To find the slope of a curved line at a point, draw a straight line *tangent* to the point. The slope of this line is the slope of the curved line at that point. Make sure that you understand the graphs that are used in the appendix in the textbook.

IV. LAGNIAPPE

The Consumption Function

The theory of the consumption function can be used to illustrate the scientific method as it is applied in economics. John Maynard Keynes developed the theory of the consumption function during the Great Depression. He identified two key variables—consumption spending and income—and hypothesized that people spend some percentage of any increase in income on goods and save the rest. Hence, consumption is a function of income. After World War II, many economists forecasted a recession on the basis of the consumption function theory. They argued that incomes would fall after the war; this would lead to reduced consumption spending, which would reduce the incomes of even more people. However, the recession did not materialize. This caused some economists to reexamine the consumption function. Milton Friedman altered the theory by pointing out that people do not respond to temporary fluctuations in their incomes by altering consumption spending greatly. Instead, they make consumption spending decisions on the basis of their expected long-term average, or permanent, income. Once the theory was modified to include longer-term considerations, it was used more successfully in making predictions.

Question to Think About: Does the percentage of income spent on consumption goods vary with age?

Heroic Self-Interest

As stated before, the assumption of self-interest does not imply that people always behave in a selfish manner. Each person defines his or her own self-interest in a different way. Most of us probably would not consider actions that are likely to lead to our death as being in our self-interest. Yet it is possible for people to believe that. The ancient Greeks wrote of heroes who valued fame more than life and who were willing to die to gain this fame. In the story of the Trojan War, the gods had foretold that the first Greek who landed on Trojan soil would die. A young man named Protesilaos jumped ashore first so that his name would go down in history. The greatest Greek hero, Achilles, faced the option of going to Troy, where he would gain great fame and die, or staying at home, where he would live a long life and remain unknown. He chose to go to Troy. Evidently, he perceived it to be in his self-interest to gain fame rather than to die an unknown.

Question to Think About: Do you think all ancient Greeks would have made the same decision that Achilles made?

V. KEY TERMS

Scarce resources
Economics
Behavioral assumption
Land
Labor
Capital
Human capital
Entrepreneurial ability
Rent
Wages
Profit
Interest
Good
Service
Scarce
Market
Product market
Resource market
Circular-flow model
Microeconomics
Macroeconomics
Rational self-interest
Marginal

Economic theory, or economic model
Variable
Other-things-constant assumption
Hypothesis
Behavior assumptions
Positive economic statement
Normative economic statement
Association-causation fallacy
Fallacy of composition
Secondary effects
Origin
Horizontal axis
Vertical axis
Graph
Time-series graph
Functional relation
Dependent variable
Independent variable
Positive, or direct, relation
Negative, or inverse, relation
Slope
Tangent

VI. QUESTIONS

A. Completion

1. _____ is the study of how individuals use their _____ resources to satisfy their _____ wants.

2. The ultimate raw material associated with labor is _____.

3. There are two kinds of capital, _____ capital and _____ capital.

4. _____ includes management and organizational skills, combined with a willingness to take risks.

5. The entrepreneur is the _____ claimant.

6. An automobile is a _____; an airplane ride is a _____.

7. Exchange is carried out in _____.

8. A key behavioral assumption concerning human economic behavior is that of
_____.

9. Economic choice usually involves a comparison of _____ benefits and costs.

10. A _____ is a simplification of economic reality that tries to capture the most important elements of the relation under consideration.

11. A _____ is a quantity that can take on different possible values.

12. _____ are conditional statements of the if-then variety.

13. A _____ economic statement represents an opinion.

14. Unintended consequences that develop slowly over time as people respond to circumstances are called _____ effects.

15. The relation between income and consumption is _____ because increases in income lead to increases in consumption.

B. True/False

_____ 1. The economic problem results from the fact that resources are scarce but human wants tend to be limitless.

_____ 2. A student's knowledge of computer programming is an example of human capital.

_____ 3. Profit goes to the owners of capital.

_____ 4. All goods are scarce but not all services are scarce.

_____ 5. Product markets refer to specific geographic locations.

_____ 6. Microeconomics is the study of the economy as a whole.

_____ 7. People who give to charity cannot be motivated by rational self-interest.

_____ 8. A decision to go to one college instead of another is an example of a marginal decision.

_____ 9. Time is a scarce resource.

_____ 10. Rational self-interest directs people to make any choice for which the total benefits exceed the total costs.

_____ 11. Good theories contain as many details as possible.

_____ 12. Assumptions are used to simplify theories by eliminating areas that are not expected to have important effects on the analysis.

_____ 13. A theory is not good if it cannot predict accurately all the time.

_____ 14. A positive statement is one that can be verified by reference to facts.

_____ 15. If one event follows another, then the first event necessarily caused the second event.

_____ 16. Policymakers generally pay close attention to both the primary and the secondary effects of policies.

_____ *17. Two variables are independent if increases in one leave the second unchanged.

_____ *18. The slope of a vertical line is zero.

C. Multiple Choice

1. Which of the following is an example of a scarce resource?
   a. coal
   b. water
   c. unskilled labor
   d. time
   e. all of the above

2. Crude oil is considered which kind of resource?
   a. land
   b. labor
   c. physical capital
   d. human capital
   e. none of the above

3. Since goods are scarce,
   a. we always have to pay money for the goods we get.
   b. we never can get what we want.
   c. everybody wants some of each good that exists.
   d. we must choose among them.
   e. a and d

4. Services differ from goods in that services
   a. do not always use scarce resources.
   b. do not always satisfy wants.
   c. often do not have a price.
   d. are intangible.
   e. are provided by the government.

5. Markets include
   a. shopping malls.
   b. arrangements by which buyers and sellers communicate their intentions.
   c. union hiring halls.
   d. all of the above
   e. a and b only

---

*Throughout this study guide, asterisks next to question numbers indicate that the material is discussed in an appendix

6. Which of the following decisions is not consistent with rational self-interest?
   a. giving money to charity
   b. choosing to work for the Peace Corps instead of for a large corporation
   c. buying a car without knowing everything about it
   d. becoming a bullfighter
   e. All are consistent with rational self-interest.

7. Economic choices are made by comparing
   a. total benefits and total costs.
   b. marginal benefits and marginal costs.
   c. average benefits and average costs.
   d. the behavior of rational people with that of irrational people.
   e. any of the above except d.

8. People are rational if they
   a. have perfect information about the future.
   b. know and understand philosophy.
   c. are selfish.
   d. make the best choices they can given their circumstances.
   e. none of the above

9. If consumers must collect information to make rational decisions, then they should collect additional information as long as
   a. it helps them make good decisions.
   b. they learn something from the additional information.
   c. the marginal cost of the information is less than the expected marginal benefit from the information.
   d. there is anything they do not know about the good.
   e. all of the above

10. A good theory is one that
    a. best replicates reality.
    b. uses the fewest assumptions.
    c. predicts more accurately than other theories.
    d. cannot be proven wrong.
    e. all of the above

11. The validity of a theory is determined by
    a. testing the reasonableness of its assumptions.
    b. testing its predictions with evidence.
    c. making sure its variables are well defined.
    d. none of the above.
    e. all of the above.

12. *Ceteris paribus* means
    a. economic man.
    b. other things constant.
    c. the fallacy of composition.
    d. secondary effects.
    e. positive economics.

13. A positive statement is one that
    a.   can be supported or rejected with reference to the facts.
    b.   states how things ought to be.
    c.   is true.
    d.   cannot be refuted.
    e.   all economists agree on.

14. Which of the following is an example of a normative statement?
    a.   The rate of inflation is lower today than it was ten years ago.
    b.   High interest rates cause lower economic growth.
    c.   Since price controls cause shortages, the government should not use price controls to combat inflation.
    d.   Per capita income is higher in the Soviet Union than in the United States.
    e.   Tariffs result in higher prices to consumers.

15. Suppose that some individual decision makers in Los Angeles decide that removing the pollution control equipment on their cars will not have a noticeable effect on pollution in the area. Several months later pollution levels are higher than ever. The decision makers have fallen into
    a.   ignoring the secondary effects.
    b.   the fallacy that association is causation.
    c.   the fallacy of composition.
    d.   irrational self-interest.
    e.   none of the above.

16. It has been found that minimum wage laws increase unemployment among teenagers. This is an example of
    a.   ignoring the secondary effects.
    b.   the fallacy that association is causation.
    c.   the fallacy of composition.
    d.   irrational self-interest.
    e.   none of the above.

*17. In Exhibit 3, the relationship between price and quantity depicted by line *ab* is
a. positive, with slope 0.4.
b. positive, with slope –0.4.
c. inverse, with slope –2.5.
d. inverse, with slope –0.4.
e. positive, with slope 2.5.

Exhibit 3

*18. The value of a dependent variable is determined by
a. the value of the independent variable.
b. the values of other dependent variables.
c. the assumptions of the model.
d. the reliability of the theory.
e. b and d.

*19. A straight line is tangent to a curve at point *A*. If the slope of the straight line is +3, the slope of the curve at *A*
a. is between 0 and +3.
b. is equal to +3.
c. is equal to –3.
d. is more than +3.
e. The slope cannot be determined without more information.

*20. If consumption is on the vertical axis and income is on the horizontal axis, a 45-degree line represents
a. the expected relation between income and consumption.
b. the marginal benefit from another dollar of income.
c. the marginal cost of another dollar of income.
d. the best combination of income and consumption for a rational consumer.
e. the combination of points where consumption equals income.

D. Discussion Questions

1. Explain how scarcity and choice are related.

2. "You can have it all!" Do you agree or disagree with the statement? Explain

3. How are human capital and entrepreneurial ability different from labor?

4. The average college student earns a higher income than the average high school graduate. An electrician with twenty years of experience usually earns a higher wage than an electrician with five years experience. Offer an economic explanation for each.

5. The text says that a study of economic aggregates must begin with an understanding of individual choice. Why is this so?

6. Explain the concept of rational decision-making.

7. Can decisions a student makes about what to take to college be said to involve rational decision-making? Explain. How would factors such as the size of the dorm room or distance from home affect the decision about what belongings to take to college? Would seniors make different decisions than freshmen? Explain.

8. "People don't really act rationally. If they did, there would never be any mistakes." Evaluate this statement.

9. Sales of automobiles increased in December 1986 and fell in January 1987. The deductibility of sales taxes ended on December 31, 1986. Did the change in the tax laws affect sales of autos in December and January? Explain.

10. The text says that a company's decision to build a plant in Taiwan can be an example of a marginal decision. Explain how such a large investment can be described as marginal.

11. A firm is losing $5 million a year. Four executives discuss whether to increase advertising spending to stimulate sales and profits. Al says, "We should increase advertising spending if it generates more sales." Beatrice says, "We should increase advertising if the extra sales revenue are greater than the extra spending on advertising. Clyde says, "We should increase advertising spending if the extra sales revenue is greater than the extra production spending plus the extra advertising spending." Deanne says, "We should increase advertising spending only if it generates positive profits." Which executive is correct? Explain.

12. People usually spend more time deciding which car to buy than they do choosing a brand of toothpaste. Can you offer an explanation for this observation?

13. Economic theory says that a rise in the price of a good will cause people to buy less of it. If the price of meat increases and John Doe buys more meat, has the theory been refuted? Explain.

14. How are economic theory and positive statements related?

15. Stacy says, "The unemployment rate is higher today than it was during the Great Depression." Shelley says, "That is just your opinion so you are making a normative statement." Stacy counters, "No, it is a positive economic statement because it is true." Who is correct and why?

16. Discuss the four steps of the scientific method.

17. How do predictions and forecasts differ?

18. An economist and a friend are playing golf. On the third hole another golfer says to the economist, "I think interest rates will go up. Do you agree?" The economist answers, "Yes." On the eighth hole another golfer says to the economist, "I think interest rates will go down. Do you agree?" The economist answers, "Yes." On the fifteenth hole, a third golfer says to the economist, "The interest rate is 5 percent, and I think the interest rate will be 5 percent. Do you agree?" The economist answers, "Yes." At the nineteenth hole, the economist's friend asks, "You agreed that interest rates would rise, fall and stay the same. How can you agree with all these statements?" The economist answers, "I didn't say when these things would happen."
Is the economist's answer reasonable? Explain.

19. If association is not the same as causation, then how can we determine when one variable affects another?

20. The Burpee Beer Company decides to increase advertising spending to generate more sales. After a year, it notes that its costs increased but its sales didn't increase. What fallacy did they make? Explain.

*21. Use the following information to answer the question below:

x =	0	2	4	6	8	10	12	14	16	18	20
y =	0	1	2	3	4	5	6	7	8	9	10

Exhibit 4

a. Graph the relation between *x* and *y* on Exhibit 4.
b. Is this a positive or a negative relation? How do you know?
c. What is the slope of the line?

*22. You are given the following information regarding the price of eggs and the quantity purchased.

Price:	$1.00	0.90	0.80	0.70	0.60	0.50	0.40
Quantity (dozens):	1	2	3	4	5	6	7

Exhibit 5

a. Graph the relation between price and quantity purchased on Exhibit 5.
b. What is the slope of the line?

*23.   In Exhibit 6, what is the slope of the curve at point *a*? point *b*? point *c*? point *d*?

Exhibit 6

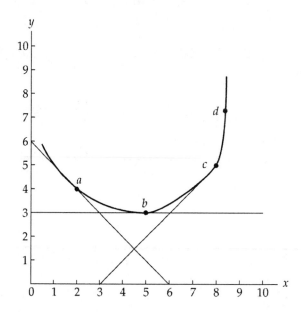

*24.   a.   Draw a curve whose slope increases with distance from the origin.
       b.   Draw a curve illustrating a direct relation whose slope decreases as the distance from the origin increases.
       c.   Draw a curve illustrating an inverse relation whose slope increases as the distance from the origin increases.
       d.   Draw a curve illustrating an inverse relation whose slope decreases as the distance from the origin increases.

VII. ANSWERS

A.   Completion

1.   Economics; scarce; unlimited
2.   time
3.   human; physical
4.   Entrepreneurial ability
5.   residual
6.   good; service
7.   markets
8.   rational self-interest
9.   marginal
10. theory (model)
11. variable
12. Predictions
13. normative
14. secondary
15. direct (positive)

B. True/False

1. True
2. True
3. False
4. False
5. False
6. False
7. False
8. True
9. True
10. False. Decisions are based on marginal benefits and marginal costs.
11. False
12. True
13. False. A theory is good not because it predicts accurately all the time but because it predicts better than other theories.
14. True
15. False
16. False
17. True
18. False

C. Multiple Choice

1.	e	6.	e	11.	b	16.	a
2.	a	7.	b	12.	b	17.	d
3.	d	8.	d	13.	a	18.	a
4.	d	9.	c	14.	c	19.	b
5.	d	10.	c	15.	c	20.	e

D. Discussion Questions

1. Scarcity implies that we cannot have everything that we want. Our resources are limited, so we must choose which of the many possible goods and services we will have. This applies to society as well as to any individual.

2. Scarcity implies that we cannot have it all. We have to make choices and decide which goods and services we will have.

3. Human capital differs from labor in that human capital involves knowledge that people acquire to increase their *ability* to produce, whereas labor refers to the human time spent in production. Entrepreneurial ability is the special talent of bringing other resources together to produce goods in new and more profitable ways.

4. Both the college graduate and the electrician with more experience have more human capital so have greater incomes than the others.

5. All choices are made by individuals. Consequently, to understand how the choices of many individuals affect the economy, it helps to know how the individual choices were made and how they interact to determine the aggregate performance.

6. Rational decision-making involves comparing the status quo with the marginal benefits and marginal costs of alternative situations. The rational individual chooses so as to make him-self or herself as well off as possible, given the constraints the individual faces.

7. A college student cannot take everything to the dorm, so the student must choose which items to take. The things that are most likely to be used at college will go; those that are less likely to be used will not go. The larger the dorm room, the more the student will take to college. Students who attend college closer to home will spend less time deciding what to take since it is relatively easy for them to make another trip home. Presumably seniors have learned what they really want and will make "better" decisions than inexperienced freshmen.

8. People do not know all possible effects of every decision. Therefore, people sometimes make mistakes. If individuals had better information, they would choose differently.

9. Yes. People who were considering the purchase of a new car were spurred to act before the end of December to avoid the tax penalty. On the margin, it was more attractive to buy a new car in December 1986 than in January 1987.

10. A new plant increases the productive capacity of a firm. If the firm wants to increase capacity, it must either build a new plant or expand an existing plant. The decision is a marginal decision since it involves a change from the status quo rather than an all-or-nothing decision.

11. Clyde is correct. Deanne is wrong because it would be better to lose $2 million than $5 million. Al is wrong because the extra costs have to be considered as well as the extra revenues. Beatrice is wrong because extra sales implies extra production, and the extra production costs have to be considered as well.

12. People make decisions on the basis of expected marginal benefits and expected marginal costs. Since the marginal costs of buying a new car are greater than those of buying a new tube of toothpaste, we expect people to inquire more about the expected benefits of the automobile.

13. No. Theory applies to people on average, not to specific individuals. There are many possible factors that could explain John Doe's behavior—he may have just quit being a vegetarian, he may have inherited a lot of money, or he may be getting ready to have a big dinner party.

14. The predictions of economic theory are positive statements, since they are capable of being tested and either upheld or refuted. Theory does not involve opinion or value judgments.

15. Both are incorrect. Stacy's statement is an example of a positive economic statement since it can be shown to be true or false by checking the facts. The statement is false, but a false statement is still a positive economic statement. Shelley is incorrect because the statement is not an opinion statement about what should be.

16. The first step is to identify and define the key economic variables. The second step is to state the assumptions, including behavioral assumptions, that specify the conditions under which the theory is to apply. Basically, this involves identifying the variables or conditions that would cause the theory not to predict as well as expected. The third step is to develop testable hypotheses about the relations among the variables. The last step is to test the theory.

17. Predictions are based on the implications of a theory and generally take the form of if-then statements. There is no expectation that the prediction will occur if the conditions are not met. A forecast is an educated guess that a certain event will actually occur.

18. The economist's answer is reasonable, even if it is not entirely satisfying. He is not making a prediction since there is not an if-then statement. The forecasts made by the three golfers were vague and each would likely come true at some point of time in the future.

19. One of the roles of theory is to identify likely causal relations. However, there will be occasions when we cannot ascertain causality.

20. This is likely the fallacy of composition. If Burpee Beer was the only brewery to increase advertising spending it is likely that their sales would have increased. But, if the other firms also increased advertising, then it is likely that the sales of all the firms would remain about the same and only their costs would have risen.

21. a.

   b.   The relation is positive because when *x* goes up, *y* goes up.
   c.   0.5

22. a.

23. Slope at point *a*: −1; at point *b*: 0; at point *c*: 1; at point *d*: infinite

24.

a. *y*

b. *y*

c. *y*

d. *y*

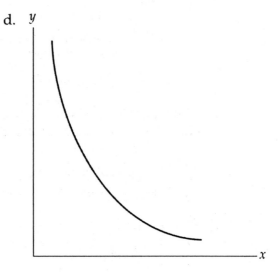

CHAPTER 2

Some Tools of Economic Analysis

I.   INTRODUCTION

The previous chapter introduced the concept of scarcity. We saw that people must make choices because of scarcity. This chapter explores the idea of choice in more detail. The cost of a choice and the tools economists use to analyze cost are discussed. The chapter also examines some of the choices that any society must make.

II.   OUTLINE

1.   Choice and Opportunity Cost

   1.1   Opportunity Cost
      a.   The opportunity cost of a choice is the benefit expected from the best alternative that is forgone.
      b.   We do what we do because we have nothing better to do. If we had something better to do, we would do it.

   1.2   *CASE STUDY:* The Opportunity Cost of College

   1.3   Opportunity Cost Is Subjective
      a.   Each individual must calculate the expected value of the best alternative for himself or herself.
      b.   Calculating opportunity cost requires time and information.
      c.   Time is the ultimate constraint.
      d.   Opportunity cost may vary with circumstance.

   1.4   Sunk Cost and Choice
      a.   A sunk cost is a cost that cannot be recovered no matter what you do.
      b.   Sunk costs should be ignored in making economic decisions.

2.   Specialization, Comparative Advantage, and Exchange

   2.1   The Law of Comparative Advantage. Combined output can increase when the individual with the lowest opportunity cost for producing a particular good specializes in producing that good.

   2.2   Absolute and Comparative Advantage
      a.   A person has an absolute advantage when he or she can perform tasks with fewer resources than another person.
      b.   A person has a comparative advantage when he or she can produce a given product at a lower opportunity cost than someone else.
      c.   Each person should specialize in the task for which he or she has a comparative advantage.

     d. The law of comparative advantage applies to firms, regions, and nations as well as to individuals.

  2.3 Specialization and Exchange
     a. *Barter* is a system in which products are exchanged directly for other products.
     b. Money is a medium of exchange because everyone is willing to accept it in exchange for goods and services. Money makes it easier to exchange goods and services.
     c. Because of comparative advantage and specialization, people do not produce most of the things they want and must enter into exchange to acquire them.

  2.4 Division of Labor and Gains from Specialization
     a. Greater specialization can be achieved through division of labor: the separating of production into various tasks and the assigning of individuals to these separate tasks.
     b. Division of labor is productive for several reasons:
       (1) Tasks can be assigned according to preferences and abilities.
       (2) As people perform the same tasks over and over, they become better at them.
       (3) There is no time lost in moving from one task to another.
       (4) Specialization of labor allows for the introduction of more sophisticated techniques.

  2.5 *CASE STUDY:* Evidence of Specialization Abounds

3.   The Economy's Production Possibilities

  3.1 Efficiency and the Production Possibilities Frontier
     a. The production possibilities frontier (PPF) describes the possible combinations of two goods that can be produced when resources are used fully and efficiently.
     b. Resources are used efficiently when they cannot be combined differently in any way that would increase the production of one good without decreasing the production of the other good.

  3.2 Inefficient and Unattainable Production
     a. Points inside the PPF represent combinations of the two goods that are produced inefficiently.
     b. Points outside the PPF represent combinations of the two goods that cannot be attained, given society's resources and technology.

  3.3 Shape of the Production Possibilities Frontier
     a. The PPF slopes down because, when resources are used fully and efficiently, more of one good can be produced only by producing less of the other good.
     b. The PPF is bowed out when not all resources are equally productive in producing both goods.
     c. The law of increasing opportunity cost applies to production of both goods: as additional units of one good are produced, more and more of the other good must be sacrificed.

  3.4 What Can Shift the Production Possibilities Frontier?
     a. Over time the PPF may shift out or in.

b. Shifts in the PPF will occur as a result of
    (1) changes in resource availability.
    (2) increases in the capital stock.
    (3) effects of technological change.

3.5 What We Can Learn from the PPF
    a. The PPF demonstrates efficiency since it describes the efficient combinations of output that are possible.
    b. The PPF demonstrates scarcity since there is a limit to what can be produced.
    c. The downward slope of the PPF indicates opportunity cost.
    d. The bowed shape of the PPF indicates the law of increasing opportunity cost.
    e. The PPF illustrates the need to make choices.
    f. Outward shifts in the PPF reflect economic growth.

3.6 Three Questions Each Economic System Must Answer
    a. What goods and services will be produced?
    b. How will goods and services be produced?
    c. For whom will goods and services be produced?
    d. These questions are interrelated, since what will be produced is often determined by the economic and social systems of the people for whom the goods are made.

4. Economic Systems

4.1 Pure Capitalism
    a. A pure capitalistic system is characterized by private ownership of resources.
    b. Coordination of economic activity is accomplished by price signals under capitalism.
    c. Markets direct decisions concerning the three economic questions.
    d. *Laissez faire* means letting people do as they choose without government intervention.

4.2 Pure Command Economy
    a. A pure command economy is an economic system characterized by public ownership of resources.
    b. Coordination is accomplished by central planning.

4.3 Mixed and Transitional Economies
    a. No society is a pure capitalist or a pure command economy.
    b. All societies mix elements of capitalism and the command economy, although the composition of the mix differs considerably.

4.4 Economies Based on Custom or Religion

III. DISCUSSION

Choice and Opportunity Cost

Everybody faces the problem of scarcity—even the very rich. Time is scarce for everyone, and any activity we engage in has an *opportunity cost* associated with it. Opportunity costs are subjective. For one student the opportunity cost of taking an economics course may be the course on Homer not taken, whereas the opportunity cost for another student may be the hours missed from work. Since the opportunity cost of any activity is the value of the best alternative choice that is forgone, and different people have different alternative choices, opportunity costs differ for different people.

The concept of opportunity cost does not mean that the choice actually made will always be the best choice. After taking economics, a student may think that she made a mistake and should have taken Homer. Often, we do not know the true value of the forsaken alternative, so occasionally we make mistakes.

Calculating opportunity costs requires time and information. The time we spend collecting information could be spent doing other things; we do not always spend enough time collecting information and we make mistakes. Opportunity costs may also vary with circumstances. The opportunity cost of studying on a rainy day is less for most people than the opportunity cost of the same activity on a beautiful Saturday afternoon.

Specialization, Comparative Advantage, and Exchange

Dividing production in accordance with the *law of comparative advantage* leads to increased production. Since all people (or firms, regions, or countries) are not equally efficient in producing all goods and services, total output is greater when each individual specializes in producing the goods or services that she or he can produce relatively more efficiently.

The law of comparative advantage applies not only to people but also to all productive resources. Suppose a farmer has two acres of land. One acre can produce 1,000 bushels of wheat, or 800 bushels of corn, or some combination of both. The second acre can produce either 600 bushels of wheat or 200 bushels of corn. Although the first acre has an *absolute advantage* in producing both crops, it has a comparative advantage in producing corn. The opportunity cost of a bushel of corn on the first acre is 1.25 bushels of wheat. For the second acre, the opportunity cost of a bushel of corn is 3 bushels of wheat. The opportunity cost of corn is less for the first acre. What about wheat? The opportunity cost of a bushel of wheat on the first acre is 0.8 bushel of corn, and the opportunity cost for the second acre is 0.33 bushel of corn. The opportunity cost of wheat is less for the second acre than for the first, so the second acre of land has a comparative advantage in producing wheat.

In order to take advantage of comparative advantage, resources must specialize. *Specialization* implies that people do not produce most of the goods and services that they wish to consume. Instead, most people specialize, exchanging a single product or service for money and then exchanging money for the goods and services that they want to consume. This specialization is generally a part of the *division of labor*. Further, most people do not produce a single product by themselves. Instead, they perform a specialized task that helps produce a good or service. In some small commuter airlines, for example, the pilot may also sell tickets, but larger airlines divide tasks and assign different individuals to perform them. As a result, the total output can be larger than it would be without division of labor.

The Economy's Production Possibilities

The *production possibilities frontier* (PPF) describes the possible combinations of two goods that can be produced with maximum efficiency. Exhibit 1 presents a PPF for an economy that produces wheat and sweaters. The curve slopes down, which indicates that the only way to get more wheat is to produce fewer sweaters. At any point on the PPF, more of one good can be produced only by producing less of the other. This is what is meant by producing the goods efficiently. The PPF is also bowed out, which reflects the *law of increasing opportunity cost*. At point *a* only sweaters are produced. If we want to produce 1,000 bushels of wheat, we see that we must give up fewer than 500 sweaters. To produce another 1,000 bushels of wheat, more than 500 sweaters must be sacrificed. Beginning at point *d*, 4,500 sweaters and 8,000 bushels of wheat, the production of sweaters must be curtailed by 2,000 units to increase wheat production by another 1,000 bushels. Between points *e* and *f*, an additional 2,500 sweaters must be sacrificed to produce yet another 1,000 bushels of wheat. In moving from point *a* to point *f*, each 1,000-bushel increase in wheat production requires sacrificing increasing numbers of sweaters. That is, the opportunity cost of wheat increases as more and more wheat is produced.

Exhibit 1

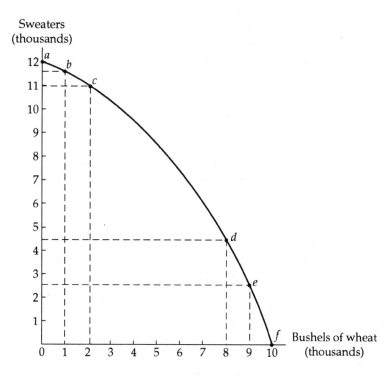

A production possibilities frontier is constructed for a given amount of resources and a given level of technology. If either the number of resources or the technology changes, the PPF shifts. The more capital a country produces in a year, the farther out the PPF shifts in future years. You should review Exhibit 2 in the text to make sure you understand these shifts.

Economic Systems

Any society must answer three basic economic questions: What goods and services will be produced and in what quantities? How will the goods be produced? For whom will the goods be produced? Not all societies answer the three basic questions in the same manner. The two extreme types of arrangement are pure capitalism and the pure command economy. Under *pure capitalism*, all productive resources are privately owned. One's income depends on the resources one owns and the prices the resources command. The more income one has, the more "votes" one has in determining the type of goods that will be produced. Markets are used to coordinate the plans of the individual members of society, and changes in prices signal individuals to alter their behavior in certain predictable ways.

A *pure command economy* operates very differently from a capitalist economy. In a pure command economy, all productive resources are owned by the government. Decisions concerning what to produce and in what quantities are made by government officials. The economy is organized so that decisions are made at the top and carried out by the people lower in the pyramid.

No society on earth today has either a pure capitalist economy or a pure command economy. Instead, all societies use a mixture of government involvement and individual decision making. In some countries, such as the United States, most exchanges are carried out through markets and most productive resources are owned by individuals. In other countries, such as the People's Republic of China, most productive resources are owned by the government and many economic decisions are made by central planners. However, there is extensive government intervention in the economy of the United States and many examples of private ownership in the People's Republic of China.

IV. LAGNIAPPE

Advantages of the Division of Labor

Adam Smith, who is credited with recognizing the advantages of the division of labor, wrote:

The great increase of the quantity of work which, in consequence of the division of labor, the same number of people are capable of performing, is owing to three different circumstances; first to the increase of dexterity in every particular workman; secondly, to the saving of the time which is commonly lost in passing from one species of work to another; and lastly, to the invention of a great number of machines which facilitate and abridge labor, and enable one man to do the work of many. [Adam Smith, *The Wealth of Nations* (Chicago: The University of Chicago Press, 1976), p. 11. Originally published in 1776.]

Question to Think About: How do these three advantages of the division of labor coincide with the four reasons given in the text?

Ricardo and Comparative Advantage

David Ricardo (1772–1823) was the first to identify comparative advantage as the source of trade. As an example, he used the production of wine and cloth in England and Portugal. If England required 100 men per year to produce cloth and 120 men per year to produce wine, and it took only 90 men per year to produce the same amount of cloth in Portugal and 80 men per year to produce the same amount of wine, then Portugal had an absolute advantage in both. However, as Ricardo noted:

It would therefore be advantageous for her (Portugal) to export wine in exchange for cloth. This exchange might even take place notwithstanding that the commodity imported by Portugal could be produced there with less labor than in England. Though she could make the cloth with the labor of 90 men, she would import it from a country where it required the labor of 100 men to produce it, because it would be advantageous to her rather to employ her capital in the production of wine, for which she would obtain more cloth from England, than she could produce by diverting a portion of her capital from the cultivation of vines to the manufacture of cloth. [David Ricardo, *The Principles of Political Economy and Taxation* (London: A. M. Dent & Sons, 1973), p. 82. Originally published in 1821.]

Question to Think About: What is the opportunity cost of wine in Portugal? in England? What is the opportunity cost of cloth in England? in Portugal?

V. KEY TERMS

Opportunity cost
Sunk cost
Law of comparative advantage
Absolute advantage
Comparative advantage
Barter
Division of labor
Specialization of labor

Production possibilities frontier (PPF)
Efficiency
Law of increasing opportunity cost
Economic system
Pure market system
Pure capitalism
Pure command economy
Mixed economy

VI. QUESTIONS

A. Completion

1. The _____ of any action is the expected benefit of the best alternative not chosen.

2. A cost that cannot be recovered no matter what you do is a _____ cost.

3. _____ is the ability to produce something with fewer resources than other producers.

4. _____ is the ability to produce something at a lower opportunity cost than other producers.

5. The _____ leads to greater output because it results in greater specialization of labor.

6. _____ is a system of exchange in which products are traded directly for other products.

7. Something that everyone is willing to accept in return for all goods and services is called a _____.

8. A society is producing on its _____ if it uses its resources fully and efficiently.

9. A bowed-out production possibilities frontier indicates that the cost of producing either good _____ as greater amounts of the good are produced.

10. Production is _____ if there is no way to rearrange resources that will allow more of one good to be produced without causing less of any other good to be produced.

11. Any economic system must decide what goods will be produced, for whom they will be produced, and _____.

12. Most societies are a mixture of _____ and _____.

13. The idea that people should be allowed to do as they choose without government interference is called _____.

14. In a command economy, resources are directed through _____.

B. True/False

_____ 1. The opportunity cost of an activity is the expected benefit from the best alternative that is forsaken.

_____ 2. The price of something is usually the best measure of the opportunity cost of the activity.

_____ 3. The opportunity cost of a given activity is usually the same for all people.

_____ 4. Opportunity cost measures the cost of the alternative given up less the expected benefit from the opportunity chosen.

_____ 5. Opportunity costs vary with circumstances.

_____ 6. Opportunity costs tend to be constant over time.

_____ 7. Comparative advantage is caused by absolute advantage.

_____ 8. The law of comparative advantage calls for specializing in the task in which one has a comparative advantage.

_____ 9. One function of money is to make it easier for exchange to take place.

_____ 10. Barter decreases as an economy becomes more specialized.

_____ 11. The division of labor allows the introduction of specialized machinery that makes workers more productive.

_____ 12. A production possibilities frontier shifts out when society moves from inefficient to efficient production.

_____ 13. A production possibilities frontier illustrates opportunity cost by sloping downward.

_____ 14. The law of increasing opportunity cost generates a production possibilities frontier that bows outward.

_____ 15. The PPF would not be bowed outward if the resources in an economy were all perfectly adaptable for the production of both goods.

_____ 16. We would expect a society's PPF to shift out over time.

_____ 17. If existing capital wears out faster than new capital is produced, the PPF will shift in over time.

_____ 18. The answer to the question of how goods are to be distributed helps shape the incentives people have to produce.

_____ 19. Under pure capitalism, market prices guide resources to their highest valued use.

_____ 20. In a pure command economy, central planners decide how a good will be produced.

C. Multiple Choice

1. The opportunity cost of a vanilla ice cream cone is
    a. a chocolate ice cream cone.
    b. a piece of apple pie.
    c. a hamburger.
    d. a gallon of gasoline.
    e. All of the above are possible.

2. Which of the following is a true statement about opportunity costs?
    a. The opportunity cost of an activity includes the expected benefit of the most attractive alternative passed up.
    b. Opportunity cost implies that people are always pleased with the decisions they make.
    c. Opportunity cost is an objective notion.
    d. When making choices, people exhaustively calculate costs and benefits for all possible alternatives.
    e. All of the above are true.

3. For a toy store, the opportunity cost of closing for a day is likely to be greatest
    a. on any given Wednesday.
    b. on any given day in February.
    c. on the second Saturday of December.
    d. on the third Friday in June.
    e. on the Fourth of July.

4. Opportunity costs are subjective because
    a. they depend on circumstances, which may vary.
    b. the best alternative may differ for different people.
    c. they do not reflect money costs.
    d. all of the above
    e. a and b only

5. Sunk costs should be ignored in making economic choices because
    a. they are usually trivial.
    b. they are marginal costs so they are not as relevant as total costs.
    c. they are not affected by the choice.
    d. they are not monetary costs.
    e. none of the above. They should not be ignored.

6. Fred and Samantha cook and clean. They have identical opportunity costs for cooking, but Samantha has an absolute advantage in cooking. We know, then, that
   a. Fred has an absolute advantage in cleaning.
   b. Fred has a comparative advantage in cleaning.
   c. Samantha has an absolute advantage in cleaning.
   d. Samantha has a comparative advantage in cleaning.
   e. None of the above. More information is needed.

7. A man has two sons, Robbie and David. Robbie can mow the lawn in 1 hour and wash the car in 50 minutes. David can mow the lawn in 40 minutes and wash the car in 30 minutes. Which statement below is true?
   a. David has an absolute advantage in both chores and a comparative advantage in mowing the lawn.
   b. David has an absolute advantage in both chores and a comparative advantage in washing cars.
   c. Robbie has an absolute advantage in both chores and a comparative advantage in mowing the lawn.
   d. Robbie has an absolute advantage in both chores and a comparative advantage in washing cars.
   e. Robbie has an absolute advantage in washing cars and David has an absolute advantage in mowing the lawn.

8. In the preceding example,
   a. Robbie should wash the car and David should mow the lawn.
   b. David should both mow the lawn and wash the car.
   c. David should wash the car and Robbie should mow the lawn.
   d. Robbie and David should share both jobs.
   e. We cannot tell who should do what chore without more information.

9. Specialization of labor implies that
   a. people must engage in exchange to acquire the goods they want.
   b. barter is an efficient way to carry out exchange.
   c. money is not a necessary part of the economy.
   d. the economy must be characterized by absolute advantage.
   e. output falls if labor is divided into too many specialized tasks.

10. Which of the following is a source of the increased productivity due to specialization of labor?
   a. People are assigned various tasks to perform so they will not get bored.
   b. Employees can be assigned tasks on the basis of the manager's preference and prejudices.
   c. People become better at a job the more they perform it.
   d. Workers can replace expensive machines in production.
   e. all of the above

11. If the opportunity cost in the United States of 1 unit of wheat is 4 units of cloth, then
   a. the opportunity cost of wheat in England is more than 4 units of cloth.
   b. the opportunity cost of wheat in England is less than 4 units of cloth.
   c. the opportunity cost of 1 unit of cloth in the United States is 1/4 unit of wheat.
   d. the United States has a comparative advantage in producing cloth.
   e. both a and d

12. If the United States has an absolute advantage in producing wheat and England has an absolute advantage in producing cloth, then
   a. neither country has a comparative advantage in either good.
   b. the United States has a comparative advantage in wheat and England has a comparative advantage in cloth.
   c. the United States should specialize in wheat and England should specialize in cloth.
   d. b and c
   e. none of the above. More information is needed.

13. Disadvantages of increased specialization include
   a. reduced standards of living.
   b. reduced contact with other people.
   c. increased job dissatisfaction.
   d. increased reliance on money.
   e. all of the above.

Exhibit 2

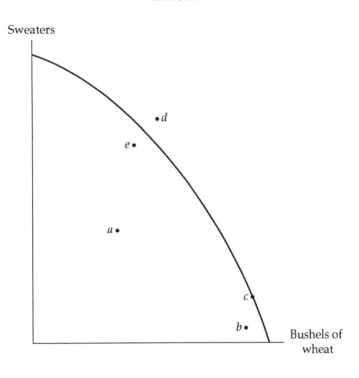

14. Which point in Exhibit 2 indicates where production is efficient?
   a. point *a*
   b. point *b*
   c. point *c*
   d. point *d*
   e. point *e*

15. Which point in Exhibit 2 cannot be attained?
    a. point *a*
    b. point *b*
    c. point *c*
    d. point *d*
    e. All points except *c* are unattainable.

Exhibit 3

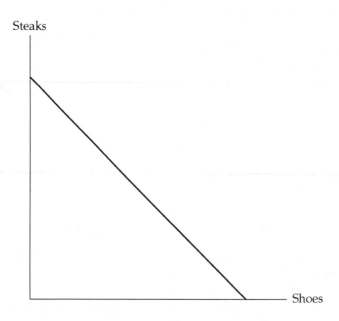

16. The production possibilities frontier in Exhibit 3 indicates
    a. the law of increasing opportunity cost.
    b. that the opportunity cost of producing shoes is constant.
    c. that production is not efficient.
    d. decreasing opportunity costs.
    e. none of the above.

17. Which of the following can cause the PPF to shift out?
    a. an increase in vacation time
    b. an increase in immigration
    c. a decrease in the retirement age
    d. migration of unskilled workers to other countries
    e. none of the above

18. In a pure capitalist economy, productive resources are owned by
    a. the government.
    b. the people collectively.
    c. individuals.
    d. the rich.
    e. the army.

19. Which of the economic questions does not have to be solved in a primitive economy?
    a. What will be produced?
    b. How will goods be produced?
    c. For whom will goods be produced?
    d. both b and c
    e. They must all be solved.

20. In which country does the government own some resources?
    a. the United States
    b. France
    c. Cuba
    d. Canada
    e. all of the above

D. Discussion Questions

1. How are opportunity cost and scarcity related?

2. The textbook says that we always do what we do because we have nothing better to do. Explain what this means.

3. Why do college enrollments often increase during economic downturns?

4. Why are the opportunity costs of law school greater than the opportunity costs of undergraduate school?

5. The textbook says, "Time is the ultimate constraint." Explain why this is so.

6. If people always choose the alternative that provides the highest expected benefit, how can mistakes ever be made?

Use the information in Exhibit 4 about production of cloth and wheat in the United States and England to answer questions 7 and 8.

Exhibit 4

Output Produced per Day by One Worker

	England	United States
Wheat	3	10
Cloth	1	2

7. a. What is the opportunity cost of wheat in England? in the United States?
    b. Which country has a comparative advantage in the production of wheat? Which has a comparative advantage in the production of cloth?
    c. If the two countries trade, which will specialize in wheat and which in cloth? Which will export wheat and which will export cloth?

8. a. Which country has an absolute advantage in wheat and which in cloth?
    b. Why is trade based on comparative advantage rather than on absolute advantage?

9. What does money have to do with specialization and comparative advantage?

10. Explain how the division of labor increases productivity.

11. Under what conditions is it possible to increase production of one good without decreasing production of another good?

12. Suppose there are two resources used in an economy: labor and capital. Capital is relatively more useful in producing wheat, whereas labor is relatively more useful in producing cloth. How will the production possibilities frontier for wheat and cloth change if the supply of capital falls by 10 percent and the supply of labor increases by 10 percent?

13. What can we learn from the production possibilities frontier?

14. Suppose 10 percent of a country's capital stock wears out every year. What will happen to the PPF in future years if the country produces new capital each year equal to 20 percent of its capital stock at the beginning of the year? if it produces new capital equal to 5 percent of its beginning capital?

15. Name the three questions all societies must answer and why they must be answered?

16. How are the three questions answered differently in a pure capitalist system and a pure command economy?

VII. ANSWERS

A. Completion

1. opportunity cost
2. sunk
3. Absolute advantage
4. Comparative advantage
5. division of labor
6. Barter
7. medium of exchange
8. production possibilities frontier
9. increases
10. efficient
11. how goods will be produced
12. capitalism; a command economy
13. laissez faire
14. central planning

B. True/False

1. True
2. False. Calculations of opportunity cost must also include the time spent away from the most valued alternative.
3. False
4. False
5. True
10. True
11. True
12. False
13. True
14. True
15. True
16. True
17. True

6.	False			18.	True		
7.	False			19.	True		
8.	True			20.	True		
9.	True						

C. Multiple Choice

1.	e	6.	c	11.	c	16.	b
2.	a	7.	b	12.	d	17.	b
3.	c	8.	c	13.	c	18.	c
4.	e	9.	a	14.	c	19.	e
5.	c	10.	c	15.	d	20.	e

D. Discussion Questions

1. Scarcity implies that we must make choices since we cannot have everything that we want. Every choice involves an opportunity cost, so opportunity costs result from scarcity.

2. At any time we have many choices available to us. The alternative that we choose is the most preferred alternative. Consequently, there is no choice better than the one we choose— we have nothing better to do. If we had something better to do, we would do it.

3. The opportunity cost of college decreases for people who lose their jobs due to the economic downturn.

4. Both law students and undergraduate students forgo earning a living while they are in school. The opportunity costs of law school are greater than those of undergraduate school, however, because undergraduate students are forgoing the relatively small salaries earned by workers with only high school diplomas, whereas law students are forgoing the salaries earned by college graduates.

5. Time is the ultimate constraint because consumption of goods and services takes time. One may have three cars but can only drive one at a time. A person can only do one thing at a time, so choices always have to be made.

6. People do not always have perfect information concerning alternatives. Information is scarce, and it takes time to collect accurate and complete information. Consequently, people sometimes make decisions that they later regret. At the time the decision is made, the person assumes it is a good decision, but events often do not turn out as expected; information can turn up later to prove a decision wrong.

7. a. Opportunity cost of wheat in England is 1/3 unit of cloth; in the United States it is 1/5 unit of cloth.
   b. The United States has a comparative advantage in the production of wheat, since the opportunity cost of producing wheat is lower in the United States. England has a comparative advantage in the production of cloth because the opportunity cost of producing cloth in England is 3 units of wheat compared to a cost of 5 units of wheat in the United States.
   c. The United States will specialize in wheat and England will specialize in cloth. The United States will export wheat and England will export cloth.

8. a. The United States has an absolute advantage in both wheat and cloth, since more of each good is produced by a worker in the United States.
   b. The cost of a good is measured not in terms of the hours of work required to produce it but rather in terms of opportunity cost, i.e., the amount of another good that must be given up to consume the first good. Basing trade on comparative advantage allows a country or producer with the lowest opportunity cost to specialize in producing a good.

9. Specialization results from comparative advantage. When people specialize, they tend to produce few of the things they consume and to consume few of the things they produce. They must rely on exchanging the goods they produce for the goods they want to consume. This would be difficult to do with a barter system, so money helps make exchange easier.

10. The division of labor allows people to work in their area of comparative advantage. By performing tasks over and over, people become better at performing them. There is also no time lost in workers' going from one task to another. Finally, the division of labor allows for the introduction of specialized machinery, which makes labor more productive.

11. We can produce more of one good without sacrificing production of another good when we are inside the PPF. If we can do so, we are either not using all available resources or not using them efficiently.

12. In the graph below, *AB* is the original PPF. The decrease in capital causes the production of wheat to fall more than the production of cloth, since capital is more efficient in producing wheat. The increase in labor causes the production of cloth to increase more than the production of wheat. The net effect is an increase in the production of cloth and a decrease in the production of wheat. *CD* is the new PPF.

Exhibit 5

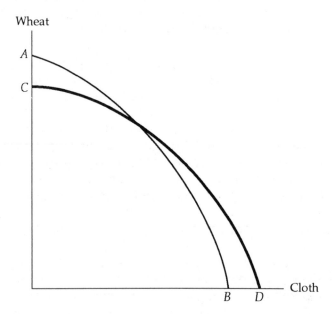

13. By showing the limits to productivity, the PPF illustrates the concept of scarcity and the need to make choices. It illustrates the concept of opportunity cost with its downward slope, and it illustrates increasing opportunity cost with its bowed-out shape. Finally, it illustrates the concept of efficiency, since there is at least one point on the PPF that is preferable to any point inside the PPF, and the concept of economic growth, since the entire PPF can shift away from the origin.

14. Annual production of new capital equal to 20 percent of the capital stock at the beginning of the year will cause the capital stock to increase by 10 percent in the future, since only 10 percent of the capital is consumed each year. The PPF will shift out the next year, indicating economic growth. A 5-percent yearly production of capital will cause the total capital stock to decrease by 5 percent in the future, since 10 percent of the capital stock is consumed each year. The PPF will shift in toward the origin.

15. Each society must decide what will be produced and in what quantities. People want goods and services, but they cannot have all they want because of scarcity. Hence, some criteria must be established to decide which goods will be produced. Different resource combinations can be used to produce a given good, so once a society decides what will be produced, it must also decide how goods will be produced. Finally, since everybody wants more than is available, society must decide who will get the goods that have been produced.

16. In a pure capitalist economy, individuals own the resources and decide how they will be used. Seeking the best places for their resources, they make their decisions on the basis of prices and changes in prices. Consumers decide what will be produced by demonstrating their willingness to pay for the goods. Entrepreneurs decide how the goods will be produced by making decisions designed to keep costs low. Goods are distributed based on incomes and the prices of the goods. The whole process is coordinated by people's responses to price changes. In a pure command economy, central planners decide what will be produced and how it will be produced. They also decide who gets what products. (The Marxist ideal is expressed by the axiom "From each according to his ability, to each according to his need.")

CHAPTER 3

Demand and Supply Analysis

I.   INTRODUCTION

The workhorses of economic analysis are the concepts of supply and demand. These tools are introduced in this chapter, although both tools will be developed much further in later chapters. Because the material in this chapter is a foundation for much of the course, be certain that you understand it and that you can use the tools developed here.

II.   OUTLINE

1.   Demand. Demand reflects the quantity of a good that people are both willing and able to buy at various prices, other things constant.

    1.1   The Law of Demand
       a.   The law of demand states that the quantity demanded of a good is inversely related to its price.
       b.   Demand differs from wants and needs.
       c.   The substitution effect of a price increase will be to encourage consumers to switch to other goods that are relatively cheaper.
       d.   A change in price also generates an income effect, since the price change affects the buying power of consumer income, or real income.

    1.2   The Demand Schedule and Demand Curve
       a.   A demand schedule indicates the quantity of a commodity that consumers wish to buy at each possible price for a given period of time.
          (1)   Demand is a rate per period of time.
          (2)   Prices of other goods are held constant.
          (3)   A demand schedule looks at the effects of a relative price change.
       b.   A demand curve provides a graphical representation of the information in a demand schedule.
       c.   *Demand* refers to the entire demand schedule or demand curve.
       d.   *Quantity demanded* refers to an individual point on the demand curve.
       e.   A change in demand occurs when the entire demand schedule or demand curve shifts.
       f.   A change in quantity demanded occurs when the price of a good changes and one moves along the demand curve.
       g.   The market demand is the sum of the individual demands of all consumers in a market.

2.   Shifts of the Demand Curve

    2.1   Changes in Consumer Income
       a.   A change in income causes the entire demand curve to shift, i.e., causes a change in demand.

    b.   If the demand for a good increases as income increases, then the good is a normal good.

    c.   If the demand for a good decreases as income increases, then the good is an inferior good.

  2.2   Changes in the Prices of Related Goods

    a.   Two goods are substitutes if they are alternative ways of satisfying a particular want.

    b.   Two goods are complements if they are used in combination to satisfy a particular want.

    c.   If an increase in the price of one good causes the demand curve for a second good to shift to the right, the two goods are substitutes.

    d.   If an increase in the price of one good causes the demand curve for a second good to shift to the left, the two goods are complements.

  2.3   Changes in Consumer Expectations

    a.   If consumers expect the price of a good to increase in the future, the demand curve for the good will shift to the right today.

    b.   If consumers expect an increase in future income, the demand curves for goods will shift to the right today.

  2.4   Changes in the Number or Composition of Consumers. The more people there are in the market, the greater the market demand.

  2.5   Changes in Consumer Tastes

    a.   Tastes are assumed to be relatively stable over time.

    b.   A change in demand cannot be attributed to a change in tastes before other possible reasons for the change are carefully considered.

3.   Supply. The law of supply states that the quantity of product supplied in a given time period is usually directly related to its price, other things constant.

  3.1   The Supply Schedule and Supply Curve

    a.   A higher price makes producers more willing to offer more for sale because they are rewarded more for doing so.

    b.   A higher price enables producers to produce more because it allows them to cover the higher marginal costs that result as quantity produced increases, according to the law of increasing opportunity costs.

    c.   The market supply is the sum of the individual supplies of all suppliers in a market.

4.   Shifts of the Supply Curve

  4.1   Changes in Technology. A technological advance is reflected by a shift to the right in the market supply curve.

  4.2   Changes in the Prices of Relevant Resources. Lower resource costs lead to a shift to the right of the supply curve.

  4.3   Changes in the Prices of Alternative Goods. An increase in the price of an alternative good raises the opportunity cost of producing other goods that use the same resources.

4.4 Changes in Producer Expectations. If producers expect the price of a good to rise in the future, current supply could increase or decrease, depending on the type of good.

4.5 Changes in the Number of Producers
   a. An increase in the number of producers increases the market supply.
   b. A change in supply is a shift of the entire supply curve; a change in the quantity supplied is a movement along a supply curve when the price of a good changes.

5. Demand and Supply Create a Market

5.1 Markets
   a. Markets coordinate the independent decisions of buyers and sellers.
   b. The transaction costs of an exchange are the costs of the time and the information required to complete the transaction.
   c. Markets reduce the transaction costs of exchange.
   d. Coordination takes place through markets by the operation of the "invisible hand" described by Adam Smith.

5.2 Market Equilibrium
   a. The equilibrium price is the price at which quantity demanded equals quantity supplied.
   b. An excess quantity supplied, or surplus, exists when the quantity supplied exceeds the quantity demanded at prices above equilibrium.
   c. An excess quantity demanded, or shortage, exists when the quantity demanded exceeds the quantity supplied at prices below equilibrium.
   d. An equilibrium is achieved through the independent actions of thousands of buyers and sellers in the economy.
   e. Markets allocate a resource to its highest valued use.

6. Changes in Equilibrium Price and Quantity

6.1 Shifts of the Demand Curve. Any shift of the demand curve, holding the supply curve constant, will change equilibrium price and quantity in the same direction as the shift of the demand curve.

6.2 Shifts of the Supply Curve. A shift in the supply curve, holding demand constant, changes equilibrium quantity in the same direction but changes equilibrium price in the opposite direction.

6.3 Simultaneous Shifts in Demand and Supply Curves
   a. When both curves shift simultaneously, the outcome depends on the nature of the shifts.
   b. If supply and demand both increase, the equilibrium quantity increases, but the effect on the equilibrium price depends on the size of the shift in demand relative to the size of the shift in supply. If both supply and demand decrease, the equilibrium quantity falls.
   c. If supply and demand shift in opposite directions, the equilibrium price rises with an increase in demand and falls with a decrease in demand. However, the effect on the equilibrium quantity depends on the size of the shift in demand relative to the size of the shift in supply.

6.4 *CASE STUDY:* The Market for Professional Basketball

7. Disequilibrium Prices

    7.1   Price Floors. Price floors, or minimum prices set by the government, tend to create surpluses.

    7.2   Price Ceilings. Price ceilings, or maximum prices set by the government, tend to create shortages.

    7.3   *CASE STUDY:* The Toy Business is Not Child's Play

III. DISCUSSION

Demand

Demand is a relation that indicates the quantity of a commodity that consumers wish to buy at all possible prices during a given time period, other things constant. The *law of demand* states that the relationship between price and quantity demanded is an inverse relationship, i.e., that fewer units are demanded at higher prices than at lower prices. Demand reflects consumers' willingness and ability to buy the commodity.

The inverse relationship between price and quantity demanded refers to the real, or relative, price of the commodity. If the price of shoes increases 10 percent but all other prices also increase by 10 percent, then the relative price of shoes has not changed and quantity demanded will not change.

A change in the price of a commodity has two effects on quantity demanded. The first is the *substitution effect*. If the price of one good increases while all other prices remain constant, then the good becomes more costly relative to other goods. Many consumers will respond by substituting a cheaper good for the now more expensive good, so the quantity demanded of the original good decreases. An increase in the price of one good encourages consumers to switch to other goods. The second effect—the *income effect*—affects consumers' ability to buy a good. If you have been buying ten hamburgers a week at $1.00 per hamburger and the price increases to $1.25, then the $10 that used to buy ten hamburgers can now buy only eight hamburgers. The higher price reduces your *real income*, or purchasing power, which has the tendency to induce you to purchase fewer units of the good.

The inverse relationship between price and quantity demanded can be shown by a demand schedule for any specific commodity. Exhibit 1 illustrates the quantities of gasoline demanded at various prices. Exhibit 2 provides the same information in the form of a *demand curve*. More units are demanded at lower prices, reflecting the law of demand. Several things are held constant: the prices of other goods and the incomes, expectations, and tastes of the consumers. A movement along the demand curve represents a *change in quantity demanded*. The market demand is found by adding up the demands of all consumers in the market.

Exhibit 1

The Demand Schedule for Gasoline

	Price per Gallon	Quantity Demanded (millions of gallons per week)
a	$1.25	8
b	1.00	10
c	.90	12
d	.80	14
e	.70	16
f	.60	20
g	.50	25

Exhibit 2

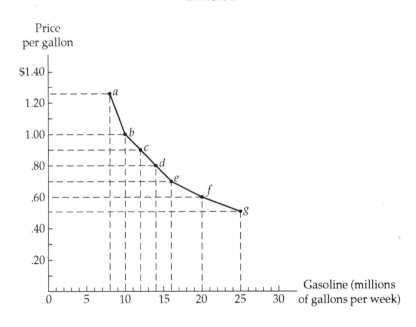

Shifts of the Demand Curve

In the demand schedule and the demand curve in Exhibits 1 and 2, only the price of gasoline varied. However, demand can be affected by factors other than the price of the good being considered, such as consumer income, the prices of substitutes and complements, consumers' expectations, the number of consumers in the market, and consumer tastes. If any one of these factors changes, the entire demand schedule changes. That is, the demand curve shifts. When this occurs, there is a *change in demand*. (Be sure you understand how a change in demand differs from a change in quantity demanded.)

An increase in income increases demand for most products. Increasing demand means that the quantity demanded at every price increases. Exhibit 3 provides an example. When consumer income averages $20,000 a year, the demand schedule for gasoline is identical to that in Exhibit 1; this demand schedule is shown in the second column of Exhibit 3. When average income increases to $30,000 a year, the demand schedule changes. At each price, consumers demand a greater quantity of gasoline when income is greater. Exhibit 4 shows this change in demand by a shift in the demand curve from D to D'.

Exhibit 3

The Demand for Gasoline

| | Price per Gallon | Quantity Demanded (millions of gallons per week) | |
		When Average Income is $20,000	When Average Income is $30,000
a	$1.25	8	10
b	1.00	10	12
c	.90	12	14
d	.80	14	16
e	.70	16	18
f	.60	20	22
g	.50	25	27

Exhibit 4

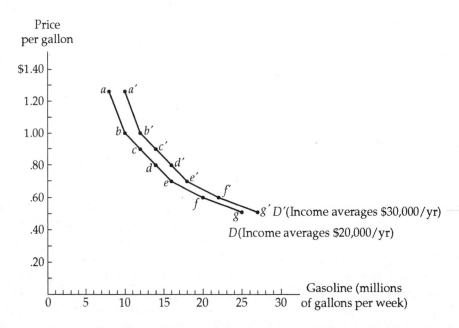

An increase in income may lead to a decrease in demand for some goods. Such goods are called *inferior goods*. People want fewer units of inferior goods when they have more income. Examples of such goods (at least for some consumers) are margarine, hamburger, bus travel, and inexpensive brands of many goods. People substitute a better product for the inferior good when they have more income. A good whose demand increases as income increases is called a *normal good*.

Any change in one of the other factors that affect demand (other than the price of the good itself) will cause a shift in the entire demand curve similar to the one shown in Exhibit 4. A change in the price of a substitute or complement will cause a shift in the demand curve. If an increase in the price of one good leads to a shift of the demand curve for another product to the right, the two goods are *substitutes*. If an increase in the price of one good leads to a shift of the demand curve for another good to the left, the two goods are *complements*. If the goods are unrelated, a change in the price of one will have no effect on the demand curve for the other.

Changes in consumer expectations about the future price of a good or future income can cause a shift in the current demand curve for the good. If price or income is expected to be higher in the future, the current demand curve will shift to the right. An increase in the number of consumers in the market will also cause an increase in market demand. A change in the composition of the population changes market demand. For example, demands change as population ages. Finally, a change in consumer tastes can cause a shift in the demand curve. Again, make sure you understand the difference between a movement along a demand curve (change in the quantity demanded) and a shift of the demand curve (change in demand). A movement along the demand curve is caused by a change in the price of the good itself; a shift in the demand curve is caused by a change in one of the other factors of demand.

Supply

The analysis of *supply* is similar to the analysis of demand. The law of supply states that the quantity of product supplied in a given time period is usually directly related to its price. An increase in quantity supplied is a result of producers' greater willingness and ability to supply more units at higher prices. Keep in mind the difference between demand and supply. The law of demand says there is an inverse relationship between price and quantity demanded, and the law of supply says there is a direct relationship between price and quantity supplied. Determination of the market supply is analogous to determination of market demand: all the supply schedules of the individual producers in a market are added up.

Shifts of the Supply Curve

A change in the price of a good causes a movement along the supply curve, or a change in quantity supplied. However, other factors affect supply. A change in one of these other factors leads to a shift of the supply curve, or a change in supply. The factors that affect supply include the state of technology, the prices of resources used to produce the good, the prices of alternative goods, producer expectations, and the number of producers. The last two have effects very similar to those discussed for demand.

An improvement in technology tends to reduce the costs of production; cheaper production costs imply that firms are willing and able to produce more for any given price. The result is a shift of the supply curve to the right, or an increase in supply. Similarly, a decrease in the price of a resource used to produce the good reduces costs and shifts the supply curve to the right. Most resources can be used to produce more than one good. For example, steel is used in autos, trucks, refrigerators, and many other goods as well as in construction. These goods are called *alternative goods*. If the price of an alternative good increases, additional resources will be shifted into production of the alternative good, increasing its supply.

Demand and Supply Create a Market

Suppliers and demanders are brought together by markets. The *transaction costs* of exchange (the cost of time and information) are reduced by markets. A market is in *equilibrium* when the quantity demanded by consumers equals the quantity supplied by producers at a given price. Exhibits 5 and 6 illustrate a supply and demand schedule and supply and demand curves, respectively. The market is in equilibrium at a price of 80 cents per gallon because the quantity demanded equals the quantity supplied at that price. Any other price will generate either a shortage or a surplus. For example, if the price of a gallon of gasoline is $1.00, quantity demanded is 10 million gallons but quantity supplied is 20 million gallons, yielding a surplus of 10 million gallons. Any time the price is greater than the equilibrium price there will be a *surplus*. If the price is 60 cents per gallon, quantity demanded is 20 million gallons and quantity supplied is 10 million gallons; there is a shortage of 10 million gallons. Any time the price is below the equilibrium price there will be a *shortage*.

Exhibit 5

Market Supply and Demand for Gasoline

Price per Gallon	Quantity Demanded (millions of gallons per week)	Quantity Supplied (millions of gallons per week)
$1.25	8	28
1.00	10	20
.90	12	16
.80	14	14
.70	16	12
.60	20	10
.50	25	6

Exhibit 6

Changes in Equilibrium Price and Quantity

A market is in *equilibrium* when no economic agent in the market has any reason to alter his or her behavior. This is the case at the equilibrium price. That is, there is no reason for price to change unless either the supply or the demand changes. An increase in demand causes the demand curve to shift out, which generates a higher price and induces suppliers to increase the quantity supplied. That is, they move along the supply curve. What can cause demand to shift? Demand shifts when income, the price of a substitute or complement, consumer expectations, population, or consumer tastes change.

Exhibit 7 shows the effects of an increase in demand for gasoline. The demand curve shifts out to *D′*, which causes the price to increase to 90 cents per gallon. The higher price encourages producers to increase the quantity supplied from 14 million gallons per week to 16 million gallons per week. That is, the new equilibrium price is 90 cents per gallon, and the new equilibrium quantity is 16 million gallons per week.

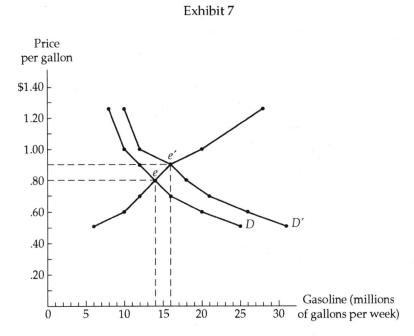

Exhibit 7

A change in supply has similar effects. An increase in supply shifts the *supply curve* to the right. Because of the increased supply, the price falls, which encourages consumers to buy more gasoline, i.e., quantity demanded increases as consumers move along their demand curves.

It is possible for several factors to change at the same time; this generates shifts in both the demand curve and the supply curve. Review Exhibits 8 and 9 in the text to make sure that you understand the impact of simultaneous shifts in supply and demand.

Disequilibrium Prices

Actual prices are not always equilibrium prices. A market is in *disequilibrium* when the price does not equate quantity demanded and quantity supplied. In free markets, such disequilibria usually do not prevail for long periods of time. However, when the disequilibrium is due to the government's imposing either price ceilings or price floors, the disequilibrium can persist. When the government mandates a price floor above the equilibrium price, the result is a surplus. When the government mandates a price ceiling below the equilibrium price, the result is a shortage.

IV. LAGNIAPPE

The Market for Calculators

In the 1960s, engineering students did calculations using slide rules. Today slide rules have been replaced by hand-held calculators. When such calculators first appeared on the market, their prices were fairly high (a minimum of $400) and their capabilities were fairly limited. During the 1970s, technological change increased the capabilities of calculators and reduced their production costs. Demand increased as calculators were designed to perform more functions, and quantity demanded increased as prices fell. Both supply and demand have increased, but the increase in supply has been much larger than the increase in demand.

Question to Think About: How do we know that the change in the supply of calculators has been much greater than the change in demand?

Stock Market Activity

The stock market has changed considerably in the last fifteen years. A typical sales volume for the New York Stock Exchange fifteen years ago ranged from 60 million to 85 million shares per day. Today it is not uncommon for a billion shares to be traded in one day. What happened? The Securities and Exchange Commission changed its rules: high commission rates were no longer permitted. Consequently, rates fell and volume increased. Also, technological changes have enabled the New York Stock Exchange to handle larger volumes.

Question to Think About: Are there any other factors that may have caused the demand for stocks to increase in the last fifteen years?

V. KEY TERMS

Demand	Law of supply
Law of demand	Supply curve
Relative price	Relevant resources
Substitution effect	Market supply
Real income	Alternative goods
Income effect	Movement along the supply curve
Demand curve	Shift of the supply curve
Market demand	Transaction costs
Normal good	Surplus
Inferior good	Shortage
Substitutes	Equilibrium
Complements	Disequilibrium
Shift of the demand curve	Price floor
Movement along the demand curve	Price ceiling
Supply	

VI. QUESTIONS

A. Completion

1. Demand is a relation indicating the quantity of a commodity that consumers are _____ and _____ to purchase at various prices during a given time period, other things constant.

2. A price increase has two effects. The _____ effect means that a consumer switches to a relatively less expensive good; the _____ effect means that the consumer's purchasing power changes.

3. Bread is a _____ good if demand for it increases when income increases.

4. Two goods are _____ if an increase in the price of one causes the demand curve for the other to shift to the right.

5. Consider a demand schedule. A change in the price of the good leads to a change in _____; a change in a relevant factor other than the price of the good leads to a change in _____.

6. Supply is a relationship between price and _____ during a given time period, other things constant.

7. An increase in price causes a(n) _____ in quantity supplied.

8. _____ are goods that are produced using the same resources.

9. A change in technology causes a shift of the _____.

10. The costs of time and information required for exchange are called _____.

11. If quantity demanded equals quantity supplied at a specific price, the market is in _____.

12. Government-imposed price floors tend to produce a _____.

13. A shortage exists when, for a given price, quantity demanded exceeds _____.

14. Price ceilings tend to produce _____.

B. True/False

_____ 1. Demand is the rate of desired and attainable purchase at each possible price, other things constant.

_____ 2. A demand schedule indicates what an individual desires.

_____ 3. Prices of all other goods are held constant for a given demand schedule.

_____ 4. An increase in the price of one good, other things constant, encourages consumers to switch to other goods.

_____ 5. A price increase results in a decrease in a consumer's real income.

_____ 6. The demand curve for a normal good slopes down, but the demand curve for an inferior good slopes up.

_____ 7. Movements along a demand curve represent changes in quantity demanded.

_____ 8. A change in income causes a movement along the demand curve.

_____ 9. Generally, economists assume that tastes change frequently and are the causes of shifts of the demand curve.

_____ 10. An increase in the price of a good provides an incentive to suppliers to switch resources from other goods and use them in producing more of the good with the higher price.

_____ 11. The market supply curve represents the sum of individual supply curves.

_____ 12. An increase in the price of a required resource shifts the supply curve of the good produced with it to the right.

_____ 13. Technological change causes a movement along the supply curve.

_____ 14. Markets reduce the transaction costs of exchange.

_____ 15. If price is above the equilibrium price, there is an excess quantity supplied.

_____ 16. An increase in demand lowers the equilibrium price.

_____ 17. An increase in the price of a required resource will cause a change in quantity demanded of the good produced with it.

_____ 18. Disequilibrium can never exist if markets are allowed to operate without government intervention.

_____ 19. A price ceiling often leads to an excess quantity demanded.

_____ 20. A shortage can occur in free markets but a surplus cannot occur in free markets.

1. Demand reflects the quantity that consumers
   a. want at alternative prices.
   b. need at alternative prices.
   c. are willing and able to buy at alternative prices.
   d. can buy at alternative prices.
   e. none of the above

2. Which of the following is not held constant in defining the demand schedule?
   a. income
   b. prices of related goods
   c. tastes
   d. price of the good in question
   e. number of consumers

3. The substitution effect of a change in the price of good X is to
   a. increase the demand for good X if its price falls.
   b. decrease the demand for good X if its price rises.
   c. increase the quantity demanded of good X if its price rises.
   d. encourage consumers to substitute more of good X for other goods if X's price falls.
   e. encourage consumers to substitute other goods for good X if X's price falls.

4. A price change
   a. affects the consumer's ability to buy the good.
   b. affects the consumer's willingness to buy the good.
   c. changes the tastes of consumers.
   d. all of the above
   e. a and b

5. The income effect of a price change will be greatest for which of the following goods?
   a. house
   b. automobile
   c. dinner at a restaurant
   d. gasoline
   e. The question cannot be answered without more information.

6. A movement along a demand curve can be caused by a change in
   a. income.
   b. the price of a substitute or complement.
   c. expectations about future prices.
   d. the price of the good in question.
   e. quantity supplied.

7. A movement along the demand curve can be caused by a change in
   a. technology.
   b. income.
   c. the price of a related good.
   d. consumer tastes.
   e. quantity supplied.

8. Which of the following will cause a shift to the right of the demand curve for an inferior good?
   a. an increase in income
   b. an increase in the price of a complement
   c. a drop in preferences for the good
   d. an increase in the number of consumers
   e. all of the above

9. Supply indicates the quantity that producers
   a. are willing and able to offer for sale at a given price.
   b. can supply for a profit at a given price.
   c. will offer for sale if technical change takes place.
   d. all of the above
   e. a and b only

10. Price and quantity supplied are usually directly related because
    a. higher prices mean that producers are rewarded more for production.
    b. the law of increasing opportunity cost applies.
    c. there is more prestige associated with producing a high-priced good.
    d. changes in technology lead to higher prices.
    e. a and b

11. Which of the following does not change supply?
    a. a change in price of the good in question
    b. a change in technology
    c. a change in producer expectations
    d. a change in the number of producers
    e. all of the above

12. A movement along a supply curve is caused by
    a. a change in the number of consumers.
    b. a change in the number of producers.
    c. technological change.
    d. a change in supply.
    e. a change in quantity demanded.

13. If the price of an alternative good falls, but the price of good X remains the same,
    a. quantity supplied of good X will increase.
    b. quantity supplied of good X will decrease.
    c. quantity demanded of good X will decrease.
    d. supply of good X will decrease.
    e. supply of good X will increase.

14. The larger the market,
    a. the greater the transaction costs.
    b. the greater the degree of specialization.
    c. the less specialization there is.
    d. the lower the price.
    e. the more likely it is that producers will be large.

Exhibit 8

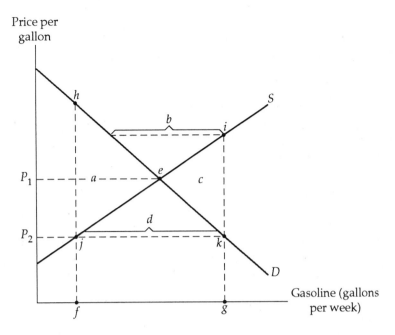

15. In Exhibit 8, equilibrium, shortage, and surplus are indicated by
    a. *e*, *d*, and *b*, respectively.
    b. *e*, *b*, and *d*, respectively.
    c. *e*, *a*, and *c*, respectively.
    d. *a*, *b*, and *d*, respectively.
    e. *c*, *d*, and *e*, respectively.

16. In Exhibit 8, if price is set by the government at P_2, the result is
    a. a surplus represented by *gf*.
    b. a surplus represented by *gi*.
    c. a shortage represented by *gf*.
    d. a shortage represented by *jh*.
    e. a shortage represented by *ke*.

17. An excess quantity demanded tends to
    a. put downward pressure on price.
    b. put upward pressure on price.
    c. cause demand to increase.
    d. cause supply to increase.
    e. b and d

18. A shift in the supply curve with demand held constant will
    a. cause equilibrium quantity to change in the same direction and equilibrium price to change in the opposite direction.
    b. cause equilibrium quantity to change in the opposite direction and equilibrium price to change in the same direction.
    c. cause both equilibrium quantity and equilibrium price to change in the same direction.
    d. cause both equilibrium quantity and equilibrium price to change in the opposite direction.
    e. cause changes that cannot be predicted without more information.

D. Discussion Questions

1. Explain why there is an inverse relationship between quantity demanded and price.

2. Explain the difference between a change in demand and a change in quantity demanded.

3. The correct answer to multiple choice question 7 is *a*. Why?

4. Explain the substitution effect and the income effect of a price change.

5. What would be the effect on the current price of coffee in this country if a period of unseasonably cold weather in Brazil destroyed a large portion of the coffee trees there?

6. In an article describing the economic life in a World War II prisoner-of-war camp, R. A. Radford noticed that Americans drank more coffee and the British drank more tea. (Note: the goods the prisoners received came from Red Cross packets. The currency that developed was cigarettes.)
   a. What accounts for the difference in consumption between the Americans and the British?
   b. Suppose someone observes the price of coffee rising while the price of tea remained constant. Take each of the determinants of demand and indicate whether a change in the determinant could have caused the price changes.
   c. Is there any factor from the supply side that could have caused the price change in coffee while the price of tea remained constant?

7. Why are economists reluctant to attribute a change in demand to a change in taste?

8. Bacon is a complement to eggs. If the price of eggs falls, what happens to the market for:
   a. Bacon
   b. beef
   c. Corn
   d. Caviar

9. Explain why there is usually a direct relationship between quantity supplied and price.

10. What is the effect on the supply of corn of an increase in the price of wheat?

11. A movement along the demand curve is caused by a change in price, and a movement along the supply curve is caused by a change in price. What causes the price to change?

12. In Exhibit 9, the demand schedules for coffee for Belle Starr and Buck Hanks and the supply schedules for Juan Hernandez and Valdez Delgado are provided.
    a. What are the equilibrium price and quantity?
    b. How much coffee does Belle Starr consume? Buck Hanks?
    c. How much coffee does Juan Hernandez sell? Valdez Delgado?
    d. Suppose Belle Starr also drinks tea. If the price of tea increases, what happens to the coffee consumption of Buck Hanks?

e. Suppose Juan Hernandez experiences equipment problems so that he can produce only one cup of coffee. What is the equilibrium price? How much coffee does each consumer drink now? How much coffee does Valdez Delgado sell now?

Exhibit 9

The Market for Coffee

		Quantities Demanded and Supplied for:		
Price	Belle Starr	Buck Hanks	Juan Hernandez	Valdez Delgado
$2.00	0	1	16	19
1.90	1	2	14	17
1.80	2	4	12	15
1.70	3	6	10	13
1.60	4	8	8	11
1.50	5	10	6	9
1.40	6	12	4	7
1.30	7	14	2	5
1.20	8	16	1	3

13. In Exhibit 10, what are the results if the government sets the price of gasoline at $1.00 per gallon? What are the results if the price is set at 50 cents a gallon? How can these results be handled by the government?

Exhibit 10

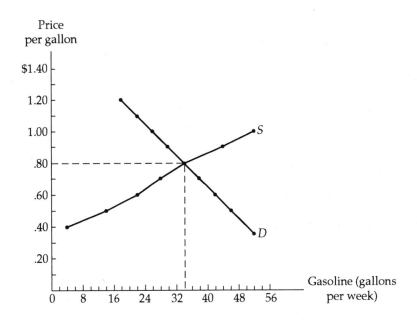

14. What are the effects on a market if demand increases and supply decreases?

15. Tickets for concerts for popular rock bands are often scalped at prices considerably above the prices printed on them. Using the concepts of supply and demand, explain why this happens.

16. Why do those who produce the concerts set such "low" prices for tickets when they know scalpers get much more?

Demand and Supply Analysis   57

17. In the mid-1970s no one had a personal computer at home. Today many people do. Using demand and supply curves, show the market for personal computers in the mid-1970s and today. Explain the difference between then and now.

18. Explain why disequilibria can occur even in markets that are allowed to operate freely.

19. The minimum wage law generates a surplus of unskilled workers. What is the surplus called? Studies find that the effect on the market of an increase in the minimum wage decreases over time. Why would this be the case?

20. Offer a brief explanation for each of the following empirical observations:
    a. Americans began importing large quantities of Japanese autos in the 1970s.
    b. The price of medical care has increased substantially in recent years.
    c. A smaller proportion of the population smokes today than did so 20 years ago.
    d. Cable TV channels that show movies for a monthly fee have been losing viewers for the last couple of years.
    e. The number of people using the services of airlines has increased substantially over the last 15 years.

VII. ANSWERS

A. Completion

1. willing; able
2. substitution; income
3. normal
4. substitutes
5. quantity demanded; demand
6. quantity supplied
7. increase
8. Alternative goods
9. supply curve
10. transaction costs
11. equilibrium
12. surplus
13. quantity supplied
14. shortages

B. True/False

1. True
2. False. Demand schedules indicate willingness and ability to buy.
3. True
4. True
5. True
6. False
7. True
8. False
9. False
10. True
11. True
12. False
13. False
14. True
15. True
16. False
17. True. The supply curve of the good shifts left, raising the price and thus reducing the quantity demanded.
18. False
19. True
20. False

C. Multiple Choice

1. c	6. d	11. a	16. c
2. d	7. a	12. a	17. b
3. d	8. d	13. e	18. a
4. e	9. a	14. b	
5. a	10. e	15. a	

D. Discussion Questions

1. There is an inverse relationship between quantity demanded and price because people are willing and able to buy more at a lower price, other things constant. People are willing to buy more because of the substitution effect—they can substitute more of the lower priced good for the higher priced good. People also are able to buy more at a lower price because of the income effect—their real incomes have increased.

2. A change in quantity demanded occurs when there is a change in the price of the good. A change in demand occurs when there is a change in any factor that affects demand other than price. Changes in income, tastes, the prices of substitutes or complements, expectations about price and income in the future, and the number or composition of consumers in the market can all cause a change in demand. In these cases, the quantity demanded at each price changes, causing a change in the entire demand schedule, which shows up as a shift of the demand curve. A change in quantity demanded is a movement along the demand curve.

3. A change in quantity demanded is caused by a change in price. The change in price must be caused by a change in supply. Technology (answer *a*) is the only choice that causes supply to change.

4. When the price of one good goes up while the prices of all other goods remain constant, the good becomes relatively more costly. Consequently, some people consume less of the more costly good and more of other goods. This is the substitution effect. A price change also affects one's real income—that is, it causes an income effect. If real income increases, the consumer will want to buy more normal goods and fewer inferior goods; if real income decreases, the opposite will occur.

5. Unseasonably cold weather in Brazil would cause the current price of coffee in this country to rise because consumers would expect a shortage of coffee and thus a higher price in the future; this expectation would increase demand today. Further, suppliers would expect a higher price in the future; this expectation would induce them to remove some coffee from the market today and keep it to sell in the future. Hence, demand would increase and supply would decrease, so price would have to increase.

6. a. Tastes
   b. The higher price could be due to an increase in demand. If income increased, price of a substitute good fell or the price of a complementary good increased, expectations about the future changed, an increase in coffee drinkers, or tastes changed, we would expect the price of coffee to rise. It is unlikely that the incomes changed since all receive the same packets and the price of tea didn't change. Most products that would be a substitute or a complement for coffee would also be substitutes or complements for tea and we would expect the price of tea to change too. The best possibility is that there was an influx of American prisoners.

c. The other cause of a price increase is a shift to the left of the supply curve, causing a movement along the demand curve for coffee. If the amount of coffee in the Red Cross packets decreased, we would observe an increase in the price of coffee. But, coffee and tea are substitutes so we should also observe an increase in the price of tea. Hence, the best explanation is an increase in the demand for coffee caused by an influx of Americans into the camp.

7. Tastes cannot be directly observed or measured. Hence, one can always attribute a change in demand to a change in taste and never be proven wrong. Because it is not observable, taste is not a good explanation of behavior. Since price and income changes can be observed, they are more useful as explanations of consumer behavior.

8. a. A decrease in the price of eggs leads to a shift to the right of the demand curve for bacon. The price of bacon will increase and the equilibrium quantity will increase.
   b. Bacon and beef are substitutes. The higher price for bacon will cause the demand curve for beef to shift to the right, causing a higher price for beef and the equilibrium quantity will increase.
   c. Corn is used to feed swine. The higher price for bacon induces farmers to move along their supply curves and increase the quantity supplied of bacon. The extra pigs need food, so the demand curve for corn will shift to the right. The price and equilibrium quantity of corn both increase.
   d. I cannot think of any effects on the market for caviar.

9. Producers are more willing and able to supply units at higher prices. They are more willing because the reward they earn by producing the product increases as price increases. They are also more able because higher prices allow them to pay the opportunity costs of resources used to produce the good. The law of increasing opportunity costs tells us that as production expands, opportunity costs increase. A higher price is required to cover these increased costs.

10. An increase in the price of wheat encourages producers to increase production of wheat, which takes resources. Some of these resources are likely to come from corn production, so the supply of corn will decrease.

11. A change in demand causes a change in price, which then causes a change in quantity supplied. A change in supply causes a change in price, which then causes a change in quantity demanded. So, price changes whenever a factor other than price causes either demand or supply to change.

12. a. Equilibrium price is $1.50 and the equilibrium quantity is 15 cups of coffee.
    b. At $1.50, Belle Starr drinks 5 cups of coffee and Buck Hanks drinks 10 cups.
    c. At $1.50, Juan Hernandez produces 6 cups of coffee and Valdez Delgado produces 9 cups.
    d. The increase in the price of tea causes Belle's demand for coffee to increase. The demand curve for coffee shifts to the right and the price of coffee increases. This induces a movement along Buck's demand curve and his coffee consumption will decrease.
    e. The new equilibrium price is $1.60. Belle Starr drinks 4 cups of coffee and Buck Hanks drinks 8 cups of coffee. Juan Hernandez supplies 1 cup of coffee and Valdez Delgado provides 11 cups of coffee to the market.

13. If the price is set at $1.00 per gallon, there is an excess quantity supplied; 52 gallons are supplied but only 26 gallons are demanded. Someone must purchase the extra 26 gallons (presumably the government). When the price is 50 cents per gallon, there is an excess quantity demanded, since 46 gallons are demanded but only 14 gallons are supplied. Some way must be found to ration these 14 gallons of gasoline among those who want it.

14. The price increases. The quantity purchased either increases or decreases, depending on whether the demand change or the supply change is greater.

15. Refer to the following exhibit. There are 60,000 tickets available, a number corresponding to the capacity of the stadium. $80 is the price that would clear the market, but the producers of the concert charge only $40. Hence, there is an excess demand for the tickets.

16. Some who get the tickets would rather make a profit by selling them for the market-clearing price, $80, than go to the game, so they scalp their tickets. The people who set the price may set it low because they do not know what price is best or because it tends to be the best price on average. Another possible explanation is that the promoters want to sell promotional materials at the concert and think that the buyers of the materials will be more likely to attend if the ticket price is lower.

17. The following exhibit illustrates the answer to this question. Demand in the 1970s is indicated by *D*; supply is indicated by *S*. The supply curve intersects the vertical axis above the point where the demand curve intersects the vertical axis. This indicates that in the 1970s the cost of producing personal computers was too high, given the demand. Because of technological changes, the supply curve has shifted out to *S′*. The demand curve has also shifted out, to *D′*, indicating increased demand. Demand has increased in part because of the increase in the availability of complementary goods such as computer games and software to make the personal computer useful in homes. The equilibrium price, $2,000, and quantity, 100,000, are indicated by point *e*.

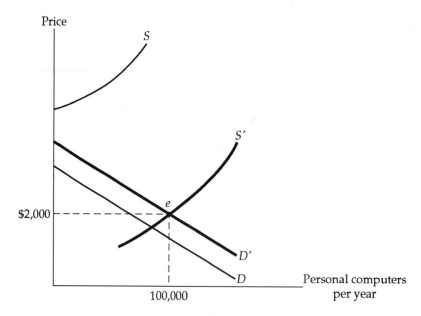

18. Disequilibrium exists whenever quantity demanded does not equal quantity supplied at the market price. If demand increases, there is an excess quantity demanded, which puts upward pressure on price. When price moves to the new equilibrium price, equilibrium is restored.

19. The surplus is called unemployment. Over time, the price level tends to increase so the real value of the minimum wage falls and the effect on unemployment diminishes.

20. a. The price of gasoline rose significantly in the 1970s, decreasing the demand for cars that use a lot of gasoline. Since Japanese cars were more fuel-efficient than American cars, imports of Japanese autos increased.
    b. Increased insurance coverage through Medicare and Medicaid programs has increased demand for medical care, raising the price. Second, technical changes have made medical treatment better, which also has caused greater expenditures on medical care.
    c. To explain the change in smoking habits, we can only argue that tastes are changing, since the relative price of cigarettes has not changed very much, and increases in income do not change smoking habits very much. The increased awareness of the link between smoking and cancer has contributed to a change in tastes.
    d. The price of a substitute good has decreased—that is, the availability of video recorders and inexpensive movie rental outlets have decreased the demand for movie channels.

e. With the deregulation of the airline industry, the price of air travel fell; this encouraged people to travel more by air. That is, there has been an increase in quantity demanded.

CHAPTER 4

Economic Decision Makers

I. INTRODUCTION

This chapter introduces the economic agents whose behavior we will analyze in the coming chapters. Of these, households are the most important because the demand for goods and services originates with households, and the resources used to produce goods and services are owned by households. Firms, governments, and the rest of the world are in some sense fictional characters—for example, there is no individual known as "Government" who makes decisions. Rather, people make decisions.

II. OUTLINE

1. The Household. The decisions of households are major factors in determining what is produced.

    1.1 The Evolution of the Household
        a. In earlier times, most households were farm families who were relatively self-reliant.
        b. Industrialization and urbanization altered the role of families in production.
        c. Since World War II married women, have entered the labor force in significant numbers.
        d. Many two-income households demand more goods and services in product markets because they produce fewer goods and services at home.

    1.2 Households Maximize Utility
        a. Households are viewed as rational decision makers.
        b. Utility maximization is based on each household's subjective goals.

    1.3 Households as Resource Suppliers
        a. All resources are owned by households.
        b. Households can use resources to produce goods and services within the home.
        c. Households can supply their resources to firms or to governments.
        d. Labor is the most valuable resource owned by most households.
        e. Government gives some households transfer payments.
        f. Transfer payments include cash transfers and in-kind transfers.

    1.4 Households as Demanders of Goods and Services
        a. Households can allocate money in three ways: (1) personal consumption expenditures, (2) savings, and (3) taxes.
        b. Personal consumption is broken down into three categories: (1) durable goods, (2) nondurable goods, and (3) services.

2. **The Firm**

2.1 **Transaction Costs and Evolution of the Firm**
   a. Most production takes place outside the home because of the benefits of specialization and comparative advantage and because transaction costs make it too costly to use markets for every transaction.
   b. During the cottage industry era, entrepreneurs arranged for production of goods and services and sold them to consumers. Production took place in the home.
   c. During the Industrial Revolution, technological developments led to the organization of work in factories.
   d. Firms are economic units formed by entrepreneurs to produce goods and services.
   e. Firms seek to maximize profits.

2.2 **Why Does Household Production Still Exist?**
   a. Households produce at home when the opportunity cost of home production is less than the opportunity cost of using the market.
   b. Some household production requires few specialized resources.
   c. People can avoid taxes by relying on household production instead of on market purchases.
   d. Household production reduces transaction costs in some cases.
   e. Technological advances have made household production more efficient in some cases.

2.3 *CASE STUDY:* The Electronic Cottage

2.4 **Types of Firms**
   a. A *sole proprietorship* is a single-owner firm.
      (1) Advantages
         (a) Owner in complete control
         (b) Easy to organize
      (2) Disadvantages
         (a) Unlimited liability
         (b) Difficult to raise money for construction and expansion
         (c) Business generally ends at death of owner.
   b. A *partnership* is two or more individuals working together in return for a share of the profit or loss.
      (1) Advantages
         (a) Relatively easy to form
         (b) Easier to raise startup funds
      (2) Disadvantages
         (a) Decision making is more difficult.
         (b) Each partner is liable for the debts of the partnership.
         (c) Death or departure of one partner necessitates reorganization.
   c. A *corporation* is a legal entity recognized by the state and treated as if it were an individual.
      (1) Advantages
         (a) Easy to amass large sums of financing
         (b) Liability for the firm's losses limited to the value of an owner's stock
      (2) Disadvantages
         (a) Individual stockholder has little control over the firm's decisions.
         (b) Corporate profits passed on to stockholders are taxed twice.

(3) The *S corporation* is a hybrid type of corporation.
  (a) The S corporation provides limited liability.
  (b) Corporate profits are taxed only once.
  (c) A firm must have no more than 35 stockholders to qualify as an S corporation.

2.5 Nonprofit Institutions

3. The Government

 3.1 The Role of Government
  a. Government establishes and enforces the rules of the game: government protects private property and enforces contracts.
  b. Antitrust laws attempt to promote competition by preventing collusion.
  c. Government regulates natural monopolies.
  d. Government produces public goods.
  e. Government deals with problems associated with externalities.
  f. Government attempts to promote a more equal distribution of income.
  g. Government attempts to promote full employment, price stability, and economic growth.

 3.2 Government's Structure and Objectives
  a. The United States has a federal system of government.
  b. It is difficult to define the objectives of the government. One useful theory is that elected officials are vote maximizers.
  c. Market exchange is based on voluntary exchange; public political choices may be enforced by the policing power of the government.
  d. Prices in the political system are not necessarily linked to costs.

 3.3 Size and Growth of U.S. Government
  a. Government spending as a percentage of gross national product has increased from 10 percent in 1929 to 35 percent in 1992, but fell back to 29 percent of GDP in 2000.
  b. The major source of growth has been federal outlays, particularly for Social Security and other transfer programs.

 3.4 Sources of Government Revenue. Most of the government's revenue comes from income, sales, and property taxes.

 3.5 Tax Principles and Tax Incidence
  a. Some think taxes should be based on the principle of ability to pay.
  b. Others think taxes should be based on the principle of benefits received.
  c. Tax incidence indicates who actually bears the burden of the tax.
  d. Important tax terms
   (1) *Marginal tax rate*: how much of each additional dollar of income must be paid in taxes
   (2) *Proportional taxes*: taxes for which the percentage of income paid is constant as income increases
   (3) *Progressive taxes*: taxes for which the percentage of income paid increases as income increases
   (4) *Regressive taxes*: taxes for which the percentage of income paid decreases as income increases

4. The Rest of the World. The rest of the world consists of the households, firms, and governments of other countries. Some countries have formed economic alliances.

    4.1   International Trade
        a.   International trade occurs because the opportunity cost of producing specific goods differs across countries.
        b.   The volume of U.S. trade with the rest of the world has increased dramatically since 1970.
        c.   The merchandise trade balance equals the value of commodities exported minus the value of commodities imported.
        d.   A nation's balance of payments is the record of transactions between its residents and the residents of the rest of the world.

    4.2   Exchange Rates
        a.   *Foreign exchange* is the currency of another country that is used to carry out international transactions.
        b.   The exchange rate measures the price of one currency in terms of another.

    4.3   Trade Restrictions
        a.   Trade restrictions include
            (1)   Tariffs, or taxes on imports and exports
            (2)   Quotas--legal limits on the quantity of a good that can be imported or exported
            (3)   Other restrictions
        b.   Restrictions tend to benefit domestic producers and to harm consumers.

    4.4   *CASE STUDY:* The Wheel of Fortune

III. DISCUSSION

The Household

Households are the most important economic agents because they are the ultimate demanders of goods and services and ultimate suppliers of all resources. Households make decisions about what goods and services to buy and what resources to sell so as to maximize *utility*. Utility is a subjective concept; activities that provide utility to one household may not be desirable to another.

Households receive income when they sell their resources to either firms or governments. The most important resource owned by most households is the labor services of family members. Labor earnings account for the majority of personal income in the United States. Most of the income received is spent on personal consumption of both durable and nondurable goods and services. The rest of the income is either saved or spent on taxes.

The Firm

A hundred years ago most households produced most of what they consumed. Today, households purchase most of the goods and services they consume from firms. Increased specialization, fueled by technological change and increased industrialization, explains much of the change in household production and consumption. Firms developed to capture many of the gains from increased specialization.

Production still takes place within the home if the task requires very few specialized resources and is easy for households to perform. Generally, households will perform tasks whenever the opportunity cost of home production is less than the opportunity cost of purchasing the good or service in the marketplace.

Firms tend to specialize in certain tasks rather than produce everything. Entrepreneurs also specialize; an entrepreneur who is good at producing automobiles may not be good at finding oil. Firm size also tends to be limited because of the costs associated with coordinating the activities of more and more people. (Make sure you are familiar with the types of firms and their relative strengths and weaknesses.)

The Government

Households and firms do not produce all goods. Voluntary exchange does not always produce all goods that society desires and does not always produce goods in an optimal manner. An economic function of government is to handle situations that the market economy cannot handle adequately. For example, government can provide an environment in which voluntary exchange can take place. The government defines and enforces property rights so that theft and failure to fulfill contracts are limited.

The government also tries to limit the effects of *monopoly* in the economy. Some goods are produced in ways that make it most efficient for a single firm to supply the entire market. The government regulates such *natural monopolies* so that firms do not charge higher prices than necessary. Firms sometimes get together to try to raise prices above the competitive level; the government enacts antitrust laws designed to limit this behavior.

Another important role for the government is to provide public goods. A *public good* is a good that is available to everyone once it is produced. Private firms usually will not produce public goods in the quantities that society wishes or needs because people who have not paid for use of public goods can still consume them. The government, however, can produce public goods and force people to pay for them through taxes. One example of a public good is national defense.

The government intervenes in the economy to correct the problems associated with *externalities*, which are unpriced by-products of consumption or production. Reckless behavior (caused by consuming too much beer) and pollution (caused by industrial production) are examples of negative externalities; increased voting rates (a by-product of consumption of education) is an example of a positive externality.

Finally, government also tries to promote equal distribution of income, full employment, price stability, and economic growth. A progressive tax system combined with *transfer payments* to the poor is used to promote the first goal; *fiscal* and *monetary policy* are used to promote the latter three goals.

The Rest of the World

People in the United States often trade with people in other countries. The rest of the world consists of all the other countries in the world. International trade occurs because the opportunity costs of producing specific goods differ across countries. A country exports goods for which its opportunity costs are relatively low. Even though international trade creates economic gains, most countries impose some sort of trade restrictions. These restrictions tend to benefit domestic producers at the expense of domestic consumers.

Trade with other countries involves using other currencies. If an American buys a sweater from an English firm, the sweater manufacturer expects to be paid in British pounds. *Foreign exchange*, the currency of other countries needed to carry out international transactions, can be bought and sold in foreign exchange markets. The *exchange rate* measures the price of one currency in terms of another. The *balance of payments* is the record of transactions between residents of one country and residents of the rest of the world.

IV. LAGNIAPPE

More on Households

We can see more clearly the role of households as suppliers of resources and buyers of goods by looking at the Jones family. Mr. Jones owns his own hardware store. Mrs. Jones works as an accountant for a corporation in the area. The family owns stock in the company where Mrs. Jones works, and they own government bonds. The family is also renting out a house they own.

Mr. Jones' income is classified as proprietor's income. Mrs. Jones earns a salary. The dividends they receive from their stock and the interest from the government bonds are other types of income. Finally, they receive rental income from the tenants who live in the house they own.

The Jones family earns money from the sale of the resources mentioned here. The family also purchases goods and services. Purchases of goods and services provide revenues for firms. The Jones's taxes provide revenue to the government, which helps pay the salaries of government workers. Their savings also are used by others: government bonds help finance government activity and the stock helps finance investments of the firm.

Question to Think About: How does government borrowing fit into the flow of expenditures and receipts discussed here?

Quasi-Public Goods

National defense is a public good because it is impossible to prevent nonpayers from receiving the benefits of the good once it is produced. Some goods do not have all the characteristics of a public good but are close enough so that the government generally provides them. For example, nonpayers can be excluded from receiving fire or police protection. But the high cost of determining whether someone who has just been mugged has paid for police protection makes it more efficient for government to provide police protection for all. Similarly, fire protection is provided for all even though it is possible not to serve nonpayers.

Question to Think About: On what other grounds besides those mentioned here might government-sponsored fire protection be extended to all citizens?

V. KEY TERMS

Utility
Transfer payments
Personal consumption
Firms
Sole proprietorship
Partnership
Corporation
Limited liability
S corporation
Market failure
Monopoly
Natural monopoly
Public good
Externality

Fiscal policy
Monetary policy
Tax incidence
Proportional taxes
Progressive taxes
Regressive taxes
Rest of the world
Merchandise trade balance
Balance of payments
Foreign exchange
Exchange rate
Tariff
Quota

VI. QUESTIONS

A. Completion

1. Households are assumed to maximize their levels of satisfaction, or _____.

2. Some households receive _____ from the government.

3. Most personal income goes to _____.

4. _____ are people who work for themselves.

5. A cab ride is an example of a _____.

6. The most common form of business is a _____.

7. Stockholders are protected in the case of bankruptcy by the idea of _____.

8. If a good is available to all once it is produced, it is a _____ good.

9. _____ externalities convey unpriced benefits.

10. The government's regulation of the money supply is called _____.

11. _____ policy involves the government's taxing and spending powers.

12. The percentage of income paid in taxes decreases as income increases under _____.

13. Legal limits on the quantities of particular goods that can be imported are called _____.

14. The _____ measures the price of one currency in terms of another.

15. The merchandise trade balance is one component of a country's _____.

16. Households demand goods and services in the _____ and supply resources in the _____.

B. True/False

_____ 1. The decisions made by households about consuming goods and services determine what is produced.

_____ 2. Utility maximization is based on an objective standard.

_____ 3. All resources are owned ultimately by households.

_____ 4. Rents and dividends make up about one-quarter of all personal income.

_____ 5. For most households, personal consumption expenditures use the largest share of personal income.

_____ 6. Farm families tend to be more self-sufficient than urban families.

_____ 7. Firms exist because of transaction costs.

_____ 8. Households with the highest opportunity cost of time tend to hire others to perform household tasks rather than to engage in household production.

_____ 9. Partnerships offer limited liability.

_____ 10. The bulk of all business sales are made by corporations.

_____ 11. Market transactions generally reflect private benefits and costs as well as external benefits and costs.

_____ 12. A natural monopoly exists when one firm controls all of a natural resource.

_____ 13. Coercion is often a part of government involvement in the economy.

_____ 14. In comparison to other industrial countries, the proportion of government spending in GDP is greater in the U.S.

_____ 15. Sales taxes provide the bulk of revenues to most states.

_____ 16. The gasoline tax is based on the principle of benefits received.

_____ 17. The marginal tax rate indicates how much of each additional dollar earned is paid in taxes.

_____ 18. Trade restrictions are imposed to benefit domestic consumers.

_____ 19. An increase in the dollar price of the yen is associated with a decrease in the yen price of the dollar.

_____ 20. It is impossible to run a deficit in all accounts in the balance of payments.

C. Multiple Choice

1. Utility is
   a. a statement about who consumes a good or service.
   b. a measure of the usefulness of a good.
   c. the satisfaction received from consuming a good or service.
   d. the satisfaction received from making a decision.
   e. none of the above.

2. Which of the following could be produced either by individual households or by firms?
   a. lawn care
   b. cleaning services
   c. cooking
   d. child care
   e. all of the above

3. The majority of personal income in the United States comes from
   a. labor earnings.
   b. ownership of land.
   c. ownership of capital.
   d. profits and dividends.
   e. the sum of b, c, and d.

4. The service sector has been growing rapidly in recent years because
   a. households are producing fewer of these services themselves.
   b. the opportunity cost of time for many households has increased.
   c. more married women are in the labor force.
   d. all of the above
   e. none of the above

5. Economists who have studied labor markets attribute the increase since World War II in the number of women who work outside the home to
   a. the high cost of living, which requires a family to have two incomes to maintain its standard of living.
   b. increasing demand for labor, which has raised wages and expanded job opportunities.
   c. inclusion of women under the Civil Rights Act.
   d. declines in the number of women who have children and delays in getting married.
   e. increasing college attendance by women relative to men.

6. Production by firms can be explained by
   a. increased specialization.
   b. increased specialization and comparative advantage.
   c. increased specialization and positive transaction costs.
   d. tax incentives.
   e. b and d.

7. Which of the following is most likely to be purchased from a firm rather than produced by the household?
   a. termite control
   b. child care
   c. washing the car
   d. painting the house
   e. putting in storm windows

8. Corporations account for the majority of sales in the economy because
   a. the corporation is the easiest form of business to begin.
   b. there are tax advantages for corporations that are not available to sole proprietorships or partnerships.
   c. corporations can more easily raise large sums for financing projects.
   d. owners have the greatest control over the decision making of the firm.
   e. a, b, and c

9. A natural monopoly evolves when
   a. there is only one firm in the industry.
   b. it is cheaper for one firm than for two or more firms to serve the market.
   c. the government establishes one firm as the only firm in a market.
   d. public goods are produced.
   e. firms successfully collude.

10. According to one theory of government behavior, elected officials attempt to maximize
   a. utility.
   b. votes.
   c. the size of their administrative agencies.
   d. profits.
   e. tax revenues.

11. Since World War II, federal government revenues have increasingly come from
   a. excise taxes.
   b. personal income taxes.
   c. corporate income taxes.
   d. payroll taxes.
   e. tariffs.

12. Which of the following sources of government revenue is based on the individual's ability to pay?
   a. the gasoline tax
   b. the toll on a government-owned bridge
   c. the progressive income tax
   d. the admission charge to a federal park
   e. all of the above

13. In the absence of trade restrictions, exchange among countries
    a. is due to cultural differences.
    b. follows the law of comparative advantage.
    c. tends to harm consumers in less developed countries.
    d. benefits only those who are engaged in international trade.
    e. has declined in importance in the last twenty years.

14. The exchange rate of a foreign currency will tend to increase if
    a. demand for that country's goods increases.
    b. the value of the dollar also increases.
    c. the supply of the foreign currency in foreign exchange markets increases.
    d. people in that country increase their import buying.
    e. all of the above

D. Discussion Questions

1. Firms often own resources—for example, many oil firms own oil wells. How, then, can the text say that all resources are owned by households?

2. Why is the household considered the most important actor in the economy?

3. Discuss the factors that have changed the household in the last hundred years. What effects have these changes had on the economy?

4. The text says that the rise of two-worker families reduces the advantages of specialized resources within the family. Explain.

5. Over the years, food prices at grocery stores have increased faster than the prices received by farmers. Can you offer a (partial) explanation for this?

6. Discuss the factors that determine whether tasks are performed by members of a household or by firms.

7. What are the weaknesses and strengths of the various forms of business? Why do corporations tend to be so much larger than sole proprietorships or partnerships?

8. Why does the government, rather than private firms, provide the judicial system?

9. What is a public good? Why does the government tend to produce public goods?

10. Why is it so difficult to determine the objectives of the government?

11. How does market exchange differ from exchange in political markets?

12. Discuss the two principles of taxation. Why are not all taxes collected on the basis of benefits received?

13. Why would a country impose trade restrictions if free trade is beneficial to the country?

14. What would be the effect of an increased demand in the United States for German goods?

15. During the 1980s, the amount of imports Americans purchased was greater than the amount of exports they sold. How was the deficit financed?

VII. ANSWERS

A. Completion

1. utility
2. transfer payments
3. personal consumption expenditures
4. Proprietors
5. service
6. sole proprietorship
7. limited liability
8. public
9. Positive
10. monetary policy
11. Fiscal
12. regressive taxation
13. quotas
14. exchange rate
15. balance of payments

B. True/False

1. True
2. False
3. True
4. False
5. True
6. True
7. True
8. True
9. False
10. True
11. False
12. False
13. True
14. False
15. True
16. True
17. True
18. False
19. True
20. True

C. Multiple Choice

1. c
2. e
3. a
4. d
5. b
6. c
7. a
8. c
9. b
10. b
11. d
12. c
13. b
14. a

D. Discussion Questions

1. Firms are owned by individual stockholders, so ultimately all resources are owned by households.

2. Households are the ultimate demanders of goods and services, and they determine what will be produced by what they are willing and able to purchase. Households also ultimately supply all resources used in production.

3. Technological change increased farm productivity, and the Industrial Revolution created opportunities for employment in cities. As people moved to cities, family size decreased and families undertook less home production of many goods and services. The increased demand for goods and services by households has been met by firms. The demand for such services increased as married women entered the labor force in larger numbers.

4. The higher opportunity cost of time for women who work outside the home implies that they will often substitute market-produced goods for home-produced goods. The reduced reliance on household production reduces the advantages of specialization in the home.

5. The increase in two-income families reduced the amount of "cooking from scratch" performed by households. Instead, families purchase foods that take less time to prepare. Such foods are already processed, at least to some degree, and this extra preparation by producers increases the price.

6. In general, a task will be performed by a household if the opportunity cost of home production is less than the opportunity cost of purchasing the good or service from a firm. The opportunity cost of home production depends on how specialized the required resources are and on the opportunity cost of time for the members of the family. A household may also perform certain tasks in order to have more control over the final products or to avoid taxes. In general, as the family income increases, more services will be bought rather than produced by members of the household.

7. Both sole proprietorships and partnerships are fairly easy to establish. The major weakness of each is the limited ability to raise financial capital for starting the company or increasing productive capacity. Owners and partners are also more exposed to risk in the case of lawsuits, and the death or departure of an owner can necessitate closing or reorganizing the firm. Corporations are more difficult to establish, but they provide limited liability and a much greater ability to raise financial capital (so they tend to be larger than other types of firms). However, corporate profits are often taxed twice, which is not true of the profits of sole proprietorships or partnerships.

8. Judicial services are not public goods, since it would be possible to exclude nonpayers from the system. However, society deems it inappropriate to rely on private firms to provide judicial services and charge people to use the system because that would put the poor at a disadvantage. A well-run judicial system provides external benefits to society, so providing judicial services is seen as a legitimate role for government.

9. Public goods are goods that nonpayers cannot be prevented from using once the goods are produced. Private firms are not likely to produce public goods because they cannot be assured of payment. The government provides such goods and requires people to pay for them by means of taxes.

10. Government is not a single entity—it includes the federal government, state governments, and local governments. Further, there are many agencies in the various branches of government. The legislative branch may have different objectives than the executive branch, and the agency heads may have different objectives yet. In addition, citizens disagree about what the objectives of the government should be.

11. Market exchange is voluntary and involves market prices. Exchange in political markets involves votes rather than dollars and often involves coercion, as in the case of the payment of taxes.

12. The two principles of taxation are the principle of ability to pay and the principle of benefits received. Proponents of the former argue that taxes should be based on one's ability to pay, i.e., the rich should pay more than the poor. Proponents of the latter argue that taxes should be related to benefits received from the government. According to this principle, schools should be supported by parents rather than by all taxpayers. Not all taxes can be collected on the basis of benefits received, however, since the actual benefits received are often very difficult to measure. In some cases, people would have an incentive to lie about the benefits they received if it meant a lower tax bill. This would especially be true in the case of public goods. Further, any programs designed to help the poor could not be financed on a benefits received principle—in such cases the people who receive the benefits are too poor to pay the taxes.

13. Countries impose trade restrictions because domestic producers that face competition from cheaper imports lobby for protection.

14. The German goods must be bought with German marks, so the demand for marks would increase. The increased demand for marks would cause the exchange rate to increase. More dollars would be needed to buy a given number of marks, so the dollar prices of the German good would increase.

15. The deficit was financed by borrowing from foreigners.

CHAPTER 5

Elasticity of Demand and Supply

I.   INTRODUCTION

We know that demand curves generally slope down and supply curves generally slope upward. Sometimes we need more information about demand and supply to be able to analyze a particular market. In this chapter, the concept of elasticity is introduced and explained. Elasticity is a very important concept in economics, so make sure that you understand the material in this chapter.

II.   OUTLINE

1.   Price Elasticity of Demand. Price elasticity of demand is a measure of the responsiveness of quantity demanded to a change in price.

  1.1   Calculating Price Elasticity of Demand
   a.   *Price elasticity of demand* equals the percentage change in quantity demanded divided by the percentage change in price.
   b.   Price elasticity is always a negative number.
   c.   Elasticity expresses a relationship between relative amounts, not absolute amounts.
   d.   The price elasticity formula is:

$$E_D = \frac{\Delta q}{(q' + q)/2} \div \frac{\Delta p}{(p' + p)/2}$$

  1.2   Categories of Price Elasticity of Demand
   a.   Inelastic: price elasticity has an absolute value between 0 and 1.0 since the percentage change in quantity demanded is less than the percentage change in price.
   b.   Unit elastic: price elasticity has an absolute value equal to 1.0 since the percentage change in quantity demanded equals the percentage change in price.
   c.   Elastic: price elasticity has an absolute value more than 1.0 since the percentage change in quantity demanded is greater than the percentage change in price.

  1.3   Elasticity and Total Revenue
   a.   *Total revenue* is the revenue the firm receives from selling its products; it equals price times the quantity sold.
   b.   Total revenue increases if price increases and demand is inelastic, or if price decreases and demand is elastic.
   c.   Total revenue decreases if price increases and demand is elastic, or if price decreases and demand is inelastic.
   d.   Total revenue is unchanged by a price change if demand is unit elastic.

1.4 Price Elasticity and the Linear Demand Curve

a. With a linear demand curve, consumers are more responsive to price changes when the price is relatively high than when the price is relatively low.

b. Demand becomes less elastic as one moves down a downward-sloping linear demand curve.

c. Demand is unit elastic at the midpoint of a downward-sloping linear demand curve.

d. Demand is elastic above the midpoint of a downward-sloping linear demand curve.

e. Demand is inelastic below the midpoint of a downward-sloping linear demand curve.

f. Along a downward-sloping linear demand curve, total revenue increases as the price is reduced until the midpoint is reached and then decreases as price falls further.

1.5 Constant-Elasticity Demand

a. A horizontal demand curve has an elasticity value of infinity and represents perfectly elastic demand.

b. A vertical demand curve has an elasticity value of zero and represents perfectly inelastic demand.

c. Demand curves can also be unit elastic at all points.

2. Determinants of the Price Elasticity of Demand

2.1 Availability of Substitutes

a. The more close substitutes for the good there are available, the more elastic the demand.

b. The number and closeness of substitutes depend on how the good is defined.

c. The more narrow the definition of a good, the more substitutes there are and the more elastic the demand.

2.2 Proportion of the Consumer's Budget Spent on a Good. The more important an item is as a percentage of a consumer's budget, the more elastic the demand.

2.3 A Matter of Time. Elasticity is greater the longer the time period involved.

2.4 Elasticity Estimates

2.5 CASE STUDY: Deterring Young Smokers

3. Price Elasticity of Supply

a. *Price elasticity of supply* is a measure of the responsiveness of quantity supplied to a change in price.

b. The price elasticity of supply is:

$$E_s = \frac{\Delta q}{(q' + q)/2} \div \frac{\Delta p}{(p' + p)/2}$$

3.1 Categories of Supply Elasticity

a. Supply is elastic if the supply elasticity has a value greater than 1.0.

b. Supply is inelastic if the supply elasticity has a value less than 1.0.

c. Supply is unit-elastic if the supply elasticity equals 1.0.

d. A horizontal supply curve represents a supply that is perfectly elastic.

e. A vertical supply curve represents a supply that is perfectly inelastic.

f. A linear supply curve that comes from the origin is of unitary elasticity.

3.2 Determinants of Supply Elasticity
   a. Elasticity of supply depends on how cost changes as output increases. The more rapidly marginal cost rises as output expands, other things constant, the more inelastic the supply.
   b. Supply is more elastic the longer the time period involved.

4. Other Elasticity Measures

   4.1 Income Elasticity of Demand
       a. *Income elasticity of demand* is a measure of how demand changes in response to a change in income, prices held constant; it measures the percentage change in quantity demanded divided by the percentage change in income.
       b. Inferior goods have a negative income elasticity of demand.
       c. Normal goods have a positive income elasticity of demand.
       d. Demand is income inelastic if the value of the elasticity is between zero and 1.0 and elastic if the value is greater than 1.0. Goods that are income inelastic are sometimes called *necessities*; those that are income elastic are sometimes called *luxuries*.

   4.2 *CASE STUDY: The Market for Food and "The Farm Problem"*
       a. Most farm products have price-inelastic demand curves.
       b. Because demand is inelastic, fluctuations in output caused by weather or other factors generate relatively large changes in prices (and therefore in farm income).
       c. The problem is compounded in the long run by the fact that demand for food also tends to be income inelastic, leading to generally declining real farm income as the economy grows over time.

   4.3 Cross-Price Elasticity of Demand
       a. *Cross-price elasticity of demand* is the percentage change in quantity demanded of one good divided by the percentage change in the price of another good; it measures the responsiveness of demand for one good to changes in the price of another good.
       b. Two goods are *substitutes* if the cross-price elasticity of demand is positive.
       c. Two goods are *complements* if the cross-price elasticity of demand is negative.

5. Appendix: Price Elastic Price Elasticity and Tax Incidence

   5.1 Demand Elasticity and Tax Incidence
       a. The effect of a tax on a good is to decrease the supply by the amount of the tax.
       b. The more elastic the demand, the more the tax is paid by the producers.

   5.2 Supply Elasticity and Tax Incidence. The more elastic the supply, the less the tax is paid by producers and the more it is passed on to consumers.

III.   DISCUSSION

Price Elasticity of Demand

If the price of a good decreases, we expect the quantity demanded to increase because a demand curve slopes downward. Government officials, consumers, and business managers are often very concerned about how much quantity demanded changes—that is, how responsive quantity demanded is to a change in price. Economists have developed a tool to help answer these questions: the concept of *price elasticity of demand*. Exhibit 1 illustrates this concept. The exhibit shows two demand curves: D_1 and D_2. At a price of $1.00, the demand curves intersect and the quantities demanded of each good are equal at 100 units each. If the price falls to 90 cents, quantity demanded of good 1 increases to 105 units (demand curve D_1) and quantity demanded of good 2 increases to 150 units (demand curve D_2). Obviously, the quantity demanded of good 1 is much less responsive to the 10-cent change in price than is the quantity demanded of good 2. Economists say that demand curve D_2 is more *elastic* than demand curve D_1.

Exhibit 1

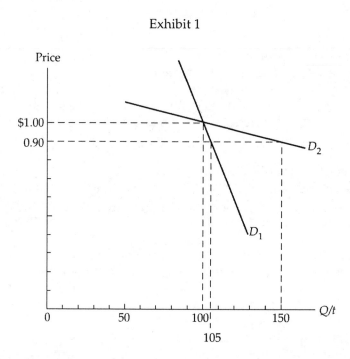

We can calculate the value of the price elasticity for each demand curve. The formula for price elasticity of demand is:

$$E_d = \frac{\Delta q}{(q' + q)/2} \div \frac{\Delta p}{(p' + p)/2}$$

In Exhibit 1, the price elasticity of D_1 is:

$$\frac{5}{(100 + 105)/2} \div \frac{0.10}{(1.00 + .90)/2} = \frac{5}{102.5} \div \frac{.10}{.95} = 0.46$$

The price elasticity of D_2 is:

$$\frac{50}{(100+150)/2} \div \frac{.10}{(1.00+.90)/2} = \frac{50}{125} \div \frac{.10}{.95} = 3.8$$

The price change is the same for both, but the quantity response is much greater for D_2 than for D_1. The result is that D_2 at a price of \$1.00 is more elastic than D_1 at a price of \$100.

Price elasticity of demand is a concept important to producers because it tells them what will happen to *total revenue* if price changes. In Exhibit 1, the total revenue at a price of \$1.00 is the same on both D_1 and D_2: \$1.00 x 100 = \$100. At a price of 90 cents, total revenue on D_1 is 0.90 x 105 = \$94.50 and total revenue on D_2 is 0.90 x 150 = \$135. The lower price caused total revenue on D_1 to fall and total revenue on D_2 to increase. Note that for this change in price, D_1 represents an *inelastic* demand and D_2 an *elastic* demand. When demand is elastic, a given percentage change in price leads to a larger percentage change in quantity demanded. Hence, when demand is elastic, a price reduction will generate so many more sales that total revenue will increase. On the other hand, if demand is inelastic, a lower price generates a smaller percentage increase in quantity, so total revenue falls.

In Exhibit 2, D_1 is steeper than D_2. Since we know that D_1 is inelastic and D_2 is elastic, it is tempting to think that a steep demand curve always represents inelastic demand and a flatter demand curve always represents elastic demand. This conclusion is false, however. Exhibit 2 illustrates why. The demand curve in panel *a* is steeper than the one in panel *b*, even though they represent the same demand for milk and the same value for price elasticity. The panels represent demand in terms of different units of measure: panel *a* shows gallons of milk demanded per time period, and panel *b* shows 8-ounce glasses demanded per time period. The difference in the slopes of the curves is due to the different scales on the horizontal axes. (With *intersecting* curves on the same graph, it is correct that the flatter demand curve represents the more elastic demand.)

Exhibit 2

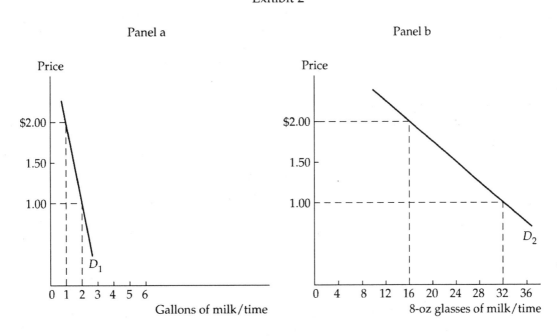

Although we cannot always use the slope of a demand curve to determine elasticity in general, there are some cases when we can use it. In the case of a downward-sloping *linear demand curve*, we know that elasticity falls as we move down the demand curve. Demand is of *unitary elasticity* at the midpoint of the demand curve, elastic above the midpoint, and inelastic below the midpoint. (Review Exhibit 2 in the text.) We also know that a horizontal demand curve is *perfectly elastic*; that is, it has an elasticity value of minus infinity everywhere. This means that any increase at all in price will cause sales to fall to zero. A vertical demand curve is *perfectly inelastic* ($E_D = 0$), which means that the same quantity is demanded regardless of the price. Finally, for a demand curve that is unit elastic at all points, total revenue is the same at every point on the demand curve.

Determinants of Price Elasticity of Demand

What characteristics of a product cause demand to be elastic or inelastic? The most important determinant of demand elasticity is the number and closeness of substitutes. If the price of a good increases and consumers believe the good is unique, then sales will not decrease by very much. If there are many other products that consumers believe are close substitutes for the good, then consumers will switch and sales will decrease sharply.

The way goods are defined affects the number and closeness of substitutes and thus the value of elasticity. The demand for gasoline is less elastic than the demand for Exxon gasoline. If all gas stations increase prices by 10 percent, studies have shown that people will reduce their purchases by less than 10 percent. If Exxon raises its price by 10 percent while all other gasoline sellers maintain the old prices, however, many Exxon consumers will switch to other brands. Note that the number and closeness of substitutes determine consumer behavior in this case. Among the substitutes for gasoline are public transportation, walking, bicycle riding, carpooling, and staying at home. All of these are also substitutes for Exxon gasoline. In addition, Shell, Mobil, Phillips, and all other brands of gasoline are very close substitutes for Exxon gasoline.

Another determinant of price elasticity of demand is the proportion of the consumer's budget spent on the good. If expenditures on a good constitute a fairly large proportion of a consumer's budget, then a price change will have a large effect on the consumer's real income. In the case of a price increase, real income falls, and the consumer is forced to cut back expenditures on the good. A 10-percent increase in the price of an automobile has a bigger impact on the budget than a 10-percent increase in the price of salt. Demand for automobiles thus tends to be more elastic than demand for salt.

The third determinant of demand elasticity, time, is also related to the number and closeness of substitutes. A sudden increase in the price of electricity may induce consumers to make sure lights are off in empty rooms and to run air conditioners at 78 degrees instead of 72 degrees. As time passes, consumers may add insulation to their houses and replace electric stoves with gas stoves. It is easier (less costly) to substitute away from electricity the longer the time period, so demand becomes more elastic.

Price Elasticity of Supply

We can also measure the responsiveness of quantity supplied to a change in price. The *price elasticity of supply* is calculated the same way as price elasticity of demand, except quantity supplied is used instead of quantity demanded. The terminology is similar, too. If the value of supply elasticity is greater than 1.0, supply is elastic; if the value is less than 1.0, supply is inelastic; and if the value equals 1.0, supply is of unitary elasticity. A vertical supply curve has a supply elasticity of zero and represents a perfectly inelastic supply; a horizontal supply curve has a supply elasticity equal to infinity and represents a perfectly elastic supply.

The elasticity of supply depends on how production costs change with output, a topic that will be examined further in later chapters. The more slowly marginal cost rises as output expands, the more elastic supply will be. A second determinant is time. The longer the time allowed for adjustment, the more elastic the supply. An increase in price will encourage existing producers to expand production and new producers to enter the market. But it takes time to build new factories and increase purchases of material inputs.

Other Elasticity Measures

There are two other useful measures of elasticity: income elasticity of demand and cross-price elasticity of demand. The *income elasticity of demand* is defined as the percentage change in quantity demanded divided by the percentage change in income. Demand for some goods falls as income increases. These goods are called *inferior goods* and they have a negative income elasticity of demand. *Normal goods* are those with a positive income elasticity of demand, which means that demand for such goods increases as income increases. Normal goods can be divided into goods that are income elastic and those that are income inelastic.

The *cross-price elasticity of demand* measures the percentage change in quantity demanded of one good divided by the percentage change in price of another good. An increase in the price of McDonald's hamburgers generates an increase in the sales of Burger King hamburgers. A positive value of cross-price elasticity of demand indicates that two goods are substitutes, and the larger the value, the more consumers consider the two goods to be close substitutes. Some pairs of goods are complements because consumption of one often involves consumption of the other. Some familiar complements are cereal and milk, gasoline and tires, and hamburgers and hamburger buns. An increase in the price of hamburger encourages people to buy less hamburger. If they buy less hamburger, they also buy fewer hamburger buns. Complements have negative values of cross-price elasticity.

Appendix: Price Elasticity and Tax Incidence

Governments impose taxes on goods in order to raise tax revenues. Examples include taxes on gasoline, cigarettes, alcoholic beverages, and airline tickets. Many people believe the sellers pass along the tax to consumers so that the consumer ultimately pays the tax. Under almost all situations, this belief is false. The tax incidence, or who ultimately pays the tax, depends on the price elasticity of demand and supply.

A tax on a good causes the price paid by consumers to increase. As long as the demand curve slopes down, the effect of this tax is both to raise price and to reduce quantity demanded. Because the higher price induces consumers to buy fewer units of the good, this price does not rise by the full amount of the tax. If the pre-tax price of a gallon of gasoline is $1.00 per gallon, then the consumer pays $1.00 per gallon and the seller receives $1.00 per gallon. If a $0.50 tax is added, the final price paid by consumers will be less than $1.50. After the seller sends $0.50 per gallon to the government, the seller receives a price less than $1.00. Suppose the final price is $1.30 per gallon, then the consumers bear 60% of the tax ($0.30 of the $0.50 tax), and sellers bear 20% of the tax ($0.20 of the $0.50 tax).

The more elastic the demand curve, the more consumers reduce consumption of gasoline after a tax is added. This implies that the final price paid by consumers rises, but not by very much. Consequently, sellers bear a relatively larger share of the tax. On the other hand, if supply is more elastic, the consumers bear a larger burden of the tax. Review carefully Exhibits 13 and 14 in the text to be sure you understand how to find the incidence of a tax on a good or service.

IV. LAGNIAPPE

Time, Elasticity, and Nuclear Power

In the 1970s, the Organization of Petroleum Exporting Countries (OPEC) increased the price of oil by curtailing production. Oil prices rose rapidly, but consumption did not fall by as large a percentage. This indicated an inelastic demand. Electricity prices rose as a result of higher oil prices. Many people feared that the increased scarcity of oil would lead to a scarcity of electricity, which would limit economic growth. One response to the problem was to increase the construction of nuclear power plants. The long-run demand for oil and electricity turned out to be more elastic than had been thought, however, and people conserved more energy than had been expected. Further, new sources of oil were discovered, which helped bring about lower oil prices.

Question to Think About: Has the decline in oil prices that started in January 1986 generated a return to the energy consumption patterns of the 1960s?

Are Children Inferior Goods?

An inferior good is one that people consume less of as their incomes increase. Economists have long noted that family size tends to decline as income increases. That is, wealthier people tend to have fewer children. It appears, then, that children are inferior goods.

Question to Think About: What are the implications of the relationship between income and family size for developing countries that currently have very high rates of population growth?

V. KEY TERMS

Price elasticity of demand
Inelastic demand
Elastic demand
Price elasticity formula
Total revenue
Linear demand curve
Perfectly elastic demand (supply) curve
Perfectly inelastic demand (supply) curve

Unit elastic demand curve
Constant elasticity of demand
Price elasticity of supply
Perfectly elastic supply curve
Perfectly inelastic supply curve
Unit elastic supply curve
Income elasticity of demand
Cross-price elasticity of demand
Tax incidence

VI. QUESTIONS

A. Completion

1. Elasticity is another word for _____.

2. If a 1-percent decrease in price leads to a 3-percent increase in quantity demanded, demand is _____.

3. A perfectly inelastic demand curve is _____.

4. A perfectly inelastic demand curve has an elasticity value of _____.

5. Demand is more price elastic the greater the number of _____.

6. If total revenue stays the same after a price increase, demand is _____.

7. The more _____ a good is defined the fewer substitutes it has.

8. The price elasticity of demand is greater the _____ the time period.

9. The elasticity of supply is _____ the longer the period of adjustment.

10. The ability of firms to alter quantity supplied in response to price changes varies across_____.

11. A good that is income inelastic is a _____.

12. Goods with an income elasticity greater than one are sometimes called _____.

13. A good with a negative income elasticity of demand is an _____ good

14. If the cross-price elasticity of demand between two goods is positive, then the goods are _____.

15. Two goods are complements if the cross-price elasticity of demand is _____.

B. True/False

_____ 1. The price elasticity of demand equals the change in quantity demanded divided by the change in price.

_____ 2. The greater the slope, the greater the elasticity of demand.

_____ 3. Price elasticity of 2 is more elastic than a ratio of 1.

_____ 4. Price elasticity of demand does not depend on the unit of measurement used.

_____ 5. If demand for a good is price elastic, the producer can increase total revenue by lowering the price of the good.

_____ 6. With a downward-sloping linear demand curve, higher prices are associated with a less elastic demand.

_____ 7. Total revenue is the same at all points regardless of price for a unit elastic demand curve.

_____ 8. Total revenue is at a maximum when the elasticity of demand is 1.0.

_____ 9. A perfectly inelastic demand curve has a slope of infinity.

_____ 10. If supply is perfectly inelastic, then an increase in price will generate less total revenue.

_____ 11. Demand is more price elastic the greater the closeness of available substitutes.

_____ 12. The greater the price elasticity of demand, the lower the price elasticity of supply.

_____ 13. The demand for personal computers is more price elastic than the demand for paper-clips.

_____ 14. The demand for food is more price elastic than the demand for steak.

_____ 15. Demand becomes more inelastic as time passes.

_____ 16. The most important determinant of elasticity of supply is the price of related goods.

_____ 17. The longer the period of time for adjustment, the greater the elasticity of supply.

_____ 18. The value of income elasticity of demand must be positive.

_____ 19. The income elasticity of demand for food is greater than one..

_____ 20. If two goods have a cross-price elasticity of demand equal to zero, the two goods are substitutes.

C.   Multiple Choice

1.   Price elasticity of demand is defined as
  a.   the change in quantity demanded divided by the change in price.
  b.   the change in price divided by the change in quantity demanded.
  c.   the percentage change in price divided by the percentage change in quantity demanded.
  d.   the percentage change in quantity demanded divided by the percentage change in price.
  e.   the percentage change in demand divided by the percentage change in supply.

2. Which of the following is true of the relationship between slope and elasticity?
   a. They are the same thing.
   b. They are unrelated.
   c. The slope affects elasticity along with the existing price and quantity demanded.
   d. The slope is the inverse of elasticity of demand.
   e. none of the above

3. If demand is price elastic, then
   a. the numerical value of price elasticity is between zero and 1.0.
   b. a price increase will generate an increase in total revenue.
   c. the demand curve is horizontal.
   d. total revenue is at a maximum.
   e. total revenue will increase if the price falls.

4. If demand is price elastic and price decreases, then
   a. the extra revenues from the extra units sold are exactly offset by the loss in revenues due to the lower price.
   b. the extra revenues from the extra units sold exceed the loss in revenues from the lower price.
   c. the extra revenues from the extra units sold are less than the loss in revenues from the lower price.
   d. more information is necessary to determine what happens to total revenue.
   e. the firm sells more units but at a loss.

5. If a demand curve has an elasticity of demand of 1.0 everywhere, then a 40-percent change in price will
   a. cause a 40-percent increase in total revenues.
   b. cause a 40-percent decrease in total revenues.
   c. cause quantity demanded to be constant.
   d. not cause a change in total revenue.
   e. none of the above

6. Price elasticity of demand is greater
   a. the more unique the product.
   b. the lower the price.
   c. the greater the availability of close substitutes.
   d. the fewer close substitutes that are available.
   e. a and d

Exhibit 3

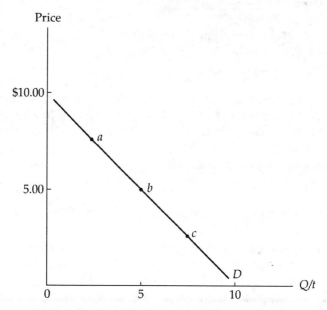

7. Demand for the good in Exhibit 3 is
   a. more elastic at point *a* than at point *b*.
   b. more elastic at point *c* than at point *b*.
   c. of unitary elasticity at point *a*.
   d. of unitary elasticity everywhere.
   e . perfectly elastic.

Exhibit 4

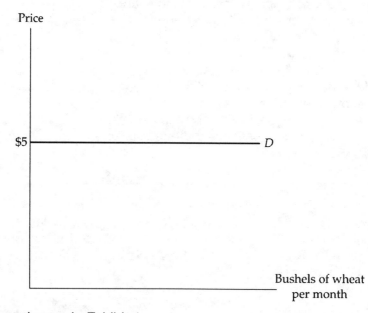

8. The demand curve in Exhibit 4
   a. is perfectly elastic.
   b. is perfectly inelastic.
   c. has a price elasticity value of infinity.
   d. has a price elasticity value of zero.
   e. a and c

9. If a firm faced the demand curve in Exhibit 4 and it raised its price,
    a. its revenues would increase.
    b. its revenues would remain constant.
    c. the quantity sold would remain constant.
    d. the quantity sold would fall to zero.
    e. none of the above

10. When expenditures on a certain good make up a large proportion of your budget,
    a. demand is price elastic because an increase in price has a large effect on your ability to buy the good.
    b. demand is price elastic because an increase in price has a large effect on your willing-ness to buy the good.
    c. demand is price inelastic because the good is very important to you.
    d. demand is price inelastic because the good must have a few close substitutes.
    e. none of the above

11. Price elasticity of demand increases over time because
    a. price increases over time.
    b. goods make up a large proportion of one's budget over time.
    c. the prices of other goods change over time.
    d. the ability to substitute away from higher-priced goods increases over time.
    e. supply elasticity increases over time.

12. Salt has a low elasticity of demand because
    a. it has few close substitutes.
    b. it is a small fraction of a consumer's budget.
    c. it is a luxury.
    d. both a and b
    e. none of the above. Salt has a high elasticity of demand.

13. Which of the following statements is correct?
    a. A vertical demand curve is perfectly inelastic, but a vertical supply curve is perfectly elastic.
    b. A vertical demand curve is perfectly elastic, but a vertical supply curve is perfectly inelastic.
    c. Both a vertical demand curve and a vertical supply curve are perfectly inelastic.
    d. A horizontal demand curve is perfectly elastic, but a horizontal supply curve is perfectly inelastic.
    e. a and d

14. Which of the following statements is correct?
    a. Total revenue falls if price goes up and supply is inelastic.
    b. Supply is more elastic the longer the time period under consideration.
    c. Supply is more elastic over time because producers are able to adjust their production plans and techniques more easily.
    d. Elasticity of supply does not depend on time.
    e. b and c

15. As time increases
    a. demand becomes more elastic and supply becomes less elastic.
    b. demand becomes less elastic and supply becomes more inelastic.
    c. both demand and supply become more elastic.
    d. both demand and supply become less elastic.
    e. demand becomes more elastic but elasticity of supply is unaffected.

16. Suppose demand increases with rising income, but by a smaller percentage than the increase in income. In this case,
    a. the income elasticity of demand is negative.
    b. the income elasticity of demand is between zero and 1.0.
    c. the income elasticity of demand is greater than 1.0
    d. the good is income elastic
    e. c and d.

17. If the income elasticity of demand is very high, we expect the price elasticity of demand to be
    a. elastic.
    b. inelastic.
    c. of unitary elasticity.
    d. perfectly elastic.
    e. perfectly inelastic.

18. The cross-price elasticity of demand indicates
    a. whether two goods are substitutes or complements.
    b. whether two goods are income elastic.
    c. whether demand for the goods is inelastic.
    d. whether the two goods are produced by the same seller.
    e. none of the above.

19. A product has a large negative cross-price elasticity with several other products. We would expect the product's price elasticity of demand to be
    a. elastic.
    b. inelastic.
    c. of unitary elasticity.
    d. perfectly elastic.
    e. perfectly inelastic.

20. If the elasticity of demand for a good X is 0.01, the cross-price elasticity of demand between X and Y is
    a. positive and large
    b. positive and small
    c. negative and large
    d. negative and small
    e. we can't tell without more information.

Exhibit 5

1.

Price	Quantity Demanded	Total Revenue	Price Elasticity
$20	.5	_____	_____
$18	1.5	_____	_____
$16	2.5	_____	_____
$14	4	_____	_____
$12	6	_____	_____
$10	8	_____	_____
$8	11	_____	_____
$6	15	_____	_____
$4	20	_____	_____
$2	26	_____	_____

a.   Calculate the values of price elasticity of demand using the information in Exhibit 5. Fill in the two columns on the right side of the table.

b.   For which prices is demand elastic? inelastic?

c.   If price decreases from $12 to $10, how much of the increased revenue is due to selling more units?

d.   What is the change in total revenue due to the lower price of units previously sold at $12?

e.   Calculate the combined effect of the above changes on total revenue.

f.   Calculate the change in revenue from increased sales, the change in revenue from the decreased price of units previously sold at a higher price, and the combined effect of these changes on total revenue when the price changes from $4 to $2.

2.   How are slope and elasticity related?

3.   Suppose you attend a meeting at work to discuss whether to change the price of your product. You think demand is elastic, but a colleague thinks it is inelastic. Does it matter whether demand is elastic or not? Explain. Is it possible that you are both right? Explain.

4. Label as a the point in Exhibit 6 where demand is unit elastic. Indicate where the demand curve is elastic and where it is inelastic.

Exhibit 6

5. Explain why price elasticity of demand is greater for goods with a large number of close substitutes than it is for goods with fewer substitutes.

6. Indicate for each pair of goods which good has the more elastic price demand and why.
   a. automobile; gasoline
   b. electricity; amusement park admission
   c. blue jeans; a pair of pants

7. Business people and vacationers both travel by airplane. Which group of customers would have the more elastic demand for air travel?

8. Explain why demand is more elastic in the long run than in the short run.

9. A state raises revenues by imposing a tax on gasoline. Other things equal, what happens to the tax revenue from the tax over time? Explain.

10. Explain why supply is more elastic in the long run.

11. Explain why the ability of firms to alter quantity supplied in response to price changes differs across industries.

12. Can a good be an inferior good for all levels of income? Explain.

13. If the demand curve for a good is vertical, what can we conclude about the income elasticity of the good?

14. Miss Muffet consumes two goods: curds and whey. If her income elasticity for curds is greater than one, what is her income elasticity for whey?

15. Robert Britt always spends one-fourth of his income on CD's. Amy spends $100 on CD's every month regardless of price or income.
    a. What is Robert's income elasticity of demand? What is his price elasticity of demand? Explain.
    b. What is Amy's income elasticity of demand? What is her price elasticity of demand? Explain.

16. Suppose that demand for good A is unit elastic everywhere along the demand curve, and that you spend all your income on good A and good B. What can we conclude about the cross-price elasticity of goods A and B?

17. Explain why the correct answer to multiple choice question 19 is *a*.

18. Explain why the correct answer to multiple choice question 20 is *e*. What do you think the cross-price elasticity of demand will equal?

19. The government requires a tax on phone services of 5 cents per call. According to a local news reporter, "The phone company is expected to pass the tax on to consumers." Is the reporter correct? Explain.

VII. ANSWERS

A. *Completion*

1. responsiveness
2. elastic
3. vertical
4. zero
5. substitutes
6. unit elastic
7. broadly
8. longer
9. greater
10. industries
11. necessity
12. luxuries
13. inferior
14. substitutes
15. negative

B. *True/False*

1. False. Price elasticity of demand measures percentage changes, not simply changes in quantity.
2. False. Elasticity and slope are not the same thing.
3. True
4. True
5. True
6. False
7. True
8. True
9. True
10. False. Total revenue will rise.
11. True
12. False. There is no fixed relationship between price elasticity of demand and price elasticity of supply.
13. True
14. False
15. False
16. False
17. True
18. False
19. False
20. False. They are unrelated.

C. Multiple Choice

1.	d	6.	c	11.	d	16.	b
2.	c	7.	a	12.	d	17.	a
3.	e	8.	e	13.	c	18.	a
4.	b	9.	d	14.	e	19.	a
5.	d	10.	a	15.	c	20.	e

D. Discussion Questions

1. a.

Price	Quantity Demanded	Total Revenue	Price Elasticity
$20	.5	$10	_____
$18	1.5	$27	9.5
$16	2.5	$40	4.25
$14	4	$56	3.46
$12	6	$72	2.6
$10	8	$80	1.57
$8	11	$88	1.42
$6	15	$90	1.08
$4	20	$80	0.71
$2	26	$52	0.39

   b. Demand is elastic at prices between $20 and $6. Demand is inelastic for prices below $6.

   c. At $10, two more units are sold, and the extra revenue that comes from selling more units is $20.

   d. The seller could have sold six units at $12 each, for $72. Now these six units are sold at $10 each, for a total of $60. Thus, total revenue declines by $12.

   e. The increase in total revenue from selling more units (part c) is $20. The decrease in total revenue resulting from the lower price on units previously sold at $12 (part d) is $12. The combined effect on total revenue is $20 – 12 = $8. That is, when price falls from $12 to $10, total revenue increases by $8, from $72 to $80.

   f. When the price drops from $4 to $2, the seller can sell six additional units at $2 each, for increase in revenue of $12. The decrease in total revenue resulting from the price decrease on units previously sold at $4 is $40. The total effect is $12 – 40, or a decrease in total revenue of $28.

2. The slope influences the elasticity of demand but not in a systematic way that can be stated as a rule. If price and quantity are held constant and slope increases, elasticity of demand also increases. But linear demand curves have a constant slope, and elasticity of demand varies along the demand curve, whereas a unitary elastic demand curve has a constant elasticity of demand but slope differs along the demand curve.

3. Yes, it matters whether demand is elastic or not. If you raise prices, total revenue will increase if demand is inelastic but decrease if demand is elastic. It is possible for demand to be inelastic in the short run but elastic when a longer time period is considered.

4.

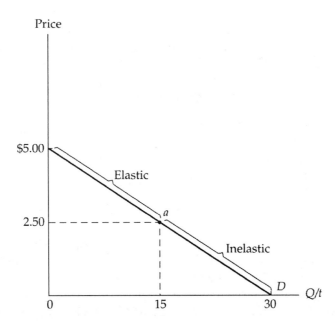

5. If a good has many close substitutes, it is easy for consumers to respond to a price increase by switching to one of the substitutes.

6. a. Demand for an automobile is more elastic because it takes up a larger proportion of a consumer's budget.
   b. Demand for amusement park admission is more elastic because there are more substitutes for it (i.e., other recreational activities) than for electricity.
   c. Demand for blue jeans is more elastic because they are a more narrowly defined good than "a pair of pants." Anything that is a substitute for a pair of pants is also a substitute for blue jeans, and other types of pants are also substitutes for blue jeans.

7. Vacationers have the more elastic demand for air travel. Elasticity is determined by the number and closeness of substitutes. A businessperson has fewer good substitutes for air travel because of the speed of air travel. Vacationers can substitute driving their car or taking the train, or they can select a vacation place closer to home.

8. Demand is more elastic in the long run than in the short run because people have more options open to them in the long run. Anything that can be done to respond to a change in price in the short run can also be done in the long run. But more adjustments can be made in the long run than in the short run.

9. Since elasticity of demand increases over time, consumers will reduce their consumption of gasoline over time and tax revenues will decline.

10. Producers are better able to adjust to changes in relative prices. Firms need time to alter the amounts of fixed inputs they use.

Elasticity of Demand and Supply   **97**

11. The ability to adjust production capacity varies across industries. For example, it takes much longer to build a new automobile assembly plant than a new fast food restaurant.

12. No. Consumption of an inferior good falls as income rises, and increases as income falls. If a consumer consumes zero units at zero income, the consumer cannot decrease consumption as income increases. All goods are normal goods at low levels of income.

13. Income elasticity must be negative. As was pointed out in the chapter titled *The Market System*, the substitution effect of a price increase is to consume less of the good. However, a vertical demand curve means that the same number of units are consumed at each price. Hence, the income effect must be negative and the good must be an inferior good, so the decrease in real income associated with a price increase has an impact opposite to that of the substitution effect.

14. Miss Muffet's income elasticity for all goods together must be one. Hence, her income elasticity for whey must be less than one.

15. a. Robert's income elasticity for CD's is unity. An 10% increase in income leads to a 10% increase in consumption of CD's. If he always spends one-fourth of his income on CD's, then the amount he spends on CD's doesn't change if the price changes. Therefore, his price elasticity of demand must equal one.
    b. Amy's income elasticity of demand is 0 since a change in income does not cause her consumption of CD's to change. Similarly, a price change does not cause her spending on CD's to change, so her price elasticity of demand is one.

16. Unit elastic means that your total expenditures on good A are the same regardless of its price. If you always spend the same amount on good A, your expenditure on good B is also constant. Thus, a change in the price of good A, other things constant, will not lead to a change in the quantity of good B purchased, and the cross-price elasticity of demand is zero.

17. If a product has a large, negative cross-price elasticity of demand with several products, then the product has several close substitutes. Hence, one would expect its price elasticity of demand to be relatively elastic.

18. We don't know if X and Y are substitutes or complements. If they are substitutes, the cross-price elasticity of demand will be positive but close to zero. If they are complements, the cross-price elasticity of demand will be negative but close to zero because the quantity of X will not change much. Hence, the value of the cross-price elasticity of demand is close to zero.

*19. The reporter is incorrect. The phone company would like to pass the entire tax on to consumers, but the demand curve slopes down. People reduce their consumption of phone services due to the tax and the phone company bears some of the tax in reduced revenues and profits.

*20. The demand for cigarettes and alcoholic beverages tend to be inelastic. This means that consumers don't reduce their consumption of cigarettes or alcoholic beverages when the tax is imposed. The government can raise a lot of revenue with these taxes. The purpose of the taxes is to raise revenue, not to alter people's behavior.

CHAPTER 6

Consumer Choice and Demand

I. INTRODUCTION

This chapter provides a closer look at consumer choice by introducing the concept of utility analysis. We will derive a downward-sloping demand curve by using numerical measures of utility. An alternative approach, indifference curve analysis, is presented in an appendix.

II. OUTLINE

1. Utility Analysis. *Utility* is the term economists use to describe the sense of pleasure or satisfaction that consumers receive from consuming goods and services. Utility is a subjective concept.

   1.1 Tastes and Preferences
      a. The utility a consumer derives from consuming a particular good depends on the consumer's tastes and preferences.
      b. Economists assume tastes are given and are relatively stable.

   1.2 The Law of Diminishing Marginal Utility
      a. *Total utility* is the total satisfaction received from consumption of a good, and *marginal utility* is the extra satisfaction received from consuming one more unit of the good.
      b. The *law of diminishing marginal utility* states that the more of a good that is consumed per time period, other things constant, the smaller the increase in total utility received from each additional unit consumed.

2. Measuring Utility

   2.1 Units of Utility
      a. *Units of utility* are imaginary numbers that allow us to assign relative weights to the utility derived from consumption.
      b. Each individual has a unique subjective utility scale.

   2.2 Utility Maximization in a World without Scarcity
      a. A consumer's objective is to maximize total utility.
      b. When the price of a good is zero, utility is maximized by consuming more of the good as long as the marginal utility from consuming an additional unit is positive.

   2.3 Utility Maximization in a World of Scarcity
      a. Consumer equilibrium occurs when the budget is completely exhausted and there is no way to increase utility by reallocating the budget.

b. To maximize utility, consumers must take into consideration their relative preferences for goods, the prices of the goods, and their incomes.

2.4 The Utility-Maximizing Conditions
a. Utility is maximized when the budget is completely exhausted and the last dollar spent on each good yields the same marginal utility, or when $MU_X/p_X = MU_Y/p_Y$ for the last unit of each good purchased.
b. In equilibrium, higher priced goods must yield more marginal utility than lower priced goods.

2.5 The Law of Demand and Marginal Utility
a. Consumer equilibrium is found for a set of prices, preferences, and income, which provides one point on an individual's demand curve.
b. The price of the good under consideration is changed and the new equilibrium is found, other things constant. This provides a second point on the demand curve.
c. The process continues for different prices until a demand curve is derived.

2.6 *CASE STUDY: Water, Water, Everywhere*

2.7 Consumer Surplus
a. Along the demand curve, the price of a good measures the dollar value to the consumer of the marginal utility derived from the last unit consumed.
b. Consumer surplus measures the difference between the value of total utility received from consuming a good and the total expenditure on the good, or between the maxi-mum amount you were willing to pay and what you actually paid.
c. Along a typical downward-sloping demand curve, consumer surplus increases as the price of a good falls.

2.8 Market Demand and Consumer Surplus
a. The *market demand curve* is the horizontal sum of the individual demand curves for all consumers in the market.
b. Consumer surplus applies to the market demand curve as well as to individual demand curves.
c. Market consumer surplus is indicated by the area whose lower boundary is the prevailing price and whose upper boundary is the demand curve.

2.9 *CASE STUDY: The Marginal Value of Free Medical Care*

3. The Role of Time in Demand. Consumption takes time. The cost of consumption has two components: the money price of a good and the time price of a good. The time price of consumption differs across individuals because individuals have different opportunity costs of time.

4. Appendix: Indifference Curves and Utility Maximization

4.1 Consumer Preferences
a. *Indifference curves* show all combinations of two goods that provide a consumer with the same total satisfaction, or total utility.
b. The *marginal rate of substitution*, MRS, indicates the maximum amount of one good a consumer is willing to give up in order to get one more unit of another good, while maintaining the same level of total utility.
c. The marginal rate of substitution equals the slope of an indifference curve.
d. Each curve in an indifference map represents a different level of utility. Curves further from the origin reflect higher levels of total utility.

e. Properties of indifference curves:
   (1) Indifference curves reflect a constant level of utility; that is, the consumer is indifferent among consumption combinations along an indifference curve.
   (2) Indifference curves slope down.
   (3) Because of the law of diminishing marginal rate of substitution, indifference curves are bowed in toward the origin.
   (4) Higher indifference curves represent higher levels of utility.
   (5) Indifference curves do not intersect.

4.2 The Budget Line
   a. The *budget line* reflects the income of the consumer and prices of the goods, indicating all combinations of the two goods that the consumer can purchase.
   b. The slope of the budget line equals minus the price of the good on the horizontal axis divided by the price of the good on the vertical axis.

4.3 Consumer Equilibrium at the Tangency
   a. The consumer wants to select a combination of goods on an indifference curve as far from the origin as possible, but must stay on or within the budget line.
   b. Equilibrium occurs when the consumption bundle selected is on an indifference curve that is tangent to the budget line.
   c. At equilibrium the MRS equals minus the ratio of the prices of the two goods.
   d. The MRS also equals minus the marginal utility of the good on the horizontal axis divided by the marginal utility of the good on the vertical axis. That is, in equilibrium, $MU_X/MU_Y = -p_X/p_Y$ or $MU_X/p_X = MU_Y/p_Y$.

4.4 Effects of a Change in Price
   a. A change in price of one good, other things constant, causes the slope of the budget line to change.
   b. The demand curve can be derived by changing the price of the good and finding the new equilibrium.

4.5 Income and Substitution Effects
   a. The impact of a change in price can be divided into an income effect and a substitution effect.
   b. The substitution effect always results in a change in quantity demanded in the opposite direction of the change in price. It is measured by movement along the same indifference curve on which equilibrium occurred before the price change, to a point where the MRS equals the new price ratio.
   c. The income effect is positive for normal goods and negative for inferior goods. It is measured as the distance between the point on the original indifference curve indicating the substitution effect to the point indicating the new equilibrium.
   d. The total effect of a price change is the sum of the substitution effect and the income effect.

Consumer Choice and Demand

III. DISCUSSION

Utility Analysis

If a consumer has a choice between buying an apple for 50 cents or an orange for 50 cents and chooses the apple, then we presume that the consumer expects to receive more enjoyment from the apple than from the orange. We call this enjoyment *utility* and state that the consumer expects to receive more utility from the apple than from the orange. If the consumer assigns a value of 5 to the utility received from the orange, then a value greater than 5, say 7, is assigned to the apple. If the consumer also buys the orange, *total utility* is 12 (7 + 5), and the *marginal utility* of the orange is 5 units of utility.

Utility is subjective. We cannot compare the utility one consumer receives from consuming an apple with the utility received by a different consumer. Utility depends on the tastes and preferences of the consumer.

The basic principle of utility analysis is the *law of diminishing marginal utility*. This law states that marginal utility eventually decreases with each additional unit of the good consumed, other things constant. Since marginal utility is the increase in total utility from consuming one more unit, total utility increases as more units are consumed, but at a decreasing rate. Keep in mind that the law of diminishing marginal utility refers to a particular period of time. You may not want another piece of cake right now if you have just eaten three pieces, but you may want another piece tomorrow.

Measuring Utility

Economists assume that people attempt to maximize their total utility. In a world without scarcity, this would mean that consumers could increase utility by consuming additional units of a good as long as marginal utility was positive. In the real world—a world with scarcity—the more a person consumes of one product, the less he or she is able to consume of other products. The consumer will consume more units of a good as long as the extra utility per dollar obtained from each additional unit is greater than the utility given up by consuming less of other products.

A consumer maximizes utility by consuming goods so that the marginal utility, MU, of the last dollar spent on each good is the same. If there are three goods—coffee, hamburgers, and pizza—then utility is maximized when the consumer's budget is completely exhausted and, for the last unit purchased of each good,

$$\frac{MU_C}{PC} = \frac{MU_H}{PH} = \frac{M_p}{Pp}$$

If people maximize utility and the law of diminishing marginal utility applies, then their demand curves for goods slope down. Exhibit 1 presents a utility schedule for a consumer's purchases of food and clothing. If the consumer has an income of $20, the price of a unit of food is $3, and the price of a unit of clothing is $2, utility is maximized by consuming 4 units of food and 4 units of clothing:

$$\frac{MU_F}{P_F} = \frac{9}{3} = 3 = \frac{6}{2} = \frac{MU_C}{P_C}$$

Exhibit 1

Units of Food/Period	Total Utility	Marginal Utility	$\frac{MU_F}{P_F}$	Units of Clothes/Period	Total Utility	Marginal Utility	$\frac{MU_C}{P_C}$
0	0	—	—	0	0	—	—
1	25	25	8.33	1	20	20	10
2	41	16	5.33	2	34	14	7
3	53	12	4	3	44	10	5
4	62	9	3	4	50	6	3
5	68	6	2	5	54	4	2
6	72	4	1.33	6	57	3	1.5

Suppose the price of food increases to $4. The consumer cannot continue to buy 4 units of each good because that would take $24 and the consumer has only $20. We also know that the consumer is no longer in equilibrium because

$$\frac{MU_F}{PF} = \frac{9}{4} = 2.25 < 3 = \frac{6}{2} = \frac{MU_C}{PC}$$

To return to equilibrium, either MU_F must increase or MU_C must fall. But MU_C will decrease only if the consumer buys more clothing. Obviously, the consumer cannot do this; spending already must be reduced by $4. Hence, the consumer must reduce the number of units of food that are purchased. By cutting back to 3 units of food, the consumer returns to equilibrium.

$$\frac{MU_F}{PF} = \frac{12}{4} = 3 = \frac{MU_C}{PC}$$

The demand curve for food is shown in Exhibit 2. Point *a* shows the amount of food purchased at $4, and *b* shows the amount at $3. The demand curve slopes down.

Exhibit 2

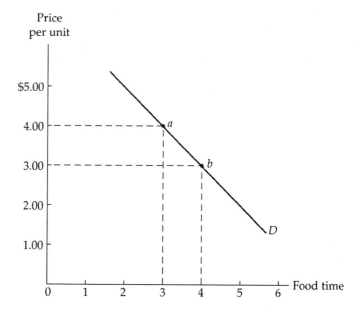

In the previous discussion, the total utility from consuming food fell as a result of the higher price for food. The consumer received 53 units of utility from spending $12 on food when $p_F = \$4$ per unit, and 62 units of utility when $p_F = \$3$ per unit. That is, the higher price for food made the consumer worse off.

Consumer surplus is the difference between the value of the total utility received from consuming a good and the total expenditure on the good. Along the demand curve, the value of the marginal utility from consuming an additional unit is the price of that unit. The law of diminishing marginal utility implies that the value of the first unit exceeds the value of the second, which exceeds the value of the third, and so on. If the consumer buys 5 units at $2, then the consumer values the fifth unit at $2. However, we know that the consumer values units 1 through 4 at more than $2. Since the consumer pays $2 for each of the 5 units, he or she receives more value than was paid for, i.e., he or she receives consumer surplus.

The market demand curve is obtained by adding up the quantities demanded by each consumer for a specific price. If Alvin will buy 5 units of a good at $2, Fred 3 units, and Sophie 6 units, then the total quantity demanded at $2 is 14 units. (Review Exhibit 7 in the text to make sure you understand the process of deriving a market demand curve.) Similarly, total consumer surplus equals the sum of individual consumer surpluses. At a price of $2, for example, consumer surplus is represented by the area below the demand curve and above a price of $2.

The Role of Time in Demand

It takes time to fix and eat a meal, to go to a movie, or to play a round of golf. That is, consumption involves time. The time price of consumption affects consumer decisions just as the money price does. The money price of a good is usually the same for all buyers, but the time price differs, since different people have different opportunity costs of time.

Appendix: Indifference Curves

The appendix to the chapter explains an alternative approach to analyzing consumer behavior: indifference curves. Since consumer choice is essentially a subjective decision, it is useful to have a tool that does not rely on measuring utility. An *indifference curve* shows all the combinations of two goods that yield the same total satisfaction or total utility to a consumer.

Suppose a consumer consumes 8 donuts and 6 cups of coffee per day. This combination of coffee and donuts yields some level of satisfaction to the consumer. Now ask the consumer, "What is the maximum number of donuts you are willing to give up to get one more cup of coffee?" Suppose the individual is willing to give up 2 donuts. Then the consumer is indifferent between a combination of 8 donuts and 6 cups of coffee and a combination of 6 donuts and 7 cups of coffee. Someone is indifferent between two combinations when he or she does not care which combination is consumed. Further, the individual's *marginal rate of substitution* (MRS) of coffee for donuts equals 2 because he or she is willing to give up 2 donuts for 1 cup of coffee.

Other combinations of coffee and donuts that yield the same total satisfaction can be found in a similar fashion by posing the same question, "What is the maximum number of donuts you are willing to give up to get one more cup of coffee?" The *law of diminishing marginal rate of substitution* indicates that the consumer will respond with a number less than 2 when he or she is already consuming 7 cups of coffee. Assume the response is 1.5. That is, the consumer is indifferent between the following combinations of coffee and donuts: 8 donuts and 6 cups of coffee; 6 donuts and 7 cups of coffee; or 4.5 donuts and 8 cups of coffee.

Exhibit 3 presents an *indifference map*. Indifference curve I_2 shows the three combinations mentioned earlier (points *a*, *b*, and *c*, respectively) as well as other combinations that yield the same total satisfaction to the consumer. The consumer is indifferent between points on the same indifference curve. Further, the consumer prefers any point on indifference curve I_2 to any point on indifference curve I_1 and prefers any point on I_3 to any point on either I_2 or I_1. The consumer wants to be on the indifference curve that is the farthest from the origin because it represents a higher level of total utility.

Exhibit 3

Earlier in the chapter, we saw that consumers maximize utility subject to their budget constraints. In indifference curve analysis, the budget constraint is represented by a *budget line*. Suppose the consumer has $6.00 a day to spend on donuts and coffee. The price of a donut is 50 cents and the price of a cup of coffee is $1.00. The consumer can buy 12 donuts or 6 cups of coffee, or a combination of the two. Exhibit 4 shows the consumer's budget line. The vertical intercept is 12 (Income/p_D) and the horizontal intercept is 6 (Income/p_C). The slope of the budget line is −2; this slope indicates the rate at which the consumer can trade donuts for coffee and is found by calculating −p_C/p_D. The consumer must be either on the budget line or closer to the origin; he or she cannot consume a combination of coffee and donuts that lies outside the area defined by the budget line.

Exhibit 4

A consumer maximizes satisfaction (or utility) by consuming a combination of the two goods that lies on the indifference curve farthest from the origin but also touching the budget line. Exhibit 5 illustrates.

Exhibit 5

Chapter 6

The budget line is line AD. The consumer can be on indifference curve I1 or I2, but not on I3. I2 is farther from the origin, so it is preferred over I1. Point e, where curve I2 is tangent to the budget line, represents the combination of coffee and donuts that maximizes the consumer's utility, given the prices and the consumer's income. At e, MRS = $-pC/pD$. That is, the rate at which the consumer is willing to exchange donuts for coffee equals the rate at which the market will allow the consumer to exchange donuts for coffee.

Make sure you understand the effects of price changes and income changes on the budget line and how to use indifference curve analysis to show why a demand curve slopes down. We can use indifference curves to analyze many types of consumer behavior. Examine the use of food stamps to subsidize food consumption. Food stamps allow recipients to buy more food than they could otherwise. Food stamps are supposed to be used to buy food and cannot be used to purchase most nonfood items, including cigarettes and alcoholic beverages.

Exhibit 6 illustrates the effects of the use of food stamps on food consumption. Originally, the consumer's budget line is *AB*, and utility is maximized at point *e* (F_1 units of food and N_1 units of nonfood). Suppose the government gives the consumer a cash grant equal to the dollar equivalent of *ef* units of food. The budget line shifts out to *CD*, and the consumer's new equilibrium is *e′*; the consumer can now consume more of both food and nonfood items. However, the government does not want the recipient to increase consumption of nonfood items and so switches from a cash grant to food stamps. That is, the recipient now receives food stamps that will allow the purchase of an additional *ef* units of food only. The new budget line is *AgD*, since the food stamps cannot be used to increase nonfood consumption above *A* (the maximum amount of nonfood items that could be purchased without food stamps). The recipient's new equilibrium is still *e′*, which allows increased consumption of both food and nonfood items. The food stamps are equivalent to a cash grant as long as the new equilibrium with a cash grant lies on the line segment *gD*.

Exhibit 6

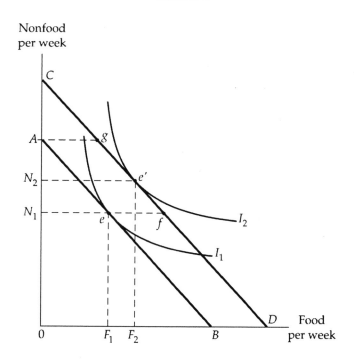

IV. LAGNIAPPE

Consumer Surplus and Sellers' Tactics

As the term implies, *consumer surplus* is the surplus value the consumer receives but does not pay for. It indicates that a consumer would be willing to pay more than he or she actually has to pay. Sellers would like to find a way to capture some of the consumer surplus for themselves. Some amusement parks charge a fee to enter the park plus a charge for each ride. The entry fee is an attempt to capture part of the consumer surplus. Similarly, some restaurants are for members only. A price is charged to join the club, and a separate price is charged for each meal. The membership fee is an attempt to capture part of the consumer surplus.

Question to Think About: Why do firms *not* use pricing tactics that allow them to capture all the consumer surplus?

Children and Time

In the last chapter, we discussed whether children are inferior goods. In this chapter, we can see part of the explanation for the tendency for higher-income families to have fewer children. Children involve time, and the opportunity cost of time is greater when income is higher. Consequently, wealthier people tend to have fewer children. Further, wealthier people will spend more on time-saving goods to help raise their children: nannies, tutors, boarding schools, and the like.

Question to Think About: Is the total cost of a child (time plus money cost) likely to be greater or smaller for a wealthy couple than for other people?

V. KEY TERMS

Tastes
Total utility
Marginal utility
Law of diminishing marginal utility
Consumer equilibrium
Marginal valuation
Consumer surplus
Time price
Indifference curve

Marginal rate of substitution (MRS)
Law of diminishing marginal rate of
  substitution
Indifference map
Budget line
Substitution effect
Income effect
Budget line

VI. QUESTIONS

A. Completion

1. _____ is the term used to describe the satisfaction derived from consuming goods.

2. _____ measures the satisfaction from eating three hamburgers; _____ measures the satisfaction from eating the third hamburger.

3. According to the _____, the greater the rate of consumption of a good during a given time period, other things constant, the smaller the increase in total utility received from each additional unit consumed.

4. A consumer wishes to maximize _____ utility.

5. A consumer's utility is _____ when the last dollar spent on each good consumed yields the same utility, and the consumer's budget is completely exhausted.

6. Consumer _____ is achieved when the budget is exhausted, and the last dollar spent on each good yields the same utility.

7. The maximum price a consumer is willing to pay for another unit of a good measures the consumer's _____ of the good.

8. The difference between the value of the total utility a consumer receives from consuming a given quantity of a good and the consumer's total expenditure on the good is called _____.

9. The market demand curve is the _____ summation of the individual demand curves for all the consumers in the market.

10. The _____ price of a good is the same for all consumers, but the _____ price of the good differs among individuals.

11. The _____ of time is greater the greater the wage a person receives.

*12. A consumer is _____ between any two points on an indifference curve.

*13. A person's utility function can be expressed graphically as an indifference _____.

*14. The _____ indicates the maximum amount of one good the consumer will give up to get an additional unit of another good while maintaining the same level of total utility.

*15. The budget line is also known as the _____ frontier.

B. True/False

_____ 1. Utility analysis provides an explanation of how consumer tastes are formed.

_____ 2. Economists assume tastes are given and never change.

_____ 3. The law of diminishing marginal utility says that total utility declines as more units of a good are consumed during a given time period.

_____ 4. Economists are working on ways to measure utility objectively.

_____ 5. At a price of zero, a consumer will maximize utility by consuming additional units of the good as long as marginal utility is positive.

_____ 6. In consumer equilibrium, the total utility received from each good consumed is the same.

_____ 7. A bundle of goods maximizes utility if any change permitted by the consumer's budget leads to lower utility.

_____ 8. If two goods have the same price, then a consumer's equilibrium implies that the marginal utility from consuming the last unit of each good is the same.

_____ 9. If a consumer is allocating income to goods A and B, and if, for the last units consumed, $MU_A/p_A > MU_B/p_B$, the consumer should consume either more A or less B.

_____ 10. Along the demand curve, price measures the value of the marginal utility derived from the last unit of consumption.

_____ 11. The height of a demand curve measures total utility.

_____ 12. At a price of zero, consumer surplus equals the value of the total utility obtained from consuming the good.

_____ 13. The market demand curve is the vertical sum of the individual demand curves of all consumers on the market.

_____ 14. Consumer surplus applies to individual demand curves but not to market demand curves.

_____ 15. The money price of a good tends to be greater for wealthier people.

_____ *16. Indifference curves have the same shape as production possibility frontiers.

_____ *17. As one moves down an indifference curve, the slope decreases.

_____ *18. Indifference curves can intersect once.

_____ *19. We can derive a downward-sloping demand curve using marginal utility analysis but not using indifference curve analysis.

_____ *20. An increase in the price of a good causes the consumer's real income to decrease.

C. Multiple Choice

1. If marginal utility is positive but diminishes as more units of a good are consumed, then total utility is
   a. increasing at a constant rate.
   b. increasing at a decreasing rate.
   c. constant.
   d. decreasing at a constant rate.
   e. decreasing at a decreasing rate.

2. Which of the following statements is true?
   a. Diminishing marginal utility is a feature of all consumption.
   b. Marginal utility can never be negative.
   c. The rate at which marginal utility falls is the same for all consumers.
   d. The law of diminishing marginal utility applies to food items only.
   e. a, b, and c

3. If total utility is decreasing, then marginal utility is
   a. positive but decreasing.
   b. negative.
   c. zero.
   d. equal to total utility.
   e. none of the above.

4. Units of utility can be used
   a. to compare the satisfaction an individual receives from different goods.
   b. to compare the marginal utility an individual receives from additional units of the same good.
   c. to compare the utility received by different consumers.
   d. all of the above
   e. a and b

5. If the price of all goods is zero, then a utility-maximizing consumer will
   a. consume all available units of the goods.
   b. consume the same number of units of all goods.
   c. consume additional units of each good as long as the good's marginal utility is positive.
   d. consume additional units of all goods as long as total utility is positive.
   e. behave consistently with the law of demand.

Use the following information to answer questions 6 through 8. p_X = $5, p_Y = $10, and the consumer's income equals $50. The consumer is in equilibrium when consuming 6 units of X and 2 units of Y.

6. If p_X increases to $8, then equilibrium will be restored when the consumer
   a. raises p_Y to $16.
   b. increases income to $80.
   c. decreases consumption of X.
   d. increases consumption of X.
   e. decreases the marginal utility of X.

7. At the original consumer equilibrium,
   a. the total utility from X must be greater than the total utility from Y.
   b. the marginal utility of the sixth unit of X equals the marginal utility of the second unit of Y.
   c. consumer surplus must be greater for X than for Y.
   d. the marginal utility of the sixth unit of X is half of the marginal utility of the second unit of Y.
   e. there is not enough information to compare either marginal or total utility.

8. If the price of X increases to $10, the new equilibrium will be characterized by
   a. an increase in consumption of Y.
   b. the purchase of an equal amount of X and Y by the consumer.
   c. a reduction in the marginal utility of X.
   d. the marginal utility of X being equal to the marginal utility of Y.
   e. a change in tastes.

9. Consumer equilibrium is reached when the consumer's budget is completely exhausted
   a. and the total utility for all goods is the same.
   b. and the marginal utility for the last unit consumed of each good is the same.
   c. and total utility divided by price is the same for the last unit consumed of each good.
   d. and marginal utility divided by price is the same for the last unit consumed of each good.
   e. none of the above

10. Suppose a consumer allocates income to goods X and Y. If MU_X = 8, p_X = $4, p_Y = $120, and the consumer is in equilibrium, then MU_Y =
   a. 16.
   b. 60.
   c. 120.
   d. 240.
   e. The question cannot be answered without more information.

11. As price falls and consumption increases, consumer surplus
   a. increases.
   b. decreases.
   c. remains constant.
   d. a, b, and c are all possible
   e. a if demand is elastic, but b if it is inelastic

Exhibit 7

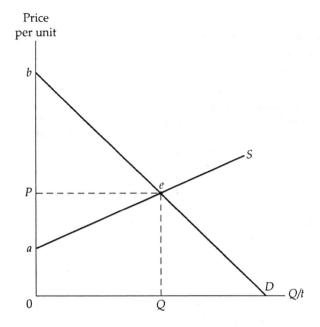

12. In Exhibit 7, consumer surplus at market equilibrium is measured by the area
    a. 0*be*.
    b. *abe*.
    c. *Pbe*.
    d. *Pea*.
    e. 0*aeQ*.

13. In Exhibit 7, the consumer surplus of the last unit equals
    a. the distance *eQ*.
    b. the distance *ae*.
    c. the distance *aP*.
    d. zero.
    e. The answer cannot be determined without more information.

14. A market demand curve is found by
    a. adding the price each person is willing to pay for a certain quantity demanded.
    b. adding the quantity demanded by each person at each price.
    c. adding the consumer surplus of each person.
    d. horizontally adding the marginal utilities of each person.
    e. none of the above.

15. Suppose there are two goods that provide the same service. Which of the following statements is true?
    a. The good with the higher time price will tend to have the lower money price.
    b. The good with the higher money price will tend to have the higher time price.
    c. There is probably no relationship between time price and money price.
    d. People will decide which one to buy on the basis of money price only.
    e. Wealthy people will tend to buy the good with the higher time price.

16. More married women work outside the home today than was true thirty years ago. One result of this change is that families:
    a. have more children.
    b. buy more pianos.
    c. buy more microwaves.
    d. take longer vacations.
    e. All of the above.

Exhibit 8

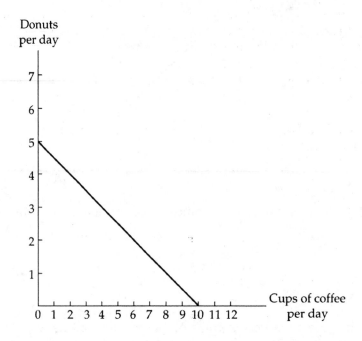

*17. In Exhibit 8, what are the prices of coffee and donuts, and what is the slope of the budget line? Income is $5 per day.
    a. p_C = 50 cents, p_D = 25 cents, slope = –2
    b. p_C = 50 cents, p_D = $1.00, slope = –2
    c. p_C = 50 cents, p_D = $1.00, slope = –1/2
    d. p_C = $1.00, p_D = 50 cents, slope = –1/2
    e. p_C = $1.00, p_D = 50 cents, slope = –2

*18. The law of diminishing marginal rate of substitution implies that indifference curves
    a. cannot intersect.
    b. are bowed in to the origin.
    c. are linear.
    d. slope downward.
    e. all of the above

19. Suppose the maximum rate at which a consumer is willing to give up gasoline for an additional movie is 3 when the consumer is in equilibrium. Which of the following are possible prices for gasoline (pG) and movies (pM)?
   a. $p_G = \$0.90$, $p_M = \$2.70$
   b. $p_G = \$3.00$, $p_M = \$1.00$
   c. $p_G = \$0.90$, $p_M = \$0.30$
   d. $p_G = \$0.25$, $p_M = \$1.00$
   e. More information is necessary to answer the question.

*20. Consider two goods, X and Y. Assuming the price of X falls,
   a. the substitution effect will cause fewer units of Y to be purchased, whereas the income effect will encourage the purchase of more units of Y.
   b. both the substitution effect and the income effect cause more X to be purchased, and the consumption of Y will be constant.
   c. both the substitution effect and the income effect cause less Y to be purchased.
   d. more Y will be purchased only if the income effect is smaller than the substitution effect.
   e. none of the above. The substitution and income effects only affect X and have no bearing on the consumption of Y.

D. Discussion Questions

1. State the law of diminishing marginal utility. What does this law have to do with explaining consumer behavior?

   Use Exhibit 9 to answer questions 2 through 4.

Exhibit 9

Units of Steak (1)	Total Utility (2)	Marginal Utility (3)	$\frac{MU}{P_1}$ (4)	$\frac{MU}{P_2}$ (5)	$\frac{MU}{P_3}$ (6)	Units of Shirts (7)	Total Utility (8)	Marginal Utility (9)	$\frac{MU}{P_4}$ (10)	$\frac{MU}{P_5}$ (11)
0	0	——	——	——	——	0	0	——	——	——
1	150	——	——	——	——	1	200	——	——	——
2	290	——	——	——	——	2	350	——	——	——
3	390	——	——	——	——	3	480	——	——	——
4	470	——	——	——	——	4	580	——	——	——
5	530	——	——	——	——	5	660	——	——	——
6	580	——	——	——	——	6	700	——	——	——

2. a. Let the price of steak (P_1) equal $6 and the price of shirts (P_4) equal $10. Complete columns (3), (4), (9), and (10).
   b. If the consumer's income is $70, how many steaks and shirts will he or she buy per time period?
   c. Suppose the price of steaks increases to $10. Complete column (5). How many steaks does the consumer buy now? how many shirts?
   d. Why does the consumer's consumption of steak fall?
   e. Suppose the price of steaks falls to $5. Complete column (6). How many steaks does the consumer buy now?
   f. Draw the demand curve for steak.

3. a. Let the price of shirts fall to $8. Complete column (11). How many shirts does the consumer buy now? Assume the price of steaks is $6.
    b. Draw the demand curve for shirts.

4. Suppose all the numbers in columns (2) and (8) are divided by 10. Will any of your responses to questions 2 and 3 change? Why or why not?

5. Without graphs, explain how a demand curve can be derived using utility theory.

6. Explain why higher-priced goods must provide more utility than lower-priced goods in equilibrium.

7. What is consumer surplus? How is consumer surplus related to the law of diminishing marginal utility?

Exhibit 10

Price per Game	Quantity Demanded
$8	1
7	2
6	4
5	6
4	8
3	11
2	15
1	20

8. Exhibit 10 shows your demand schedule for golf games.
    a. If the price of a game is $4, how many golf games will you play a month?
    b. Suppose the golf course charges $10 to be a member and $4 per game played. How many golf games per month will you play in that case?
    c. Suppose the golf course charges $6 for the first four games per month and $4 for all other games played. How many will you play?
    d. What are your total expenditures on golf for a month under the three pricing arrangements?
    e. What is your consumer surplus under each of these arrangements?
    f. Why are the same number of golf games purchased under each situation in *a-c*?
    g. What is the maximum price you would pay to be able to buy as many games of golf as you wanted at $4.00 per game?

Exhibit 11

		Quantity Demanded		
Price	Art	Bill	Carla	Market
$10	1	0	0	____
9	2	0	1	____
8	3	0	3	____
7	4	1	6	____
6	5	2	9	____
5	6	3	15	____
4	7	4	22	____
3	8	5	30	____
2	9	6	40	____
1	10	8	50	____

9. Exhibit 11 shows individual demand schedules for three people.
    a. Fill in the blanks to determine the market demand.
    b. Draw all four demand curves on Exhibit 12.
    c. Shade in the total consumer surplus when the price is $6.

Exhibit 12

10. In real terms, the prices of food in grocery stores have risen the last several decades while the price received by farmers has not changed very much. Why?

11. Everybody has the same number of hours in a day, so how can the time price of consumption differ from person to person?

*12. What does the slope of an indifference curve measure?

*13. Using indifference curves, show that a consumer will buy less food at a higher price for food. (Hint: Put food on the horizontal axis.)

*14. Using indifference curves, show the income and substitution effects of a price increase.

*15. If a consumer is in equilibrium and then income increases, the new equilibrium will involve the same marginal rate of substitution. Why? Will the marginal utilities of the goods also be the same? Explain.

VII. ANSWERS

A. Completion

1. Utility
2. Total utility; marginal utility
3. law of diminishing marginal utility
4. total
5. maximized
6. equilibrium
7. marginal valuation
8. consumer surplus
9. horizontal
10. money; time
11. opportunity cost
12. indifferent
13. map
14. marginal rate of substitution
15. consumption possibilities

B. True/False

1. False
2. False
3. False. Total utility increases but at a decreasing rate.
4. False
5. True
6. False
7. True
8. True
9. True
10. True
11. False
12. True
13. False. It is the horizontal sum.
14. False
15. False
16. False
17. True
18. False
19. False
20. True

C. Multiple Choice

1. b
2. a
3. b
4. e
5. c
6. c
7. d
8. d
9. d
10. d
11. a
12. c
13. d
14. b
15. a. If the combined money and time price of one good is more than the other, everyone would buy the other good.
16. c
17. c
18. b
19. a
20. a

D. Discussion Questions

1. The law of diminishing marginal utility states that the greater the rate of consumption of a particular good during a given time period, other things constant, the smaller the increase in total utility received from each additional unit consumed. This law helps explain why demand curves slope down. If additional units of a good provide smaller increases in utility, then a consumer will not pay as much per unit for additional units as he or she was willing to pay for previous units.

2. a.

Units of Steak	Total Utility	Marginal Utility	$MU \over P_1$	$MU \over P_2$	$MU \over P_3$	Units of Shirts	Total Utility	Marginal Utility	$MU \over P_4$	$MU \over P_5$
(1)	(2)	(3)	(4)	(5)	(6)	(7)	(8)	(9)	(10)	(11)
0	0		–	–	–	0	0	–	–	–
1	150	150	25	15	30	1	200	200	20	25
2	290	140	23.33	14	28	2	350	150	15	18.75
3	390	100	16.67	10	20	3	480	130	13	16.25
4	470	80	13.33	8	16	4	580	100	10	12.50
5	530	60	10	6	12	5	660	80	8	10
6	580	50	8.33	5	10	6	700	40	4	5

   b. Five steaks and four shirts

   c. Three steaks and four shirts

   d. At the higher price for steak, MU/p = 6 for the fifth steak, which is less than MU/p for the fourth shirt. The consumer cannot continue buying five shirts, since that would take $90 and income is only $70. To return to equilibrium, the consumer needs to increase the utility per dollar spent on steak. This is accomplished by buying fewer steaks, since the marginal utility of the third steak is greater than the marginal utility of the fifth steak. At three steaks, MU/p = 10, which is the same as that for the fourth shirt, and the entire $70 is used up.

   e. Six steaks

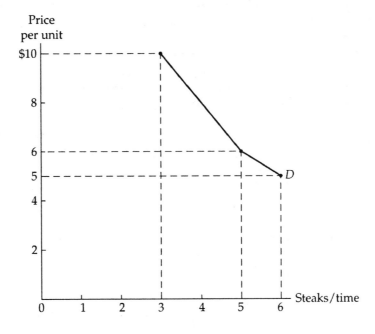

3. a. Five shirts

    b.

4. No. Since all the numbers on the table are divided by the same amount, 10, the ratios will not be changed by the change in scale of utility.

5. In a consumer equilibrium, the marginal utility of the last dollar spent on each good is the same. If we take one good, X, then some number of units are consumed at the existing price. If the price of X increases, the consumer is no longer in equilibrium because $MU/_p$ of X has fallen. To get back to an equilibrium condition, the consumer must reduce consumption of X because of the law of diminishing marginal utility. Since MU falls as consumption increases, reducing consumption will yield a higher marginal utility. The reduced consumption of X generates a higher MU of X, raising $MU/_p$.

6. In equilibrium, the marginal utility per dollar spent is the same for each good, i.e., $MU_X/p_X = MU_X/p_Y$. If the price of X is less than the price of Y, then the marginal utility of X must also be less than the marginal utility of Y. That is, for a consumer to buy the more costly good, it must provide more utility than lower-priced goods.

7. Consumer surplus is the difference between the value of the total utility received from consuming a good and the total expenditures for the good. Along the demand curve, the per-unit price paid for the good equals the value of the marginal utility of the last unit purchased. But this is also the price paid for all the units purchased. We know that the marginal utility of the previous units exceeds the marginal utility of the last unit consumed because of the law of diminishing marginal utility. Hence, the consumer receives more value than the per-unit price paid on all units except the last unit. This extra value is consumer surplus.

8. a. Eight golf games
   b. Eight games. The total value of utility is still greater than total expenditure.
   c. Eight games
   d. $32; $42; $40
   e. $8 + $7 + (2 x $6) + (2 x $5) + (2 x $4) = $45 = value of total utility. Consumer surplus under the arrangement in part a is $45 – $32 = $13; under the arrangement in part b, it is $45 – $42 = $3; and under the arrangement in part c, it is $45 – 40 = $5.
   f. The decision of how many games to play is made by comparing the marginal value from an additional game played with the price. The price of the eighth game is $4.00 in each case.
   g. The maximum total payment you are willing to pay for 8 games is $45, as shown in *e* above. Eight games at $4.00 each is $32, so the maximum you would pay to join the club is $15.

9. a.

		Quantity Demanded		
Price	Art	Bill	Carla	Market
$10	1	0	0	1
9	2	0	1	3
8	3	0	3	6
7	4	1	6	11
6	5	2	9	16
5	6	3	15	24
4	7	4	22	33
3	8	5	30	43
2	9	6	40	55
1	10	8	50	68

b. and c.

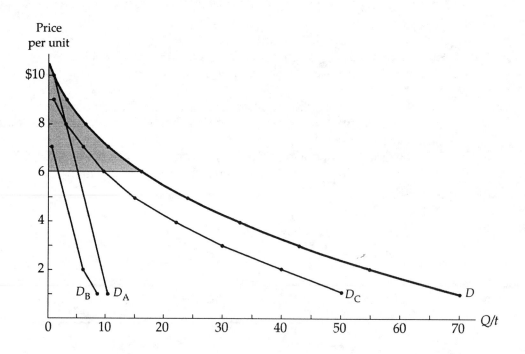

10. The value of time has increased as wages increase and more women work outside the home. To save time, more customers purchase more pre-processed foods rather than preparing food from scratch. The pre-processed food has a higher price because of the processing regardless of the price farmers receive.

11. The value of time differs for different people because different people have different opportunity costs of time. The greater the opportunity cost, the more valuable the time and the more people look for time-saving products.

12. The slope equals the marginal rate of substitution, which measures the maximum rate at which a consumer is willing to exchange one good for an additional unit of another good while maintaining the same level of satisfaction. It represents the consumer's subjective valuation of one good in terms of the other good.

13. In the following graph, the original budget line is AB and the original equilibrium is e. A higher price for food shifts the budget line to AC. The consumer cannot reach equilibrium at e any longer; the new equilibrium is e´. Consumption of food falls from F1 to F2.

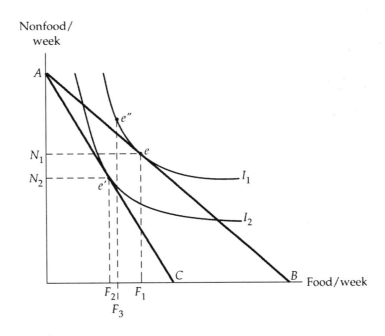

14. The substitution effect is found by finding the point where a line with the same slope as *AC* would be tangent to I_1. In the graph in answer 12, this is point e□, associated with F_3. The substitution effect is $F_1 - F_3$ and the income effect is $F_3 - F_2$.

15. The marginal rate of substitution does not change because the prices of the two goods do not change. At the new equilibrium, the marginal rate of substitution equals the ratio of the prices. Since the prices did not change, MRS does not change. The marginal utility of each good does change, though, because of the law of diminishing marginal utility. More of both goods are consumed at the higher income, so marginal utility falls for both goods. In fact, the marginal utilities fall proportionately because the ratio of the marginal utilities is the same at the new equilibrium as at the old. (Recall that in equilibrium MRS = p_X/p_Y = MU_X/MU_Y.)

CHAPTER 7

Production and Cost in the Firm

I. INTRODUCTION

In this chapter, we turn our attention to the supply side of the market. Firms produce goods and services by combining various resource inputs and then selling the finished goods to consumers or other firms. Production involves technical processes and physical relationships; for example, steel is produced by using iron ore, coal, and other materials. Costs are related to production because all resources have opportunity costs. The costs of production are then related to supply curves. The analysis in this chapter applies to all firms. The next three chapters consider additional features to show how certain types of firms behave.

II. OUTLINE

1. Cost and Profit

   1.1 Explicit and Implicit Costs
       a. Whether a resource is owned by the firm or hired in resource markets, the use of the resource involves an opportunity cost.
       b. *Explicit costs* are actual cash payments for resources purchased in resource markets.
       c. *Implicit costs* are opportunity costs to the firm of using resources owned by the firm or provided by the firm's owners.

   1.2 Alternative Measures of Profit
       a. *Accounting profit* is total revenue minus explicit costs.
       b. *Economic profit* is total revenue minus explicit and implicit costs.
       c. *Normal profit* is the profit required to induce the firm's owners to employ their resources in the firm.

2. Production in the Short Run

   2.1 Fixed and Variable Resources
       a. *Variable resources* are inputs that can be quickly varied to increase or decrease the rate of production.
       b. *Fixed resources* are resources that cannot be varied in the short run.
       c. The *short run* is a period of time during which at least one resource is fixed.
       d. The *long run* is a period of time during which all resources can be varied.

   2.2 The Law of Diminishing Marginal Returns
       a. The *total product* is the total output of goods or services produced by the firm.
       b. The *marginal product* is the amount by which total product (output) increases with each additional unit of a resource, all other resources constant.
       c. Increasing marginal returns: Marginal product often increases with the first units hired because of increased specialization among units of the resource.

        d.   The law of diminishing marginal returns: As additional quantities of a variable resource are combined with a given amount of a fixed resource, a point is eventually reached when the additional units of the variable resource yield a smaller and smaller marginal physical product.

        e.   The law of diminishing marginal returns is the most important feature of firm production in the short run.

    2.3   The Total and Marginal Product Curves

        a.   The total product curve increases at an increasing rate when marginal returns are increasing.

        b.   The total product curve increases at a decreasing rate when marginal returns are decreasing but still positive.

        c.   The total product curve decreases when marginal returns are negative.

3.   Costs in the Short Run. *Fixed costs* are costs that must be paid even if no output is produced. They do not vary as output changes. *Variable costs* vary directly with changes in output. They equal \$0 when output is zero.

    3.1   Total Cost and Marginal Cost in the Short Run

        a.   There are three types of total cost:

           (1)   Total fixed cost (*TFC*)

           (2)   Total variable cost (*TVC*)

           (3)   Total cost (*TC*) = *TFC* + *TVC*

        b.   *Marginal cost* is the change in total cost that occurs as output changes by one unit. It equals the slope of the *TC* curve at each level of output.

        c.   Marginal cost is the key to decision making in the short run.

        d.   Changes in marginal cost reflect changes in marginal product of the variable input.

        e.   Marginal cost falls when the marginal product of the variable resource increases and rises when the marginal product of the variable resource declines, i.e., when diminishing marginal returns set in.

    3.2   Average Cost in the Short Run

        a.   There are three types of average cost:

           (1)   Average fixed cost (*AFC*) = *TFC*/*q*, where *q* = level of output

           (2)   Average variable cost (*AVC*) = *TVC*/*q*

           (3)   Average total cost (*ATC*) = *TC*/*q* = *AFC* + *AVC*

        b.   The U-shaped form of the average variable cost curve and the average total cost curve is determined by the shape of the marginal cost curve.

    3.3   The Relationship between Marginal Cost and Average Cost

        a.   If marginal cost lies below average cost, it pulls average cost down; if marginal cost lies above average cost, it pulls average cost up.

        b.   The marginal cost curve intersects both the average variable cost curve and the average total cost curve from below, where the average curves are at a minimum.

    3.4   Summary of Short-Run Cost Curves

        a.   The level of the firm's fixed cost, the price of variable resources, and the law of diminishing marginal returns determine the shapes of all the short-run cost curves.

        b.   The shapes of the average variable cost and average total cost curves are determined by marginal cost, which is determined by the shape of the variable resource's marginal product curve.

4. Costs in the Long Run

    4.1   The Long-Run Average Cost Curve
        a.   The long-run average cost curve is the "envelope curve," or planning curve, made up of the segments of short-run average total cost curves for various sizes of plant that represent the lowest cost per unit for each output level.
        b.   Each short-run cost curve is tangent to the planning curve.

    4.2   Economies of Scale
        a.   Economies of scale exist when long-run average cost declines as plant size increases.
        b.   Economies of scale can result from increased opportunities for specialization.

    4.3   Diseconomies of Scale
        a.   Diseconomies of scale exist when long-run average cost rises as plant size increases.
        b.   Diseconomies arise as a result of
            (1)   The information problems associated with a large bureaucracy
            (2)   The firm's lack of control over some resources
        c.   The *minimum efficient scale* is the lowest rate of output at which the firm can take full advantage of economies of scale.

    4.4   *CASE STUDY:* At the Movies

    4.5   Economies and Diseconomies of Scale at the Firm Level. To this point, the text discussion on economies of scale has referred mainly to a particular plant rather than to a firm.

    4.6   *CASE STUDY:* Billions and Billions of Burgers
        a.   McDonald's experiences economies of scale at the firm level.
        b.   Standardized menus and operating procedures, centralized management training programs, and advertising lead to economies of scale.

5. Appendix: A Closer Look at Production and Costs

    5.1   The Production Function and Efficiency
        a.   The production function identifies the maximum quantity of a particular good or service that can be produced per time period by various combinations of resources, for a given level of technology.
        b.   It is assumed that the firm produces the maximum possible output given the combination of resources employed; that is, it is assumed that production is *technologically efficient.*
        c.   Firms that maximize profits will be efficient.

    5.2   Isoquants
        a.   An *isoquant* is a curve that shows all the technologically efficient combinations of two resources that can produce a certain amount of output.
        b.   Properties of isoquants
            (1)   Isoquants farther from the origin represent higher output levels.
            (2)   Isoquants slope down and to the right as long as both resources have a positive marginal physical product.
            (3)   Isoquants do not intersect.
            (4)   Isoquants are usually convex to the origin.

c. The slope of an isoquant is the marginal rate of technical substitution (*MRTS*) and equals (minus) the ratio of the marginal physical products of two resources. The *MRTS* indicates the rate at which one resource can be substituted for the other resource while the same level of output is maintained.

5.3 Isocost Lines
a. An *isocost line* identifies all combinations of two resources that can be purchased for a given total cost.
b. The slope of an isocost line equals minus the price of the resource on the horizontal axis divided by the price of the resource on the vertical axis.
c. A firm is not limited to a particular isocost line the way a consumer is limited to a budget line.

5.4 The Choice of Input Combinations
a. The efficient (and profit-maximizing) combination of resources for a given total cost is found at the point of tangency between an isoquant and the isocost line.
b. At an efficient combination, *MRTS* = ratio of resource prices.

5.5 The Expansion Path
a. The *expansion path* traces least-cost combinations of two resources that produce various quantities of output, holding prices of resources constant.
b. The expansion path is closely linked to the firm's long-run average cost curve.
c. Changes in relative prices of resources cause the firm's expansion path to change.

III. DISCUSSION

Cost and Profit

Resources used by firms to produce goods and services can be classified in several ways. One classification distinguishes between resources that are hired or purchased by the firm and those that are owned by the firm (or by the firm's owners). Both types of resources have opportunity costs, but they are treated differently by accountants. The actual cash payments for resources purchased in resource markets are called *explicit costs* and are treated as costs by both economists and accountants. The opportunity costs for resources owned by the firm or provided by the firm's owners are called *implicit costs* and generally are not treated as costs by accountants.

Accounting profits and *economic profits* differ in their treatment of implicit costs. Accounting profit equals total revenue minus explicit costs; economic profit equals accounting profit minus implicit costs. When a firm makes zero economic profit, it is said to be making a *normal profit* because all relevant opportunity costs are exactly covered. A firm will go out of business if it cannot cover all relevant opportunity costs.

Production in the Short Run

Another system of classifying inputs distinguishes between fixed and variable resources. A *fixed resource* is one that cannot be varied in the short run. The *short run* is defined as the period for which at least one resource is fixed. A *variable resource* is one that is easily varied. In the *long run*, all inputs are variable resources.

In the short run, the most important feature of production is the *law of diminishing marginal returns.* Remember, in the short run at least one resource is fixed. To increase output in the short run, the firm must change one or more of its variable inputs. As larger amounts of a variable resource are combined with the fixed resource, output increases. The extra output produced when an additional unit of a variable resource is combined with a fixed resource is called the *marginal product* of that variable resource. The law of diminishing returns states that eventually marginal physical product will get smaller as additional units of the variable resource are combined with the fixed resource. Make sure you understand Exhibit 3 in the text, and especially make sure that you know where diminishing returns begin.

Costs in the Short Run

In the short run, we distinguish between fixed and variable costs. *Fixed costs* are obligations that exist even if the firm is not producing any output and that do not change as output increases. *Variable costs* are zero when output is zero and increase as output increases. *Total cost* is the sum of fixed and variable costs. An important type of cost is *marginal cost*, which is the change in total cost that results when output changes by one unit. Marginal cost is the key to decision making by the firm in the short run since the firm can alter variable and total costs by changing output.

Exhibit 1

Land	Labor	Total Product (Bushels of wheat)	Marginal Product	FC	VC	TC	AVC	ATC	MC
5	0	0		$5000		5000	-	-	-
5	1	100	100	5000	1000	6000	10.00	60.00	10.00
5	2	400	300	5000	2000	7000	5.00	17.50	3.33
5	3	1000	600	5000	3000	8000	3.00	8.00	1.67
5	4	1500	500	5000	4000	9000	2.67	6.00	2.00
5	5	1900	400	5000	5000	10000	2.64	5.38	2.50
5	6	2200	300	5000	6000	11000	2.72	5.00	3.33
5	7	2400	200	5000	7000	12000	2.92	5.00	5.00
5	8	2500	100	5000	8000	13000	3.20	5.20	10.00

Exhibit 1 illustrates the connection between short-run production and short-run costs. Land is fixed at 5 units, and costs $1,000 per unit, so total fixed costs are $5,000. A unit of labor also costs $1,000. Marginal product increases at first, but diminishing marginal returns begin with the fourth worker. Variable costs equal $1,000 times the number of workers hired. Total costs equal total fixed costs plus total variable costs. To calculate average variable costs, we take variable costs and divide by total output (not by the number of workers). So, at 1000 bushels of wheat, average variable costs are $3000/1000 bushels of wheat = $3.00. Marginal cost is found by taking the change in variable costs and dividing by the change in total product. With the fourth worker, additional costs are $1,000 and additional output is 500 units, so marginal cost is $2.00. Note that marginal costs decline while marginal returns are increasing, but increase when marginal returns decline.

Exhibit 5 in the text illustrates total and marginal cost curves, and Exhibit 7 illustrates average and marginal cost curves. The shape of each curve (except the curves for fixed costs) reflects the law of diminishing marginal returns. When marginal cost increases, total cost increases at an increasing rate. Since average costs are found by dividing total cost by output, average costs also owe their shape to the law of diminishing returns.

Costs in the Long Run

In the long run, there are neither fixed resources nor fixed costs. The long run is a planning period during which all inputs can be varied, a new firm can be started, or a firm can go out of business. In the long run, the firm can determine the best method of production for every possible rate of output and select the scale of plant that is best for the desired rate of output. Hence, the long-run planning curve is the envelope of the least-cost segments of the short-run average cost curves for each output level. Review Exhibits 8 and 9 in the text to be sure that you understand the derivation of the planning curve.

The *long-run average cost curve* (or planning curve) tends to be U-shaped. As output expands, the firm is able to use more specialized equipment and workers; this enables it to produce more output at a lower per-unit cost. Eventually, however, the firm may become so large that it becomes unwieldy to run. Per-unit costs may now increase as the firm experiences *diseconomies of scale*. Many studies have found a large range of output for which average costs are constant as output increases; at such levels of output there are neither *economies of scale* nor diseconomies of scale.

Appendix: A Closer Look at Production and Costs

There are many ways to produce the same good. Automobiles can be produced by hand, using very little capital equipment, or they can be produced by very capital-intensive methods. Further, the amount of steel can be varied by substituting aluminum or even plastic for some auto parts. A *production function* identifies the maximum quantity of a good that can be produced by various combinations of resources. Note that less of one resource and more of another resource can be used to produce the same total quantity of output. Make sure you understand the production function given in Exhibit 11 in the text. Remember, the numbers in each row show how output changes when one resource is fixed.

Tools similar to those developed in the appendix to the previous chapter can be used to analyze production. An *isoquant* is a curve defined by points that indicate various combinations of two inputs that yield the same quantity of output. The farther an isoquant is from the origin, the greater the output. Isoquants slope downward, are bowed in to the origin, and cannot intersect. The slope of an isoquant indicates the *marginal rate of technical substitution* of one resource for the other, and also equals the negative of the ratio of the marginal physical products of the resources.

An *isocost line* is similar to a consumer's budget line. It identifies all combinations of two resources the firm can buy for a given total cost. Its slope is minus the ratio of the prices of the resources.

Although the firm's equilibrium is similar to the consumer equilibrium described in the last chapter, there are some important differences. The consumer wants to maximize utility, but the firm wants to maximize profits, not output. Hence, the firm has no desire to get to the isoquant farthest from the origin. Instead, the firm wants to minimize the cost of producing a given amount of output. Alternatively, we can say the firm seeks to maximize output for a given total cost. Both approaches yield the same solution: a tangency between an isoquant and an isocost line. Review Exhibit 14 in the text to be sure you understand these concepts.

A firm may decide to expand production. Presumably, it does so because it believes profits can be greater if it produces a higher rate of output. If prices of resources do not change, the isocost line shifts out to a parallel position, and a new point of tangency with a different isoquant curve is established. This point of tangency represents the firm's new minimum total cost to produce the higher rate of output. The line connecting all such tangencies is the *expansion path*. If the price of a resource changes, then the slope of the isocost line changes. The firm will alter its use of resources to use more of the relatively cheaper resource and less of the relatively expensive resource.

IV. LAGNIAPPE

Be Careful with the Terms

Several new terms have been introduced in this chapter, and it is easy to make mistakes by using the terms incorrectly or carelessly. For example, it is easy to associate fixed resources with fixed costs. Although fixed inputs often generate fixed costs, there is not a one-to-one correspondence between them. For example, coaches at both the college and professional levels are often given multiyear contracts. The coach is not a fixed resource, though, as demonstrated by the fact that coaches are often fired before their contracts have expired. The team owners are still obligated to pay the coach's salary for the length of the contract, however. Hence, the coach's salary is a fixed cost.

The boundary between the short run and the long run is also fuzzy. Generally, the short run is defined as the period of time in which at least one resource is fixed, and the long run is the period of time in which all resources are variable. But the time it takes to alter all resources depends on economic factors, too. A factory can be built slowly for less money or faster for more money by having construction crews work around the clock.

Question to Think About: What factors might encourage a firm to build a new plant very quickly, but at a high cost?

Adam Smith on Specialization of Labor

An important source of economies of scale is the productivity that results from increased specialization of labor. Adam Smith pointed this out in 1776:

To take an example, therefore, from a very trifling manufacture; but one in which the division of labor has been very often taken notice of, the trade of the pinmaker; a workman not educated to this business (which the division of labor has rendered a distinct trade), nor acquainted with the use of the machinery employed in it... could scarce... make one pin in a day, and certainly could not make twenty. But in the way in which this business is now carried on... it is divided into a number of branches, of which the greater part are... peculiar trades. One man draws out the wire, another straights it, a third cuts it, a fourth points it, a fifth grinds it at the top for receiving the head; to make the head requires two or three distinct operations; to put it on is a peculiar business, to whiten the pins is another; it is even a trade by itself to put them into the paper; and the important business of making a pin, is, in this manner divided into about eighteen distinct operations.... I have seen a small manufactory of this kind where ten men only were employed, and where some of them consequently performed two or three distinct operations. But though they were very poor, and therefore but indifferently accommodated with the necessary machinery, they could, when they exerted themselves, make among them about twelve pounds of pins in a day. There are in a pound upwards of four thousand pins of a middling size. Those ten persons, therefore, could make among them upwards of forty-eight thousand pins in a day. Each person... might be considered as making four thousand eight hundred pins in a day. But if they had all wrought separately and independently... they certainly could not each of them have made twenty, perhaps not one pin in a day; that is, certainly, not... what they are at present capable of performing, in consequence of a proper division and combination of their different operations. [Adam Smith, *The Wealth of Nations*. Edited by Edwin Cannan. (Chicago: University of Chicago Press, 1976), 8-9.]

Question to Think About: What limits the advantages of specialization of labor?

V. KEY TERMS

Explicit cost
Implicit cost
Accounting profit
Economic profit
Normal profit
Variable resource
Fixed resource
Short run
Long run
Total product
Marginal product
Increasing marginal returns
Law of diminishing marginal returns
Fixed cost
Variable cost
Total cost

Marginal cost
Average fixed cost
Average variable cost
Average total cost
Lost-run average cost curve
Economies of scale
Diseconomies of scale
Minimum efficient scale
Production function
Technologically efficient
Isoquant
Marginal rate of technical substitution (MRTS)
Isocost line
Expansion path

VI. QUESTIONS

A. Completion

1. The opportunity costs to the firm of using resources owned by the firm are _____ costs.

2. Economic profit equals _____ minus _____.

3. If economic profits are zero, _____ profits equal accounting profits.

4. All resources can be varied by the firm in the _____.

5. The amount by which total product increases with each additional unit of the variable resource that is combined with a fixed resource is called _____.

6. The _____ is the most important feature of production in the short run.

7. Costs that do not change when output changes are called _____ costs.

8. _____ is the change in total cost as output increases by one unit.

9. Average fixed costs _____ with output.

10. The _____ curve always intersects both the _____ curve and the _____ curve at their minimum points.

11. If the long-run average cost curve slopes downward, then _____ are being realized.

12. The lowest rate of output at which economies of scale are achieved fully is the _____.

*13. The slope of an isoquant measures the _____.

*14. The slope of an isocost line measures the _____ prices of the inputs.

*15. The line connecting least-cost combinations of inputs (holding input prices constant) for several output levels is the _____.

B. True/False

_____ 1. Implicit costs are opportunity costs, but explicit costs are not.

_____ 2. The difference between accounting profit and economic profit is in the treatment of implicit costs.

_____ 3. A normal profit is zero.

_____ 4. The short run is the time period during which at least one resource is fixed.

_____ 5. Marginal product can decrease but can never become negative.

_____ 6. Production in the short run tends to be characterized by diminishing marginal returns at first and increasing marginal returns later.

_____ 7. The marginal product curve reaches its peak at the same quantity of the variable input as the total physical product curve.

_____ 8. At a zero rate of output, total cost equals fixed cost in the short run.

_____ 9. Fixed costs increase as marginal cost increases.

_____ 10. Marginal cost can be derived from the total variable cost curve but not from the total cost curve.

_____ 11. Marginal cost decreases when there are increasing marginal returns and increases when there are diminishing marginal returns.

_____ 12. In the short run, the key to economic decision making is marginal cost.

_____ 13. The shapes of the short-run variable cost and total cost curves are determined by the increasing and decreasing returns to the variable inputs.

_____ 14. The long-run average cost curve is the envelope of the minimum points on the short-run average total cost curves.

_____ 15. The shape of the long-run average cost curve is determined by the law of diminishing returns.

_____ 16. Average costs are minimized at the minimum efficient scale.

_____ 17. Many firms operate on the upward-sloping portion of their long-run average cost curves.

_____ *18. Any point on an isoquant is technologically efficient.

_____ *19. Isoquants differ from indifference curves in that isoquants can intersect.

_____ *20. A change in the relative prices of resources generates a new expansion path.

C. Multiple Choice

1. The difference between explicit costs and implicit costs is that
   a. implicit costs are opportunity costs and explicit costs are not.
   b. explicit costs are associated with variable resources and implicit costs with fixed resources.
   c. explicit costs are short-run costs and implicit costs are long-run costs.
   d. explicit costs are associated with resources hired by the firm and implicit costs with resources owned by the firm or provided by the firm's owners.
   e. b and c

2. If accounting profit is $45,000 and economic profit is $20,000, then
   a. normal profit is $20,000.
   b. explicit costs are $25,000.
   c. implicit costs are $25,000.
   d. fixed costs are $25,000.
   e. the firm is not maximizing profit.

3. In question 2, if the owner paid herself a salary of $25,000, then
   a. normal profit would be zero.
   b. implicit costs would increase by $25,000.
   c. economic profit would still be $20,000.
   d. economic profit would equal normal profit.
   e. accounting profit would fall to zero.

4. In Exhibit 2, diminishing marginal returns begin with worker number
   a. 1.
   b. 2.
   c. 3.
   d. 4.
   e. 5.

Exhibit 2

Acres of Land	Workers	Bushels of Corn
5	0	0
5	1	200
5	2	500
5	3	900
5	4	1,200
5	5	1,400

5. If the marginal product of the eighth worker is zero, then
   a. diminishing marginal returns begin with the eighth worker.
   b. total product is at a maximum when eight workers are hired.
   c. the marginal product of the ninth worker is positive.
   d. diseconomies of scale are beginning.
   e. total product will begin increasing at a decreasing rate.

6. When marginal product begins to decline,
   a. additional units of the variable input are unproductive.
   b. total product begins to decline, too.
   c. average product begins to decline.
   d. total product increases at a decreasing rate.
   e. both b and c

7. In the short run, total cost is expected eventually to
   a. increase at a decreasing rate.
   b. increase at an increasing rate.
   c. increase at a constant rate.
   d. decrease.
   e. be constant.

8. When the firm experiences increasing marginal returns,
   a. marginal costs are increasing.
   b. marginal costs are decreasing.
   c. marginal costs are constant.
   d. total costs are decreasing.
   e. The question cannot be answered without more information.

9. The minimum point of the average total cost curve is
   a. at the same rate of output as the minimum of the average variable cost curve.
   b. to the left of the minimum of the average variable cost curve.
   c. to the right of the minimum of the average variable cost curve.
   d. below the minimum point of the average variable cost curve.
   e. a and d.

10. If marginal cost is less than average total cost but is rising, then
    a. average total cost is rising.
    b. average total cost is constant.
    c. average total cost is falling.
    d. average total cost is at a minimum.
    e. total cost is at a minimum.

11. If the long-run average cost curve is a horizontal line, then
    a. there are economies of scale at all rates of output.
    b. every plant size has the same minimum average cost.
    c. total costs increase at a constant rate.
    d. all of the above
    e. b and c

12. Every point on a long-run average cost curve
    a. represents the least-cost way of producing that level of output.
    b. involves a tangency between the short-run average cost curve and the long-run average cost curve.
    c. represents a different plant size.
    d. all of the above
    e. a and b only

13. One factor that gives rise to economies of scale is
    a. diminishing marginal returns.
    b. increased specialization of labor.
    c. information problems.
    d. many fixed inputs.
    e. none of the above.

14. In the long run, if 1,000 units are produced at a cost of $8,000 and 1,200 units at a cost of $9,200, then in this output range there are
    a. diseconomies of scale
    b. economies of scale.
    c. increasing marginal returns.
    d. diminishing marginal returns.
    e. decreasing marginal costs.

15. Which of the following statements is true?
    a. Most large firms produce where there are diseconomies of scale.
    b. The minimum efficient scale is the rate of output where diminishing marginal returns begin.
    c. Long-run average cost curves must be U-shaped.
    d. The minimum efficient scale occurs at the rate of output that takes advantage of all economies of scale.
    e. c and d

*16. Which of the following is held constant in a production function?
    a. tastes
    b. labor
    c. capital
    d. technology
    e. b, c, and d

*17. Profit maximization implies that firms
   a. maximize output.
   b. produce efficiently.
   c. minimize costs of production of a given output.
   d. all of the above
   e. b and c

*18. Along a particular isoquant,
   a. the amount of output is constant.
   b. the amount of labor is constant.
   c. the amount of capital is constant.
   d. the marginal physical product of each resource is constant.
   e. total cost is constant.

*19. If a firm selects a combination of capital and labor that minimizes costs of producing a given output level, then
   a. $MPP_L/MPP_C = w/r$.
   b. $MRTS = w/r$.
   c. $MRTS = MPP_L MPPC$.
   d. all of the above
   e. a and b

*20. Along an expansion path,
   a. prices of resources are constant.
   b. the scale of the plant is constant.
   c. output decreases if there are diseconomies of scale.
   d. output increases at a constant rate.
   e. none of the above.

D. Discussion Questions

1. In a meeting about whether to store inventory in a company-owned warehouse or rent a warehouse, a colleague says, "We should use our own warehouse and save the cost of renting one." Do you agree or disagree? Explain.

2. Suppose you own your own business and have the following costs:

Salaries	$30,000
Materials	15,000
Electricity	2,000
Phones	2,000
Rent	12,000

   You use your own car instead of renting a similar make for $4,000 a year, and you could earn $20,000 working for someone else. Total revenue is $80,000.
   a. What is your accounting profit?
   b. What is your economic profit?
   c. What is your normal profit?
   d. Should you stay in business?

3. Explain why true/false question 3 is false.

4. Fred goes to an expensive private college, paying $25,000 a year for tuition. After graduation, he goes to a state university for law school, paying $12,000 a year tuition. Fred's friend, Barney, tells him that his cost of law school is more due to his cost of college. Do you agree or disagree? Why?

5. Why would anyone stay in business if they made zero economic profit?

Use Exhibit 3 to answer questions 6 and 7.

Exhibit 3

Acres of Land (1)	Workers (2)	Bushels of Wheat (3)	Marginal Product (4)	Total Fixed Cost (5)	Total Variable Cost (6)	Total Cost (7)	Marginal Cost (8)	AFC (9)	AVC (10)	ATC (11)
3	0	0	——	——	——	——	——	——	——	——
3	1	50	——	——	——	——	——	——	——	——
3	2	125	——	——	——	——	——	——	——	——
3	3	225	——	——	——	——	——	——	——	——
3	4	315	——	——	——	——	——	——	——	——
3	5	385	——	——	——	——	——	——	——	——
3	6	445	——	——	——	——	——	——	——	——
3	7	490	——	——	——	——	——	——	——	——
3	8	520	——	——	——	——	——	——	——	——
3	9	540	——	——	——	——	——	——	——	——
3	10	550	——	——	——	——	——	——	——	——

6. a. Complete column (4).
   b. Where do diminishing marginal returns begin?
   c. Draw the total product curve and the marginal product curve.

7. Suppose land rents for $500 an acre and workers receive $100 per time period.
   a. Complete the remaining columns in the table.
   b. Draw the total cost curves on one graph and the average cost curves and marginal cost curves on another.
   c. At what output rate does marginal cost begin to rise? How many workers are associated with this rate of output?

8. According to the text, the shapes of the short-run average variable cost curve, the short-run average total cost curve, and the marginal cost curve are determined by the increasing and decreasing returns of the variable inputs. Explain why this is so.

9. Dave has a summer business mowing lawns with the following schedule for variable costs:

Quantity of Lawns Mowed	1	2	3	4	5	6	7	8
Variable Costs	$10	$15	$25	$40	$60	$85	$115	$150

If fixed costs are $150, what are average fixed costs, average variable costs, average total costs, and marginal costs?

10. Women in a Central American village make hammocks using one worker and one loom to make one hammock a day. Due to advertising on the internet, the village wants to increase production but still use the same production techniques. Will the village experience increasing, decreasing, or constant returns to scale? With it experience economies of scale or diseconomies of scale in constant average costs? Explain.

Refer to Exhibit 4 to answer questions 11 and 12.

Exhibit 4

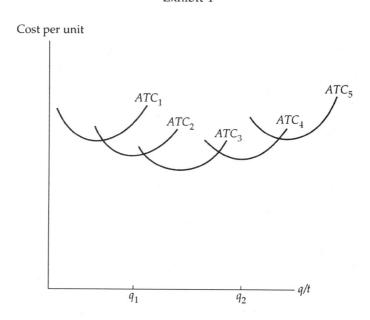

11. There are five short-run average total cost curves in Exhibit 4. Indicate what the long-run average cost curve associated with these short-run curves looks like. Which size plant should be built if the firm wants to produce q_1 units? q_2 units?

12. Indicate where the firm experiences economies of scale and diseconomies of scale. What is the minimum efficient scale?

13. Below are long-run total costs for three firms. For each, state whether it experiences economies of scale or diseconomies of scale. What is the output here where the minimum efficient scale exists?

	Quantity							
	1	2	3	4	5	6	7	8
Firm X	$100	$120	$140	$160	$180	$200	$220	$240
Firm Y	$50	$100	$150	$200	$250	$300	$350	$400
Firm Z	$75	$110	$145	$180	$220	$270	$330	$400

14. Explain what causes economies of scale.

15. Can economies of scale and diminishing marginal returns apply to the same firm? Explain.

Use the production function for wheat shown in Exhibit 5 in answering question 16.

Exhibit 5

Number of Acres Cultivated per Year	Tons of Fertilizer per Year					
	1	2	3	4	5	6
1	90	135	170	200	225	245
2	135	200	245	285	315	340
3	170	245	300	340	375	405
4	200	285	340	390	430	465
5	225	315	375	430	480	510
6	245	340	405	460	510	550

*16. a. Draw isoquants for 200, 225, 245, and 340 bushels of wheat.
  b. Does the production function display the law of diminishing marginal returns? How do you know?
  c. Suppose that the farmer wants to produce 200 bushels of wheat, land costs $200 an acre, and fertilizer is $200 per ton. Add the isocost line to your graph. How many tons of fertilizer would the farmer buy and how much land would she use? What are the total costs of production?
  d. What does the expansion path look like? How much fertilizer and land would the farmer use to produce 400 bushels of wheat? 500 bushels?

*17. If $MRTS_{LC} > -w/r$, is the firm maximizing profits? Explain. What should the firm do?

*18. How are the expansion path and the long-run average cost curve related?

VII. ANSWERS

A. Completion

1. implicit
2. accounting profit; implicit costs (or, total revenue; explicit and implicit costs)
3. normal
4. long run
5. the marginal product
6. law of diminishing marginal returns
7. fixed
8. Marginal cost
9. decrease
10. marginal cost; average variable cost; average total cost
11. economies of scale
12. minimum efficient scale
13. marginal rate of technical substitution
14. relative
15. expansion path

B. True/False

1. False
2. True
3. False
4. True
5. False
6. False. Diminishing marginal returns typically follow increasing marginal returns.
7. False
8. True
9. False
10. False. Total costs include total variable costs, so marginal cost can be derived from either one.
11. True
12. True
13. True
14. False. It is the envelope of the portion of each short-run average total cost curve that represents the lowest cost per unit for each output level.
15. False
16. True
17. False
18. True
19. False
20. True

C. Multiple Choice

1. d
2. c
3. c
4. d
5. b
6. d
7. b
8. b
9. c
10. c
11. e
12. d
13. b
14. b
15. d
16. d
17. e
18. a
19. d
20. a

D. Discussion Questions

1. You should disagree with your colleague's reasoning. The company-owned warehouse could be rented to another company for a fee. If the inventory is stored there, the firm bears the opportunity cost of the forgone rental payments. If the explicit cost of renting a different warehouse is greater than the implicit cost of using the company-owned warehouse (i.e., the forgone rental payments), the company-owned warehouse should be used.

2. a. Accounting profit = $80,000 − $61,000 = $19,000
   b. Economic profit = $19,000 − $24,000 = −$5,000
   c. Normal profit = $4,000 + $20,000 = $24,000
   d. You should not remain in business if you want to maximize your wealth.

3. A normal profit is the accounting profit when zero economic profits are made. That is, normal profits equal the implicit costs.

4. I agree with Barney. As a college graduate, Fred could make a much higher wage than he could as a high school graduate, so this tuition plus the loss in compensation is probably greater for law school than for college.

5. Zero economic profit occurs when the firm covers all relevant opportunity costs, including the opportunity cost of the owner's capital investment and time. Thus, the firm is making a normal profit when it makes zero economic profits. The owners of the firm are doing as well as they would do in their next best alternatives.

6. a.

Acres of Land (1)	Workers (2)	Bushels of Wheat (3)	Marginal Product (4)	Total Fixed Cost (5)	Total Variable Cost (6)	Total Cost (7)	Marginal Cost (8)	AFC (9)	AVC (10)	ATC (11)
3	0	0		$1,500	$0	$1,500				
3	1	50	50	$1,500	$100	$1,600	$2.00	$30.00	$2.00	$32.00
3	2	125	75	$1,500	$200	$1,700	$1.33	$12.00	$1.60	$13.60
3	3	225	100	$1,500	$300	$1,800	$1.00	$6.67	$1.33	$8.00
3	4	315	90	$1,500	$400	$1,900	$1.11	$4.76	$1.27	$6.03
3	5	385	70	$1,500	$500	$2,000	$1.43	$3.90	$1.30	$5.20
3	6	445	60	$1,500	$600	$2,100	$1.67	$3.37	$1.35	$4.72
3	7	490	45	$1,500	$700	$2,200	$2.22	$3.06	$1.43	$4.49
3	8	520	30	$1,500	$800	$2,300	$3.33	$2.88	$1.54	$4.42
3	9	540	20	$1,500	$900	$2,400	$5.00	$2.78	$1.67	$4.45
3	10	550	10	$1,500	$1,000	$2,500	$10.00	$2.73	$1.82	$4.55

b. Diminishing marginal returns begin with the fourth worker.

c.

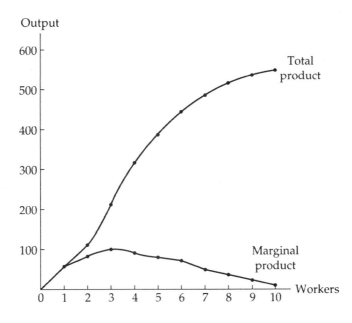

7. a. See the table in the answer to part a of question 6. Note: For columns 8 through 10, you should have used output and not the number of workers. For example, marginal cost equals the change in cost divided by the change in output. The first figure in column 8 is $2.00 because the change in total costs is $100 ($1,600 − $1,500) and the change in output is 50 (50 − 0).

b.

c. Marginal cost begins to rise at output of 315 bushels of wheat; four workers are associated with this rate of output.

8. When returns are increasing and extra workers are hired, additions to output increase; i.e., the marginal physical product increases. The addition to cost is the same for each worker hired, however. Therefore, the marginal cost of output must be falling. When returns are diminishing, each additional worker generates smaller increases in output. Since costs increase by the same amount for each worker and output increases are getting smaller, marginal costs must be increasing. The shape of the marginal cost curve determines the shape of the total variable cost curve and the total cost curve since marginal cost is the additional cost of producing an additional unit of output. Thus, marginal cost also determines the shape of the average variable cost curve and the average total cost curve.

9.

Quantity of Lawns Mowed								
AFC	$50	$25	$16.67	$12.50	$10	$8.33	$7.14	$6.25
AVC	$10	$7.50	$8.33	$10	$12	$14.17	$16.43	$18.75
ATC	$60	$32.50	$25.00	$22.50	$22	$22.50	$23.57	$25.00
MC	$10	$5	$10	$15	$20	$25	$30	$35

10. They would experience constant returns to scale since the technique is the same. They are not engaged in increasing specialization. If the price of a loom and wage for a worker remains constant, average cost would be constant. But, if they had to pay more for a new worker, they would have diseconomies of scale.

11.

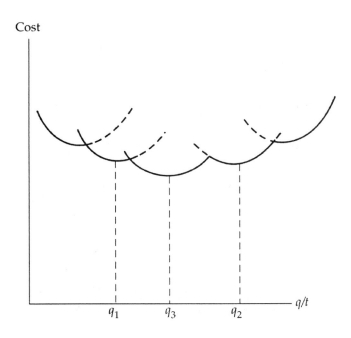

The long-run average cost curve is the solid line shown here. The firm should build a plant of size 2 if it wants to produce q_1 units; it should build a plant of size 4 if it wants to produce q_2 units.

12. Economies of scale prevail up to an output rate of q3 units; diseconomies of scale exist for output rates greater than q3. The minimum efficient scale is plant size 3, since q3 is associated with the lowest of all ATC curves.

13. Firm X experiences economies of scale. Its marginal cost is less than long-run average cost so long-run average cost is falling throughout the range. Maximum efficiency scale has not been reached yet. Firm Y has a horizontal long-run average cost so there are neither economies of scale nor diseconomies of scale. Minimum efficient scale is one. For firm Z, long-run average costs decline to the 5th unit and then rise, so there are economies of scale to the 5th unit and then diseconomies of scale. Five is the minimum efficient scale.

14. Economies of scale are due to the use of more specialized machines and the greater specialization of labor that is possible in larger plants. As a result, output increases at a faster rate than costs increase.

15. Yes. Economies of scale is a long-run phenomenon; diminishing marginal returns is a short-run phenomenon. They are unrelated, so the same firm could experience both.

16. a.

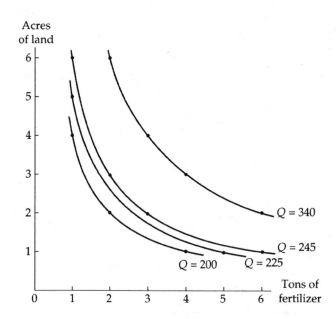

b. Yes, the production function does illustrate the law of diminishing marginal returns because changes in output get smaller along every row and along every column.

c. Under these conditions, the farmer would buy 2 tons of fertilizer and use 2 acres of land. Total costs = $400 + $400 = $800.

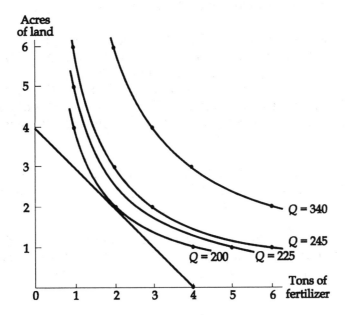

d. The expansion path is a straight line through the origin that connects 2 tons and 2 acres, 3 tons and 3 acres, and so forth. The farmer would use 4 tons of fertilizer and 4 acres of land to produce 400 bushels of wheat, and 5 tons of fertilizer and 5 acres of land to produce 500 bushels.

17. No, the firm is not producing in the least costly way. It can adjust its input mix (i.e., its employment of labor relative to capital) in a way that will produce the output at a lower cost. The firm should increase its use of labor relative to capital, lowering $MRTS$ until $MRTS = -w/r$.

18. The expansion path shows the lowest-cost combination of inputs for each rate of output. The long-run average cost curve also shows the lowest average cost for each output level. Hence, every point on an expansion path coincides with a point on the long-run average cost curve.

CHAPTER 8

Perfect Competition

I. INTRODUCTION

This chapter introduces the model of perfect competition. The model of perfect competition is an abstraction from reality, since it does not describe many actual industries. Even so, it is useful because it allows us to focus on the essential question of how firms adjust the quantity they produce when prices change. That is, what lies behind the firm and industry supply curves? The perfect competition model is also an important benchmark for evaluating the efficiency of other market structures.

II. OUTLINE

1. An Introduction to Perfect Competition. The decisions a firm faces depend on the structure of the market in which it operates. *Market structure* describes the main features of the market: number of firms, type of product, ease of entry, and the like.

    1.1 Perfectly Competitive Market Structure
        a. Assumptions of the model of perfect competition:
            (1) There are many buyers and sellers.
            (2) All firms produce a homogeneous product.
            (3) All participants in the market are fully informed about prices, the availability of inputs and outputs, and production processes.
            (4) Firms and all resources are freely mobile.
        b. Firms are price takers—they have no control over price.
        c. Firms can vary only the amount of the product they offer for sale.

    1.2 Demand under Perfect Competition
        a. The demand curve for the output of an individual firm is horizontal at the market price.
        b. There is no price competition among firms—all are price takers.

2. Short-Run Profit Maximization. Economists assume the firm's goal is to maximize economic profit. Since the firm cannot affect price, the question of how to maximize profit becomes a question of which rate of output to produce.

    2.1 Total Revenue Minus Total Cost
        a. The firm can find an output level that maximizes profit by calculating the difference between total revenue and total cost for each possible output level.
        b. The profit-maximizing level of output is the point where total revenue exceeds total cost by the greatest amount.

    2.2 Marginal Revenue Equals Marginal Cost in Equilibrium
        a. *Marginal revenue* is the extra revenue a firm receives from selling one more unit of output.

149

b. In perfect competition, marginal revenue equals price.
c. If marginal revenue exceeds marginal cost, the firm will expand output.
d. If marginal revenue is less than marginal cost, the firm will contract output.
e. The *golden rule of profit maximization* is that the firm should produce where marginal revenue equals marginal cost.

2.3 Economic Profit in the Short Run
a. Marginal revenue also equals *average revenue* for a perfectly competitive firm.
b. Profit per unit of output is found by comparing average revenue and average cost at the profit-maximizing rate of output.
c. Total profit equals average profit multiplied by output. It is indicated by the vertical distance between the total revenue and total cost curves.

3. Minimizing Short-Run Losses. It is possible for the market price to be so low that no level of output will yield a profit. Faced with losses at all levels of output, a firm can either continue to produce at a loss or shut down.

3.1 Fixed Cost and Minimizing Losses
a. If a firm shuts down, its losses will equal its fixed costs.
b. The firm's losses will be less if there is a rate of output where revenues cover all variable costs and some of the fixed costs.
c. If the total cost curve lies above the total revenue curve at all output rates, losses are minimized where the vertical distance between the curves is minimized.

3.2 Marginal Cost Equals Marginal Revenue
a. The firm should consider expanding the rate of output as long as marginal revenue exceeds marginal cost.
b. If price is greater than average variable cost at this rate of output, the firm should produce.

3.3 Shutting Down in the Short Run
a. If price falls below the lowest point on the average variable cost curve, the firm should shut down.
b. By shutting down, the firm limits its losses to its fixed costs.

4. The Firm and Industry Short-Run Supply Curves

4.1 The Short Run Firm Supply Curve
a. As price changes, a firm varies its output to equate marginal revenue and marginal cost as long as the price allows the firm to cover its average variable costs.
b. The firm's *short-run supply curve* is the portion of its marginal cost curve that is equal to or that rises above the minimum of the average variable cost curve.

4.2 The Short-Run Industry Supply Curve. The *industry supply curve* is the horizontal sum of the supply curves of all firms in the industry.

4.3 Firm's Supply and Market Equilibrium. A perfectly competitive firm selects the short-run output that maximizes profit or minimizes loss. Sometimes minimizing loss implies the firm shuts down.

4.4 *CASE STUDY:* Auction Markets

5. **Perfect Competition in the Long Run.** Short-run economic profits attract new entrants, and losses encourage firms to leave. In the long run, the entry and exit of firms eliminate economic profits and losses.

    5.1   Zero Economic Profit in the Long Run
        a.   The industry is in long-run equilibrium when firms make zero economic profit.
        b.   Each firm adjusts its scale of operations until average cost is minimized.

    5.2   The Long-Run Adjustment to a Change in Demand
        a.   Effects of an increase in demand: existing firms make profits as the price rises and new firms enter, which increases short-run supply in the industry and lowers price until profits return to the normal level.
        b.   Effects of a decrease in demand: existing firms suffer losses as the price falls and some firms leave the industry, which decreases short-run supply in the industry and raises price until remaining firms are earning a normal profit.

6. **The Long-Run Industry Supply Curve**

    6.1   Constant-Cost Industries
        a.   In constant-cost industries, cost curves do not change as firms enter or leave the industry.
        b.   The long-run industry supply curve is horizontal, or perfectly elastic, for such industries.

    6.2   Increasing-Cost Industries
        a.   In increasing-cost industries, production costs increase for all firms as new firms enter the industry.
        b.   The long-run industry supply curve slopes upward because higher production costs mean that firms require a higher price to earn a normal profit.

7. **Perfect Competition and Efficiency**

    7.1   Productive Efficiency: Making Stuff Right
        a.   Productive efficiency occurs when a firm produces at the minimum point of its long-run average cost curve.
        b.   The entry and exit of firms in perfect competition ensures that firms produce at the minimum point of long-run average cost in the long run.

    7.2   Allocative Efficiency: Making the Right Stuff
        a.   The goods produced are those most preferred by consumers.
        b.   Allocative efficiency is achieved when price equals the marginal cost of the last unit sold, which occurs at equilibrium in perfect competition.

    7.3   What's so perfect about Perfect Competition?
        a.   Market exchange usually benefits both consumers and producers.
        b.   Consumers gain because they receive consumer surplus whenever they would be willing to pay more than the market price for some units of the good consumed.
        c.   Producers also gain because they receive producer surplus when the amount they receive for their output exceeds the minimum amount required to supply the good.
        d.   In the short run, *producer surplus* is the total revenue received minus total variable costs for producing the good.

e. The combination of consumer surplus and producer surplus shows the gains from voluntary exchange.
f. Producer surplus is not the same as profit
g. There is no producer surplus in perfectly competitive industries in the long run, except possibly in increasing-cost industries.

7.4 CASE STUDY: Experimental Economics

8. Conclusion
a. Many buyers and sellers are necessary in a perfectly competitive market to prevent any individual buyer or seller from influencing price.
b. Firms must produce a homogeneous product so consumers only care about price.
c. All market participants must have full information so only one price prevails.
d. Free entry and exit must be ensured so that the long-run equilibrium condition of zero profits is achieved.

III. DISCUSSION

Perfect Competition

The model of *perfect competition* is characterized by two important features: first, firms are *price takers*, and second, firms make zero economic profits in the long run. The perfect competition model rests on four assumptions. (1) There are many buyers and sellers, which means that no single buyer or seller can affect price. (2) All firms produce a homogeneous product, which implies that customers only care about the price charged by one seller or another. (3) All market participants have access to all relevant information, so no consumer mistakenly pays a price higher than the market price, and no firm mistakenly pays more for resources than other firms pay. (4) Firms and resources are free to enter or leave the industry at will. The last assumption ensures that firms will make only a normal profit in the long run. New firms enter the industry as long as firms in the industry are making economic profits. Perfectly competitive firms are price takers, i.e., they face a horizontal demand curve at the market price.

Short-Run Profit Maximization

We assume that firms seek to maximize profits. Under perfect competition, the firm has no control over price. The only thing the firm can decide is the level of output it will produce. There are two ways the firm can determine the profit-maximizing output. Fortunately, they both yield the same output level. The first method is for the firm to calculate total revenue and total cost for every possible output and then choose to produce the output for which the difference between total revenue and total cost is the greatest. Review Exhibits 2 and 3 in the text to make sure you understand this method.

The second method of finding the profit-maximizing output is to expand output as long as *marginal revenue* exceeds marginal cost and stop expanding output before marginal cost exceeds marginal revenue. If the marginal revenue from producing one more unit is greater than the marginal cost of the unit, the firm's profits will increase if it produces that unit. On the other hand, if marginal cost is greater than marginal revenue, the extra unit should not be produced, since it will raise costs by more than it increases revenues. The firm will maximize profits by producing at the level of output where marginal revenue equals marginal cost.

Minimizing Short-Run Losses

If the price is too low to allow a firm to make a profit at any output, it will try to make its losses as small as possible. The firm has two decisions to make in this situation. First, the firm must decide whether to produce or not. By shutting down, the firm limits its losses to its fixed costs. However, if there is an output level for which total revenue exceeds total variable costs, then the firm should produce at that output level. If total revenue exceeds total variable costs, then the variable costs of producing the output are covered. There is then some revenue left over to apply to fixed costs, and the firm is better off producing.

The firm faces a second decision if it decides to produce: it must choose the output level that minimizes losses. The way the firm finds this output level is similar to what it does when it is making a profit. It either finds the output that minimizes the difference between total cost and total revenue, or it finds the output level where marginal revenue equals marginal cost. Again, either approach yields the same solution.

The Firm and Industry Short-Run Supply Curve

We know the firm produces the level of output where marginal revenue equals marginal cost. For a perfectly competitive firm, marginal revenue equals the price of the good. That is, since the firm's price is constant, the extra revenue from selling one more unit will be the price received. The firm's short-run supply curve, then, is the portion of its marginal cost curve that is at or above the minimum point of its average variable cost curve. In Exhibit 6 in the text, the short-run supply curve begins at point 2 and includes all of the marginal cost curve above point 2. The industry supply curve is found by adding up the quantities produced by each firm at each price. (Note that this is similar to the way the industry demand curve was determined from the individual demand curves.)

Exhibit 1

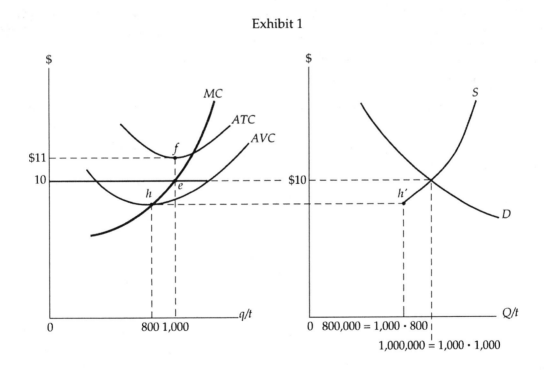

- a -   - b -

Exhibit 1 illustrates a short-run equilibrium. The right-hand panel shows the industry supply and demand curves. The market price is $10 and output is 1,000,000. The left-hand side shows the situation of an individual firm in this industry. Its demand curve is horizontal at $10. The firm's supply curve begins at point h, where the firm produces 800 units. We assume that all firms are identical and that there are 1,000 firms in the industry. Hence, the industry supply curve begins at h', with an output of 800,000. The firm is producing 1,000 units because that is where $MR = MC$. The firm loses $1,000, which is less than it would lose by shutting down, since the price is above the minimum point on the AVC curve.

Perfect Competition in the Long Run

Over time, firms can enter or leave an industry. If firms are making economic profits, new firms will enter the industry. This will continue until economic profits are zero. If firms are losing money, some firms will leave. Again, this will continue until economic profits are zero. With zero economic profits, or a normal profit, firms have no incentive either to leave or to enter the industry. Long-run equilibrium under perfect competition is characterized by zero economic profits. Exhibit 9 in the text illustrates a long-run equilibrium.

The Long-Run Industry Supply Curve

In some cases, entering firms may be able to pay the same for inputs as the firms that are already in the industry. Then the new firms' costs will be the same as those of the existing firms, and the new equilibrium price will be the same as the original equilibrium price. The long-run supply curve of a *constant-cost industry* is horizontal.

Suppose an industry is initially in long-run equilibrium, and then demand increases. The increase in demand causes prices to increase, and firms already in the industry begin earning economic profits. Over time, new firms enter the industry. These firms must hire labor, raw materials, and other inputs to produce the good. If these inputs are already employed elsewhere, the new firms may have to bid up prices in order to hire them. Thus, costs for these firms will be higher than costs were for the original firms. However, costs for existing firms also increase as a result of the entry of new firms. This is because firms already in the industry will have to match the higher prices the entering firms paid for inputs or lose their supplies of these inputs. The new long-run equilibrium price must be high enough to cover the higher costs, so the new equilibrium will be established at a higher price than the original equilibrium. Exhibit 12 in the text illustrates this process. Such an industry is known as an *increasing-cost industry*, and its long-run supply curve slopes upward.

Perfect Competition and Efficiency

Perfect competition is efficient. In the long run, firms are at the minimum points on their long-run average cost curves, so goods cannot be produced at a lower cost. This implies that resources are not being wasted and *productive efficiency* is being achieved. *Allocative efficiency* also is achieved by perfectly competitive industries when the goods consumers want most are actually produced. The value of a good is measured by its price; marginal cost measures the value of the resources used to produce an extra unit of the good. If $p = MC$, the value of the resources used in producing the good equals their value in producing their next best alternative. When this occurs, consumers will not be any better off if either more or less of the good is produced. At equilibrium under perfect competition, $p = MC$.

Exchange is usually beneficial to both consumers and producers. Consumers receive consumer surplus, which was defined and illustrated in the preceding chapter. *Producer surplus* is a parallel concept. An upward-sloping supply curve implies that the firm is willing to supply more units for higher prices. The producer is also willing to supply some units at a lower price, however.

Hence, the producer is receiving more revenues from supplying some units than would be required to get the producer to supply the units. This difference is producer surplus. It is calculated by subtracting total variable cost from total revenue. Graphically, producer surplus is the area above the firm's (or industry's) supply curve and below the market price.

IV. LAGNIAPPE

Profits over Time

The model of perfect competition assumes that additional firms enter an industry when existing firms in the industry are making economic profits. By entering an industry, new firms cause economic profits in the industry to decline. The economic function of profits is to direct entrepreneurs to use resources as society wants them to be used. But the process eliminates the profits that attracted the new firms.

If firms in the real world behaved as described by our model, we should observe a tendency for profits of all firms to gravitate toward the national average. In fact, studies have found that firms making high profits one year tend to have profit rates closer to the average several years later. We do not expect this process to produce zero profits for all firms for several reasons. First, accounting profits and not economic profits are measured. Second, the risk borne by firms differs across industries. Finally, the economy is constantly changing, causing demand and costs to shift.

Question to Think About: What would happen if new firms could not enter an industry?

Resource Mobility and Profits

Resources tend to move from unprofitable to profitable ventures. Sometimes we can see this process at work by looking at the movement of people. In the 1990s, high oil prices encouraged many people to move to oil states such as Louisiana, Texas, and Alaska. In the 1980s, oil prices fell sharply, and people moved away from these areas. Both Dallas and Houston experienced very high vacancy rates in office space. It was even difficult to find a U-Haul truck in these states.

A more recent example involves the computer and internet fields in the 1990's. Many bright college students took jobs in computer and internet firms. When these markets declined in 2000-2001, many of these same people sought work in other industries or returned to universities for graduate work or law school.

Question to Think About: What factors would cause labor not to be perfectly mobile?

V. KEY TERMS

Market structure	Long-run industry supply curve
Perfect competition	Constant-cost industry
Homogeneous product	Increasing-cost industry
Price taker	Decreasing-cost industry
Marginal revenue	Productive efficiency
Average revenue	Allocative efficiency
Short-run firm and industry supply curves	Producer surplus

VI. QUESTIONS

A. Completion

1. Market _____ describes the important features of a market, such as the number of firms in the market.

2. When the product of one firm is identical to the product of other firms in the market, the product is said to be _____ .

3. Resources are freely _____ if firms can enter and exit an industry easily.

4. A firm is a _____ if it faces a horizontal demand curve for its product.

5. Under perfect competition, price always equals _____ and _____.

6. As long as price at least covers variable costs, a profit-maximizing firm produces where _____ equals _____.

7. If marginal cost exceeds marginal revenue, the firm should _____ its output level.

8. The short-run supply curve of a perfectly competitive firm is the portion of its _____ curve that lies above the minimum point of its _____ curve.

9. Long-run equilibrium in perfect competition is characterized by _____ economic profits.

10. In long-run equilibrium in perfect competition, each firm produces at the _____ of the long-run average cost curve.

11. A _____ -cost industry can decrease output and not see resource prices fall.

12. If new firms entering an industry have higher production costs than existing firms, the industry is a(n) _____-cost industry.

13. _____ efficiency is achieved when firms produce the goods society values the most.

14. Allocative efficiency occurs when firms produce at the rate of output where _____ equals _____.

15. If the amount producers receive for their output is greater than the minimum amount they require to produce the output, then producers receive _____.

B. True/False

_____ 1. The decisions a firm makes depend on the structure of the market in which it operates.

_____ 2. Under perfect competition, each firm only has to decide how much of a good to produce.

_____ 3. The product of one producer is identical to the products of all other producers in the market under perfect competition.

_____ 4. Under perfect competition, a firm will not advertise its product.

_____ 5. Perfectly competitive firms try to change the profit-maximizing price.

_____ 6. Firms compete vigorously with each other under perfect competition.

_____ 7. The slope of the perfectly competitive firm's total revenue curve is the price of the good.

_____ 8. For a firm in a perfectly competitive industry, marginal revenue equals the market price.

_____ 9. Firms maximize profits by producing where total revenue equals total cost.

_____ 10. In the short run, perfectly competitive firms can make economic profits or losses.

_____ 11. In the short run, a firm should never have to lose more than its fixed costs.

_____ 12. If price is greater than average variable cost for some range of output, the firm should produce in the short run.

_____ 13. The firm's marginal cost curve is also its short-run supply curve.

_____ 14. If the market demand curve and the market supply curve intersect at a price of $5, the minimum point of the *AVC* curve must be below $5.

_____ 15. In the long run, perfectly competitive firms can make economic profits.

_____ 16. In long-run equilibrium, the competitive firm produces at the minimum point of its long-run average cost curve.

_____ 17. A decrease in market demand causes some competitive firms to leave the industry in the long run.

_____ 18. The industry long-run supply curve always slopes upward.

_____ 19. Where there is productive efficiency there must also be allocative efficiency.

_____ 20. Producer surplus is positive only when economic profits are positive.

1. Which of the following is not a feature of perfectly competitive markets?
   a. differentiated products
   b. many buyers
   c. many sellers
   d. fully informed participants in the market
   e. resource mobility

2. A price taker is a firm that
   a. faces a downward-sloping demand curve.
   b. faces a perfectly elastic demand curve.
   c. is large relative to other firms in the market.
   d. has only limited control over price.
   e. none of the above

3. Firms that seek to maximize profits will
   a. never experience losses.
   b. choose the level of output where total revenue equals total cost.
   c. choose the level of output where the difference between marginal revenue and marginal cost is the greatest.
   d. choose the level of output where the difference between price and marginal cost is the greatest.
   e. choose the level of output where the difference between total revenue and total cost is the greatest.

4. Marginal revenue in perfect competition equals
   a. marginal cost at every rate of output.
   b. price.
   c. the change in total revenue from producing one more unit.
   d. b and c.
   e. a and c.

Exhibit 2

5. In Exhibit 2, the profit-maximizing firm will produce how many units?
   a. q_1
   b. q_2
   c. q_3
   d. q_4
   e. q_5

6. In Exhibit 2, if price increases, profits
   a. increase.
   b. decrease.
   c. remain constant.
   d. We cannot tell without knowing what happens to costs.
   e. We cannot tell without knowing what the market demand curve looks like.

Exhibit 3

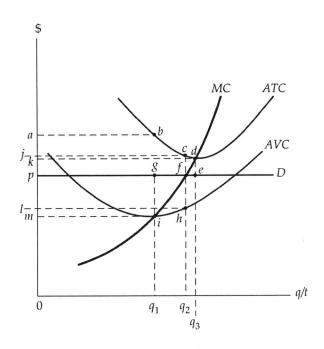

7. In Exhibit 3, losses at equilibrium are equal to area
   a. *abgp.*
   b. *kdep.*
   c. *jcfp.*
   d. *pfhl.*
   e. *pgim.*

8. In Exhibit 3, if price falls to *m*, the firm's losses will
   a. exceed total fixed costs.
   b. be less than total fixed costs.
   c. equal total fixed costs.
   d. equal *migp.*
   e. The question cannot be answered without more information.

9. Profits in the short run are
   a. overstated because fixed costs are not included.
   b. equal to the difference between marginal revenue and marginal cost times the number of units sold.
   c. equal to the difference between price and average total cost times the number of units sold.
   d. only normal profits and not economic profits.
   e. accounting profits only.

10. The firm should shut down in the short run if price falls below the minimum point of
    a. marginal cost.
    b. marginal revenue.
    c. average total costs.
    d. fixed costs.
    e. average variable cost.

Exhibit 4

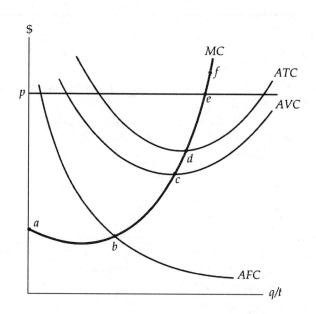

11. In Exhibit 4, the perfectly competitive firm's short-run supply curve is
    a. *abcdef.*
    b. *bcdef.*
    c. *cdef.*
    d. the marginal cost curve.
    e. *bcde.*

12. If perfectly competitive firms are making economic profits, then
    a. wages will always be bid up until the profits are gone.
    b. the firms must be superior and will continue to make profits.
    c. new firms will enter the industry.
    d. they are not equating marginal revenue and marginal cost.
    e. none of the above

13. Suppose a constant-cost, perfectly competitive industry is in long-run equilibrium, and then demand increases. Eventually, a new long-run equilibrium is reached. Output for a firm originally in the industry
    a. initially increases and then returns to its original level.
    b. initially increases and remains at its higher level.
    c. initially increases and then decreases to a higher level than it was at originally.
    d. initially increases some and then increases more later.
    e. stays the same throughout.

14. A decrease in demand causes the long-run equilibrium price to fall. One result is
    a. a reduction in long-run profits.
    b. reduced profits for firms entering the industry.
    c. reduced prices for some resource owners.
    d. an increase in the minimum efficient scale.
    e. none of the above.

15. In an increasing-cost, perfectly competitive industry,
    a. the long-run supply curve slopes upward.
    b. new entrants bid up the price of resources used in the industry.
    c. economic profits are zero in long-run equilibrium.
    d. existing firms' costs increase as output increases.
    e. all of the above

16. Along a long-run industry supply curve in perfect competition,
    a. economic profits are zero.
    b. economic profits can be positive, negative, or zero.
    c. the number of firms in the industry is constant.
    d. normal profit is zero.
    e. none of the above

17. Productive efficiency is achieved when
    a. firms produce at the lowest possible marginal cost.
    b. $p = MC$.
    c. firms produce at the minimum point of their long-run average cost curves.
    d. firms produce the goods consumers want.
    e. economic profits are being made.

18. Allocative efficiency is achieved when
    a. firms produce at the lowest possible cost.
    b. economic profits are being made.
    c. $p = MC$.
    d. marginal cost is at a minimum.
    e. a and b

19. Producer surplus is greater in the short run than in the long run because
    a. there are no profits in the long run.
    b. there is never any producer surplus in the long run.
    c. the short-run supply curve is more inelastic than the long-run supply curve.
    d. a and b
    e. none of the above

20. Producer surplus is zero
    a. when the long-run supply curve is elastic.
    b. when economic profits are zero.
    c. when all workers receive the same wage rate.
    d. when a constant-cost industry is in long-run equilibrium.
    e. none of the above

D. Discussion Questions

1. Perfectly competitive firms are called price takers. What does this mean? Why are they price takers?

2. Show that price equals both marginal revenue and average revenue for a perfectly competitive firm.

Exhibit 5

Price	Quantity	Total Revenue	Total Cost	Marginal Cost	Marginal Revenue	Average Variable Cost	Average Total Cost	Economic Profit
$4	0	—	$10.00	—	—	—	—	___
$4	1	___	$14.20	___	___	___	___	___
$4	2	___	$17.80	___	___	___	___	___
$4	3	___	$20.60	___	___	___	___	___
$4	4	___	$23.10	___	___	___	___	___
$4	5	___	$25.70	___	___	___	___	___
$4	6	___	$28.50	___	___	___	___	___
$4	7	___	$31.50	___	___	___	___	___
$4	8	___	$34.70	___	___	___	___	___
$4	9	___	$38.10	___	___	___	___	___
$4	10	___	$41.70	___	___	___	___	___
$4	11	___	$45.50	___	___	___	___	___
$4	12	___	$49.50	___	___	___	___	___
$4	13	___	$53.70	___	___	___	___	___
$4	14	___	$58.20	___	___	___	___	___
$4	15	___	$63.20	___	___	___	___	___

3. a. Fill in the blanks in Exhibit 5.
   b. At what level of output are profits maximized? Explain two methods of determining this level of output. What is the firm's profit?
   c. Is this level of output a long-run equilibrium? How do you know?
   d. Suppose price increases to $4.50. How many units will the firm produce? What will its profit be?
   e. How far would price have to fall before the firm would shut down?
   f. What adjustments will the industry make in the long run?

4. Suppose there are 1,000 firms in the industry of the firm described in the previous question.
    a. Draw the industry supply curve in the right-hand grid of Exhibit 6. Add a demand curve that intersects the supply curve at the correct place.
    b. Draw the relevant curves for the firm in the left-hand grid.
    c. Indicate the firm's profits or losses.

Exhibit 6

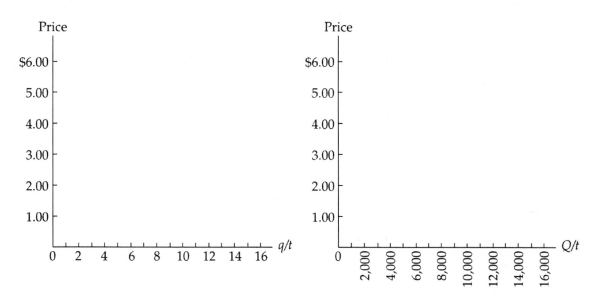

5. What is the golden rule of profit maximization? Explain why the rule maximizes profits.

6. Why does a firm ever produce when it is losing money?

7. Why are economic profits zero all along a long-run supply curve in perfect competition?

8. The floppy disk industry is perfectly competitive. Each firm produces 500,000 disks at an average total cost of 60 cents. The disks sell for 75 cents.
    a. Is the industry in long-run equilibrium?
    b. What is the marginal cost of a disk? How do you know?

9. Suppose the textile industry is perfectly competitive and in long-run equilibrium. If the price of cotton rises, what happens to the costs of firms and to profits? What will happen over time? If the industry is an increasing cost industry, what is the new long-run equilibrium like? (Assume the industry is increasing cost because of labor costs.)

10. Explain what determines the shape of an industry long-run supply curve.

11. Why are profits so important in the perfect competition model when they are always zero in the long run?

12. There once was an empire that produced and consumed two goods—bread and entertainment (circuses). Initially, 60% of workers and 70% of land was used to produce bread, with the remaining land and labor used to produce public entertainment. Both industries are perfectly competitive and in long-run equilibrium. Then, a new ruler arrives who wants more entertainment, and the demand for entertainment increases. What happens in the short-run and in the long run? What share of the labor force and land are in the entertainment industry? (Note: you cannot give an exact number. Instead, relate whether one good has an increase or decrease).

13. What is productive efficiency? How does perfect competition guarantee productive efficiency?

14. What is allocative efficiency? How does perfect competition guarantee allocative efficiency?

15. Under perfect competition, the marginal cost of supplying a good exactly equals the marginal benefit of the good to consumers. Firms also make zero profits in the long run. Does this mean that market exchange provides no benefits to participants? Explain.

VII. ANSWERS

A. Completion

1. structure
2. homogeneous
3. mobile
4. price taker
5. marginal revenue; average revenue
6. marginal revenue; marginal cost
7. decrease
8. marginal cost; average variable cost
9. zero
10. minimum
11. constant
12. increasing
13. Allocative
14. price; marginal cost
15. producer surplus

B. True/False

1. True
2. True
3. True
4. True
5. False. They have to take whatever market price prevails.
6. False. The output decisions of one firm have no effect on the other firms.
7. True
8. True
9. False
10. True
11. True. The firm can always limit losses to its fixed costs by shutting down.
12. True
13. False. The firm's short-run supply curve is only that portion of the *MC* curve that is at or above the minimum point of the average variable cost curve.
14. True. The supply curve of a firm is the portion of its marginal cost curve that lies above the minimum point of the average variable cost curve. The market supply curve is the horizontal summation of the supply curves of all the firms in the industry.
15. False
16. True
17. True
18. False. The statement is true only for increasing-cost industries.
19. False
20. False

C. Multiple Choice

1. a	6. a	11. c	16. a
2. b	7. c	12. c	17. c
3. e	8. c	13. a	18. c
4. d	9. c	14. c	19. c
5. d	10. e	15. e	20. d

D. Discussion Questions

1. Perfectly competitive firms are called price takers because they have no individual control over price. A firm can sell as many units as it wants at the market price. In perfect competition, there are so many firms that any changes in output a firm makes will not affect the market price. In addition, the goods produced by such firms are homogeneous, so buyers do not care which seller they buy from—they only care about getting the best price. (We assume the consumers know what the market price is.)

2. Total revenue equals price times quantity ($p \times q$). Marginal revenue equals the change in total revenue from selling one more unit. Since price does not change, total revenue increases by the price when one more unit is sold. Average revenue equals total revenue divided by quantity, or $pq/q = p$.

3a.

Price	Quantity	Total Revenue	Total Cost	Marginal Cost	Marginal Revenue	Average Variable Cost	Average Total Cost	Economic Profit
$4	0	—	$10.00	—	—	—	—	-$10.00
$4	1	$4	$14.20	$4.20	$4	$4.20	$14.20	-$10.20
$4	2	$8	$17.80	$3.60	$4	$3.90	$8.90	-$9.80
$4	3	$12	$20.60	$2.80	$4	$3.53	$6.87	-$8.60
$4	4	$16	$23.10	$2.50	$4	$3.28	$5.78	-$7.10
$4	5	$20	$25.70	$2.60	$4	$3.14	$5.14	-$5.70
$4	6	$24	$28.50	$2.80	$4	$3.08	$4.75	-$4.50
$4	7	$28	$31.50	$3.00	$4	$3.07	$4.50	-$3.50
$4	8	$32	$34.70	$3.20	$4	$3.09	$4.34	-$2.70
$4	9	$36	$38.10	$3.40	$4	$3.12	$4.23	-$2.10
$4	10	$40	$41.70	$3.60	$4	$3.17	$4.17	-$1.70
$4	11	$44	$45.50	$3.80	$4	$3.23	$4.14	-$1.50
$4	12	$48	$49.50	$4.00	$4	$3.29	$4.13	-$1.50
$4	13	$52	$53.70	$4.20	$4	$3.36	$4.13	-$1.70
$4	14	$56	$58.20	$4.50	$4	$3.44	$4.16	-$2.20
$4	15	$60	$63.20	$5.00	$4	$3.55	$4.21	-$3.20

b. Profits are maximized at 12 units of output. Calculating the difference between total revenue and total cost is one method of determining this output; this method yields a minimum loss of $1.50. Also, $MR = MC$ at 12 units of output. The firm's profit is −$1.50.

c. No, this level of output is not a long-run equilibrium because the firm is losing money.

d. The firm will produce 14 units and make a profit of $4.80.

e. Price would have to fall below $3.07, which is the minimum of average variable cost.

f. In the long run, some firms will leave the industry.

4.

5. The golden rule of profit maximization is that the firm should expand output as long as marginal revenue exceeds marginal cost and should stop expanding output when marginal cost exceeds marginal revenue. In other words, it should produce at the output level where marginal revenue equals marginal cost. This maximizes profits because the firm will increase profits by producing an additional unit whenever marginal revenue is greater than marginal cost. When this happens, revenues increase more than costs when the extra unit is produced. If marginal cost is greater than marginal revenue, reducing output by one unit will cause costs to fall more than revenues, again increasing the profits. If the firm expands whenever $MR > MC$ and contracts whenever $MR < MC$, then it will produce when $MR = MC$.

6. In the short run, the firm has to pay its fixed costs whether it produces or not. It will produce any time its losses, when it produces, are less than its fixed costs. This will be the case whenever price is above average variable cost at some level of output.

7. The long-run supply curve applies when all firms have made all adjustments they wish to make. Hence, every point on a long-run supply curve is a long-run equilibrium, which is characterized by zero economic profits.

8. a. The industry is not in long-run equilibrium because firms are making profits (P>ATC).
   b. Marginal cost is 75 cents because profit-maximizing firms produce where marginal revenue (price) equals marginal cost.
   c. Less than 500,000 units. Since MC > ATC at 500,000 units and long-run equilibrium occurs when ATC is at a minimum and where MC = ATC, the long-run equilibrium output must be less than 500,000.

9. The increased price of an input raises average costs and marginal costs. Firms lose money in the short run. Over time, some firms will exit the industry. For the new long-run equilibrium, there will be fewer firms and profits will be zero. Textile workers will receive lower wages than before.

10. New firms entering an industry must obtain the necessary resources in order to produce the goods. If they can hire the resources for the same prices that existing firms pay, industry costs remain constant and the long-run supply curve is horizontal. If the have to bid up the prices of resources, their costs rise. However, the costs to existing firms also rise in that case. The new long-run equilibrium price is thus higher than the old one, and the long-run supply curve slopes upward. If production costs fall as industry output expands, the long-run supply curve slopes downward.

11. Profits (or losses) induce entrepreneurs to move resources from one area to another. If profits can be made in a market, entrepreneurs will enter the market to capture some of these profits. These actions result in a reduction of profits until all firms receive zero economic profits.

12. Price of entertainment rises. Entertainment firms can make a profit by offering more entertainment. They use their land more intensively by adding more shows and working their workers more or hiring some new workers. Over time, new firms enter the industry. They hire workers from the bread industry and buy land from bread firms. In the new long run equilibrium, a higher share of workers and land are employed in the entertainment industry and fewer in the bread industry. That is, some resources have been reallocated from bread production to the production of entertainment.

13. Productive efficiency is using the least-cost combination of inputs to produce a good. That is, with productive efficiency, inputs are not wasted. In the long run under perfect competition, firms produce at the minimum point of their long-run average cost curve, so they are efficient.

14. Allocative efficiency is the production of goods that consumers want. The price of a good reflects the value consumers attach to the last unit they consume. The marginal cost of the last unit measures the value of the resources used to produce the good in their best alternative use. When $p = MC$, the marginal cost of producing the last unit of output exactly equals the marginal benefit consumers receive from that unit. The right amount of the good is produced when $p = MC$. Under perfect competition, firms are in equilibrium when price equals marginal cost.

15. No, because consumers usually receive some consumer surplus and producers usually receive producer surplus. This will be true if demand curves slope down and supply curves slope up.

CHAPTER 9

Monopoly

I. INTRODUCTION

This chapter analyzes monopoly. Like the model of perfect competition, the model of monopoly is a tool used to analyze markets, not a descriptive model of real-world firms. Pure monopoly is very rare, just as perfect competition is very rare. The next chapter examines two intermediate market structures: monopolistic competition and oligopoly.

II. OUTLINE

1. Barriers to Entry. *Barriers to entry* are restrictions on the entry of new firms into an industry.

   1.1 Legal Restrictions. The government can make it illegal for another firm to enter a market.
   a. *Patents* award the developers of new products the exclusive rights to production for seventeen years.
   b. Patent laws are designed to be incentives for inventors to allocate resources to developing inventions.
   c. The government also restricts entry into some areas by licenses and other restrictions.

   1.2 Economies of Scale
   a. A monopoly can emerge when a firm experiences declining average costs over the entire range of output demanded by consumers.
   b. When this occurs, the firm is said to be a *natural monopoly*.

   1.3 Control of Essential Resources
   a. A firm that controls the supply of a nonreproducible resource critical to production can restrict entry.
   b. Over time, technological change tends to break down barriers to entry.

   1.4 *CASE STUDY:* Is a Diamond Forever?

2. Revenue for the Monopolist. The demand curve for a monopolist is identical to the market demand curve, so the monopolist faces a downward-sloping demand curve.

   2.1 Demand, Average Revenue, and Marginal Revenue
   a. The demand curve is also the monopolist's average revenue curve.
   b. Marginal revenue for a monopolist is less than price.

   2.2 The Gains and Loss From Selling One More Unit
   a. There is a gain in revenue from selling one additional unit.
   b. There is also a loss associated with an additional unit—the loss from recovering a lower price on the previous units.

2.3 **Revenue Schedule.** As the price declines, the gap between price and marginal revenue become less from selling all units at a lower price increases.

2.4 **Revenue Curves**
   a. A monopolist's marginal revenue curve lies below the demand curve.
   b. Total revenue is maximized when marginal revenue equals zero.
   c. When marginal revenue is positive, demand is price elastic; when marginal revenue is negative, demand is price inelastic.

3. **The Firm's Costs and Profit Maximization**

   3.1 **Profit Maximization**
      a. The monopolist can find the rate of output for which the difference between total revenue and total cost is the greatest. If economic profit is possible, that output will maximize profit.
      b. Alternatively, the monopolist can expand output as long as marginal revenue exceeds marginal cost but stop before marginal cost exceeds marginal revenue.
      c. Monopolies always produce on the elastic portion of the demand curve.

   3.2 **Short-Run Losses and the Shutdown Decision**
      a. The monopolist will continue to produce at a loss if marginal cost equals marginal revenue where price exceeds average variable cost but is below average total cost.
      b. A monopoly will shut down if revenue fails to cover variable costs at all output levels.
      c. Since the monopolist produces where $MR = MC$, but MR does not equal price, the marginal cost curve does not show the relation between price and quantity supplied.
      d. Since there is not a unique relationship between price and output, the monopolist does not have a supply curve.

   3.3 **Long-Run Profit Maximization**
      a. Because there are barriers to entry into a monopoly industry, economic profits can persist in the long run.
      b. A monopolist seeks to find the scale of the firm that maximizes profit.
      c. If a monopolist that is suffering losses cannot eliminate the losses in the long run, the firm will leave the industry.

4. **Monopoly and the Allocation of Resources**

   4.1 **Price and Output under Perfect Competition**
      a. Price equals marginal cost at equilibrium under perfect competition.
      b. At equilibrium, the marginal cost to society of producing the final unit of output equals the marginal benefit consumers assign to that unit.

   4.2 **Price and Output under Monopoly**
      a. At equilibrium, marginal revenue equals marginal cost for a monopoly, but price exceeds marginal revenue.
      b. Therefore, price exceeds marginal cost, and consumers value an additional unit of output at more than the marginal cost to society of producing the unit of output.

   4.3 **Allocative and Distributive Effects**
      a. As long as it does not have significant economies of scale, a monopolist produces a smaller rate of output and charges a higher price than a firm under perfect competition.

       b.   Monopoly profits are a transfer from consumers to the monopolist of what would be consumer surplus under perfect competition.

       c.   The welfare loss, or *deadweight loss*, of a monopoly is measured by the lost consumer surplus that is not transferred to anyone else.

5.   Problems Estimating the Welfare Cost of Monopoly

    5.1   Why the Welfare Loss of Monopoly Might Be Lower
       a.   If a monopolist experiences significant economies of scale, the price under monopoly could be lower than under competition.
       b.   Fear of potential rivals: high profits might attract new entrants, which would reduce future profits, so the monopolist does not raise price as much as it could.
       c.   Fear of public intervention: high profits and a high price might result in the government's stepping in and taxing profits or setting prices.

    5.2   Why the Welfare Loss of Monopoly Might Be Higher
       a.   A monopolist could grow lazy and fail to minimize the costs of production or be generally lacking in innovation. However, the market for corporate control limits these tendencies.
       b.   Monopolists may expend resources to obtain and maintain the monopoly. This is called *rent seeking*.

    5.3   *CASE STUDY:* The Mail Monopoly

6.   Models of Price Discrimination

    6.1   Conditions for Price Discrimination
       a.   A producer must face a downward-sloping demand curve.
       b.   There must be at least two identifiable classes of customers with different elasticities of demand.
       c.   The monopolist must be able to distinguish easily between customers in the two groups.
       c.   The monopolist must be able to prevent buyers who face the lower price from reselling to buyers who face the higher price.

    6.2   A Model of Price Discrimination
       a.   For each class of customers, the monopolist sets a rate of output where marginal revenue equals marginal cost.
       d.   The group with the more price elastic demand will face the lower price.

    6.3   Examples of Price Discrimination
       a.   Airlines and telephone utilities charge businesses higher prices than they charge households.
       b.   Many businesses give price discounts to students or senior citizens.

    6.4   Perfect Price Discrimination: The Monopolist's Dream
       a.   *Perfect price discrimination* involves charging a different price for each unit of output sold.
       b.   If monopolists could perfectly price discriminate, all the consumer surplus under perfect competition would be transferred to the monopolist in the form of profits.
       c.   Perfect price discrimination would result in allocative efficiency and there would be no deadweight loss.

III. DISCUSSION

Barriers to Entry

A *monopoly* is the sole seller of a good that has no close substitutes. Monopolists often earn economic profits. We saw in the previous chapter that profits usually attract new firms to enter the market. A monopoly must prevent such entry from taking place. Factors that prevent new firms from profitably entering are called *barriers to entry*.

There are three types of barriers to entry. First, the government can create legal barriers that restrict other firms from entering the industry. *Patents* are an example of a legal barrier, although patents are justified on the grounds that they create incentives for firms to spend time and resources on inventive activity. In other cases, the government may restrict entry to only those firms or individuals with a certain type of license and then limit the number of licenses. Second, production may be characterized by significant economies of scale. In such cases, a single firm can attain lower average costs by expanding production and underpricing other firms. The result is called a *natural monopoly*. The third type of barrier to entry is control of an essential resource.

Revenue for the Monopolist

The demand curve faced by a monopolist is the market demand curve because there are no other firms in the industry. All the differences between monopoly and perfect competition derive from the facts that the monopolist faces a downward-sloping demand curve and the entry of new firms is restricted. Since the demand curve slopes downward, the monopolist must lower price to sell additional units of output. This implies that the monopolist's marginal revenue curve lies below its demand curve. Recall that for a competitive firm, the demand curve is also the marginal revenue curve. Exhibit 1 shows a demand schedule and other revenue schedules for a monopolist.

Exhibit 1

Price	Quantity Demanded	Total Revenue	Average Revenue	Marginal Revenue
$5.00	10	$ 50.00	$ 5.00	$ 5.00
4.80	20	96.00	4.80	4.60
4.60	30	138.00	4.60	4.20
4.40	40	176.00	4.40	3.80
4.20	50	210.00	4.20	3.40
4.00	60	240.00	4.00	3.00
3.80	70	266.00	3.80	2.60
3.60	80	288.00	3.60	2.20
3.40	90	306.00	3.40	1.80
3.20	100	320.00	3.20	1.40

Average revenue equals $TR/q = pq/q = p$, so price is always the same as average revenue. The key difference between monopoly and perfect competition is that marginal revenue does not equal price.

Suppose a firm is selling 50 units a week at $4.20 per unit. Its total revenue is $210.00. If it lowers price to $4.00, the firm can sell an additional 10 units and obtain an additional $40.00 from those units. However, this is not the only effect of the price reduction. The 50 units that the firm used to sell at $4.20 now sell for $4.00 each. Instead of receiving $210.00 for the 50 units, the firm now receives $200.00— $10.00 less than before. Thus, the price decrease has two effects. The sale of additional units increases revenues, but the lower price reduces the revenue from those units that formerly were sold at the higher price. The change in total revenues from selling the additional 10 units is the sum of the two effects: $40.00 + (−$10.00) = $30.00. Marginal revenue is $3.00, which is less than the price of $4.00. Hence, the marginal revenue curve lies below the demand curve.

The Firm's Costs and Profit Maximization

The golden rule of profit maximization is the same for the monopolist as it is for the perfectly competitive firm: find the rate of output for which marginal revenue equals marginal cost. In the case of perfect competition, this rule implies that the firm sets price equal to marginal cost. This is not true for the monopolist because price is greater than marginal revenue. Hence, in equilibrium, the monopolist's price is greater than its marginal cost. Make sure that you understand Exhibits 5 and 6 in the textbook as well as the discussion that accompanies those exhibits.

Monopolists do not always make positive profits, and may face the decision of whether to produce at a loss or to shut down in the short run. The procedure for deciding is identical to that used by a competitive firm. If there is no price that is greater than average variable cost, the firm should shut down and minimize its losses by limiting them to the amount of the fixed costs. The firm should produce if there is some rate of output at which all variable costs and some fixed costs are covered.

We saw in the last chapter that when competitive firms make profits in the short run, new firms enter the industry in the long run until all firms make zero profits. In monopoly, new firms are prevented from entering the industry, so the distinction between the long run and the short run is not as clear. Still, all resources can vary in the long run, so the monopolist will alter the scale of the firm so as to maximize profits.

Monopoly and the Allocation of Resources

Unless it experiences significant economies of scale, an industry that is a monopoly produces a smaller rate of output and charges a higher price than an industry under perfect competition. The restricted output and higher price imply that consumer surplus is smaller under monopoly than it is under perfect competition. Some of the consumer surplus is transferred to the monopolist in the form of profits, and some is lost to society. This loss is known as the *deadweight loss* of monopoly. Under perfect competition, price equals marginal cost; under monopoly, price exceeds marginal cost. Consequently, the allocation of resources is different when production is carried on in a perfectly competitive industry than it is when production is carried on in a monopoly.

Problems Estimating the Welfare Cost of Monopoly

The actual social cost of monopoly may be larger or smaller than the deadweight loss of monopoly described. A monopolist may not charge the short-run profit-maximizing price for fear that the large economic profits it would earn would attract new entrants or would attract the attention of government officials. To the extent this is true, the deadweight loss of monopoly is less than that indicated in Exhibit 8 in the text. On the other hand, monopolies may not minimize the cost of production and may spend resources to obtain or maintain the monopoly. When either of these situations occurs, the true social cost of monopoly is greater than that indicated by Exhibit 8.

Models of Price Discrimination

Monopolists can often increase profits by practicing *price discrimination*: charging different prices to different customers or charging the same consumer different prices for different units of the same good. To price discriminate, a firm must face a downward-sloping demand curve, must have at least two different groups of customers with different elasticities of demand, must be able to identify members of the different groups easily, and must be able to prevent resale of its products between members of the groups.

To maximize profits by price discriminating, the monopolist equates marginal revenue for each group of customers with the marginal cost of supplying the good. The group with the more price inelastic demand will pay the higher price.

In the best of all worlds (for a monopolist), the firm could practice perfect price discrimination: it could charge a different price for each unit of the good sold. In this way, every dollar of consumer surplus would be converted to profit for the monopolist. However, no monopolist is able to perfectly price discriminate, since the necessary information about individual demand schedules is impossible to obtain.

IV. LAGNIAPPE

Barriers to Entry and Time

Barriers to entry often last for a relatively short time. In the United States, patents have a legal life of seventeen years. In most European countries, firms must renew patents annually and pay a substantial fee to renew. Studies have found that the average duration of a European patent is closer to seven years than seventeen. That is, firms often do not find it profitable to renew the patent after seven years because the patent has lost its value. A patent loses its value when new discoveries make the patented product or process obsolete or less unique.

Another barrier to entry—control of a key resource—also tends to be weakened over time. Few resources are in such limited supply that one firm can capture all of the supplies. Even when this does occur, other firms are likely to search for alternative sources of the resource or for other resources that can be used as substitutes. For example, over time, discoveries of bauxite reduced Alcoa's control of bauxite. Similarly, at one time U.S. Steel controlled most of the high-quality iron ore reserves in the country. Depletion of those reserves, combined with new discoveries of rich iron ore reserves elsewhere in the world, have broken down this barrier to entry.

In contrast, economies of scale can have long-lasting effects, since they are based on technical considerations and not on economic behavior. Government restrictions can also be long lasting, although the protected firms may have to spend resources (that is, engage in *rent seeking*) to maintain their privileged position.

Question to Think About: How could a firm that experiences significant economies of scale ever lose its monopoly position?

Price Elasticity and Price Discrimination

We learned from the text that a monopolist that price discriminates charges a higher price to the group of customers with the less elastic demand. Price elasticity of demand is determined by the number and closeness of substitutes. Hence, the monopolist is charging the group with fewer alternatives a higher price. If the firm tried to charge the higher price to the group with the more elastic demand, people would switch to substitutes.

The relationship between substitutes and price discrimination can be seen by examining prices set by local phone companies and by local electric utilities. Most electric utilities charge a higher rate to residential customers than to industrial customers. To some extent, this difference reflects lower costs of servicing industrial customers. However, it also reflects the fact that industrial customers have more substitutes for the utility's electricity than residential customers have.

Residential customers have very few options other than conservation if electricity rates increase; industrial users can often generate their own electricity.

Most phone companies charge business users a higher rate than they charge residential users. Again, the rate differential is due to the availability of substitutes. Residential users can always use pay phones or a neighbor's phone if rates go up—or they can do without a phone. Businesses cannot do without a phone as easily. It's not good for a business's image if prospective customers must call a neighboring establishment to do business! Consequently, business demand for phone service is more inelastic.

Question to Think About: What are other examples of price discrimination? How do elasticities of demand and the availability of substitutes relate to the different prices in such examples?

V. KEY TERMS

Barrier to entry
Patent
Innovation
Price searcher

Deadweight loss
Rent-seeking
Price discrimination
Perfectly discriminating monopolist

VI. QUESTIONS

A. Completion

1. To have a monopoly, it is necessary to prevent new firms from profitably entering the market, which requires some kind of _____

2. To encourage innovation, the government awards _____ that grant exclusive rights to produce a product for seventeen years.

3. State _____ are required in order to provide some types of services, such as haircuts and legal assistance.

4. When there are significant economies of scale over the full range of market demand, the result is a _____ monopoly.

5. The demand curve for a monopoly is the _____ demand curve.

6. The marginal revenue curve for a monopoly that does not perfectly discriminate lies _____ the demand curve.

7. Marginal revenue is negative when the demand curve is _____.

8. A monopoly maximizes profits by producing where _____ equals marginal cost.

9. A monopoly produces on the _____ portion of the demand curve.

10. A monopoly does not have a _____ curve.

11. Because there are _____, a monopoly can earn long-run economic profits.

12. When a monopoly restricts output and raises prices, it creates a _____ loss to society.

13. Firms engage in _____ activity when they lobby politicians for economic transfers.

14. Monopolies practice _____ when they charge different prices to different groups of customers.

15. There is no deadweight loss if a monopolist is able to engage in _____ price discrimination.

B.   True/False

_____   1. A barrier to entry is something that prevents new firms from profitably entering an industry.

_____   2. Local utilities usually are monopolies because they control essential resources.

_____   3. Technological change sometimes helps break down barriers to entry.

_____   4. A major difference between a monopolistic firm and a competitive firm is that the monopolist faces a downward-sloping demand curve, whereas a competitive firm faces a horizontal demand curve.

_____   5. Under monopoly, price is greater than average revenue but lower than marginal revenue.

_____   6. The monopolist's demand curve is also its average revenue curve.

_____   7. Unless it perfectly price discriminates, the monopolist's marginal revenue curve lies below its demand curve because the demand curve slopes down.

_____   8. Marginal revenue is positive whenever the price elasticity of demand is less than one.

_____   9. A monopolist maximizes profit by selecting the rate of output where price equals marginal cost.

_____   10. The supply curve of a monopoly is less elastic than the supply curve of a perfectly competitive industry.

_____   11. All monopolists make an economic profit.

_____   12. Most monopolists try to charge the highest price possible.

_____   13. The more elastic the demand curve a monopoly faces, the higher the price it charges.

_____   14. Monopoly profits represent a transfer from consumers to the monopolist producer.

_____   15. The deadweight loss of monopoly is measured by the economic profit of the monopoly.

16. Monopolists may not charge the monopoly price if they fear government intervention.

_____ 17. The welfare loss of monopoly is greater the more rent seeking that occurs.

_____ 18. To be able to price discriminate, a monopolist must be able to prevent resale of its product between customers.

_____ 19. The group with the more elastic demand faces the higher price when price discrimination occurs.

_____ 20. Perfect price discrimination is inefficient because profits are so great.

C. Multiple Choice

1. In states where the government runs liquor stores, the monopoly results from
   a. economies of scale relative to the market demand.
   b. control of an essential resource.
   c. patents.
   d. legal restrictions.
   e. none of the above.

2. If a small town has only one grocery store, the grocer has a monopoly as a result of
   a. economies of scale relative to the market demand.
   b. control of an essential resource.
   c. licenses.
   d. legal restrictions.
   e. none of the above.

3. For a monopolist that does not perfectly price discriminate, marginal revenue is less than price because
   a. the firm must lower price on all units to sell additional units.
   b. the firm faces a downward-sloping demand curve.
   c. average revenue is less than price.
   d. marginal cost is less than price.
   e. a and b

4. Total revenue for a monopolist is at a maximum when
   a. marginal revenue equals marginal cost.
   b. price equals marginal revenue.
   c. price equals marginal cost.
   d. marginal revenue equals zero.
   e. marginal revenue equals average revenue.

5. If a monopoly lowers price to sell additional units, its revenues increase if
   a. the number of units sold is greater than the drop in price.
   b. the percentage increase in units sold is greater than the percentage decrease in price.
   c. the monopolist faces no close substitutes.
   d. it is losing money at its current rate of output.
   e. average revenue is above marginal cost.

Monopoly

6. A monopolist always produces
   a. where price is at a maximum.
   b. where total revenue is at a maximum.
   (c.) on the elastic portion of the demand curve.
   d. on the unitary elastic portion of the demand curve.
   e. on the inelastic portion of the demand curve.

Exhibit 2

7. A monopolist will maximize profits at which rate of output in Exhibit 2?
   a. Q_1
   (b) Q_2
   c. Q_3
   d. Q_4
   e. Q_5

8. In Exhibit 2, what will the profit-maximizing rate of output be if fixed costs increase?
   a. Q_1
   (b.) Q_2
   c. Q_3
   d. Q_4
   e. The question cannot be answered without more information.

Chapter 9

Exhibit 3

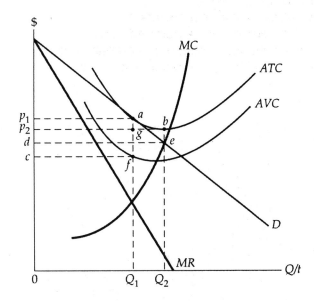

9. In Exhibit 3, the monopolist's economic profits are
   a. the area p_1agp_2.
   b. the area p_1afc.
   c. the area p_2bed.
   d. zero.
   e. Profits cannot be determined without more information.

10. In Exhibit 3, a monopoly that perfectly price discriminates will
    a. produce Q_1 units.
    b. produce Q_2 units.
    c. make zero profits.
    d. charge p_1 to some customers and p_2 to other customers.
    e. The question cannot be answered without more information.

11. In Exhibit 3, what could cause the *ATC* curve to shift down to the *AVC* curve without affecting the *MC* curve?
    a. a change in the price of the good
    b. a change in the price of labor
    c. a reduction of fixed costs by 50 percent
    d. elimination of fixed costs
    e. none of the above

12. The fundamental difference between a monopoly and a firm in perfect competition is that
    a. a monopoly is large.
    b. a monopoly can make more profits.
    c. a monopoly can price discriminate.
    d. a monopoly faces a downward-sloping demand curve.
    e. a monopoly tries to maximize profits.

13. In the long run, a monopolist will
    a. expand the size of the firm until it makes zero profits.
    b. adjust the scale of the firm to maximize profits.
    c. go out of business if it makes zero profits.
    d. charge a higher price than in the short run.
    e. b and d

Exhibit 4

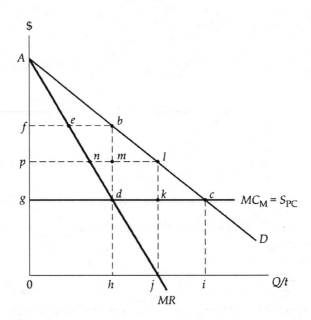

14. Consider Exhibit 4. What is the price–output combination if the industry is perfectly competitive? if it is a monopoly that does not price discriminate?
    a. Perfect competition: quantity = j, price = p
       Monopoly: quantity = h, price = f
    b. Perfect competition: quantity = j, price = g
       Monopoly: quantity = j, price = p
    c. Perfect competition: quantity = i, price = g
       Monopoly: quantity = j, price = p
    d. Perfect competition: quantity = i, price = g
       Monopoly: quantity = h, price = f
    e. none of the above

15. The monopoly in Exhibit 4 does not price discriminate. What is its deadweight loss?
    a. lkc
    b. bml
    c. bdc
    d. djl
    e. $fbdg$

16. In Exhibit 4, what are the profits of a monopolist that is able to perfectly price discriminate?
    a. $fbdg$
    b. Acg
    c. $fbcg$
    d. $fbdg + lkc$
    e. Adg

17. In Exhibit 4, what are the deadweight losses if the firm perfectly price discriminates?
    a. *fdbg*
    b. *Abf*
    c. *Acg*
    d. *bdc*
    e. zero

18. Which of the following could make actual deadweight losses different from what is indicated by a typical graphical analysis?
    a. fear of potential rivals
    b. fear of public intervention
    c. failure to minimize costs
    d. rent-seeking activity
    e. all of the above

19. Which of the following is not a requirement for price discrimination?
    a. monopoly power
    b. economies of scale
    c. different groups of customers with different elasticities of demand
    d. ability to easily identify members of different customer groups
    e. ability to keep the members of different customer groups separate

20. A price-discriminating monopolist charges the highest price to
    a. the group with the largest demand.
    b. the group with the most elastic demand.
    c. the group with the least elastic demand.
    d. the group with demand that is of unitary elasticity.
    e. the oldest group.

D. Discussion Questions

1. Indicate the source of the monopoly in each of the following cases:
   a. U.S. Post Office
   b. Local phone company
   c. State-owned liquor store
   d. The National Football League
   e. Taxi company in a major city
   f. Local cable TV company
   g. Madonna
   h. OPEC

2. Explain what a natural monopoly is.

3. Discuss the types of barriers to entry, and explain whether each type is likely to provide long-term monopoly power.

4. The Grand Rapids Whitecaps are a minor league baseball team in Grand Rapids, Michigan. They are the only professional baseball team in Grand Rapids.
   a. Do the owners of the team have a monopoly? Explain.
   b. Suppose an inexpensive, high-speed train is built that connects Grand Rapids and Detroit. What happens to the monopoly position of the Grand Rapids Whitecaps?

Monopoly

Use the information in Exhibit 5 about a monopoly to answer question 5.

Exhibit 5

Price	Qty	TR	MR	AR	TVC	TC	AVC	ATC	MC
$12	0	—	—	—	—	$5	—	—	—
11	1	—	—	—	$13	—	—	—	—
10	2	—	—	—	16	—	—	—	—
9	3	—	—	—	20	—	—	—	—
8	4	—	—	—	25	—	—	—	—
7	5	—	—	—	31	—	—	—	—
6	6	—	—	—	38	—	—	—	—
5	7	—	—	—	46	—	—	—	—
4	8	—	—	—	56	—	—	—	—
3	9	—	—	—	68	—	—	—	—
2	10	—	—	—	82	—	—	—	—
1	11	—	—	—	99	—	—	—	—

5. a. Fill in the blanks in the table.
    b. Draw the demand curve, marginal revenue curve, average variable cost curve, average total cost curve, and marginal cost curve on the graph in Exhibit 6.

Exhibit 6

    c. What are the profit-maximizing rates of output and price? Indicate your answer on the graph.
    d. What is the profit for the monopolist?
    e. Suppose variable costs increase by $2 at every rate of output. What are the new profit-maximizing rates of output and price? What are the profits now?
    f. Assume variable costs are as indicated in Exhibit 5 and that fixed costs increase by $2. What are the new profit-maximizing rates of output and price? What are the new profits?

6. Roberto Luna just finished producing his new classical guitar CD. The recording company paid Roberto a $1,000,000 recording fee. The company can produce a CD at a constant variable cost of $4.00. The record company's estimate of demand for the CD is:

Price	Number of CD's Sold	Total Revenue	Marginal Revenue (per CD)
$26	0		
24	20,000		
22	40,000		
20	60,000		
18	80,000		
16	100,000		
14	120,000		
12	140,000		
10	160,000		
8	180,000		
6	200,000		

    a. Complete the above table.
    b. What are the profit-maximizing output and price? What are the profits?
    c. If Roberto received a $2 million fee, what would happen to the profit-maximizing quantity, price, and to the value of the recording company's profits?

7. If there are no rivals for a monopolist's product, how can it ever lose money?

8. Explain why a monopoly does not have a supply curve.

9. What are the allocative and distributive differences between monopoly and perfect competition? What causes these differences?

10. Exhibit 8 in the text illustrates the welfare loss of monopoly. Discuss the factors that could make the actual welfare loss of monopoly either greater or less than the amount *bce* shown in that exhibit.

11. "If it engages in rent-seeking activity, a monopolist's economic profits may actually be zero." Is this statement true or false? Why?

12. Firms can compete to obtain a monopoly. For example, a city can accept bids from rival cable-TV companies and grant the license to the firm that pays the highest fee to the city.
    a. If firms compete in this way to obtain the monopoly position, what will happen to the monopoly profits?
    b. Will cable-TV users be better off than if the license was not granted to the highest bidder?
    c. Who would be better off?
    d. Is there a way consumers can be better off?

13. Most cases of price discrimination involve services rather than goods. Can you offer an explanation for this observation?

14. Why does a price-discriminating monopolist charge a higher price to the customers with the most inelastic demand?

15. Indicate in Exhibit 7 the price charged and output supplied to submarket A and submarket B by a price-discriminating monopolist.

Exhibit 7

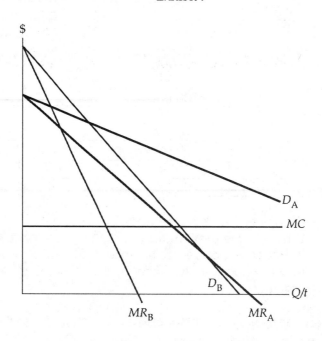

16. What is perfect price discrimination? What is the deadweight loss associated with perfect price discrimination?

17. Explain why true/false question 20 is false.

18. If perfect price discrimination is so profitable, why do firms not engage in it more?

VII. ANSWERS

A. Completion

1.	barrier to entry	8.	marginal revenue
2.	Patents	9.	Elastic
3.	Licenses	10.	Supply
4.	Natural	11.	barriers to entry
5.	Market	12.	deadweight (or welfare)
6.	Below	13.	rent-seeking
7.	Inelastic	14.	price discrimination
		15.	perfect

B.   True/False

1.	True	11.	False
2.	False	12.	False
3.	True	13.	False
4.	True	14.	True
5.	False	15.	False
6.	True	16.	True
7.	True	17.	True
8.	False	18.	True
9.	False	19.	False
10.	False. A monopolist does not	20.	False
	a supply curve.		

C.   Multiple Choice

1.	d	6.	c	11.	d	16.	b
2.	a	7.	b	12.	d	17.	e
3.	e	8.	b	13.	b	18.	e
4.	d	9.	d	14.	d	19.	b
5.	b	10.	b	15.	c	20.	c

D.   Discussion Questions

1. a. Legal restrictions
    b. Economies of scale
    c. Legal restrictions
    d. Control of essential resources
    e. Legal restrictions
    f. Natural monopoly
    g. Control of an essential resource (her talent)
    h. Control of an essential resource

2. A natural monopoly exists when economies of scale generate declining average costs over the entire range of market demand. In such situations, there is only room for one producer in the market.

3. Barriers to entry include legal restrictions (such as patents and licenses), economies of scale, and control of essential resources. Economies of scale are likely to provide long-term monopoly power, although sometimes technological change produces new products that are close substitutes for the product supplied by monopoly. Control of essential resources often diminishes over time because new sources are found or technological change develops substitutes. Patents expire after seventeen years, but license requirements by the government can be long lasting.

4. a. There is a monopoly, but the monopoly power may not be very great. There are other minor league teams in cities that are not far from Grand Rapids. Further, baseball fans can go to major league games in Detroit or Chicago. Finally, there are other types of entertainment and sports in the Grand Rapids area.
    b. The monopoly power is weakened since it is now easier to see a major league baseball game in Detroit.

5. a.

Price	Qty	TR	MR	AR	TVC	TC	AVC	ATC	MC
$12	0	$0	$\overline{}$	$\overline{}$		$5	$\overline{}$	$\overline{}$	$\overline{}$
11	1	11	$11	$11	$13	18	$13.00	$18.00	$13
10	2	20	9	10	16	21	8.00	10.50	3
9	3	27	7	9	20	25	6.67	8.33	4
8	4	32	5	8	25	30	6.25	7.50	5
7	5	35	3	7	31	36	6.20	7.20	6
6	6	36	1	6	38	43	6.33	7.17	7
5	7	35	-1	5	46	51	6.57	7.29	8
4	8	32	-3	4	56	61	7.00	7.63	10
3	9	27	-5	3	68	73	7.56	8.11	12
2	10	20	-7	2	82	87	8.20	8.70	14
1	11	11	-9	1	99	104	9.00	9.45	17

b.

c. $Q = 4$, $p = \$8$; see point e on the graph.
d. The monopolist's profit is $2.
e. $Q = 3$, $p = \$9$; profits = 0.
f. $Q = 4$, $p = \$8$; profits = 0.

6. a.

Price	Number of CD's Sold	Total Revenue	Marginal Revenue (per CD)
$26	0	0	--
24	20,000	480,000	24
22	40,000	880,000	20
20	60,000	1,200,000	16
18	80,000	1,440,000	12
16	100,000	1,600,000	8
14	120,000	1,680,000	4
12	140,000	1,680,000	0
10	160,000	1,600,000	-4
8	180,000	1,440,000	-8
6	200,000	1,200,000	-12

  b. Q = 12,000 CD's; Price = $14.00; Profits = $680,000
  c. Nothing would happen to the number of CD's produced and sold, or to the price. The firm would lose $320,000.

7. A monopolist will lose money whenever the costs of production exceed the revenues from sales. This happens whenever average costs are above the demand curve at all points. Having a monopoly is no guarantee of making economic or even normal profits.

8. A supply curve expresses a direct relationship between price and quantity supplied. A monopolist chooses its output level by equating marginal revenue and marginal cost and then finds price on the demand curve. A change in demand generates a new marginal revenue curve, which must be used to find the profit-maximizing output level, and then again price is found on the demand curve. There is not a direct relationship between price and quantity supplied. In fact, depending on how demand shifts, it is possible for a new price to be associated with the old quantity supplied.

9. Unless it experiences substantial economies of scale, a monopolist produces fewer units of output and charges a higher price than does a firm under perfect competition; output is less than the allocatively efficient level. There is also a transfer of consumer surplus from consumers to the monopolist producer in the form of profits and a loss of consumer surplus that nobody captures and that results from the higher prices and the restricted output associated with monopoly.

10. The actual welfare loss of a monopoly may be less when the firm has substantial economies of scale or when it does not charge the full monopoly price because of the fear of potential rivals or government intervention. In this case, the monopolist is willing to sacrifice some current profits for continuing long-run profits. The actual welfare loss may be greater if the monopolist becomes lazy because it faces no competition. In this case, the monopolist fails to produce in the least costly manner. Another factor that may cause welfare losses to be higher is rent-seeking activity.

11. True. The profits available to a monopoly are the rewards from successfully lobbying and being awarded the monopoly. A firm might be willing to spend up to the value of the monopoly profits, so the successful firm could find that it has actually earned zero profits when it considers the resources it spent in obtaining the monopoly.

Monopoly

12. a. The monopoly profits will be lower or even disappear as the competitive bidding transfers the profits to the city.
b. No. they would still be paying higher profits.
c. If the revenue raised by the city allows lower taxes, then the tax payers would be better off. If the city used the funds for other expenditure, then the citizens do benefit from the new expenditures and are better off.
d. If the city could have let the rival firms compete by offering the lowest prices for the cable services.

13. In order to price discriminate, a monopolist must be able to prevent the customers who pay a low price from reselling to the customers who pay a high price. Goods are sometimes easy to resell, but services cannot be resold.

14. Customers with elastic demand will reduce consumption more than those with inelastic demand for a given price increase. Therefore, the monopolist will charge the group with the more inelastic demand the higher price.

15.

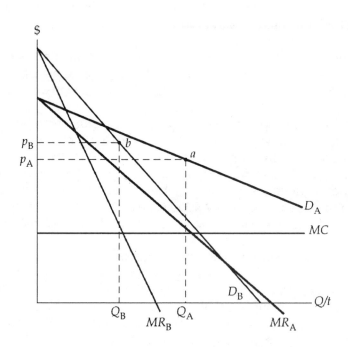

16. Perfect price discrimination occurs when a monopolist charges a different price for every unit sold. There is no deadweight loss in such situations because all consumer surplus is transferred to the monopolist in the form of monopoly profits.

17. Deadweight loss has to do with reduced output to raise price and not with whether the firm makes profits or not. A monopoly engaged in perfect price discrimination produces as many units as would be produced under perfect competition, so there is no deadweight loss.

18. Firms do not engage in more perfect price discrimination because they lack the information about the demand curves of each customer. Further, many firms find it very difficult to prevent resale of their products by those who buy units at a low price.

CHAPTER 10

Monopolistic Competition and Oligopoly

I. INTRODUCTION

Two models of markets are introduced in this chapter: monopolistic competition and oligopoly. Both are intended to describe real-world market structures more closely than do the polar models of perfect competition and monopoly. Monopolistic competition is similar to perfect competition in that both are characterized by many firms, each of which is too small to affect the decisions of rivals. Monopolistic competition differs from perfect competition in that in the former, firms produce differentiated products, whereas in the latter, firms produce homogeneous products. Oligopoly (few sellers) is closer to monopoly (one seller) in that the firms tend to be large and to have considerable influence over price.

II. OUTLINE

1. Monopolistic Competition

   1.1 Characteristics of Monopolistic Competition
       a. There is a large number of producers.
       b. Producers offer products that differ slightly, so each firm faces a downward-sloping demand curve; each firm has some control over the price it charges.
       c. Each firm is too small to have any significant impact on other firms; each firm acts independently.
       d. Firms can enter or leave the market with relative ease.

   1.2 Product Differentiation. Producers differentiate their products in four ways:
       a. Physical characteristics of goods
       b. The number and variety of locations where the product is available
       c. Services accompanying the product
       d. Product image

   1.3 Short-Run Profit Maximization or Loss Minimization
       a. Because of product differentiation, the firm faces a downward-sloping demand curve. The firm's demand curve will be more elastic the greater the number of competing firms and the less differentiated the firm's product.
       b. If the firm can at least cover its variable cost, it produces at the rate of output where $MR = MC$.
       c. The firm seeks to maximize profits and may earn profits in the short run.
       d. The firm will minimize losses in the short run by shutting down if $p < AVC$ at all output levels.

   1.4 Zero Economic Profit in the Long Run
       a. Since there are no barriers to entry or exit, firms make a normal profit in the long run.
       b. Monopolistic competition is similar to perfect competition in this way.

1.5 *CASE STUDY:* Fast Forward

1.6 Monopolistic Competition and Perfect Competition Compared
    a. In monopolistic competition, a firm does not produce at the minimum of the average total cost curve.
    b. In monopolistic competition, a firm produces where price exceeds marginal cost; under perfect competition, price equals marginal cost.
    c. Firms under monopolistic competition may spend resources on advertising or other methods of differentiating their products; perfectly competitive firms need not do so.

2. An Introduction to Oligopoly. This type of market includes only a few sellers, which implies that the firms are interdependent.

    2.1 Varieties of Oligopoly
        a. Some oligopolistic industries produce a homogeneous product; others produce differentiated products.
        b. The interdependence of firms makes it difficult to analyze the behavior of a firm in an oligopolistic industry.
        c. Each firm knows that any change in its own policies will affect its rivals and probably cause a reaction by the rivals.
        d. Some type of barrier to entry usually is associated with oligopoly.

    2.2 *CASE STUDY:* The Unfriendly Skies

    2.3 Economies of Scale. Many oligopolies are characterized by extreme economies of scale which make entry difficult.

    2.4 High Cost of Entry. High start-up costs and the need for costly promotional efforts may discourage entry into a market by causing production costs to be higher than they would be otherwise.

3. Models of Oligopoly. Because of the interdependence of firms in this type of market, there is no single model of oligopoly.

    3.1 Collusion
        a. A *cartel* is a group of firms that agree to coordinate production and pricing decisions to maximize joint profits.
        b. Firms in a cartel want to replicate the monopoly price-output decision.
        c. The joint profit-maximizing rate of output is determined by equating the marginal cost of production for the cartel and the market's marginal revenue.
        d. The cartel then must allocate output among the firms.
        e. It is difficult to maintain a cartel under certain conditions:
            (1) if there are significant differences in costs of production among firms;
            (2) if the number of firms is large;
            (3) if output is differentiated across firms;
            (4) if entry barriers to the industry are low;
            (5) if cheating on the agreement becomes widespread;
        f. The fundamental problem of a cartel is to prevent cheating by the members.
        g. A cartel cannot survive if new entry into the industry is easy.

3.2   Price Leadership
    a.   *Price leader* is a firm that sets prices for the rest of the industry.
    b.   Price leadership is a type of informal, or tacit, collusion.

3.3   Game Theory
    a.   *Game theory* examines oligopolistic behavior as a series of strategic moves and counter-moves among rivals.
    b.   Game theory focuses on the players' incentives to cooperate or compete.
    c.   There are several strategies that can be considered in game theory.

3.4   Comparison of Oligopoly and Perfect Competition
    a.   Prices are usually higher under oligopoly.
    b.   Profits are usually higher in the long run under oligopoly because of barriers to entry.
    c.   The *prisoner's dilemma* is a game that illustrates game theory.
    d.   A *strategy* is the player's game plan.
    e.   *A pay off matrix* lists the rewards or penalties that can be expected based on the strategy chosen by the players.
    f.   A *dominant strategy* for a player is one where the player's best strategy is the same regardless of the strategy selected by the other players.
    g.   When each player has a dominant strategy, there is a *dominant-strategy equilibrium.*
    h.   The prisoner's dilemma can be applied to a *duopoly* situation where two firms are setting prices.
    i.   The cola war game is another illustration.
    j.   The prisoners' dilemma is a *one-shot* game.
    k.   Players can establish reputation in *repeated games.*
    l.   The *tit-for-tat* strategy is to generate the highest payoff in repeated games.

III.   DISCUSSION

Monopolistic Competition

The key characteristic of *monopolistic competition* is product differentiation. Under perfect competition, all firms produce an identical, homogeneous product, but the product produced by a monopolistically competitive firm differs slightly from the products of other firms in the industry. As an example, consider milk sold in retail stores; assume the milk is chemically identical in all stores. If the retail market is perfectly competitive, then store A cannot raise its price above the price charged by all other retail stores. If it did it would lose all its sales to the other stores. However, if the retail market is characterized by monopolistic competition, store A can raise price by a small amount and lose some, but not all, of its sales.

Why would anyone pay more at store A? Consumers would willingly pay a higher price at store A if the store were closer to their homes so they spent less time and money on travel, or if its checkout person were quicker, or if it were open all night. Hence, convenience stores are able to charge higher prices than some other retail outlets because consumers view their products as slightly different (in this case because of the convenience that accompanies the product). Note, though, that the convenience store might lose all sales if it tried to raise price by too much.

The short-run price and output combination of a firm under monopolistic competition is found as it is under monopoly. Each firm faces a downward-sloping demand curve, which implies that its marginal revenue curve slopes down and lies below the demand curve. The firm chooses its output rate (assuming the demand curve lies above average variable cost at some point) by finding the rate of output for which $MR = MC$. Exhibit 1 illustrates the situation of a firm in monopolistic competition that is making positive profits. In the long run, new firms that are attracted by the profits enter the industry, drawing customers away from existing firms and reducing the demand facing each firm. Long-run equilibrium is achieved when firms make zero profits, just as in perfect competition.

Exhibit 1

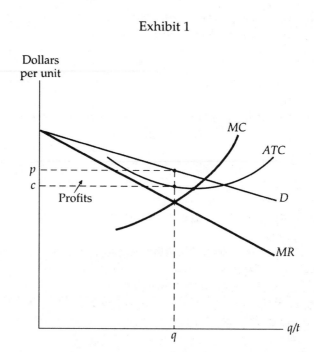

The difference between the long-run equilibrium condition of the firm in perfect competition and that of the firm in monopolistic competition is illustrated in Exhibit 2. Both panels show that the long-run equilibrium is characterized by a tangency between the firm's demand curve and the average total cost curve. The perfectly competitive firm's demand curve is horizontal, so the tangency occurs at the minimum point of the average total cost curve; the firm in monopolistic competition faces a downward-sloping demand curve, so the tangency occurs to the left of the minimum point of the average total cost curve. Hence, the firm in monopolistic competition is not producing at the lowest point on its average total cost curve. If we compared a perfectly competitive industry and a monopolistically competitive industry, we would find that there were more firms in the monopolistically competitive industry and each firm produced a smaller rate of output. That is, monopolistic competition is characterized by excess capacity. Some economists argue that this excess capacity is wasteful, but others argue that the excess capacity is not wasted because it is associated with increased choice for consumers.

Exhibit 2

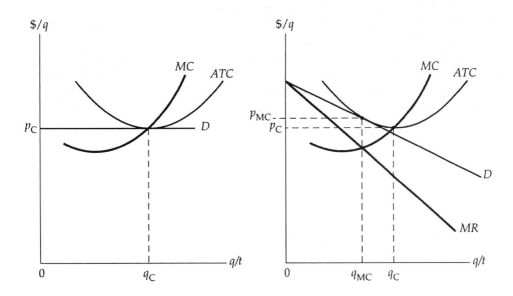

An Introduction to Oligopoly

The key characteristic of *oligopoly* is the interdependence of firms in such an industry. Since oligopoly is a market dominated by a few large firms, each firm recognizes that its price-output decisions affect the other firms and that the other firms are likely to respond to changes in their rivals' behavior. Thus, each firm must take into consideration the likely responses of its rivals. (Note that only in oligopoly does a firm have rivals. In perfect competition and in monopolistic competition, firms can behave as if their actions had no effect on other firms. There is no interdependent behavior.) Consequently, it is very difficult to develop a model of oligopoly markets, for the firms can respond to each other in a variety of ways. There are many models of oligopoly, and the text examines a few of the better-known models.

Models of Oligopoly

A monopoly is able to earn above-normal profits by restricting output and raising price above the perfectly competitive price. A group of firms can increase profits by cooperating and agreeing to restrict output and to raise prices. Such cooperative behavior on the part of firms is called *collusion*. The firms maximize joint profits by determining the industry marginal revenue curve, horizontally summing all the firms' marginal cost curves, and setting the aggregated marginal cost equal to marginal revenue. The problem then is to assign output quotas to each firm, since each would like to sell more at the higher price. Firms in *cartels* have incentive to cheat (either to sell some extra units secretly or to sell units at a price lower than the cartel price, or both). Cheating can cause prices to fall. Collusion is illegal in the United States. Firms may try to avoid collusion by following a *price leader*, a single firm that establishes a price that the other firms follow. If the price set is the monopoly price, the incentive to cheat is still strong.

Game theory provides another approach to oligopoly. Firms establish strategies in the face of interdependence. Moves and countermoves are planned by rival firms. A game involves players, strategies, and payoffs. The prisoners' dilemma is a game that is widely used in economics. It is an example of a noncompetitive game because each player is interested in only his or her own welfare and not in the welfare of the other player. In the prisoner's dilemma, the players are two prisoners who the police believe committed a crime together. The police offer a deal to each prisoner if the prisoner will confess and provide evidence against the other prisoner. Each prisoner has two possible strategies—keep quiet or confess and provide evidence against the other prisoner. The "payoff matrix" provides the listing of the rewards or penalties. In Exhibit 6 in the textbook, the payoffs are 1 year in prison if both remain silent, 5 years in prison if both confess, and 0 years in prison for the one who confesses and 10 years for the one who doesn't confess.

Each prisoner has a dominant strategy, that is, a strategy to use that is best regardless of the strategy chosen by the other. Each prisoner wants to minimize his own jail term. Jerry minimizes his jail time by confessing—if Ben confesses Jerry serves 5 years by confessing but 10 years by not confessing. If Ben doesn't confess, Jerry serves no jail term by confessing and one year by not confessing. So, Jerry minimizes his jail time by confessing regardless if Ben confesses or doesn't confess. Confessing is Jerry's dominant strategy. The optimal strategy equilibrium is where each confess and serve five years in prison. If the two co-operated and remained silent, they each serve only one year, but they confess.

The application of the prisoner's dilemma to firms is straightforward. The strategies involve decisions about the prices, output, advertising, expenditures, or other variables outside the firm's control. Payoffs involved profits. In Exhibit 7 in the textbook two firms each must decide whether to charge a low price or a higher price. The high price is the price if the firms collude, and the

Since there is not a single model of oligopoly, comparisons of oligopoly and perfect competition are difficult. In general, price, costs associated with product differentiation, and long-run profit tend to be higher in oligopoly than in perfect competition.

IV. LAGNIAPPE

Monopolistic Competition and College

U.S. colleges and universities can be seen as "firms" in a monopolistically competitive industry. Each produces a similar product (education), but the products are not identical. A college can raise price (tuition) without losing all of its students. The product differs by location (students tend to attend colleges relatively close to home), extent of services (prestige, good sports teams, partying, contacts), quality, and image (Harvard's image differs from UCLA's).

Question to Think About: As "firms" in a monopolistically competitive industry, are colleges characterized by excess capacity?

Cheating on Collusive Agreements

Collusive agreements are often difficult to establish and maintain, since it is profitable to cheat. Suppose you are head of a corporation that has made a collusive agreement to set the price of your product at $40, which is above marginal cost. A potential customer wants to buy 10,000 units of the product at $34 each, which also is greater than marginal cost. If you accept, your profits will be greater than if you do not get the sale. Further, the customer informs you that another firm that is in on the collusive agreement has offered to sell the product at $36 per unit. You have to decide whether the customer is telling you the truth and whether to cheat on the agreement yourself. Collusion is profitable, but cheating on the agreement can be even more profitable.

Question to Think About: Would you be more willing to cheat if the order were large than if it were small? How would you determine if other firms were cheating on the agreement?

V. KEY TERMS

Monopolistic competition
Product differentiation
Excess capacity
Oligopoly
Interdependence
Duopoloy
Collusion
Cartel
Price Leader

Game Theory
Duopoly
Strategy
Payoff Matrix
Prisoner's Dilemma
Dominant Strategy
Dominant-Strategy Equilibrium
Repeated Games
Tit for Tat Strategy

VI. QUESTIONS

A. Completion

1. _____ is an industry made up of many relatively small firms producing goods that are relatively close substitutes.

2. A firm in monopolistic competition makes output and price decisions _____ of other firms.

3. A firm in monopolistic competition is not a price _____.

4. For a firm in monopolistic competition that can at least cover its variable costs, marginal cost equals _____ in equilibrium.

5. Firms in monopolistic competition make _____ economic profits in the long run.

6. Monopolistic competition is characterized by _____; that is, firms produce to the left of the minimum point on the average total cost curve.

7. The key characteristic of monopolistic competition is _____; the key characteristic of oligopoly is the _____ of firms.

8. In oligopoly, a change in policies by one firm will produce a _____ from its rivals.

9. A _____ is a group of firms that agree to coordinate production and pricing decisions.

10. The fundamental problem of a cartel is _____.

11. Price leadership is a type of _____ collusion.

12. _____ examines oligopolistic behavior as a series of strategic decisions.

13. When firms agree to restrict output and raise price, they are involved in
_____.

14. A game theory that is often used in oligopoly is known as _____.

15. Regardless of market structure, profit maximization encourages firms to produce the rate of output where _____ equals _____.

B. True/False

_____ 1. Monopolistic competition is similar to perfect competition, since firms in both market structures produce homogeneous products.

_____ 2. Because monopolistically competitive firms are small and numerous, they act as price takers.

_____ 3. Product differentiation implies that the firm's demand curve slopes down.

_____ 4. Product differentiation refers to differences in the physical properties of goods.

_____ 5. The monopolistically competitive firm that can cover its variable costs produces at the rate of output at which marginal cost equals price.

_____ 6. Firms in monopolistic competition behave like monopolists when it comes to setting price and output.

_____ 7. The difference in the long-run equilibrium for perfect competition and the long-run equilibrium in monopolistic competition is due to differences in the shapes of the demand curves faced by the firms.

_____ 8. Long-run equilibrium under monopolistic competition is characterized by excess capacity.

_____ 9. Long-run equilibrium under monopolistic competition is characterized by positive economic profits.

_____ 10. Oligopoly differs from other market structures in that each firm has to be concerned with reactions to its decisions from the other firms in the industry.

_____ 11. Oligopolies tend to be industries in which production is characterized by substantial economies of scale.

_____ 12. Firms in oligopolistic industries that produce homogeneous products tend to be more interdependent than firms in oligopolistic industries that produce differentiated products.

_____ 13. The biggest problem facing cartels is how to prevent cheating.

_____ 14. Cartels often practice price leadership.

_____ 15. Game theory is used to analyze behavior of firms that cooperate but not firms that compete.

_____ 16. The equilibrium for a prisoner's dilemma game is the collusive solution.

_____ 17. The prisoner's dilemma is an example of a repeated game.

_____ 18. The most likely strategy for a repeated game is the tit-for-tat strategy.

C. Multiple Choice

1. Which of the following is not a characteristic of monopolistic competition?
   a. many firms
   b. product differentiation
   c. excess capacity
   d. downward-sloping demand curve
   e. interdependence

2. Product differentiation is an important characteristic of monopolistic competition because
   a. most products are differentiated.
   b. it generates downward-sloping demand curves for firms.
   c. it results in firms' producing at too high a level of output.
   d. it generates the long-run equilibrium condition of zero profits.
   e. none of the above

3. Which of the following is a way in which sellers can differentiate their products?
   a. color
   b. location
   c. hours of operation
   d. provision of extra services
   e. all of the above

4. Monopolistic competition is like perfect competition except that
   a. firms in monopolistic competition can make long-run profits.
   b. there are substantial economies of scale with monopolistic competition.
   c. firms are large in monopolistic competition.
   d. firms in monopolistic competition face downward-sloping demand curves.
   e. both b and c

Exhibit 3

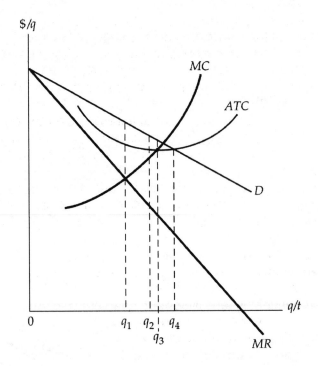

5. In Exhibit 3, the profit-maximizing output rate is
    a. $q1$.
    b. $q2$.
    c. $q3$.
    d. $q4$.
    e. zero.

6. The monopolistically competitive firm in Exhibit 3 is in
    a. short-run equilibrium, making positive economic profits.
    b. short-run equilibrium, experiencing economic losses.
    c. long-run equilibrium, making zero economic profits.
    d. long-run equilibrium, making positive economic profits.
    e. neither short-run nor long-run equilibrium.

7. Long-run equilibrium under monopolistic competition is
    a. similar to that in perfect competition in that the firms produce at the minimum point
        of their average cost curves.
    b. similar to that in monopoly in that profits are being made.
    c. similar to that in oligopoly in that anything can happen.
    d. similar to that in perfect competition in that firms make zero economic profits.
    e. similar to that in perfect competition in that price equals marginal cost.

8. Which of the following is true of monopolistic competition in long-run equilibrium?
    a. $p = MR$ and $p = MC$
    b. $p > ATC$ and $MR = MC$
    c. $p = ATC$ and $MR = MC$
    d. $p = ATC$ and $p = MC$
    e. $p > ATC$ and $p > MR$

9. Under monopolistic competition, there is excess capacity because
    a.   firms are wasteful.
    b.   there are not enough firms.
    c.   there are substantial economies of scale.
    d.   the firm's demand curve slopes down, and the firm makes zero economic profits in long-run equilibrium.
    e.   firms may want to produce more in the future if demand increases.

10. Which of the following statements about a firm in long-run equilibrium is true?
    a. $p > AR$ under monopolistic competition and $p = ATC$ under perfect competition.
    b. $p = MC$ under both, but price under monopolistic competition is higher than it is under perfect competition.
    c. $p > MC$ under monopolistic competition and $p = MC$ under perfect competition.
    d. $p = MC = ATC$ under perfect competition but $p < MC = ATC$ under monopolistic competition.
    e.   a and b

11. Interdependence means that
    a.   firms face the same demand curve.
    b.   firms are considering merging.
    c.   firms depend on each other for business.
    d.   the actions of one firm affect other firms.
    e.   all of the above

12. Which of the following is a source of oligopoly?
    a.   economies of scale
    b.   control over an essential resource
    c.   product differentiation
    d.   inelastic demand curves
    e.   a and b

13. Firms in a cartel increase profits by
    a.   working together to produce a better profit.
    b.   jointly restricting output to raise price.
    c.   setting up joint advertising campaigns.
    d.   working to make their demand curves more elastic.
    e.   working to make themselves less interdependent.

14. Which of the following makes it easier to reach a collusive agreement?
    a.   few firms in the industry
    b.   different costs among the firms
    c.   product differentiation
    d.   frequent shifts in demand
    e.   none of the above

15. Which of the following statements is true of the oligopolist that can cover its variable costs and is in equilibrium?
    a. $p = MC = ATC$
    b. $p > MC$
    c. $p > MR$ and $p = MC$
    d. $p < MC$ and $MR = MC$
    e.   a is true, but only in the long run

16. According to the game theory
    a. oligopolist firms always avoid the worst outcome.
    (b) outcomes can be volatile.
    c. oligopolistic firms collude.
    d. police wars are the normal situation.
    e. oligopolistic firms merge.

17. Suppose there are two airlines with flights from Chicago to Denver—United and Northwest. They can charge $400 a ticket or $200 a ticket. If they each charge $400, they each receive a month's profits for $50,000. If they each charge $200, they receive monthly profits of $30,000 each. If one charges $400 and the other $200, the one charging the lower price received $60,000 profit while the other earns $20,000 profit a month. The dominant strategy for United is to charge _____, and the dominant strategy for Northwest is to charge _____.
    a. $400;$400
    b. $400;$200
    c. $200;$400
    (d) $200;$200
    e. Cannot tell without more information.

18. If the scenario in question 17 is repeated indefinitely, it is likely the equilibrium will be
    (a) each charges $400.
    b. United charges $400 and Northwest charges $200.
    c. United charges $200 and Northwest charges $400.
    d. Both charge $200.
    e. One firm drives the other out of business.

19. The prisoner's dilemma can be used
    a. to analyze criminal situations only.
    b. to analyze cooperative behavior.
    (c) to analyze non-cooperative behavior.
    d. To analyze markets with many firms and many decision variables.
    e. Both b and d.

20. Under oligopoly
    a. Price is always higher than under perfect competition.
    b. Price is always higher than under monopolistic competition.
    (c) Price can be higher or lower than under perfect competition.
    d. both a and b only.
    e. none of the above.

D. Discussion Questions

1. Explain why product differentiation leads to differences between monopolistic competition and perfect competition.

2. Explain why true/false question 4 is false.

3. How is monopolistic competition like monopoly? How is it different?

4. What is excess capacity? Why are firms characterized by excess capacity under monopolistic competition?

5. Is excess capacity necessarily wasteful?

6. How is oligopoly like monopoly? How is it different?

7. Explain why it is difficult to analyze the behavior of a firm under oligopoly.

8. Explain how oligopoly is the only market structure characterized by rivalry among firms.

9. Explain how collusion can be profitable. Explain how cheating on a collusive agreement can be profitable.

10. If collusion is profitable, why don't all firms collude?

11. Is collusion more likely in the steel industry or in the auto industry? Why?

12. Contrast perfect competition and oligopoly.

13. Describe game theory.

13. How does the kinked demand curve model explain price rigidity?

14.

		Alitalia	
		$1,000	**$2,000**
AirCanada	**$1,000**	$20,000 $20,000	$5,000 $75,000
	$2,000	$75,000 $5,000	$50,000 $50,000

The payoff matrix is for Alitalia and AirCanada on rates between Toronto and Rome.
a. What is AirCanada's dominant strategy? Explain.
b. What is Alitalia's dominant strategy? Explain.
c. Suppose AirCanada pursues a tit-for-tat strategy. What will it do if it observes Alitalia charging $1,000? $2,000?
d. If the tit-for-tat strategy is used over time, what price will each firm probably charge? Why?

15. In the payoff matrix above, suppose Alitalia's profits differ, such that it earns $35,000 if it charges $2,000 and Air Canada charges $2,000.
a. What is Alitalia's dominant strategy?
b. What is AirCanada's dominant strategy?
c. Given AirCanada's situation, does Alitalia have an optimal strategy?

Monopolistic Competition and Oligopoly

VII. ANSWERS

A. Completion

1. Monopolistic competition
2. independently
3. taker
4. marginal revenue
5. zero
6. excess capacity
7. product differentiation; interdependence
8. reaction
9. cartel
10. cheating
11. tacit
12. Game theory
13. collusion
14. prisoner's dilemma
15. marginal revenue; marginal cost

B. True/False

1. False
2. False
3. True
4. False
5. False. *MR = MC.*
6. True
7. True
8. True
9. False
10. True
11. True
12. True
13. True
14. False. Cartels are formal agreements to work together; price leadership is an informal, or tacit, collusive tactic. Cartels are illegal in the United States.
15. False
16. False
17. False.
18. True

C. Multiple Choice

1. e
2. b
3. e
4. d
5. a
6. a
7. d
8. c
9. d
10. c
11. d
12. e
13. b
14. a
15. b
16. b
17. d
18. a
19. c
20. c

D. Discussion Questions

1. Product differentiation implies that each firm can raise its price a little without losing all its customers. That is, the firm faces a downward-sloping demand curve. All the differences between perfect competition and monopolistic competition are due to the downward-sloping demand curve. A downward-sloping demand curve implies that the marginal revenue curve lies below the demand curve (under perfect competition, the demand curve and the marginal revenue curve are equal). Thus, when the firm sets $MR = MC$, $p > MC$. Since the demand curve slopes down, the zero-profit long-run equilibrium condition implies that the average total cost curve is tangent to the demand curve to the left of the minimum point of the average total cost curve. That is, there is excess capacity.

2. Product differentiation can occur even if the products are physically identical. Products can differ by location, by services, or by image. In other words, physical differences are only one way to differentiate products.

3. Monopolistic competition is like monopoly in that firms face downward-sloping demand curves and, in equilibrium, $p > MC$. The two market structures differ in that free entry under monopolistic competition leads to zero economic profits in the long run. The products offered by a monopoly have no close substitutes, whereas the products of the firms under monopolistic competition are close, but not perfect, substitutes. A monopoly can earn positive economic profits in the long run.

4. Excess capacity occurs when a firm could lower its average total costs by expanding production, i.e., the firm produces to the left of the minimum of its average total cost curve. Firms are characterized by excess capacity under monopolistic competition because the long-run equilibrium condition of zero economic profits implies that the firm produces at the rate of output where the demand curve is tangent to the average total cost curve. Since the demand curve slopes down, this must be to the left of the minimum of the average total cost curve.

5. Excess capacity is not necessarily wasteful, since consumers value product variety and excess capacity is a necessary result of product differentiation.

6. Oligopoly and monopoly are alike in that firms under both market structures tend to be large, there is some sort of barrier to entry, and firms have considerable influence on price. They differ in that firms under oligopoly are interdependent; each must consider possible reactions of the other firms to any change it makes in price or output.

7. Interdependence among firms makes it difficult to analyze the behavior of a firm under oligopoly. Since firms can react in many ways, each firm may make plans and adjustments in many ways. There is no single type of behavior.

8. The choices of output levels made by a firm under perfect competition have no effect on any other firms in the industry. Firms make decisions independently of one another. The same is true for monopolistic competition—decisions are made independently. Under monopoly, a firm has no rivals. Only under oligopoly are firms interdependent and take into consideration how rivals may respond to changes they make in price–output policies.

Monopolistic Competition and Oligopoly

9. Collusion can be profitable because the colluding firms stop trying to compete, agree to restrict output, and raise prices to the level a monopoly would charge. That is, firms collectively act as if they were a monopoly. A collusive agreement sets $p > MC$ and $p > ATC$, so that firms maximize their joint profits. Since $p > MC$, an individual firm can increase its profits by selling additional units as long as the price received exceeds the marginal cost of the units. Each firm faces this temptation to cheat. If firms do cheat, prices will tend to fall and the collusive agreement will fall apart.

10. Collusion can be profitable, but it is often not feasible. In many industries there are too many firms for collusion to be practical. In addition, if firms collude, raise prices, and make economic profits, new firms may enter the industry. It is also more difficult to collude when costs differ greatly and when the products are differentiated. Finally, collusion is illegal in the United States, which deters some firms from trying to collude.

11. Collusion is more likely in the steel industry than in the auto industry because steel is more homogeneous than autos. The product heterogeneity of autos makes it more difficult to come to an agreement about each dimension of the products (price, quality, standard features, etc.), and it is harder to observe and prevent cheating.

12. Perfect competition and oligopoly differ in several ways. Perfect competition is characterized by many firms; in oligopoly there are only a few firms. Firms under perfect competition face horizontal demand curves; oligopolists face downward-sloping demand curves with slopes that depend upon the reactions of other firms in the industry. Firms under perfect competition make decisions independently of each other; oligopolists are interdependent. In long-run equilibrium under perfect competition, $p = MC$ and the firm produces at the minimum of its average total cost curve. Under oligopoly, $p > MC$ and a firm may or may not produce at the minimum of its average total cost curve. Some oligopolists also have the added costs of product differentiation. Finally, oligopolists are likely to earn above-normal profits; competitive firms earn zero profits in long-run equilibrium.

13. Game theory examines oligopolistic behavior as a series of strategic moves among rivals. A strategy reflects a player's operational plan and the payoff matrix lists the profits that each of the rivals can expect based on the strategy each firm adopts.

14. a. AirCanada's dominant strategy is to charge $1,000. If Alitalia's price is $2,000, AirCanada's profits are greater by charging $1,000 ($75,000 instead of $50,000). If Alitalia's price is $1,000, AirCanada's profits are greater by charging $1,000 ($20,000 instead of $5,000). Therefore, AirCanada's dominant strategy is to charge $1,000.
   b. $1,000. Logic same as a.
   c. AirCanada will charge $1,000 when Alitalia charges $1,000 and $2,000 when Alitalia charges $2,000.
   d. $2,000 for each. Each can develop a reputation for honoring the agreement to charge $2,000.

15. a. Alitalia doesn't have a dominant strategy. It should charge $1,000 when AirCanada charges $1,000 and $2,000 when AirCanada charges $2,000.
   b. AirCanada's dominant strategy is to charge $1,000.
   c. Since Alitalia knows AirCanada will charge $1,000, Alitalia's best strategy is to charge $1,000 also.

CHAPTER 11

Resource Markets

I. INTRODUCTION

Up to this point, we have focused on product markets—the markets for goods and services. We now change our emphasis and begin to analyze resource markets—the markets for such resources as labor, land, and capital. The material in this chapter applies to all resources. In the next chapter, we will examine labor markets in more detail.

II. OUTLINE

1. The Once-Over

    1.1 Resource Demand. Additional units of a resource will be demanded as long as the extra revenue generated exceeds the extra cost.

    1.2 Resource Supply. Resource owners will supply additional units as long as doing so increases their utility.

2. The Demand and Supply of Resources. In product markets, households are demanders and firms are suppliers; in resource markets, households are suppliers and firms are demanders. The supply and demand for resources depend on the willingness and ability of buyers and sellers to participate in the market.

    2.1 The Market Demand for Resources
        a. Firms demand resources because the resources are needed to make the good or service the firm produces.
        b. The demand for a resource is a derived demand—it is derived from the value of the final product.
        c. The demand curve for a resource slopes downward because as the price of a resource falls, producers are more willing and more able to employ the resource.
            (1) As the price of a resource declines, other things constant, the firm is more willing to use the resource, since it is cheaper relative to other resources than it used to be.
            (2) At a lower price, the producer can hire more resources for the same total cost, so its ability to buy more has increased.

    2.2 The Market Supply for Resources
        a. The supply curve of a resource slopes upward because resource owners are more willing and able to supply the resource at a higher price.
        b. The owner of a resource is more willing to supply it at a higher price, other things constant, because the higher price increases his or her real income.
        c. The owner is more able to supply the resource at a higher price, since the higher price enables the owner to incur the higher costs of supplying more of the resource.

2.3 Temporary and Permanent Resource Price Differences
   a. We expect the prices paid for identical resources to tend toward equality over time, regardless of the market to which the resource is being supplied.
   b. Sometimes resource prices are not the same because the resource market is in a transitory state of disequilibrium but is moving toward equilibrium.
   c. There can be permanent differences in resources; these do not induce a reallocation of resources.
   d. Permanent resource price differences occur when
      (1) resources are immobile.
      (2) there are differences in resource quality.
      (3) the training requirements of resources differ.
      (4) nonmonetary rewards of jobs differ.

2.4 Opportunity Cost and Economic Rent
   a. The minimum amount the owner of a resource must receive to supply the resource for a particular use is the *opportunity cost* of the resource.
   b. *Economic rent* is the amount the resource owner receives above the opportunity cost.
   c. When supply is perfectly inelastic, all earnings are economic rent.
   d. When supply is perfectly elastic, all earnings are opportunity costs.
   e. When the supply curve slopes upward, resource owners collect both opportunity costs and economic rent.

3. A Closer Look at Resource Demand

3.1 The Firm's Demand for a Resource. The law of diminishing marginal returns states that the marginal physical product declines as more of a variable resource is combined with a given quantity of other resources.

3.2 Marginal Revenue Product
   a. The marginal revenue product (*MRP*) of labor is the amount by which total revenue increases as a result of hiring one more worker. It depends on:
      (1) The amount of additional output produced—the marginal physical product of labor
      (2) The price of the output
   b. For the perfectly competitive firm, *MRP* equals the price times the marginal physical product of labor.
   c. For a firm with market power, *MRP* equals the change in total revenue that results from hiring an additional unit of labor. *MRP* declines both because of diminishing marginal physical product and because the selling price of the good must fall if the firm is to sell additional units.

3.3 Marginal Resource Cost
   a. The marginal resource cost (*MRC*) is the change in total cost that results from hiring one more unit of a resource.
   b. If a firm is a price taker in the resource market, *MRC* equals the price of the input.
   c. A profit-maximizing firm employs each resource up to the point where its marginal resource cost equals its marginal revenue product.
   d. The firm's marginal revenue product curve is viewed as its demand curve for that resource when the firm buys resources in a competitive market.
   e. The profit-maximizing level of output can be found by either this method or finding where *MR* = *MC*.

3.4 Shifts in the Demand for Resources. The demand for resources will shift when
    a. there are changes in the prices of other resources used;
        1.) If two resources are substitutes, an increase in the price of one causes the demand for the other to increase.
        2.) If two resources are complement, an increase in the price of one causes the demand for the other to decrease.
    b. there is a change in technology or training;
    c. demand for the final product changes.

3.5 *CASE STUDY:* The Derived Demand for Architects

3.6 Optimal Use: More than One Resource. To maximize profits, the firm should employ resources so that the marginal revenue product equals the marginal resource cost of each resource.

3.7 *CASE STUDY:* The McMinimum Wage

4. Distribution of Resource Earnings. Wages and salaries represent the largest share of U.S. national income. Labor's share of total income has increased also.

III. DISCUSSION

The Demand and Supply of Resources

Firms require resources to produce goods and services. Households own the resources. A firm will hire quantities of various resources to maximize profits, and households will supply resources so as to maximize utility. The demand for a resource is a *derived demand*; it is derived from the value of the final product.

The demand curve for a resource slopes downward. Resources can be combined in different amounts to produce a product. If the price of one resource falls, other things constant, the firm will hire more of that resource. At a lower price, the firm is able to hire more of the resource.

The supply curve of a resource slopes upward. At a higher price, other things constant, the owner is willing and able to supply more because of the extra real income he or she receives.

Other things equal, resource owners will supply their resources to the firm offering the highest price. Consequently, in theory, identical resources tend to receive the same price in all markets. Differences in prices induce resource owners to move their resources to the higher-paying uses.

In the real world, however, we often observe that similar resources do not receive the same price. In some cases, the inequality of resource prices indicates that the resource market is in disequilibrium. Things are often changing in product and resource markets, and changes generate temporary differences in resource prices. Over time, the prices will move back toward equality. In other cases, differences in resource prices can persist, even in a market in equilibrium. It may be that the resources are not mobile, so they cannot move to higher-paying firms; the resources may differ in quality of training; or the nonmonetary aspects of jobs may differ.

Economic rent is a concept students often find confusing, but it need not be. The opportunity cost of a resource is the minimum amount a resource owner must receive to supply a resource to a particular use. Any earnings above opportunity costs are called economic rent. Review Exhibit 3 in the text to be sure you understand the relationships among supply, opportunity costs, and economic rent.

A Closer Look at Resource Demand

A firm can increase output by hiring more resources. Suppose we focus on one resource, say labor. We know that because of the law of diminishing marginal returns, output eventually increases by smaller amounts as additional workers are hired. The firm sells the extra output produced by an additional worker at the market price. The additional revenue received is the *marginal revenue product* of labor. If the firm is a competitive firm, or price taker, in the output market, it can sell as many units of the final good as it wants without affecting the market price. The firm's marginal revenue product (*MRP*) falls as additional workers are hired because of the law of diminishing marginal returns. If the firm is not a competitive firm—if it is a price maker in the output market—then it can sell additional units of output only by lowering the price of the output. The *MRP* of such a firm falls for two reasons: (1) the law of diminishing marginal returns and (2) the fact that the firm must lower price on all units sold in order to sell more units of its product. You should compare Exhibits 4 and 5 in the text carefully to be sure you understand these differences between the two types of firms.

When the firm buys labor in a competitive market, its marginal revenue product curve for labor is also its demand curve for labor. The additional revenue gained from hiring an additional worker is the most that the firm is willing to pay for the additional worker. The extra cost to the firm of hiring an additional worker is called the *marginal resource cost* (*MRC*) of labor. If the firm is a *price taker* in resource markets, *MRC* equals the market wage for labor. For such firms, the supply curve of labor is perfectly elastic. The firm maximizes profits by hiring workers up to the level where marginal resource cost equals marginal revenue product (*MRC = MRP*).

We have seen that the demand curve for labor is also the firm's *MRP* curve in a competitive labor market, and that *MRP* depends on the price of the good produced and the marginal physical product of labor. Anything that causes either the price of the final product or the marginal physical product of labor to change will cause the demand curve for labor to shift. In Exhibit 1, the firm's demand curve for labor (D_1) intersects the firm's supply curve at 10 units of labor. Assume that the marginal physical product of the tenth worker is 2 units of output per day, the product price is $10, and the daily wage is $20. *MRP* is $20 when 10 workers are hired; point *a* represents the equilibrium. If the price of the firm's product increases to $15, then the marginal revenue product of the tenth worker increases to $30 ($15 x 2). The demand curve for labor shifts up to D_2 and passes through point *b*. Now *MRP* > *MRC*, and the firm will hire more workers.

Exhibit 1

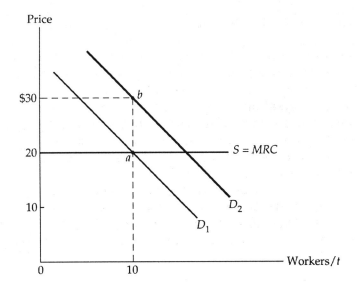

The demand curve for labor could also shift from D_1 to D_2 if the price of the product stayed at $10 but labor became more productive. Suppose the firm purchases more units of other inputs. If these *other* inputs and labor are complements, the marginal physical product of labor will increase. Say the marginal physical product of the tenth worker increases to 3 units of output. Now $MRP = $10 \times 3 = 30, and demand shifts to D_2. The productivity of labor could also increase if technological improvements occurred or if labor received additional training. In both cases, labor is more productive and therefore more valuable.

A profit -maximizing firm hires each input up to the point where the marginal revenue product of the input *equals* the marginal resource cost. This implies that the choice of the combination of inputs to use depends on the relative costs of each.

IV. LAGNIAPPE

Optimal Resource Use

Firms can combine resources in many different ways. The technique they use depends on the prices of resources. Firms combine resources in a way that conserves the more costly resources. In Louisiana, rice farmers use a lot of capital equipment and relatively little labor; in Thailand, rice farmers use relatively more labor. The reason is that labor is much cheaper in Thailand than it is in the United States. Electric utilities produce electricity using water power in the Pacific Northwest and coal in Ohio. The output of wheat per acre is greater in Great Britain than it is in the United States. Because good farmland is scarce in Great Britain, British farmers use relatively more of other inputs on an acre and produce more wheat on the acre than do U.S. farmers.

Question to Think About: What changes did firms make as a result of the decline in prices of computers over the last decade?

The Demand Curve for Labor Slopes Down?

There are some in society who believe the number of jobs available is constant, that is they believe the demand curve for labor is vertical. If the demand curve for labor is downward sloping, more jobs are available when wages are lower. Pollicies such as minimum wages or the "living wage" reduce the number of jobs available. Of course, the supply curve of labor slopes up so lower wages can increase the jobs available but not the jobs accepted.

Question to Think about: What factors other than government policy affect the wages available to low-skilled workers?

V. KEY TERMS

Derived demand
Economic rent
Marginal revenue product

Marginal resource cost
Resource substitutes
Resource complements

VI. QUESTIONS

A. Completion

1. Households _____ resources and _____ products; firms _____ products and _____ resources.

2. The firm's demand for resources arises from the demand for the good produced with them, so the demand for resources is a _____ demand.

3. Wage differentials for similar workers that induce workers to relocate are called _____ differentials.

4. Wage differentials for similar workers that do not trigger a shift of resources to other uses are called _____ differentials.

5. The minimum price necessary to get a resource owner to supply his or her resource is its _____.

6. The amount of earnings above the opportunity cost of a resource is called _____.

7. All earnings are opportunity costs when the resource's supply curve is _____.

8. When the supply curve is vertical, _____ determines the equilibrium price.

9. A profit-maximizing firm will hire an additional worker if the wage is less than labor's _____.

10. The marginal revenue product in perfect competition is also called the _____ of the marginal product.

11. The competitive firm's demand curve for labor slopes down because of the _____.

12. The additional cost of buying an additional unit of a resource is its _____.

13. A reduction in the price of one resource will lead to an increase in demand for another resource if the resources are _____.

14. The marginal revenue product curve can be thought of as the firm's _____ for the resource.

15. The additional cost of hiring one more unit of labor is the _____ of labor.

B. True/False

_____ 1. In deciding between two jobs, a worker always chooses the higher-paying job.

_____ 2. A firm has a demand for a resource because of the resource's ability to produce goods and services.

_____ 3. As the price of a resource falls, other things constant, producers are more willing and more able to employ that resource.

_____ 4. As the price of a resource increases, other things constant, resource owners are more willing to supply more of the resource, and are more able to do so.

_____ 5. Resource markets operate so that the price of a homogeneous resource tends toward equality across markets over time, *ceteris paribus*.

_____ 6. If wages are not the same for identical labor, then this indicates a temporary resource price differential.

_____ 7. Resource price differences can reflect differences in the nonmonetary aspects of similar jobs.

_____ 8. Both temporary resource price differentials and permanent resource price differentials spur movement of resources away from lower-priced uses toward higher-priced uses.

_____ 9. The opportunity cost of a resource equals its economic rent.

_____ 10. How resource returns are divided between economic rent and opportunity costs depends on the shape of the supply curve.

_____ 11. When the supply of a resource is perfectly inelastic, demand determines the equilibrium price.

_____ 12. The demand curve for a resource slopes down because of the law of diminishing marginal returns.

_____ 13. If the price of the good produced with it increases, the marginal revenue product of labor increases.

_____ 14. For price-taking firms in the resource market, the price paid for each unit of a resource equals its marginal resource cost.

_____ 15. A profit-maximizing firm employs each resource up to the point where its marginal resource cost equals its marginal revenue product.

_____ 16. A firm with market power in its product market faces an upward-sloping supply curve for a resource.

_____ 17. If demand for a final product increases, demand for inputs used to produce the good also increases.

_____ 18. If the price of capital increases and the demand for labor falls, labor and capital are substitutes.

C. Multiple Choice

1. We assume that in the market for resources,
   a. firms seek to maximize profits and resource owners seek to maximize utility.
   b. firms seek to maximize profits and resource owners seek to maximize income.
   c. firms and resource owners seek to maximize utility.
   d. firms seek to minimize costs and resource owners seek to maximize income.
   e. none of the above

2. In assuming that profit maximization motivates firms, we assume that the firms
   a. choose the most efficient production process.
   b. choose the least costly combination of resources.
   c. restrict output to increase profits.
   d. all of the above
   e. a and b only

3. The perfectly competitive firm's demand curve for a resource slopes down because
   a. the demand curve for the final product slopes down.
   b. there are fewer resources available at lower prices.
   c. there are diseconomies of scale.
   d. firms will substitute away from a resource if its price increases.
   e. firms are willing to use more of a resource at a higher price.

4. Which of the following is held constant along a demand curve for an input?
   a. technology
   b. quantity of other inputs used by the firm
   c. prices of other inputs used by the firm
   d. price of the product produced by the firm
   e. all of the above

5. Which of the following is likely to happen if salaries for schoolteachers increase, other things constant?
   a. Some housewives become teachers.
   b. Some part-time teachers become full-time teachers.
   c. Some people in other occupations switch to teaching.
   d. Enrollments in education courses in colleges increase.
   e. all of the above

6. The example in question 5 is an illustration of what happens when
   a. people are greedy.
   b. workers differ in productivity.
   c. there are temporary resource price differentials for labor.
   d. there are permanent resource price differentials for labor.
   e. jobs differ in attractiveness.

7. If two identical workers earn different salaries, then
   a. one worker must have more training than another.
   b. one worker must be more skillful than another.
   c. the nonmonetary aspects of their jobs may differ.
   d. the market may not be in equilibrium.
   e. c and d

8. The division of resource earnings between opportunity costs and economic rent depends on
   a. the demand for the resource.
   b. nonmonetary aspects of the job.
   c. the resource owner's elasticity of supply.
   d. the elasticity of supply of the good produced.
   e. a and c.

9. The marginal revenue product of a resource depends on
   a. the price of the resource.
   b. the supply of the resource.
   c. the price of the firm's output.
   d. the marginal physical product of the resource.
   e. c and d.

10. For a price taker in the output market, the marginal revenue product curve slopes down because
    a. the demand curve for the final product slopes down.
    b. marginal revenue curves slope down.
    c. of diminishing marginal returns.
    d. the marginal resource cost slopes down.
    e. a and b

Exhibit 2

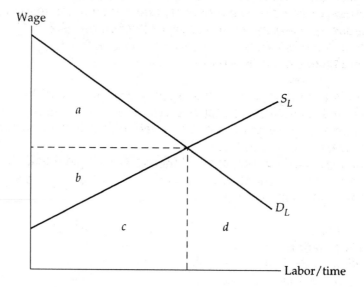

11. In Exhibit 2, at equilibrium, opportunity costs are represented by area _____ and economic rent by area _____.
    a. *a; b*
    b. *b; c*
    c. *b; d*
    d. *c; a*
    e. *c; b*

12. In Exhibit 2, if the supply curve became more elastic but still intersected the demand curve at the same point,
    a. opportunity costs would increase.
    b. opportunity costs would decrease.
    c. economic rent would increase.
    d. consumer surplus would increase.
    e. none of the above

13. Labor and capital are used to produce good X. An increase in the demand for labor can be due to
    a. an increase in the wage rate.
    b. an increase in the price of X.
    c. an increase in the productivity of labor.
    d. all of the above.
    e. b and c only.

14. An increase in the amount of capital used by the firm will
    a. make all labor more productive.
    b. increase the demand for labor that is a substitute for the capital.
    c. increase the demand for labor that is a complement to the capital.
    d. have no effect on labor.
    e. decrease the productivity of all labor in the firm.

15. A technological improvement that increases the marginal productivity of a resource will
    a. cause an increase in the demand for the resource.
    b. cause a decrease in the quantity demanded of the resource.
    c. cause an increase in the supply of a resource.
    d. lead to a lower wage.
    e. lead to less economic rent.

16. To maximize profit, the firm should employ resources so that
    a. the ratio of labor to capital equals one.
    b. the marginal revenue product of labor equals the marginal revenue product of capital.
    c. the marginal revenue product equals the marginal resource cost for each input.
    d. the marginal product of all resources equals one.
    e. none of the above

17. A profit-maximizing firm employs labor and capital such that
    a. $MRP_L = MRC_k$
    b. $MRP_L = MRP_K$
    c. $MRC_L = MRC_K$
    d. $MRP_L = MRC_L$; $MRP_K/MRC_K = 0$
    e. both b and c.

18. Suppose there is an influx of people into the labor force. These people will be able to find jobs
    a. only if there is an increase in the demand for labor.
    b. only if they are highly skilled.
    c. since the increase in the supply of labor causes the wage rate to fall.
    d. since the government will hire those who can't find jobs in the private sector.
    e. None of the above. Most of them won't be able to find jobs.

D. Discussion Questions

1. What does it mean to say that the demand for a resource is a derived demand?

2. Why does the supply curve of a resource slope upward?

3. Why do we expect that the price paid for identical resources of production will tend toward equality across markets over time?

4. How do temporary resource price differentials and permanent resource price differentials differ in their effects on labor markets?

5. Would you expect to find a greater permanent price differential in the price of coal or in the wages of clerks across firms? Explain.

6. Would you expect garbage truck drivers to receive the same wage as delivery truck drivers? Explain.

7. Suppose the labor supply schedule is as shown in Exhibit 3, and the market wage is $70 per day. What are the opportunity costs and economic rent of each worker hired?

Exhibit 3

Salary/Day	Workers
$50	1
55	2
60	3
65	4
70	5
75	6

8. Why does the division of resource earnings into economic rent and opportunity costs depend on the resource owner's elasticity of supply?

9. a. Fill in the blanks in Exhibit 4.

Exhibit 4

Units of Labor	Total Physical Product	Marginal Physical Product	Product Price	Marginal Revenue Product
0	0	---	$5	---
1	20	_____	5	_____
2	38	_____	5	_____
3	54	_____	5	_____
4	68	_____	5	_____
5	80	_____	5	_____
6	90	_____	5	_____
7	98	_____	5	_____
8	104	_____	5	_____

   b. If the firm is a resource price taker, how many workers does it hire at a market wage of $60?

   c. Suppose product price falls to $3. How many workers are hired?

10. What can cause the demand for a resource to shift?

11. Suppose you own your own firm, and you hire two workers at $10 an hour. A new housing area opens causing demand for your service to increase. What will happen to the number of workers you hire and to their wage?

12. Why do workers in the United States earn more, on average, than workers in Mexico?

13. Why do stores in suburban shopping centers provide free parking, whereas stores in downtown areas of cities do not?

14. Suppose a firm is hiring workers and capital so that $MRP_L = 20$, $MRP_K = 50$, $MRC_L = \$18$, and $MRC_K = \$55$. Is the firm maximizing profits? If not, what should the firm do?

VII. ANSWERS

A. Completion

1. supply; demand; supply; demand
2. derived
3. temporary resource price
4. permanent
5. opportunity cost
6. economic rent
7. horizontal (perfectly elastic)
8. demand
9. marginal revenue product
10. value
11. law of diminishing marginal returns
12. marginal resource cost
13. complements
14. demand curve
15. marginal resource cost

B. True/False

1. False
2. True
3. True
4. True
5. True
6. False
7. True
8. False
9. False
10. True
11. True
12. True
13. True
14. True
15. True
16. False
17. True
18. False

C. Multiple Choice

1. a
2. e
3. d
4. e
5. e
6. c
7. e. Note that if either a or b is true, the workers are not identical.
8. c
9. e
10. c
11. e
12. a
13. e
14. c
15. a
16. c
17. d
18. d

D. Discussion Questions

1. Firms do not demand resources for the same reasons consumers demand goods and services. The firm values resources because the resources produce the goods and services that the firm sells. The value of a resource to the firm is derived from the value of the product the resource helps produce.

2. Resource owners are more willing and more able to supply a good as price increases, other things constant. They are more willing because the higher price means they will be able to buy more goods and services. They are more able because they can supply resources that have higher opportunity costs when the price is higher.

3. A resource owner who was receiving a lower price than those working for a different firm or industry in jobs with the same nonmonetary benefits will move to the higher-paying area. This process will continue until all identical resources receive the same price.

4. Temporary resource price differentials for labor encourage those receiving the lower wages to move to occupations or locations where wages are better. Permanent resource price differentials do not induce workers to change jobs.

5. The wages of clerks are likely to vary more. Nonmonetary differences may generate wage differences for clerks, but coal owners will not be concerned about nonmonetary factors.

6. No. Working on a garbage truck is more unpleasant than driving a delivery truck. Drivers will demand more pay to work on the garbage truck.

7.

Worker	Opportunity Costs	Economic Rent
1	$50	$20
2	55	15
3	60	10
4	65	5
5	70	0

Note that the sixth worker is not hired if the market wage is $70 per day.

8. If supply is perfectly elastic, the resource can earn as much in its best alternative use as in its current use. Any reduction in earnings in the current use will induce the resource to go elsewhere, so there is no economic rent. When supply is perfectly inelastic, the resource has no other use, so its opportunity costs are zero. Thus, the proportion of resource earnings that is opportunity costs is greater the more elastic the supply of the resource.

9. a.

Units of Labor	Total Physical Product	Marginal Physical Product	Product Price	Marginal Revenue Product
0	0	---	$5	---
1	20	20	5	$100
2	38	18	5	90
3	54	16	5	80
4	68	14	5	70
5	80	12	5	60
6	90	10	5	50
7	98	8	5	40
8	104	6	5	30

b. 5 workers
c. 1 worker

10. The demand for a resource is determined by its marginal revenue product, which depends on the price of the good produced and the productivity of the resource. Anything that causes the product price to change or the resource's productivity to change will cause the resource's demand curve to shift.

11. The number of workers hired will probably increase, but the wage won't change since you presumably are a price-taker in the labor market.

12. Workers in the United States are more productive, on average, than workers in Mexico. This is so for at least two reasons. First, U.S. workers tend to have more capital to work with, and second, U.S. workers tend to be better educated and trained.

13. Land is more expensive in downtown areas than it is in suburbs, so suburban shopping centers can better afford to provide free parking.

14. No, the firm is not maximizing profits. It should employ resources so that $MRP_L = MRC_L$ and the $MRP_K = MRC_K$. Since $MRP_L > MRC_L$, the firm should hire more labor. Since $MRP_K < MRC_K$, the firm should employ fewer units of capital.

CHAPTER 12

Labor Markets and Labor Unions

I. INTRODUCTION

The last chapter examined resource markets in general. This chapter focuses attention on labor markets. The chapter derives the individual worker's labor supply curve and the market supply curve. Wage determination and factors causing wage differences are also examined. An examination of labor unions follows.

II. OUTLINE

1. Labor Supply. Each worker has a labor supply curve for each possible use of his or her labor. The individual worker's supply curves for each use of labor depend on the opportunity costs of his or her time in other activities.

  1.1 Labor Supply and Utility Maximization
    a. There are two sources of utility that are of interest in discussions of labor supply:
      (1) Consumption of goods and services
      (2) Leisure activities
    b. There are three uses of time:
      (1) Market work: selling time in labor markets for money
      (2) Nonmarket work: producing goods and services for oneself or acquiring skills and education
      (3) Leisure
    c. Work can be a source of disutility.
    d. The *net utility of work* (the utility of the consumption that work makes possible less the disutility of the work itself) makes work an attractive use of time.
    e. Utility maximization: consumers attempt to allocate time so that the expected marginal utility of the last unit of time spent in each activity is identical.
    f. Some implications of the model of time allocation are:
      (1) Individuals use nonmarket work to produce those goods they can provide more cheaply than the market can.
      (2) The higher the expected earnings for a high school graduate, the greater the opportunity cost of college.

  1.2 Wages and Individual Labor Supply
    a. Substitution and income effects of a wage increase
      (1) Substitution effect: the consumer supplies more time to market work.
      (2) Income effect: the consumer supplies more time to leisure and less time to market work.

b. Backward-bending labor supply curve: eventually the income effect outweighs the substitution effect.

1.3 Nonwage Determinants of Labor Supply
a. The greater the other sources of income, the less market work one will perform.
b. The better the amenities of the job, the more likely one is to perform market work.
c. The more a job provides experience that will increase future income, the more likely one is to perform market work.
d. The more a job accords with one's tastes, the more likely one is to perform market work.

1.4 Market Supply of Labor. The supply of labor to a particular market the horizontal sum of all the individual supply curves.

1.5 Why Wages Differ
a. Some jobs pay more because they require a long training period. To induce people to pay the costs of the training, the job has to pay more.
b. Similarly, people with more education usually receive a higher wage.
c. Workers with more experience receive a higher wage, other things equal.
d. Differences in ability cause difference in wages too.
e. Winner-Take-All Labor Markets.
f. Other things equal, riskier jobs pay higher wages.
g. There can be differences in wages due to geographic location.
h. Discrimination can be a source of differences in wages.
i. Union workers earn higher wages than non-union workers, other things equal.

2. Unions and Collective Bargaining

2.1 Types of Unions
a. The first unions in the United States were *craft unions*—unions made up of workers in particular crafts, such as carpenters or masons.
b. The American Federation of Labor (1886) was an organization made up of craft unions whose focus was on economic issues.
c. An industrial union includes all unskilled, semi-skilled, and skilled workers in an industry.
d. The Congress of Industrial Organizations (1935) was a national organization of unions in mass-production industries such as automobiles and steel.

2.2 Collective Bargaining
a. Collective bargaining: union and management negotiate a mutually acceptable contract.
b. Mediation and arbitration
(1) *With mediation*, an impartial observer (mediator) listens to both sides and makes suggestions for resolving differences.
(2) With *binding arbitration*, an arbitrator is appointed and empowered to issue a decision that both sides must accept.

2.3 The Strike. A union withholds labor from the firm.

3. Union Wages and Employment

    3.1 Inclusive, or Industrial, Unions
        a. The union negotiates a wage above the equilibrium wage.
        b. Excess supply of labor results.
        c. This model characterizes strong industrial unions.
        d. Wage gains come at the cost of reduced total employment compared to the level that would prevail without a union.
        e. Nonunion wages tend to fall as the supply of labor in the nonunion sector increases.

    3.2 Exclusive, or Craft, Unions
        a. The union shifts the supply curve to the left.
        b. The restricted supply pushes wages up.
        c. This model characterizes craft unions, assuming they can restrict membership and force all employers in the market to hire only union members.

    3.3 Increasing Demand for Union Labor
        a. Unions can increase demand for labor by appealing to consumers to buy union-made products.
        b. Unions can increase demand for labor by restricting the supply of products that compete with union-made products.
        c. The demand for labor is increased if unions generate increased productivity.
        d. *Featherbedding* is the practice of requiring producers to hire more union workers than they need.

    3.4 Recent Trends in Union Membership
        a. Union membership as a percentage of the U.S. work force has declined over the last 50 years.
        b. The decline is due in part to structural changes in the economy that have arisen because the service sector is less unionized than the industrial sector.
        c. The United States has a lower level of union participation than other industrialized nations.

    3.5 *CASE STUDY:* Technology Workers Unionizing Information

III. DISCUSSION

Labor Supply

It is a basic axiom of economics that people seek to maximize utility. An earlier chapter discussed utility maximization as it relates to the consumption of goods and services. But consumption takes time. A television or a stereo provides very little utility to a person who has no time to use it. Leisure time is time spent relaxing, sleeping, and consuming goods and services. Leisure is considered to be a normal good and is subject to the law of diminishing marginal utility.

There are three ways to spend time: in market work, nonmarket work, or leisure. *Market work* involves time spent working for money. *Nonmarket work* may be as laborious as market work but does not involve monetary payments. Time not spent in one form of work or another is considered *leisure*. Of the three types of activities, only leisure is assumed to provide utility directly. Market work provides income that is used to purchase goods and services that provide utility, but market work itself generally does not provide utility. Nonmarket work also does not provide utility directly but is often necessary in order to receive utility from goods. Cooking a meal may not provide utility, but eating it does. The net utility of market work is the utility of the consumption made possible through work minus the disutility of the work itself. Rational consumers maximize utility by allocating their time so that the expected marginal utility of the last unit of time spent in each activity is identical. (Compare this to the rule concerning utility maximization and consumption of goods derived in the chapter titled *Consumer Choice and Demand*.)

What happens when someone's wage rate increases? That person may substitute more market work for nonmarket work, since the opportunity cost of nonmarket work has increased. Instead of repairing the car, the person may take it to a mechanic and work longer at the office. The person may also decide to spend more time on leisure activities— for example, eating out more.

An increase in the wage rate has two opposing effects on an individual worker. On one hand, the higher wage raises the opportunity cost of both nonmarket work and leisure, so the person will want to supply more hours to market work. This is called the *substitution effect* of a wage increase. On the other hand, a higher wage rate increases the individual's income. As income increases, the person will most likely want to consume more leisure. To do so, the worker must devote fewer hours to market work or to nonmarket work. The income effect of a higher wage rate is to reduce the number of hours supplied to market work. Typically, the substitution effect is stronger at relatively low wage rates, but eventually the income effect dominates. Once the income effect dominates, a higher wage rate leads to a smaller quantity of market labor supplied, and the individual's labor supply curve bends backward, as shown in Exhibit 1 in the text. The market supply curve is derived from the individual supply curves. (You should also review Exhibit 2 in the text.)

The last chapter discussed the demand factors that generate wage differentials. This chapter discusses wage differentials that relate to the supply of labor. People have different tastes. Jobs that are boring or repugnant to one person might appeal to another. Even so, some occupations are so universally disliked that employers must compensate employees in those jobs with higher wages. In some cases, the undesirability of a job may arise from the risk associated with it. Occupations with a higher probability of causing a worker's injury or death tend to be characterized by higher wages.

Individual differences also account for differences in wages. Some jobs require considerable training and education. During the training period, the person's income is less than it would be if the person worked at another job and gave up the training. For people to give up income during the training years, they must receive higher salaries later. People also differ with respect to ability. Sometimes people have to move in order to find a better wage. Geographic differences in wages encourage people to migrate. Individual wages can also differ because of racial or gender discrimination. Finally, labor union members usually earn more than similar nonunion workers.

Unions and Collective Bargaining

A labor union is a group of workers who join together to improve their terms of employment. A craft union is made up of workers with a particular skill, such as plumbers or carpenters. An industrial union includes all workers (unskilled, semi-skilled and skilled) in an industry, such as all autoworkers.

A union represents the workers in a firm or industry in negotiations with management on wages and other issues. Most of the time, the two sides reach an agreement through *collective bargaining*. If the two sides are unable to reach an agreement, however, the union can *strike*. The goal of a strike is to withhold labor from the firm so the firm is not able to produce and sell its products. In some cases, negotiations must be resolved through *mediation*, in which a *mediator*, an impartial observer, attempts to bring about a compromise. In other cases, *binding arbitration* is used. Under binding arbitration, the two sides agree to be bound by the decisions of the arbitrator.

Union Wages and Employment

Clearly, an important objective of unions is to raise the wages of their members. There are three ways to raise wages above the market wage. First, the union can negotiate a higher wage and let the firm hire as many workers as it wishes at that wage. (Review Exhibit 4 in the text.) For the entire industry, the higher wage reduces the quantity of labor demanded and increases the quantity supplied, generating an excess supply of labor. The union must find some way to allocate jobs among its members.

Second, unions can raise wages by restricting supply. To do this, a union must be able to restrict membership and prevent employers from hiring nonunion workers. If the union is successful, the supply curve of labor shifts to the left and wages increase. (See Exhibit 5 in the text.) There is not an excess supply of labor as there was in the first case, but this is because the union has restricted entry into the union. There are fewer people employed than there would be otherwise.

The final method of raising wages involves increasing the demand for union workers. This can involve advertising union-made goods, restricting imports from abroad, or *featherbedding*. Some economists argue that union workers are more productive than nonunion workers, so their higher wages merely reflect these differences in productivity. This increased productivity may come from workers' greater confidence and security because the union is monitoring the employer's treatment of workers, handling of pension funds, and the like.

The 1970s saw an increase in public employee unions but a decline in traditional union strongholds in the United States. U.S. unions are finding it more difficult to increase wages and prevent competition by nonunion workers because of structural changes in the economy and increased competition from imports.

IV. LAGNIAPPE

Time, Wage Rates, and Labor Supply

The theory developed in the first part of the chapter explains why an individual's labor supply curve bends backward. Some may question the assertion that the substitution effect dominates at lower wage rates and the income effect at higher wage rates. One reason this may be the case is that the worker may be substituting market work for nonmarket work rather than for leisure. As the wage rate increases, additional time spent in market work need not come out of leisure. In fact, it is possible for both leisure and market work to increase as the individual reduces nonmarket work. Eventually, though, leisure time may be affected. One cannot work all 24 hours of every day, and it is impossible for an individual's labor supply curve to continually slope upward.

There is evidence for a backward-bending supply curve. Employers' practice of offering time-and-a-half pay for overtime work is consistent with a backward-bending labor supply curve, since the firm is greatly increasing the opportunity cost of nonmarket work and of leisure in order to induce employees to work more hours. The observation that the length of the work week has decreased as incomes have increased also supports the theory.

Question to Think About: Can you think of any evidence to contradict the notion of a backward-bending labor supply curve?

Unions, Environmentalists, and NAFTA

The textbook points out that a method now used by unions to promote their interests is to team up with other organizations. A good example of this is the opposition to the North American Free Trade Agreement (NAFTA). This agreement reduced barriers to trade and capital mobility among Canada, Mexico, and the United States. Union leaders believe the agreement will precipitate a decline in employment of union members in the United States as some plants and factories move to Mexico because of the lower Mexican wages. Environmentalists argue that firms will move productive facilities to Mexico to avoid tougher environmental laws in the United States. The cooperation between union members and environmentalists in opposing NAFTA was a surprise to many of those involved in the negotiations. The arguments of the unions may seem self-serving to some, but by teaming up with environmentalist arguments, the unions can appear less self-interested.

Question to Think About: What position would you expect union leaders to take in domestic disputes involving the loss of jobs to protect the environment?

V. KEY TERMS

Market work
Nonmarket work
Leisure
Labor union
Craft union
American Federation of Labor
Congress of Industrial Organizations
Industrial union

Backward-bending supply curve of labor
Comparable worth
Entrepreneur
Collective bargaining
Mediator
Binding arbitration
Strike
Featherbedding

VI. QUESTIONS

A. Completion

1. Any time not spent in market work is spent in _____ or _____.

2. Economists treat time spent working as a source of _____.

3. A rational individual will allocate his or her time so that the expected marginal utility of the last hour of leisure equals the expected net marginal utility of the last hour of _____, which equals the expected net marginal utility of the last hour of _____.

4. The _____ effect of a higher wage encourages a person to work fewer hours.

5. The _____ effect of a higher wage encourages a person to work more hours.

6. An individual's labor supply curve begins bending backward when the _____ effect dominates the _____ effect.

7. Because the individual must be present to provide labor, _____ of the job are important determinants of labor supply.

8. A job that provides more valuable job experience, other things constant, tends to pay _____ wages.

9. Jobs associated with a higher probability of injury are _____ and have higher wages, other things constant.

10. Imperfect labor _____ leads to different wages across regions.

11. The American Federation of Labor was made up of _____ unions and the Congress of Industrial Organizations was made up of _____ unions.

12. Labor and management negotiate a mutually acceptable contract through _____.

13. A _____ tries to resolve differences between labor and management by listening to both sides and making suggestions about how each side could adjust its position.

14. _____ is a method of solving union-management problems whereby a third party listens to both sides and comes to a decision, and both sides are committed to abiding by the decision.

15. A _____ is a union's attempt to withhold labor from the firm.

16. _____ is an attempt to force employers to hire more union workers than they would prefer.

B. True/False

_____ 1. Each individual has only one labor supply curve.

_____ 2. Market work does not provide utility, but nonmarket work and leisure do provide utility.

_____ 3. A rational individual maximizes utility by maximizing leisure time.

_____ 4. Doing homework is a type of nonmarket work.

_____ 5. People who maximize utility use nonmarket work to provide goods and services they can produce more cheaply than the market can.

_____ 6. A higher market wage increases a person's opportunity cost of repairing his or her own car.

_____ 7. The substitution effect of a higher market wage is to work less because the worker can substitute more goods and services for work.

_____ 8. If leisure were an inferior good, the income effect and substitution effect of an increase in the market wage would be the same.

_____ 9. People who are wealthy are willing to supply more hours of market work than people who are not wealthy, other things constant.

_____ 10. Owning labor is different from owning other resources, such as land, because an individual must be present to provide labor.

_____ 11. The supply of labor to a particular job will be greater the more attractive the amenities of the job.

_____ 12. Economists assume that tastes for work are homogeneous across workers.

_____ 13. The market supply curve for labor must bend backward.

_____ 14. Occupations that include frequent periods of unemployment pay lower wages than other occupations, other things constant.

_____ 15. Labor migration reduces wage differentials.

_____ 16. Other things constant, jobs with low status pay less than jobs with higher status.

_____ 17. Collective bargaining agreements can include all aspects of employment.

_____ 18. An arbitrator has more authority to bring labor negotiations to a close than a mediator.

_____ 19. A strike imposes great costs on employers but few costs on the union membership.

_____ 20. Most labor negotiations in the United States end in strikes.

_____ 21. Craft unions typically try to raise wages by increasing the demand for their services.

_____ 22. A union can obtain higher wages for its members only by accepting reduced employment.

C. Multiple Choice

1. The primary sources of utility are
   a. the consumption of goods and services.
   b. leisure.
   c. nonmarket work.
   d. all of the above.
   e. a and b.

2. Leisure is a
   a. normal good.
   b. inferior good.
   c. a normal good for people who do not engage in market work and an inferior good for everyone else.
   d. a normal good for people who do not engage in nonmarket work and an inferior good for everyone else.
   e. None of the above. It is not treated as a good at all.

3. The difference between market work and nonmarket work is that
   a. market work is not enjoyable and nonmarket work is.
   b. one receives money for market work but not for nonmarket work.
   c. one obtains utility from nonmarket work but not from market work.
   d. nonmarket work is done only when one is unemployed.
   e. b and c.

4. Market work is an attractive use of time because
   a. it provides utility.
   b. it provides meaning to life.
   c. it enables one to avoid nonmarket work which has more disutility than market work.
   d. it permits one to buy goods and services which provide utility.
   e. none of the above. It is not an attractive use of time.

5. Rational consumers
   a. balance their time among market work, nonmarket work, and leisure in order to maximize utility.
   b. divide their time so that the expected net marginal utility of the last hour spent on nonmarket work equals the expected marginal utility of the last hour of leisure, which equals the expected net marginal utility of the last hour spent on market work.
   c. attempt to maximize utility by allocating time so that the expected marginal utility of the last unit of time spent in each activity is identical.
   d. all of the above.
   e. b and d.

6. Which of the following is an example of a leisure activity?
   a. going to college
   b. repairing the car
   c. doing dishes
   d. mowing the lawn
   e. none of the above

7. Which of the following is a possible response to a reduction in the wage rate?
   a. go to college
   b. go fishing more often
   c. work fewer hours
   d. paint the house
   e. all of the above

8. An individual's labor supply curve bends backward because
   a. leisure is a normal good.
   b. of a progressive income tax.
   c. people are basically lazy.
   d. market work is an inferior good.
   e. nonmarket work is a normal good.

9. Suppose an individual's labor supply curve is vertical at 40 hours a week. We know that
   a. the substitution effect and income effect offset each other at this number of hours.
   b. the income effect is always zero.
   c. the substitution effect is always zero.
   d. leisure is an inferior good.
   e. the substitution effect always dominates the income effect.

10. Which of the following would cause a person's labor supply to decrease?
    a. The person gets a new supervisor, who allows more personal freedom at work.
    b. The person's best friend gets a job at the company.
    c. The workplace is air-conditioned.
    d. The individual wins a lottery.
    e. none of the above.

11. Most law clerks to Supreme Court justices receive lower wages than they could get in other work. The reason people take these jobs is
    a. they cannot get better jobs.
    b. they have better sources of additional income and wealth.
    c. the value of the job experience increases expected future earnings.
    d. because they desire to live in Washington, D.C.
    e. none of the above.

12. The market supply curve of labor need not bend backward because
    a. different individuals have different opportunity costs and different tastes for work.
    b. some people do not have backward-bending labor supply curves.
    c. women are working more now.
    d. there are laws against job discrimination.
    e. the market supply curve has nothing to do with the labor supply curves of individuals.

13. Wage differentials are due to
    a. differences in risk among jobs.
    b. differences in amenities among jobs.
    c. differences in training.
    d. differences in ability.
    e. all of the above.

14. Factors that help narrow wage differentials include
    a. labor migration.
    b. differences in ability.
    c. differences in risk.
    d. immigration quotas.
    e. a and b.

15. Construction workers on skyscrapers receive higher wages the higher up they work. This wage differential is due to the greater risk with the higher jobs. The wage premium for risk is narrowed by
    a. monopsony power of the employers.
    b. labor migration.
    c. the extra status workers receive for showing the courage to work at the jobs.
    d. sorting by workers so that those less adverse to risk tend to take the riskier jobs.
    e. none of the above.

16. The United Auto Workers is an example of
    a. a craft union.
    b. an industrial union.
    c. a closed shop.
    d. a union that endorses the right-to-work.
    e. none of the above.

17. An impartial observer who attempts to resolve differences between union and management but cannot impose a settlement is a(n)
    a. arbitrator.
    b. mediator.
    c. member of the National Labor Relations Board.
    d. judge.
    e. none of the above.

18. Collective bargaining can focus on which of the following issues?
    a. wages
    b. working conditions
    c. pension plans
    d. layoff procedures
    e. all of the above.

19. Which of the following would aid unions in a strike?
    a. unemployment benefits for strikers
    b. prohibiting picketing at the plant site
    c. police protection for nonstriking workers
    d. large inventories of the good produced by the firm
    e. a and d

Labor Markets and Labor Unions

20. A strike is costly to both sides, but
    a. each side must act as if it could endure a strike rather than give in to the other side.
    b. each side must want a strike for it to occur.
    c. generally a strike hurts the firm more than it does union members.
    d. generally a strike hurts union members more than it does the firm.
    e. none of the above.

21. Which of the following would not increase the wage rate of union workers?
    a. negotiating a wage that was 20 percent above the market wage
    b. establishing high membership fees to join the union
    c. toughening standards for getting a license or a union card
    d. increasing immigration quotas
    e. repealing right-to-work laws

22. If a union negotiates a wage above the competitive wage, employment tends to fall. The reduction in employment will be greater the more
    a. elastic the supply curve of labor.
    b. inelastic the supply curve of labor.
    c. elastic the demand curve for labor.
    d. inelastic the demand curve for labor.
    e. The question cannot be answered without more information.

23. Increased wages can accompany increased employment among union workers if
    a. wages for nonunion workers decline.
    b. the union makes it more difficult for people to join the union.
    c. union labor's productivity increases.
    d. demand for the final product falls.
    e. the union is negotiating with a monopolist producer.

24. U.S. union membership has declined in recent years because
    a. the government has made it more difficult for public employees to join unions.
    b. many union workers have retired in recent years.
    c. yellow-dog contracts are legal again.
    d. the economy has changed and now includes more high-tech industries, and unions have not been successful at organizing high-tech workers.
    e. all of the above.

D. Discussion Questions

1. What is the price of an hour of leisure? An hour of nonmarket work?

2. What does it mean to say that leisure is a normal good?

3. If work provides disutility, why do people ever engage in either market work or nonmarket work?

4. "Some people live to work and others work to live." What does this mean in light of the analysis presented in this chapter?

5. Since it costs about $10 to change the oil in your own car and about $25 to have a garage change the oil, you are being irrational if you do not change the oil yourself. Is the statement true or false? Why?

6. Explain the substitution and income effects of a wage decrease.

7. Bill earns $378 a week at $9 an hour, and $410 a week at $10 an hour. Which is greater for Bill in this range of wages, the substitution effect or the income effect?

8. Why does the individual's labor supply curve bend backward?

9. A new lawyer has one job offer from a law firm and another job offer to work as a clerk for a judge. The latter pays $10,000 less than the former. Why would anyone accept the latter offer?

10. Why doesn't the market supply curve for labor bend backward?

11. There is a growing trend for college students to work as an intern at some time during their college career. Often, internships pay less than other work opportunities, or pay nothing at all.
    a. What is the cost of the internship to the student?
    b. What are the benefits of the internship to the student?

12. At most large universities, professors of finance earn more than professors of economics, but professors of economics earn more than professors of history.
    a. Why would this be the case?
    b. If some colleges pay all faculty with the same degree the same pay, regardless of discipline, what are the likely effects?
    c. Many colleges with a strong religion dimension pay college faculty less than colleges without the religion connection. Why would faculty accept the lower wage?

13. Explain why differences in taste help narrow wage differences.

14. Why are wages for a given occupation not the same in all parts of the country?

15. Distinguish between craft unions and industrial unions.

16. Distinguish between mediation and arbitration.

17. Other things equal, a strike is less costly to schoolteachers than to airline pilots. Explain why.

18. Explain how industrial unions tend to raise wages. Use a graph to illustrate why this approach to increasing wages generates an excess supply of labor. Explain why unemployed workers do not offer to work for less money.

19. Many states have wage laws that require any government job to pay union wage rates whether or not union labor is hired. Who would favor such a law? What are its effects?

20. Explain how being in unions might increase workers' productivity.

VII. ANSWERS

A. Completion

1. nonmarket work; leisure
2. disutility
3. market work; nonmarket work
4. income
5. substitution
6. income; substitution
7. nonmonetary factors
8. lower
9. riskier
10. mobility
11. craft; industrial
12. collective bargaining
13. mediator
14. Binding arbitration
15. Strike
16. Featherbedding

B. True/False

1. False. Each person has as many supply curves as there are labor markets.
2. False
3. False
4. True
5. True
6. True
7. False
8. True
9. False
10. True
11. True
12. False
13. False
14. False
15. True
16. False
17. True
18. True
19. False
20. False
21. False
22. False. Increased labor demand generates higher wages and higher employment.

C. Multiple Choice

1. e
2. a
3. b
4. d
5. d
6. e
7. e
8. a
9. a
10. d
11. c
12. a
13. e
14. a
15. d
16. b
17. b
18. e
19. a
20. a
21. d
22. c
23. c
24. d

D. Discussion Questions

1. The price of both is the same—it is the income one could earn in an hour of market work.

2. Leisure is a good, so people want to consume more of it. People typically are willing and able to consume more leisure as their incomes increase, which makes leisure a normal good by definition.

3. People engage in market work to earn money to buy goods and services, which provide utility. People engage in nonmarket work to produce some goods and services rather than buying them in the marketplace. In either case, it is the goods and services that become available through work that ultimately provide utility to people.

4. The first part of the statement contradicts the analysis of this chapter, for it is saying that some people like to work a lot—that is, they obtain utility directly from work. The second type of people mentioned in the statement conforms to the analysis used in this chapter.

5. False. It takes time to change the oil, and your opportunity cost of time and the disutility of doing it yourself may be greater than the $15 difference in monetary price.

6. If wages decrease, the opportunity cost of leisure and of nonmarket work both decrease. Consequently, people substitute more leisure and/or nonmarket work for market work. The substitution effect of a wage decrease is that the worker devotes fewer hours to market work. The lower wage also lowers one's income. Since leisure is a normal good, less time will be spent in leisure activities at a lower wage rate. The income effect of a wage decrease is that the worker provides more hours to market work. Because the two effects are in conflict, we cannot say for sure how the individual will respond to the wage decrease.

7. The income effect is larger. Bill works 42 hours a week at $9 an hour and 41 hours a week at $10 an hour—that is, at a higher income Bill works fewer hours.

8. The substitution effect of a higher wage is to work more, and the income effect is to work less. At lower wage rates, the substitution effect dominates, and the labor supply curve slopes up. The income effect eventually dominates at higher wages, however, so fewer hours are worked and the labor supply curve bends backward.

9. The clerkship provides experience that will increase the lawyer's market value in future years. A lawyer who thinks the value of this experience is more than $10,000 will accept the clerkship.

10. The market supply curve is the horizontal sum of individual labor supply curves. As wages increase, some people's labor supply curves bend backward, but those of others do not. In addition, at higher wages some people may just be entering the labor market; individuals in other labor markets may switch over if the wage rises enough. All these new entrants keep the market labor supply curve sloping upward.

11. a. The cost is the difference in earnings the student could have received at a job and the earnings received at the internship.
   b. The student obtains valuable experience, which should translate into higher earnings upon graduation.

12. a. The opportunities outside academia are greater for economists and finance professors than for historians. Further, the opportunities for higher incomes in the private sector are greater for finance professors than economics professors.
   b. The pool of candidates for jobs will be much larger in the history department than in the Economics or Finance Departments. The History Department is more likely to get faculty from more prestigious graduate schools than for the Economics or Finance Departments.
   c. The faculty may be willing to accept lower salaries to teach at a college that supports their religious views. The amenities associated with the job would be greater.

13. Some people dislike physical labor and like office work. If everyone were like this, work involving physical labor would pay more and office work less. But some people dislike working at a desk all day and prefer physical labor. Since those who like physical labor tend to seek that type of work and those who like office work tend to seek office jobs, wage differentials are not as wide as they would be if all workers were alike and everyone wanted to do some kinds of work and no one wanted to do other kinds.

14. Wage rates can differ geographically. If people in the lower wage areas migrate to the higher wage areas, then wages will equalize. But if not enough people are willing and able to relocate, wage differences can persist.

15. Craft unions and unions that include people who perform a specific task or craft. Examples would be plumbers, carpenters, and other construction trades. Industrial unions organize workers of all types and skills that work in a particular industry. Examples would include the United Auto Workers and the United Steel Workers.

16. In both mediation and arbitration, an outside party enters the negotiations. A mediator has no power to force an agreement; rather, a mediator offers suggestions that may help the two sides reach an agreement. An arbitrator has the power to force compromises and bring about an agreement.

17. People on strike lose their incomes for the time period they are on strike. For many union workers, the lost wages are gone forever. This would be the case for airline pilots. Teachers, however, usually end up teaching the same number of days, so their annual income would not fall as a result of the strike.

18. Industrial unions tend to negotiate a wage above the market wage. The firm can then hire as many workers as it wants at the negotiated wage. The following graph illustrates the situation. At a negotiated wage of W^*, firms want to hire fewer workers ($L_3 < L_1$), but more workers are willing to work in this market ($L_2 > L_1$). Consequently, there is an excess supply of labor of $L_2 - L_3$. Because the wage was agreed to collectively by the firm and the union members, the firm cannot hire anyone for less than W^*, nor can individual workers offer to work for less.

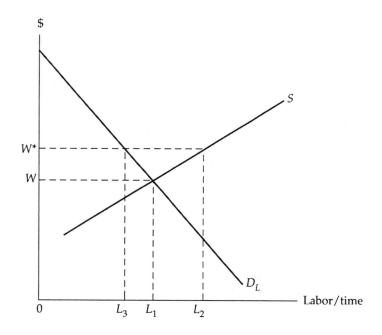

19. Union workers would favor such a law. If the government must pay union wage rates, it may decide to hire union workers. This increases the demand for union workers and helps keep union wage rates above the competitive level.

20. Conflict between workers and management can reduce worker productivity. Workers may also be less productive if they worry about whether the employer is handling such benefits as pension plans properly. If a union reduces these conflicts and worries, the workers may become more productive.

CHAPTER 13

Capital, Interest, and Corporate Finance

I. INTRODUCTION

In the last few chapters, we examined the demand for resources in general as well as the way wages and the return to labor are determined. In this chapter, we examine the returns to capital and returns to other resource owners.

II. OUTLINE

1. The Role of Time in Consumption and Production

   1.1 Production, Saving, and Time
      a. Production takes time.
      b. Producers must rely on savings to survive during the time that production is going on—when the product is not yet completed and ready to consume or sell.
      c. Producers must rely on savings in order to invest in capital.
      d. Production with money and financial markets
         (1) Due to the existence of financial markets that transfer money between savers and borrowers, a producer does not have to rely on his or her own savings.
         (2) Money is not a resource but is demanded because it can be used to purchase productive resources.

   1.2 Consumption, Saving, and Time
      a. Present consumption is valued more than future consumption.
      b. Households must be rewarded if they are to save.
      c. Interest is the reward offered to forgo present consumption.
      d. The quantity of loanable funds supplied is greater at higher interest rates, other things constant.

   1.3 Optimal Investment
      a. In a perfectly competitive output market, the marginal revenue product of capital equals the marginal physical product of capital multiplied by the price of the good purchased.
      b. If capital is expected to last indefinitely, operating expenses are negligible, and output prices are expected to remain constant in the future, the marginal rate of return on investment is equal to the marginal revenue product of capital divided by its marginal resource cost.
      c. A producer will buy capital equipment up to the point where the marginal rate of return on investment equals the market rate of interest.
      d. The firm's demand curve for investment slopes downward and is the same as its marginal rate of return on investment curve.
      e. The market demand curve for investment also slopes downward.

f. The analysis used to determine the optimal investment is the same whether the firm must borrow funds for the investment or already has the funds from past profits.

1.4   *CASE STUDY:* The Value of a Good Idea – Intellectual Property

1.5   The Market for Loanable Funds
a.   The demand curve for loanable funds slopes downward.
b.   The supply curve for loans slopes upward.
c.   The intersection of the supply and demand curves determines the quantity of loans and the interest rate.

1.6   Why Interest Rates Differ
a.   There are many interest rates in the economy.
b.   Several factors cause interest rates to differ.
   (1)   Interest rates are higher the greater the risk of default.
   (2)   The longer the duration of the loan, the greater the risk of higher-than-expected inflation and the higher the interest rate.
   (3)   The larger the loan, the lower the cost of administering it relative to the total cost of the loan; thus, the interest rate may be lower for larger loans.
c.   Differences in the tax treatment of different types of loans affect the interest rate.

2.   Present Value and Discounting

2.1   Present Value of Payment One Year Hence
a.   The value today of a sum of money payable in the future is the sum's *present value.*
b.   The present value discounts a payment to be received in one year by dividing it by 1.0 plus the relevant interest rate; $PV = M/(1 + i)$.
c.   The present value of a sum falls as the interest rate increases.

2.2   Present Value for Payments in Later Years
a. $PV = M/(1 + i)^t$, where M equals the dollars received t years from now and i is the interest rate.
b.   The present value of a given amount of money falls the further into the future the amount is to be paid.

2.3   Present Value of an Income Stream. The present value of an income stream equals the sum of the discounted stream of payments.

2.4   Present Value of an Annuity
a.   An *annuity* is a given sum of money paid each year for a specified number of years.
b.   The present value of an infinite annuity, or perpetuity, is $PV = A/i$, where A is the amount received each year.

2.5   *CASE STUDY:* The Million-Dollar Lottery

3.   Corporate Finance. Corporations acquire funds for investment in three ways: by selling stock, by retaining some profit, and by borrowing.

3.1 Corporate Stock and Retained Earnings
   a. Corporations float new stock issues to raise money for working capital and to buy new plants and equipment.
   b. A share of stock represents a claim on a share of the firm's earnings and assets.
   c. The initial sale of stock to the public is called an initial public offering (IPO).
   d. Shareholders often receive dividends out of the corporation's after-tax profits.
   e. Retained earnings are reinvested profits, which allow the firm to finance expansion.

3.2 Corporate Bonds
   a. A *bond* is a promise to pay the holder a fixed sum of money at a specified maturity date plus an annual interest payment, or coupon.
   b. The payment stream for bonds is more predictable than that for stocks.

3.3 Securities Exchanges
   a. Holders of stocks or bonds (securities) can sell them on security exchanges.
   b. The New York Stock Exchange is the largest security exchange in the United States.
   c. Securities markets allocate funds more readily to successful firms than to firms in financial difficulty.

III. DISCUSSION

The Role of Time in Consumption and Production

All economic activity takes place over time. For example, it takes time to travel to a restaurant, to order, to wait for a meal, to eat the meal, to pay the bill, and to return home. Time affects the decisions of both consumers and producers. Consider a banana. Today it may be ripe and very appealing. In a week, it will turn brown and mushy. Time has changed the banana. A consumer prefers today's banana to the same banana a week from now. In a week, the consumer may be sick and unable to eat the banana, or next week's banana may not actually be as good as today's. Present consumption is valued more than future consumption. In other words, consumers have a *positive rate of time preference*.

Without additional compensation, consumers are not willing to give up consumption of a specific good today in return for consumption of an identical good a year from now. People must receive a reward to postpone consumption. The *interest rate* is the amount of the reward offered to savers. Suppose the interest rate is 8 percent. Then an individual who saves $100 reduces current consumption by $100. A year later, the individual has $108 and is able to consume $108 worth of goods at that time. If the interest rate is 12 percent instead of 8 percent, then the individual can consume $112 worth of goods in the future. The opportunity cost of $100 of current consumption is $108 of future consumption when the interest rate is 8 percent and $112 when the interest rate is 12 percent. The cost of current consumption is greater the higher the interest rate, other things constant, so the quantity of savings supplied increases as interest rates increase.

Production cannot take place without savings. There are at least two reasons for this. First, production takes time, which implies that there is a lag between the time the decision to produce a good is made and the time it is made and consumed or sold. Meanwhile, the owners of the resources used to produce the good must live. In order to purchase inputs and pay labor costs, the producer needs money. The producer either must have previously saved money or must borrow it from others who have saved.

Second, production generally involves *capital goods*—goods that are used to produce other goods and services. Capital goods are made from resources that could have been used to produce consumption goods. Thus, if more capital goods are produced, fewer consumption goods are made in the present. Capital goods enable producers to produce more in the future than could be produced without the capital goods.

Producers can borrow money in the market for loans to finance production and can purchase capital goods in the marketplace. The firm's demand for capital goods is like the demand for any productive resource. In a perfectly competitive output market, the marginal revenue product of capital is found by multiplying the price of the good produced by the marginal physical product of capital. The firm's demand curve for capital slopes down because the law of diminishing marginal returns applies to capital just as it does to labor. The opportunity cost of the money used to purchase the capital equipment is measured by the interest rate, *i*. The purchaser will want to earn at least *i*. In the simple model presented in the text, the *marginal rate of return on investment* equals the marginal revenue product of capital divided by its marginal resource cost. As long as the marginal rate of return on investment exceeds the market interest rate, the firm is better off buying the capital equipment than placing its money in savings. The optimal amount of capital is determined at the point where the marginal rate of return on investment equals the market interest rate. This is true also if the firm must borrow the money, since the interest rate still measures the opportunity cost of the funds.

The market rate of interest is found by bringing the *demand for loanable funds* and the *supply of loanable funds* together. The interest rate is a price, and it is determined by the interaction of demand and supply just like other prices. An increase in the demand for loans leads to a higher interest rate, and an increase in the supply of loans leads to a lower interest rate.

There are actually many interest rates in the economy. Interest rates differ depending on several factors: risk, the duration of the loan, the cost of administering the loan, and how the loan is treated with regard to taxes.

Present Value and Discounting

If we wish to compare monetary values in different time periods, or income flows of various lengths, we must adjust money figures to account for the effect of time. The *present value* of a sum to be received in the future is the value of that sum today. How much is that $100 you expect to get from your grandmother a year from now worth today? The answer depends on the interest rate. Let the interest rate be 8 percent. Put $92.59 in a savings account at 8 percent interest and it will grow to $100 in a year. Hence, the present value of $100 a year from now at 8 percent is $92.59. ($92.59 x 1.08 = $100.) The present value of $100 a year from now is found by dividing $100 by 1 plus the interest rate:

$$\frac{100}{(1+0.08)} = \frac{\$100}{1.08}$$

We can also calculate the present value of $100 at 10 percent interest ($90.91) or at 5 percent interest ($95.24). The present value of $100 a year from now falls as the interest rate rises.

Present value also falls as the time period increases. The present value of $100 today at 8 percent interest is $100; its present value a year from now is $92.59; its present value two years from now is $85.73. The present value of *M* dollars *t* years from now is $M/(1 + i)^t$.

Corporate Finance

The industrial revolution created both capital-intensive, large-scale production and the need for large sums of money to purchase equipment. The corporation evolved in response to these requirements and is a legal creation of the state. A corporation can own property, incur debt, and earn profits. Shareholders own a portion of the firm. A corporation acquires funds for investment in three ways: by selling shares, by borrowing, and by retaining a portion of the firm's profits.

Corporations issue new stock to raise funds. Each share of stock represents a share of the company's profits and assets. Another source of funds is debt. Corporations raise funds by issuing *bonds*, which are basically IOUs. People who buy bonds are loaning the company money. They expect the principal to be paid back at a specified date in the future and to earn annual interest payments. The third method of acquiring funds for investment is to take part of the firm's profits and reinvest them in the firm rather than return them to the stockholders as dividend payments.

People are less likely to buy shares of stock if they cannot get rid of them later if they decide to do so. *Security exchanges* are places where stocks and/or bonds can be bought and sold. Sales of stock on stock exchanges involve stocks already held by the public rather than new issues of stock; a security exchange is like a market for used shares of stocks and bonds. There is a link between stocks sold on exchanges and new issues of stocks or bonds, however. The price of a share of stock on an exchange depends on the profitability of the company. If a firm does poorly in the market, its stock price usually falls. If such a company wants to issue new stock, it will get a relatively low price for each share and have a more difficult time raising funds. On the other hand, a profitable firm is able to acquire funds more easily and get a better price on its new issue of shares or a lower interest rate on its new issue of bonds. So even though they do not deal in new issues, security exchanges affect the prices a firm can get on its newly issued stocks and bonds.

Question to Think About: Are the time and expenditures involved in obtaining a college education investment or saving?

IV. LAGNIAPPE

Additional Thoughts on Time

A little reflection can demonstrate the importance of time in investment and production decisions. The acquisition of human capital takes time—including the time you are spending in college. I am writing this in October, but the book will not be in print until next spring. Salespeople on commission often have lags of several months from the time of the sale until they receive their commission check, especially if the firm has to bill the client first. Magazine editors make plans for the Christmas issue in April. People who build their own homes have to either obtain short-term financing or sell their current house and rent while the new home is being built. Finally, farmers are entrepreneurs who know about the importance of time.

Question to Think About: Is saving necessary for all the examples above?

Investment and Saving

There are many television shows about the stock markets. They generally refer to the buying and selling of stocks and bonds as investing. Actually, the buying of stocks and bonds is saving, not investing. Savings occurs when someone does not consume their entire disposable income. Investing occurs when firms buy new capital goods that increase their ability to produce in the future.

Question to Think About: Are the time and expenditures involved in obtaining a college education investment or saving?

V.   KEY TERMS

Positive rate of time preference
Interest rate
Marginal rate of return on investment
Loanable funds market
Supply of loanable funds
Demand for loanable funds
Term structure of interest rates
Present Value
Discounting

Discount rate
Annuity
Initial Public Offering (IPO)
Stock
Dividends
Retained Earnings
Bond
Entrepreneur

VII. QUESTIONS

A.   *Completion*

1.   Production cannot occur without _____.

2.   _____ production involves the production of capital goods.

3.   Interest rates are positive because consumers have a _____.

4.   _____ is the reward to forgo present consumption.

5.   The _____ equals the market interest rate when the firm is investing optimally.

6.   _____ is the current value of a payment to be received in the future.

7.   The _____ refers to the relationship between the interest rate and the duration of the loan.

8.   The interest rate used for _____, or expressing the value of future dollars in terms of current dollars, is called the _____.

9.   A(n) _____ is a sum of money received each year for a given number of years.

10. The owners of _____ are liable for debts of the firm only to the extent of their investment in the firm.

11. Reinvested profits are called _____.

12. A _____ is a debt security, a firm's promise to pay the holder a fixed sum of money on a designated _____ date.

13. The initial sale of stock to the public is known as an _____.

14. By providing a secondary market for securities, exchange enhances the _____ of the securities.

B. True/False

_____ 1. Roundabout production is an important source of the greater labor productivity in industrialized nations.

_____ 2. The greater the current level of investment in an economy, the less current consumption there is.

_____ 3. Present consumption is valued more than future consumption.

_____ 4. The greater the interest rate, the greater the opportunity cost of future consumption in terms of present consumption.

_____ 5. The marginal revenue product curve for capital falls because of the law of diminishing marginal returns.

_____ 6. Because capital differs from other inputs, the rules for the optimal use of capital differ from those for other inputs.

_____ 7. In the simple model in the textbook, the greater the marginal resource cost of capital, the greater the marginal rate of return on investment.

_____ 8. An increase in the demand for loans will increase the interest rate.

_____ 9. Since human capital involves people, the tools used to analyze investment decisions cannot be used to analyze human capital decisions.

_____ 10. Human capital investments tend to be risky, but physical capital investments are not.

_____ 11. Other things equal, larger loans have greater interest rates.

_____ 12. Interest rates tend to increase as the duration of the loan increases.

_____ 13. The greater the interest rate, the greater the present value of a dollar in the future.

_____ 14. The present value of a perpetuity of $100 a year is greater than the present value of a twenty-year annuity of $100 a year.

_____ 15. If a corporation purchases new equipment with retained earnings, other things constant, stockholder dividends will be less.

_____ 16. Investors consider bonds to be less risky than stocks.

_____ 17. Capital markets allocate funds to more successful firms more readily than to firms in financial difficulty.

_____ 18. When a person buys 100 shares of IBM on the New York Stock Exchange, IBM receives the proceeds less a commission.

_____ 19. When a firm issues an IPO, the firm receives the proceeds of the sale.

_____ 20. Institutional investors account for one half the trading volume of the major exchanges.

C. Multiple Choice

1. Roundabout production requires
    a. savings.
    b. time.
    c. capital equipment.
    d. all of the above.
    e. a and b only.

2. Which of the following does not indicate that consumers value current consumption more than future consumption?
    a. The interest rate is greater than zero.
    b. Hardback books cost more than paperback books.
    c. Overnight film developing costs more than two-day developing.
    d. College graduates earn more than high school graduates.
    e. A family stores cash in a cookie jar for emergencies.

3. If an individual is willing to give up $50 today for $53.50 a year from now, the interest rate is
    a. 3.5 percent.
    b. 5.0 percent.
    c. 107 percent.
    d. 7 percent.
    e. none of the above.

4. Direct production requires
    a. time.
    b. savings.
    c. capital equipment.
    d. all of the above.
    e. a and b.

5. Roundabout production
    a. is generally more efficient than producing goods directly.
    b. is less efficient than producing goods directly because it takes longer.
    c. increases productivity on farms but not in factories.
    d. requires less saving than producing goods directly.
    e. b and c

6. In a modern economy, a producer does not have to save in order to produce because
   a. the capital goods are already produced.
   b. time is not as important in manufacturing as it is in farming.
   c. a producer can use his or her own money to finance production.
   d. money is not a factor of production.
   e. producers can borrow money in the market for loanable funds.

7. When buying capital, a producer should purchase additional capital until
   a. total product is at a maximum.
   b. the marginal revenue product equals the marginal resource cost.
   c. the average revenue product equals the average resource cost.
   d. the marginal rate of return on investment equals the market rate of interest.
   e. the marginal revenue product equals the market rate of interest.

8. Which of the following would cause the marginal rate of return on investment to increase?
   a. The price of capital increases.
   b. The marginal product of capital increases.
   c. The price of the good produced increases.
   d. The price of capital decreases.
   e. b, c, and d

9. Which of the following could cause the demand for loanable funds to increase?
   a. The marginal product of capital increases.
   b. The interest rate falls.
   c. The rate of savings increases.
   d. The marginal rate of return on investment decreases.
   e. all of the above

10. An increase in the interest rate can be caused by
    a. a decrease in the demand for loanable funds.
    b. an increase in the demand for loanable funds.
    c. a decrease in the supply of loanable funds.
    d. an increase in the supply of loanable funds.
    e. both b and c.

11. Interest rates are higher
    a. the longer the duration of a loan.
    b. the greater the reliability of the borrower.
    c. the larger the size of the loan.
    d. the lower the expected rate of inflation.
    e. none of the above

12. The present value of $100 to be received in the future is greater
    a. the shorter the time before the $100 is received.
    b. the longer the time before the $100 is received.
    c. the lower the interest rate.
    d. b and c
    e. a and c

13. The present value of a $1,000 perpetuity at a 5 percent interest rate is
    a. infinite.
    b. $10,000.
    c. $5,000.
    d. $20,000.
    e. $50,000.

14. The present value of a given payment in the future will
    a. get smaller the further in the future the payment is to be received.
    b. get smaller the greater the interest rate.
    c. get larger the greater the interest rate.
    d. get larger if the expected inflation rate increases over time.
    e. a and b only

15. A corporation may do all of the following except
    a. vote.
    b. own property.
    c. sue someone.
    d. incur debt.
    e. none of the above.

16. Corporations acquire funds by
    a. issuing stock.
    b. selling bonds.
    c. retaining part of their profit.
    d. receiving dividends.
    e. a, b, and c only.

17. The existence of securities markets makes the allocation of capital more efficient by
    a. providing a market for corporations to sell new stock issues.
    b. enhancing the liquidity of the securities once they are issued and sold.
    c. providing information about the value of the corporation.
    d. regulating the investments of the managers of the corporation.
    e. b and c.

18. Which of the following activities are investment activities?
    a. Buying 100 shares of General Electric stock
    b. Buying a $1000 bond of GE
    c. Receiving dividends
    d. All of the above.
    e. None of the above.

19. Which of the following reduce the likelihood that managers will behave in ways detrimental to stockholders?
    a. stock options for executives
    b. the rigors of competition
    c. stockholder voting
    d. the threat of a takeover
    e. all of the above

20. The market for corporate control will work well when
    a. the incumbent managers fight takeover vigorously.
    b. the value of the assets of a firm is easily determined by outsiders.
    c. the government prohibits takeovers.
    d. all of the above
    e. none of the above

D. Discussion Questions

1. "Time is important in roundabout production but not in direct production." Is this statement true or false? Explain.

2. Explain why producers must rely on their own or another's savings to produce.

   Use Exhibit 1 to answer questions 3 and 4.

Exhibit 1

Units of Capital	Total Product	Marginal Product	Total Resource Cost	Marginal Resource Cost	Marginal Revenue Product	Marginal Rate of Return on Investment
0	0	___	$0	___	___	___
1	500	___	___	___	___	___
2	950	___	___	___	___	___
3	1,350	___	___	___	___	___
4	1,700	___	___	___	___	___
5	2,000	___	___	___	___	___
6	2,250	___	___	___	___	___
7	2,450	___	___	___	___	___
8	2,600	___	___	___	___	___

3. a. A unit of capital costs $15,000, the interest rate is 10 percent, and the price of output is $5.00. Assume that the capital is expected to last indefinitely and operating costs are negligible. Fill in the blanks in Exhibit 1.
   b. How many units of capital will the producer buy? How do you know?
   c. If the interest rate increased to 15 percent, how many units would the producer buy?

Exhibit 2

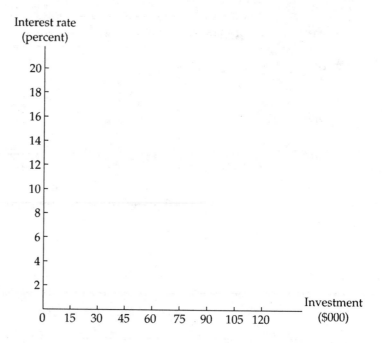

4. In Exhibit 2, draw the marginal rate of return on investment curve. Indicate the optimal amount of investment if the market rate of interest is 10 percent.
5. Explain why the demand curve for loanable funds slope down.

6. Explain why the supply curve for loanable funds slopes upward.

7. Many private schools in the country cost three to four times more than many state universities. Why would a rational student choose to go to an expensive school?

8. Suppose college graduates earn $20,000 a year more than high school graduates.
   a. Describe how you would estimate the present value of the college degree relative to a high school degree. (For this question, ignore the costs of college.)
   b. To make an estimate, use an 8 percent interest rate and use the formula for a perpetuity.
   c. Is the estimate in b larger or smaller than the true value, assuming and 8% interest rate?
   d. What is the present value of the college education if the interest rate is 5%?

9. Explain why there is more than one interest rate in a market economy.

Exhibit 3

Number of Years from Today	Project A		Project B	
	Payments	*Receipts*	*Payments*	*Receipts*
0	$10,000	$0	$6,000	$0
1	10,000	2,000	0	0
2	0	5,000	0	0
3	0	5,000	0	4,000
4	0	10,000	0	4,000
5	0	10,000	0	4,000
6	0	5,000	0	4,000
7	0	0	0	1,000

10. Exhibit 3 shows the income and payment schedules of two research projects. If the interest rate is 10 percent, what is the present value of each?

11. Suppose a third project will cost $20,000 today and yield a return of $2,500 a year indefinitely. What is the present value of the project? What is the present value if the interest rate increases to 20 percent?

12. Suppose an entrepreneur starts and runs a new firm. The firm generates $50,000 in revenues in excess of payments to other resource owners. The entrepreneur supplies $50,000 worth of capital that could be leased for $5,000 a year and manages the firm instead of hiring a manager for $25,000 a year. What is the economic profit? How much is the reward to the entrepreneur for supplying entrepreneurial ability?

13. Suppose the firm in question 10 is expected to perform at that level forever. If the interest rate is 10 percent, how much could the entrepreneur sell the firm for?

14. Explain how security exchanges affect the allocation of investment funds even though only secondhand securities are sold on the exchanges.

15. The textbook said the market value of General Electric in July 2001 was about $470 billion. What would happen to that value if something happened that made people think the future was riskier than it was before?

16. How is the model of corporate finance developed in the second part of the chapter related to the model developed in the first part of the chapter concerning roundabout production and the market for loanable funds?

VII. ANSWERS

A. Completion

1. savings
2. Roundabout
3. positive rate of time preference
4. Interest
5. marginal rate of return on investment
6. Present value
7. term structure of interest rates
8. discounting; discount rate
9. annuity
10. corporations
11. retained earnings
12. bond; maturity
13. initial public offering
14. liquidity

B. True/False

1. True
2. True
3. True
4. False. The greater the interest rate, the greater the opportunity cost of *present consumption.*
5. True
6. False
7. False
8. True
9. False
10. False
11. False
12. True
13. False
14. True
15. True
16. True
17. True
18. False
19. True
20. True

C. Multiple Choice

1. d
2. e
3. d
4. e
5. a
6. e
7. d
8. e
9. a. Answers b and c are not correct because they cause an increase in the quantity demanded. The demand curve does not shift.
10. e
11. a
12. e
13. d
14. e
15. a
16. e
17. e
18. e

Discussion Questions

1. False. Time is also important in direct production. All production involves time, not just roundabout production. A seed planted by hand takes as much time to grow as a seed planted with capital equipment like tractors and tillers.

2. Production takes time, so producers must have access to savings in order to produce. The producer must be able to compensate owners of resources used in production before the goods are sold. Further, capital equipment reduces current consumption, so savings must exist before capital goods can be produced.

3. a.

Units of Capital	Total Product	Marginal Product	Total Resource Cost	Marginal Resource Cost	Marginal Revenue Product	Marginal Rate of Return on Investment
0	0	---	$ 0	---	---	---
1	500	500	15,000	15,000	$2,500	16.67%
2	950	450	30,000	15,000	2,250	15
3	1,350	400	45,000	15,000	2,000	13.33
4	1,700	350	60,000	15,000	1,750	11.67
5	2,000	300	75,000	15,000	1,500	10
6	2,250	250	90,000	15,000	1,250	8.33
7	2,450	200	105,000	15,000	1,000	6.67
8	2,600	150	120,000	15,000	750	5

b. 5 units of capital, because at that point the marginal rate of return on investment equals the market rate of interest

c. 2 units

4.

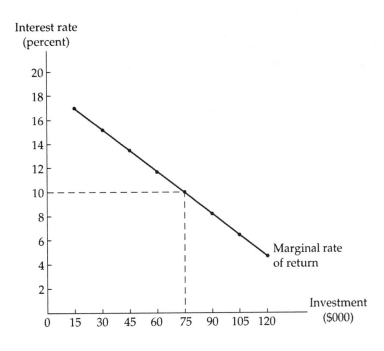

5. There are two types of borrowed funds—business and households. The demand curve for loanable funds for producers slopes down because the marginal rate of return for investment declines. The demand curve for loanable funds for households slopes down because households value present consumption more than future consumption.

6. The supply curve for loanable funds slopes upward because present consumption is valued more than future consumption. Consequently, people must be compensated to save, and the interest rate determines their compensation. The greater the interest rate, the greater one's claim on future resources, the greater the opportunity cost of present consumption, and therefore, the greater the savings.

7. The extra cost of the private schools can be thought of as a higher marginal resource cost. If everyone faces the same interest rate, then all will invest in school until the marginal rate of return on investment equals the interest rate. The marginal rate of return on investment equals the marginal revenue product divided by the marginal resource cost. If the marginal revenue product of the private schools is at least three to four times greater than the marginal revenue product of the state universities, then it is rational to attend the more expensive schools.

8. a. The present value of the college education is:

$$\frac{\$20,000}{1.08} + \frac{\$20,000}{1.08^2} +...+ \frac{\$20,000}{1.08^t}$$

The value of t is needed and depends on the average retirement age.

b. $PV = \frac{\$20,000}{0.08} = \$400,000$; A + 12%: $\frac{\$20,000}{0.12} = \$166,667$.

c. Larger. People retire and don't work forever. Since the present value of $1 to be received 50 years or more is very low, the size of the overestimate is not great.

d. At 5%: $\frac{\$20,000}{0.08} - \$400,000$; at 12%: $\frac{\$20,000}{0.12} = \$166,667$.

9. The main reason there is more than one interest rate is that loans differ in riskiness. Less reliable borrowers are riskier to lend to, so lenders require a higher interest rate. The longer the duration of the loan the greater the risk of higher-than-expected inflation, so the higher the interest rate. The dollar cost of processing a loan tends to be the same regardless of the size of the loan, so small loans have a higher relative cost and require higher interest rates. Finally, lenders are interested in their after-tax rate of return, so loans made to organizations that are not taxable will carry lower interest rates.

10. Present value of Project A

$$= -\$10,000 - \frac{8,000}{(1.1)^1} + \frac{5,000}{(1.1)^2} + \frac{5,000}{(1.1)^3} + \frac{10,000}{(1.1)^4} + \frac{10,000}{(1.1)^5} + \frac{5,000}{(1.1)^6}$$

$$= -\$10,000 - 7,272.73 + 4,132.23 + 3,756.57 + 6,830.13 + 6,209.21 + 2,822.37$$

$$= \$6,477.78$$

Present value of Project B

$$= -\$6,000 + \frac{4,000}{(1.1)^3} + \frac{4,000}{(1.1)^4} + \frac{4,000}{(1.1)^5} + \frac{4,000}{(1.1)^6} + \frac{1,000}{(1.1)^7}$$

$$= -\$6,000 + 3,005.26 + 2,732.05 + 2,483.69 + 2,257.90 + 513.16$$

$$= \$4,992.06$$

11. At an interest rate of 10 percent, the present value of the third project =

$$\frac{\$2,500}{0.10} - 20,000 = \$25,000 - 20,000 = \$5,000$$

If the interest rate rises to 20 percent, the project's present value =

$$\frac{\$2,500}{0.20} - \$20,000 = 12,500 - 20,000 = -\$7,500$$

12. $5,000 should be counted as the return to those supplying capital and $25,000 as the return to the entrepreneur for managing the firm. Economic profit is then $50,000 − $5,000 − $25,000 = $20,000. The return to the entrepreneur for supplying entrepreneurial ability is also $20,000, the economic profit.

13. $$\frac{\$20,000}{0.10} = \$200,000$$

14. The prices of securities on the exchanges reflect the profitability of the firms. The price of the stock of a company whose performance declines will fall. The lower price makes it more difficult for the firm to raise new financial capital because it will have to sell more shares of stock to receive a certain level of funds. Successful firms will receive a higher price for their new issues and will find it easier to raise the investment funds they want. Thus, the information provided by the security exchanges affects the allocation of capital.

15. The $470 billion is the present value of the expected future earnings of General Electric. If people had a change in belief and thought the future was riskier then the present value calculation should use a higher interest rate. The market value of GE would be lower.

16. Corporations raise funds for investing by selling stock, selling bonds, or investing retained earnings. The determination of whether profitable investment opportunities exist will utilize the ideas developed in the first part of the chapter—calculating the marginal rate of return on the projects and comparing that with the interest rate. Once the investment projects are identified, the firm has to finance them. It can either use retained earnings to do so or enter the capital markets, what was called earlier in the chapter the *market for loanable funds*. It can borrow (sell bonds) or it can raise equity capital (sell shares of stock). If the firm does not have enough investment projects that it expects to be profitable, it could also lend some of its retained earnings in the market for loanable funds.

CHAPTER 14

Transaction Costs, Imperfect Information, and Market Behavior

I. INTRODUCTION

In this chapter, we examine more closely the effects of imperfect information on the behavior of firms and consumers. We will investigate why firms exist and discuss the factors that affect the internal structure of firms. Since consumers do not know all information needed to make the best decisions, we will examine how imperfect information affects their decisions. Finally, the chapter briefly discusses some market responses to the problems of imperfect information.

II. OUTLINE

1. Rationale for the Firm and the Scope of Its Operation. The model of perfect competition assumes that all participants in the market possess all the information they need about prices, technology, inputs, and the like. If perfect information, frictionless exchange, and perfect competition actually existed, entrepreneurs would not be needed, and production would not be performed by firms.

   1.1 Firms Reduce Transaction Costs
       a. In the 1930s, Ronald Coase recognized that the firm may often be more efficient than market exchange because production requires the coordination of many resource owners.
       b. The costs of organizing production through market transactions often exceed the costs of undertaking production within the firm.
       c. There are costs involved in using markets to make transactions.
          (1) Costs of determining what resources are needed
          (2) Costs of negotiating separate contracts with each resource owner
       d. When the transaction costs of using the market are relatively high, households buy from a firm rather than directly hire the inputs.
       e. The more complicated the task, the greater the ability to economize on transaction costs through specialization.

   1.2 The Bounds of the Firm
       a. Firms are a way to minimize the sum of the transaction costs and the production costs of economic activity.
       b. Vertical integration is expansion of a firm into earlier or later stages of production. Other things equal, firms should buy an input in the market when the cost of doing so is lower than it would be if the input were produced internally.
       c. Internal production and markets are alternative ways of organizing transactions.
       d. Firms use specific criteria to determine whether to purchase a particular component or to produce it.

(1) Bounded Rationality of managers: a manager can understand only a limited amount of information.

(2) Minimum efficient scale: the larger the minimum efficient scale of producing a component, the more likely a firm is to buy it from another firm that specializes in producing the component.

(3) Easily observable quality: when an inpit is well defined and quality is easily determined, the firm is more likely to purchase the input.

(4) Number of suppliers: the more suppliers there are, the more likely the firm is to purchase an input.

1.3 *CASE STUDY:* The Trend Toward Outsourcing

1.4 Economies of Scope
a. If it is cheaper to produce two or more product lines at the same time than to produce them separately, the firm is more likely to do so.
b. Per-unit production costs fall as the firm produces additional types of products when there are economies of scope.

2. Market Behavior with Imperfect Information

2.1 Optimal Search with Imperfect Information
a. People often obtain information about a product before they purchase it.
b. The primary cost of gathering information is the opportunity cost of a consumer's time.
c. The marginal cost of search increases as the search for information widens.
d. The marginal benefit from obtaining additional information decreases as the search for information widens.
e. Optimal search occurs when the marginal benefit of searching for additional information exactly equals the marginal cost of search for additional information.
f. Search costs generate price dispersion and quality differences across sellers.

2.2 The Winner's Curse
a. The "winner's curse" refers to a situation in which the winner in a bidding contest for an asset loses money by winning the bid.
b. The winner's curse can occur when the true value of the asset is unknown and the most optimistic bidder wins. Sometimes the winner was too optimistic.

3. Asymmetric Information in Product Markets
a. There is *asymmetric information* in a situation when one participant in a transaction has more reliable information than the other participant.
b. Characteristics of a product may be hidden from one of the participants, or actions taken by one party may be hidden from the other.

3.1 Hidden Characteristics: Adverse Selection
a. The seller of a product often knows more about the characteristics of the product than the potential buyer.
b. When buyers know that the quality of a product varies across units and are unable to judge the quality before buying the good, the maximum price they will pay is below what the price sellers of the higher quality units must receive to induce them to sell.
c. Owners of higher quality units will pull their units off the market, so the only units still for sale in the market are the lowest quality units.
d. The end result can be that only the "lemons" end up for sale in the market.

  e. *Adverse selection* occurs when those on the informed side of the market can self-select in a way harmful to those on the uninformed side of the market.

 3.2 Hidden Actions: Principal-Agent Problem
  a. A *principal-agent* contractual relationship exists when one person (the *agent*) acts on behalf of another person (the *principal*).
  b. If the agent's goals are incompatible with the principal's goals, the agent can pursue hidden actions that are costly to the principal.

 3.3 Asymmetric Information in Insurance Markets
  a. Adverse selection creates problems in insurance markets because those who are more likely to use the insurance benefits are more likely to purchase insurance; this causes insurance rates to increase and drive out those who are less likely to use the insurance benefits.
  b. In insurance markets, people with insurance coverage may alter their behavior in ways that make it more likely the event insured against will occur. This is the *moral hazard* problem.
  c. Moral hazard arises on the part of the person who can engage in hidden actions.

 3.4 Coping with Asymmetric Information. Ways of reducing the costs of asymmetric information have been found in many markets.

4. Asymmetric Information in Labor Markets. It is more difficult to relate compensation to the marginal productivity of workers when labor is heterogeneous and production requires the coordinated efforts of several workers.

 4.1 Adverse Selection Problems in Labor Markets
  a. Before a worker is hired, the worker's true abilities are hidden from the employer.
  b. A given advertised wage tends to reflect the average marginal revenue product of all workers in the market and thus to attract the least productive workers in the pool.
  c. Employers must often rely on proxy information, such as education, to determine the most qualified applicant.
  d. Sometimes employers pay a higher wage, called *efficiency wages*, to attract higher quality workers into the labor pool.

 4.2 Signaling and Screening
  a. A *signal* is a proxy measure of the unobservable characteristics of a potential employee.
  b. Education is often used as a signal.
  c. Employers often use a screening device to determine who is more likely to be a productive worker.

 4.3 *CASE STUDY:* The Reputation of a Big Mac

III. DISCUSSION

Rationale for the Firm and the Scope of Its Operation

Previous chapters assumed that the firm exists in order to transform inputs into outputs. In a world of perfect competition and frictionless exchange, there would be no reason for firms to exist, however. Ronald Coase argued that firms exist because market transactions are costly. Economic activity can be carried on by firms or by markets. When the marginal cost of a transaction using direct managerial controls in a firm is less than the marginal cost of using the price system to allocate resources, then a firm will carry out the transaction. As the cost of using firms to organize economic activities falls, firms get larger.

The extent of the firm's activities will be determined by comparing the costs of using markets with the costs of internal production and coordination. The scope of the firm is determined by considering factors such as the point where the *bounded rationality* of managers creates diseconomies, the minimum efficient scale for producing inputs, how easily the quality of inputs can be determined, and the number of suppliers of inputs there are. Some firms realize *economies of scope*, which make it cheaper to combine two or more product lines in one firm than to produce them separately.

Market Behavior with Imperfect Information

Information is a scarce good that is costly to acquire. This is true for both consumers and producers. A consumer will collect information about a product before making the purchase. This information may include data about the characteristics of various brands and makes, the prices at different stores, warranty information, reliability, and so on. The more extensive the search for information, the greater the costs of the search. The costs include explicit costs such as purchase of magazines that provide information and gasoline used to drive to several stores. The major cost usually is the opportunity cost of the consumer's time spent in search activity. The marginal cost of search for additional information increases as the search process continues. The marginal benefits from acquiring additional information include the lower prices discovered during the search process and the higher quality obtained by the additional search. The marginal benefit will eventually decline as the search process continues. The optimal search occurs where the marginal costs of additional search for information exactly equal the marginal benefits from additional search for information. Search costs generate price dispersion and quality differences for the same product.

Imperfect information can cause another problem in the case of bidding on assets when the true value of the asset is unknown. Examples of such assets would include off-shore oil leases, movie rights to a book, and broadcast rights to sporting events. Since the true value of the asset is unknown, people have to estimate the value and base their bids on their estimates. The highest bid obtains the asset. It is possible that the highest bidder will have overestimated the true value of the asset, in which case the winner will actually suffer losses on the asset. This phenomenon is referred to as the *winner's curse*.

Asymmetric Information in Product Markets

Another problem that can develop in some markets is the problem of asymmetric information— the situation when one side of a transaction has better information than the other side. There are two types of information that a market participant may lack: information about the characteristics of the product and information about the actions of the other participant in the market activity.

The problem of the hidden characteristics of a product is sometimes referred to as the "lemon" problem. Keep in mind the conditions that are necessary for this to be a problem. The product's quality must vary across units and important characteristics of the product must be hidden from the potential buyer. Potential buyers would then make an estimate of the expected or average quality of the units and would be willing to pay a price no higher than the price of the average quality of the product. But when the owners know the true quality of the units they have, they will not offer for sale their higher quality units because what the price buyers will pay is too low. Hence, only lower quality units, or "lemons," appear on the market. As buyers realize this, they lower their offer prices accordingly until the lemons have driven all the higher quality units out of the market.

The problem of the lemon can show up in many different market contexts. In insurance markets, the buyer often has better information about the likelihood of actually using the insurance benefits than the insurance company. Suppose the insurance company sets rates based on the average medical expenses of families in the country. Those families that expected to generate medical costs equal to or greater than this average would definitely buy the insurance, whereas those that knew they would generate medical costs below this would not. That is, the people self-select on the basis of their better information. If this occurs, the actual premiums received by the insurance company will not cover the medical costs generated by policyholders. If the insurance company increases rates, more people leave the system. In insurance markets, this behavior is referred to as *adverse selection*. It is easy to see that adverse selection is another form of the lemon problem.

Market participants have developed some methods of reducing the costs associated with asymmetric information. Warranties and guarantees are used to alleviate the hidden characteristics problem in many product markets; the development of a reputation for quality has been used in other markets. Insurance companies try to obtain health histories of people in order to assess the riskiness of individuals and families and set a range of prices that depend on these estimates of risk. These practices do not eliminate the costs associated with adverse selection and lemons, but they do reduce these costs.

The second type of asymmetric information problem is due to hidden actions, or the *principal-agent problem*. Again, this problem occurs in many market settings. A *principal* is one party in a contractual relationship who obtains the services of another party, known as the *agent*. The agent is to act on the behalf of the principal and has some discretion in doing so. For example, business managers represent athletes or entertainers; the managers of a firm (agents) act on behalf of the owners of the corporation (principals); employees carry out the wishes of employers; auto mechanics act in a sense as agents for the car owners; and doctors act on behalf of patients. The problem develops when the interests of the agent are not the same as the interests of the principal. An extreme case would be a business manager who embezzled funds from his or her principal. A more benign case occurs when a worker takes a longer coffee break than company rules allow.

There is a similar phenomenon, known as *moral hazard*, in insurance markets. Suppose a family purchases fire insurance for their home that will compensate them fully for a fire (including all "psychic" costs). The likelihood of a fire is dependent, at least to some degree, on the behavior of the members of the family. With the insurance, they may not be as cautious as they would otherwise, which increases the probability of a fire. Insurance companies respond to this possibility by refusing to insure many activities fully. Instead, they have deductibles so the insured bear a part of the cost of a loss. In this way, the insured have an incentive to behave in a way that minimizes the likelihood that the event insured against will occur.

Asymmetric Information in Labor Markets

Adverse selection can occur in labor markets too. A firm advertises for workers at a certain wage. Workers who know that the value of their marginal product exceeds the wage will not apply for the job. The people who apply are those whose value of marginal product is less than or equal to the announced wage. Firms sometimes offer higher wages than necessary in order to attract higher quality workers. Further, potential employers screen applicants, and workers may offer signals, such as education, to provide evidence of their productivity.

Other solutions to asymmetric information problems is signaling and screening. Signaling is an attempt by the informed side of the market to communicate information to the other side. Education is an example. Screening is an attempt by the uninformed side to obtain better information.

IV. LAGNIAPPE

Size of Firms

Corporations became important phenomena in the late nineteenth century. As firms grew larger, their capital requirements became so large that a few individuals could no longer provide all of the necessary capital. Firms also became larger because of changes in the fields of communication and transportation. Railroads made it possible for goods to be shipped over longer distances, which expanded markets and enabled individual plants to be made larger. Telegraphs and then telephones made it possible for firms to have offices in various parts of the country. Improvements in communication and information also lowered the marginal cost of carrying out an activity within the firm relative to using the marketplace.

Other factors also encouraged the expansion of firms. Inflation raises the cost of using markets by making it more difficult to determine the real price of a good or service. Price controls also raise the cost of using markets, encouraging firms to handle additional activities internally.

Question to Think About: How might tax policy encourage expansion of firms?

Using Up a Reputation

The idea that a reputation for quality can be a "hostage" that ensures quality has become widely used in economics. It is helpful in explaining market behavior concerning franchising, advertising, and finance. However, there is always one problem that must be dealt with: the problem of the final period. Once a reputation for quality has been established, it may be profitable to cheat and produce products or services of lesser quality than you have in the past. The incentive to do so is especially great if you will not be around in the future. That is, if there is a last period to the life of a firm, there is a strong incentive to consume the "reputation capital" in the last period. Given that potential consumers know this, they will not believe that you will produce the higher quality in the last period and will not pay the higher price for higher quality goods in the last period. If this is so, then the next-to-last period becomes just like the last period. The logic of the last-period problem eventually leads to the conclusion that the firm will never provide the higher quality good. What often prevents this type of behavior from actually taking place is that for most business firms, especially corporations, the last period is unknown. Hence, the firms always have a future to be concerned with and thus have an incentive to maintain their reputations.

Question to Think About: Could a similar problem apply to workers as they approach retirement age?

V. KEY TERMS

Vertical integration
Bounded rationality
Economies of scope
Winner's curse
Asymmetric information
Hidden characteristics
Hidden actions
Adverse selection

Principal-agent problem
Principal
Agent
Moral hazard
Efficiency wage theory
Signaling
Screening

VI. QUESTIONS

A. Completion

1. Ronald Coase argues that economic activity is best understood in terms of the _____ costs involved in exchange.

2. Firms exist because entrepreneurs are trying to reduce _____.

3. The expansion of a firm into earlier or later stages of production is called _____.

4. Internal production and _____ are alternative ways of organizing transactions.

5. Management has _____ because it can comprehend only a limited amount of information.

6. _____ exist when it is cheaper to combine two or more product lines within one firm than it is for separate firms to produce them.

7. In real-world markets, reliable information is _____ for consumers and producers.

8. Price dispersion is the result of _____ costs.

9. The _____ often afflicts those who offer the highest bid on assets of unknown value.

10. When one side of a transaction has more reliable information than the other, the situation involves _____.

11. In the doctor-patient relationship, the doctor is known as the _____ and the patient is the _____.

12. The problem of hidden characteristics in insurance markets generates the problem of _____.

13. _____ occurs when the behavior of one party to a transaction affects the likelihood of an unfavorable outcome.

14. A proxy measure, which is an observable indicator of a hidden characteristic, is called a(n) _____.

15. An attempt by an employer to obtain information about the hidden characteristics of a potential employee is called _____.

B. True/False

_____ 1. Firms would not exist in a world of perfect competition, perfect information, and frictionless exchange.

_____ 2. According to Coase, firms exist to economize on transaction costs.

_____ 3. The exchange relationship between individuals using markets is contractual in nature, but relationships within a firm are not contractual.

_____ 4. Resources are allocated by prices within a firm.

_____ 5. Firms minimize the sum of production and transaction costs.

_____ 6. When exchange is characterized by incomplete contracts, firms often produce a good directly rather than buy it from another firm.

_____ 7. The easier it is to determine the quality of an input, the more likely the firm that uses the input is to produce the input itself.

_____ 8. Economies of scope are another name for economies of scale.

_____ 9. In market activities, reliable information is more costly for consumers than for producers.

_____ 10. The primary cost of search for information is the opportunity cost of the person's time.

_____ 11. A rational person will search more when buying a car than when buying tires.

_____ 12. Optimal search occurs when the difference between the marginal benefit of additional search and the marginal cost of additional search is at a maximum.

_____ 13. Search costs associated with buying a product will be greater for a couple when both spouses work outside the home than when only one of the spouses works outside the home.

_____ 14. The winner's curse applies to all cases of bidding.

_____ 15. In a market characterized by asymmetric information about the characteristics of a good, buyers usually pay more for lower quality goods than the goods are worth.

_____ 16. The principal-agent problem is an example of adverse selection.

_____ 17. Health insurance is affected more by adverse selection problems than moral hazard problems.

_____ 18. Moral hazard arises on the part of the agent.

_____ 19. Firms sometimes pay higher wages to improve the productivity of their work force.

_____ 20. A signal that can be acquired easily by all workers does not make a good signaling device.

C. Multiple Choice

1. Firms exist because of
    a. greed.
    b. transaction costs.
    c. perfect information.
    d. diminishing marginal returns.
    e. all of the above.

2. Transactions that are carried on within the hierarchy of the firm are often more efficient than transactions carried out through markets because
    a. production is costly.
    b. production often requires the coordination of many transactions among many resource owners.
    c. markets generally allocate resources inefficiently.
    d. production involves many stages, and it is always better to perform all stages at one location.
    e. b, c, and d

3. Which of the following statements is correct?
    a. Firms arise because transaction costs are greater than production costs.
    b. The choice between using internal production and using markets is determined by government regulation.
    c. Incomplete contracts are problems for firms so markets generally are used in such cases.
    d. Where inputs are easily measured, priced, and hired, production tends to be carried out by firms.
    e. One advantage of market transactions is that they do not require as much conscious effort as direct controls in a firm.

4. Which of the following would be an example of vertical integration?
    a. A steel company buys interest in a coal company.
    b. A steel company buys interest in an automobile manufacturer.
    c. Two competing steel companies merge.
    d. all of the above
    e. a and b only

5. The costs of organizing an additional transaction within the firm increase as the size of the firm increases because
    a. it gets more difficult to determine the quality of inputs.
    b. communication within the firm gets more difficult.
    c. the transactions get more complex.
    d. all of the above
    e. none of the above. The costs do not increase as the firm gets larger.

6. Suppose that research done by an R&D lab can improve two different products. This would be an example of
   a. economies of scope.
   b. vertical integration.
   c. economies of scale.
   d. increasing returns to scale.
   e. a and b only.

7. Based on the information in question 6, can we conclude that the firm will produce both product lines?
   a. No, because the economies of scope could be small relative to other production or transaction costs that would make it more costly to produce both products in one firm.
   b. No, because it will be cheaper for the R&D lab to be separate from the firm that produces the product lines.
   c. Yes, because the economies of scope will lower the costs of producing the two product lines when they are produced within the same firm.
   d. Yes, because vertical integration between the firm producing the goods and the R&D lab will generate lower costs of production.
   e. Yes, but we cannot tell without more information whether c or d provides the best reason.

8. The primary cost of searching for information on a product is
   a. the cost of advertising the product.
   b. the opportunity cost of the consumer's time.
   c. the wear and tear on the consumer's automobile.
   d. the price of magazines and reports that provide information about the product.
   e. the psychic costs associated with making the wrong decision.

9. Optimal search for information occurs when
   a. the consumer has the same amount of information as there would be if information were perfect.
   b. the marginal benefit from additional search equals zero.
   c. the costs of search are minimized.
   d. the marginal benefit of additional search equals the marginal cost of additional search.
   e. the total benefits of additional search equal the total costs of additional search.

10. An implication of Stigler's search model is that
    a. more information will be gathered by consumers on homogeneous products than on heterogeneous products.
    b. consumers' search for information will be more extensive as levels of education increase.
    c. the price dispersion of high-priced items will be less than the price dispersion of low-priced goods.
    d. the price dispersion of a good will be less, the less time people spend searching for information about the good.
    e. the marginal cost of additional search is less for lower priced goods than for higher priced goods.

11. Which of the following would be an example of the winner's curse?
    a. CBS wins the rights to the World Series and the teams end up in St. Louis and Kansas City.
    b. A publishing company outbids other companies to publish a new textbook written by a young economist.
    c. A Japanese business person outbids all others for a Van Gogh sold by a Dutch museum.
    d. All of the above are possible examples of the winner's curse.
    e. Only a and b are possible examples of the winner's curse.

12. Asymmetric information is associated with
    a. any product for which certain characteristics are hidden.
    b. products for which some characteristics are hidden from the buyer but known by the seller.
    c. products of variable quality.
    d. all insurance markets.
    e. all of the above.

13. Suppose 20 percent of the cars produced are "lemons." The value of a high-quality car after a year is $10,000, and the value of the lemon after a year is $4,000. The probable price for a year-old used car is
    a. $10,000 for good cars and $4,000 for lemons.
    b. $10,000.
    c. $8,800.
    d. $7,000.
    e. $4,000.

14. The principal-agent problem arises whenever
    a. one person acts on the behalf of another.
    b. the goals of the principal and the agent are incompatible.
    c. the actions of the agent can be hidden from the principal.
    d. all of the above
    e. b and c only

15. Adverse selection will not be a problem in the insurance industry when
    a. the event insured against is equally likely to affect anyone.
    b. the insurance company cannot charge different customers different prices.
    c. the insurance company cannot inquire into the characteristics of the customers.
    d. the insurance pool is small.
    e. none of the above

16. Moral hazard affects all of the following except
    a. fire insurance.
    b. theft insurance.
    c. auto insurance.
    d. flight insurance.
    e. health insurance.

17. Insurance companies require the insured to pay a portion of a loss to reduce the problem of
    a. adverse selection.
    b. moral hazard.
    c. screening.
    d. hidden characteristics.
    e. a, b, and d

18. If a proxy measure is to be a good signal for some hidden characteristic, it must be
    a. valuable in its own right.
    b. easily obtained by the one wanting to give the signal.
    c. difficult to obtain by those not having the hidden characteristics.
    d. perfectly correlated with the hidden characteristic.
    e. all of the above.

19. Adverse selection in labor markets leads to
    a. signaling.
    b. employers screening applicants.
    c. both signaling and screening.
    d. using reputation as a hostage.
    e. moral hazard.

20. Suppose a firm has built up a reputation for high quality and then reduces quality to increase profits. The cost to the firm of doing this is
    a. lost profits in the future after consumers realize the actual quality level.
    b. lower profits right away because people instantaneously realize that the quality is lower.
    c. higher screening costs in the future.
    d. increased moral hazard on the part of consumers.
    e. zero. The firm can always increase quality later and regain its reputation.

D. Discussion Questions

1. Explain why production would not have to be carried out by firms if the marginal product of all inputs could be measured without cost, if prices for all inputs could be identified without cost, and if transactions were without cost.

2. Describe Coase's theory of the firm.

3. What is vertical integration?

4. What determines the extent of vertical integration in a firm?

5. If market transactions are costly, why isn't all production carried on by one giant firm?

6. Firms often produce some of the inputs they use and buy other inputs. What characteristics of the inputs are important in determining whether the firm will make the input itself or purchase it from a supplier?

7. What are economies of scope? How do they differ from economies of scale?

8. Explain why the marginal cost of search for information increases as search activity increases.

9. Apply the model of optimal search to the search for a college to attend. Can the model also be applied to the search for a job?

10. What effect has the computer and the internet had on the cost and benefits of searching for goods? What empirical evidence would support this?

11. In an English auction, the price starts low and people bid the price up until no one is willing to bid higher than the last bid made. In a Dutch auction, the price starts high and comes down until someone says he or she will buy it at that price. Once someone says they will buy it, the auction stops. Suppose there are 10 people bidding on a painting. Each places a different value on the painting, ranging from $10,000 to $25,000, according to the following scale.

Andrew	$10,000
Betty	11,000
Camille	25,000
David	18,000
Edwina	18,850
Frank	16,500
Gwen	18,900
Henry	15,000
Iodine	17,500
Jacqueline	17,900

   a. Who would buy the painting under an English auction?
   b. Who would buy the painting under a Dutch auction?
   c. If you were the seller, which type of auction would likely provide you with the most money? Explain.
   d. Suppose Camille didn't show up for the auction. What would be the likely prices for the English and the Dutch auctions respectively?
   e. The Flower Auction in Amsterdam uses a Dutch auction. Would you expect the results to be very different if an English auction were used?
   f. Under which type of auction is the Winner's Curse more likely?

12. What economic differences are there between the effects of imperfect information and asymmetric information?

13. Explain why the correct answer to multiple choice question 13 is e.

14. How is the lemon problem related to insurance markets? What are some things insurance companies can do to reduce the costs of the problem?

15. The "Lemon Model" refers to used cars. Is there a similar problem for new cars? Why or why not?

16. Owners of firms usually raise some financial capital by borrowing. Lenders generally require the owner to have some of his or her own money in the company to prevent moral hazard. How could moral hazard be a problem if the owner used debt exclusively to finance the company?

17. Is adverse selection likely to be a greater problem when hiring a welder or when hiring a personnel manager? Why?

18. What must be true if signaling is to solve the adverse selection problem?

19. Based on information in this chapter, can you offer an economic justification for trademarks and brand names?

20. Can the problems of imperfect and asymmetric information be used to enrich Coase's theory of the firm? How?

VII. ANSWERS

A. Completion

1. transaction
2. transaction costs
3. vertical integration
4. markets
5. bounded rationality
6. Economies of scope
7. costly
8. search
9. winner's curse
10. asymmetric information
11. agent; principal
12. adverse selection
13. Moral hazard
14. signal
15. screening

B. True/False

1. True
2. True
3. False
4. False
5. True
6. True
7. False
8. False
9. False
10. True
11. True
12. False
13. True
14. False. The winner's curse applies only when the actual value of the asset is unknown.
15. False
16. True
17. False
18. False. It can arise on the part of either the agent or the principal, depending on circumstances.
19. True
20. True

C. Multiple Choice

1. b
2. b
3. e
4. e
5. b
6. a
7. a
8. b
9. d
10. c
11. e
12. b
13. e
14. e
15. a
16. d
17. b
18. c
19. c
20. a

D. Discussion Questions

1. Markets transmit information quickly and efficiently. Firms are used when there are costs to using markets. If there were no costs to using markets, then firms would not be needed. Each input owner would contract directly with anyone who wanted to use the input. If the price of each input were known by all and the marginal product of each input were also known, market transactions would be used to produce all goods.

2. Coase points out that there are costs to using markets. The prices and productivity of all inputs are not known with certainty. When the costs of discovering prices and productivity and contracting with resource owners are high, consumers will purchase from firms rather than contracting with all input owners. Firms will take on activities as long as the additional cost of performing each activity within the firm is less than the cost of using the market.

3. Vertical integration is the expansion of a firm into stages of production earlier or later than those in which the firm has specialized.

4. The firm will expand production into an earlier or later stage of production if its combined costs are less than if it carried on the extra transactions by using markets.

5. There are also costs to carrying on activities within the firm and coordinating transactions by managers. The amount of information managers have is often limited, as are their abilities to assimilate the information, and communication among members of the firm gets more difficult the larger the firm becomes.

6. The easier it is to determine the quality of an input by examining it, the more likely the firm will be to purchase the input from a supplier rather than produce it itself. The more suppliers of the input there are, the more likely the firm will be to purchase the input because the firm can be less concerned with interruptions in delivery of the input.

7. Economies of scope exist when it is cheaper to combine two or more products in the same firm than to produce them in separate firms. Generally, economies of scope rely on the sharing of some activities of the firm such as advertising or research and development. Economies of scale differ in that they are cost savings associated with producing more of one product.

8. As search expands, the consumer travels farther or searches longer for more data. The easiest places to obtain information will be searched first, more difficult places later. The opportunity cost of time can be thought of as constant so the increasing additions of time needed to expand search imply the marginal costs of search increase.

9. The benefits of additional search include the probability of finding a school that matches your interests more closely or finding a school that is cheaper. When searching for a college, you can use guidebooks and high school counselors to obtain a lot of information at a relatively low cost. To get more information about schools requires further effort: trips to the campus; interviews with students, faculty, and alumni; careful examination of the library; and so on. The marginal benefits of additional search soon begin to diminish and the marginal costs increase, so the optimal stopping point is when the marginal cost of additional information equals the marginal benefit.

The model can also be applied to the search for employment, where the benefit of additional search is the possibility of finding a better job. Again, marginal benefits of additional search will diminish and the marginal costs will increase, so an optimal stopping point exists.

10. The Internet has reduced the cost of searching for many products. Empirical evidence that could test this is to see if price dispersion is less today than it was in the past.

11. a. Camille
    b. Camille
    c. Dutch auction. The price received can be higher.
    d. English—between $18,500 and $18,900; Dutch—$18,500
    e. No. The buyers are all known knowledgeable and their estimates of value should be similar.
    f. Dutch auction

12. Imperfect information requires people to search for more information. Asymmetric information adds the possibility of undesirable behavior on the part of other participants in the market. The price of an asset whose value is not known to anyone at the time of the sale will be around the expected value of the asset, whereas the price of an asset when the seller has better information than the buyer will tend to be near the price of the lowest quality units of the good. In insurance markets, a price based on probabilities of an undesirable event occurring will prevail when the event is truly random but will not be an equilibrium price if the actions of those insured can affect the probability of the undesired event happening.

13. $4,000 is the value of the lowest quality cars. Potential buyers know that if they pay more than $4,000 for a used car, the only cars that will be offered for sale are those whose true value is equal to or less than the offered price. Hence, the buyers know that it is likely they will end up paying more than the car is worth. They will not do this, though, so only the lowest-valued cars will end up in the market and people will not pay more than $4,000 for a used car. The lower-quality cars have driven the higher-quality cars out of the market.

14. The lemon problem is called adverse selection in insurance markets. For a given price for insurance coverage, customers will self-select on the basis of their risk characteristics. Customers who are good risks are less likely to buy the insurance. Customers who are poor risks are more likely to buy the insurance. If the less risky customers do not buy, then the price for the insurance will not generate enough revenues to pay the claims of the poorer risks who did buy the insurance. If the company raises premiums, it drives out the better risks that had bought insurance. In the extreme, the company can be left with only high-risk customers. The adverse selection problem is handled by offering different premiums on the basis of the riskiness of the customer. To determine the riskiness, insurance companies have to collect information about the customers that is related the riskiness of the client. People often have to obtain a physical from a physician before obtaining life or medical insurance; similarly, a person's driving record and other characteristics that are statistically related to the likelihood of an accident (age, gender, education) are used to set rates for auto insurance.

15. No. There is no asymmetric information. The new car dealers don't have better information than the buyers as to the performance of specific cars on their lots.

16. The owner of the firm is the residual claimant. If the owner uses debt to finance the entire investment, then the owner has a greater incentive to undertake very risky projects. These projects have a very high return if they succeed, which implies that the owner will receive a very large residual. If the projects fail, the lenders lose and the owner ends up with zero, which is where the owner started. That is, the downside risk is borne by the lenders in this case, but the upside gains are reaped by the owner. Lenders are aware of the moral hazard problem, so they require the owner to have a sizable investment of his or her own in the firm to reduce the incentive to undertake risky projects.

17. Adverse selection would be more of a problem when selecting a personnel manager. It is easier to observe whether an individual has the qualities desired in a welder than it is to see whether the person would be a good personnel manager.

18. It must be more difficult for the less productive group to acquire the signal than for the more productive group to do so.

19. Trademarks and brand names symbolize a firm's reputation for quality, which can be used by customers as a hostage to encourage the firm to maintain its quality standards. For reputation to be effective as an incentive to maintain quality, customers must know what firm is producing the goods they buy so they can reward the high-quality firms with repeat business and punish firms that do not provide the quality they promised by boycotting them in the future.

20. Yes. The material on asymmetric information and principal-agent problems demonstrates the costs of carrying on transactions within the firm. The greater the problems within the firm of either adverse selection or moral hazard, the more likely it is that the transaction will be carried on by means of markets rather than within the firm.

CHAPTER 15

Economic Regulation and Antitrust Activity

I.   INTRODUCTION

In this chapter, we will apply what we have learned about market structure to some real-world phenomena. If firms seek to maximize profits, then they are likely to attempt to collude or use some other method to make monopoly profits. Government policies sometimes aid and sometimes hinder collusive behavior. This chapter examines government regulation and antitrust policies, both of which have changed considerably in recent years.

II.   OUTLINE

1.   Business Behavior and Public Policy. *Market power* is the ability to maintain a price above the competitive level. The exercise of market power causes a misallocation of resources.

   1.1   Government Regulation of Business
      a.   *Social regulation* consists of government controls related to health and safety.
      b.   *Economic regulation* controls price, output, and entry in industries where monopoly is inevitable or desirable.
      c.   *Antitrust activity* includes measures designed to curb monopoly and to promote competition.

2.   Regulating Natural Monopolies

   2.1   Unregulated Profit Maximization
      a.   With a natural monopoly, the lowest average total cost is achieved if one firm serves the entire market.
      b.   Because price exceeds marginal cost, there is an underallocation of resources to production of the good.
      c.   Government has four options for dealing with natural monopoly:
         (1)   Do nothing and let the unregulated price stand.
         (2)   Own and operate the monopoly itself.
         (3)   Regulate the privately owned natural monopoly.
      d.   Regulated natural monopolies are known as *public utilities*.

   2.2   Setting Price Equal to Marginal Cost
      a.   The government sets price equal to marginal cost if it wants to achieve allocative efficiency.
      b.   If the government sets price equal to marginal cost, the utility will suffer losses and go out of business in the long run.

   2.3   Subsidizing the Natural Monopolist. Government can subsidize the utility and make it charge marginal cost

   2.4   Setting Price Equal to Average Cost. Government can set price equal to average cost, and the utility will make a normal profit.

2.5   The Regulatory Dilemma. The regulatory dilemma is whether to set the allocatively efficient price (marginal cost) or to set price equal to average cost.

3.   Alternative Theories of Economic Regulation. Economic regulation is in the public interest, according to some. Economic regulation is in the special interest of producers, according to many economists.

   3.1   Producers Have a Special Interest in Economic Regulation
      a.   Producers have a strong interest in matters that affect their income.
      b.   Consumers buy many goods and services and have no special interest in legislation that affects one good or service.
      c.   Producer interests in matters relating to regulation tend to be stronger than consumer interests.
      d.   There are two variants of the special-interest theory:
         (1)   Capture theory: over time the regulating machinery acts more in accord with producer interests.
         (2)   The special interest theory of regulation says that producer interests dominate and regulation benefits the producers.

   3.2   CASE STUDY: Airline Regulation and Deregulation
      a.   The Civil Aeronautics Board (CAB) controlled entry and prices beginning in 1938.
      b.   No new entry was allowed by the CAB for forty years.
      c.   Nonprice competition was used extensively in the industry.
      d.   Deregulation began in the late 1970s.
      e.   Prices have fallen, as have wages in the industry.
      f.   Air travel has increased substantially, but airport capacity has not increased, which has retarded competition to some extent.

4.   Antitrust Laws. Antitrust laws attempt to promote a market structure that encourages competition. Antitrust laws attempt to eliminate anticompetitive behavior.

   4.1   Origins of Antitrust Policy
      a.   In the second half of the nineteenth century, technological change led to larger firms in many U.S. industries.
      b.   The growth of railroads lowered the costs of transportation, extending markets and allowing firms to grow.
      c.   Depressions caused concern among manufacturing firms, with the result that many of them began colluding and forming trusts.
      d.   Antitrust legislation was passed in response to these developments. The important U.S. laws are
         (1)   The Sherman Antitrust Act of 1890, which prohibits collusion and monopolization
         (2)   The Clayton Act of 1914, which outlawed certain anticompetitive practices
         (3)   The Federal Trade Commission Act of 1914, which established the Federal Trade Commission
         (4)   The 1950 Celler-Kefauver Anti-Merger Act, which prevents one firm from buying the assets of another if the effect is to reduce competition

   4.2   Antitrust Law Enforcement
      a.   Government agencies often initiate action against a firm because of a complaint from a customer or competitor.
      b.   A firm can sign a consent decree whereby it agrees to discontinue the alleged offense without admitting guilt.

c. If the case goes to trial and the firm loses, it can pay fines totaling three times the amount of the damages.

4.3 Per Se Illegality and the Rule of Reason
   a. Some practices are illegal *per se*, which means that no economic rationale can be used to justify the practice.
   b. Other practices fall under a *rule of reason*, which means that the aim or the effect of the practice must be unreasonable for the firm to be guilty.

4.4 Mergers and Public Policy
   a. In looking at the possible harm of a merger, the Justice Department examines the concentration of the industry.
   b. To measure concentration, the Justice Department uses the Herfindahl index.
   c. The *Herfindahl index* is the sum of the squared percentage market shares of all firms in the market.
   d. The Justice Department's guidelines on mergers distinguish between horizontal mergers and non-horizontal mergers.

4.5 Merger Movements. There have been four major merger waves in the last 100 years.
   a. The first wave involved mostly horizontal mergers, and took place from 1887 to 1904.
   b. The second wave was from 1916 to 1929 and involved primarily vertical mergers.
   c. The third wave, from 1948 to 1969, involved mostly conglomerate mergers.
   d. The fourth wave began in the 1980's and is still going on.
   e. In recent years there have been fewer objections to mergers from regulatory officials.

5. Competitive Trends in the U.S. Economy

5.1 Market Competition over Time
   a. A recent study concludes that there was an increase in the competitiveness of the U.S. economy from 1958 to 1988.
   b. Reasons for the growth of competition from 1958 to 1980:
      (1) Increased imports from abroad
      (2) Deregulation
      (3) Antitrust activity

5.2 CASE STUDY: Microsoft Trial

5.3 Recent Competitive Trends
   a. International competition has intensified.
   b. Some important markets are growing more competitive because of technological change.
   c. Some believe that recent problems in airlines, banking, and electricity are due to deregulation.

5.4 Problems with Antitrust Legislation
   a. Many cases take years to settle.
   b. There is too much reliance on the model of perfect competition.
   c. Treble damage suits may be anticompetitive.
   d. International competition is becoming more important and is often overlooked in evaluating the domestic market.

5.5 CASE STUDY: Windows '98 sold with Microsoft Browser

III. DISCUSSION

Business Behavior and Public Policy

Market power is the ability to raise price and maintain it above the competitive level. The market structure of an industry affects the conduct of firms in the industry. The fewer firms in an industry, the easier it is for them to collude and raise prices above the competitive level. If this occurs, economists say the firms are performing poorly because production is not allocated efficiently.

Regulating Natural Monopolies

A natural monopoly has a downward-sloping long-run average cost curve throughout the entire range of market demand. Regulators do not want the natural monopoly to set the monopoly price. The socially optimal price is found by setting price equal to marginal cost. Unfortunately, if the regulatory agency sets this price, the firm loses money and goes out of business in the long run because marginal cost is less than average cost. The government could require marginal cost pricing and then subsidize the utility so it would not lose money. Generally, this is not done. Instead, regulators typically set price equal to average cost. Average cost pricing is a compromise between the more efficient marginal cost pricing and monopoly pricing.

Alternative Theories of Economic Regulation

Economic regulation involves the control of price, output, entry and exit, and the quality of services in an industry. Ideally, economic regulation is designed to promote social welfare by controlling natural monopolies and promoting competition in some industries. In reality, however, economic regulation often creates what amounts to a government-enforced cartel.

Economists tend to view regulation as the result of competition among interest groups. Interest groups seek favors from the government in the form of subsidies, tariffs, or regulation. Government officials provide the favors, depending on the effectiveness of the lobbying efforts of the interest groups and the likely effects of the officials' actions on the probability of reelection. Within this framework, it is often likely that producer interests will be expressed more forcefully than consumer interests. The producers that are able to gain control of the regulatory process are often able to earn monopoly profits as the government restricts entry into the industry.

The ICC and the CAB are two examples of regulatory agencies that have shaped U.S. industries so that they resemble government-sponsored cartels. The ICC restricted entry into the trucking industry, and the CAB restricted entry into the airline industry. For forty years, the CAB permitted no entry into the interstate airline industry. Prices were set to allow profits, although the firms did not always earn monopoly profits, for two reasons. First, nonprice competition often eroded the profits. For example, in the airline industry, firms competed by offering more flights, roomier seats, and complimentary food or drinks. Second, the regulatory agencies often required firms to maintain unprofitable routes along with the profitable ones.

Deregulation of the U.S. railroad, trucking, and airline industries occurred during the 1980s. Consequently, rates have fallen as entry and output have expanded. Some carriers that had been able to survive in the protected, regulated environment have gone bankrupt. Wages have fallen in these industries as competition has increased. Economic efficiency has increased as a result of deregulation, but producers and employees who have been negatively affected by these changes are still lobbying for a return to regulation.

Antitrust Laws

Antitrust laws attempt to promote competition in the marketplace. The Sherman Antitrust Act makes it illegal for firms to conspire to restrict trade and to attempt to monopolize an industry. The Clayton Act prohibits certain practices associated with monopoly or monopolization if they substantially lessen competition: price discrimination, *tying contracts*, *exclusive dealing*, and *interlocking directorates*. The Federal Trade Commission was established in 1914 to prevent unfair methods of competition.

The courts have used two criteria in interpreting the antitrust laws. Some activities—price fixing, for example—are illegal *per se*. If the government can show that a firm committed the forbidden act, then the firm is found guilty. Depending on the view of the Supreme Court, other activities fall under the *rule of reason*. Under the rule of reason, not only must a complainant show that the firm committed the practice, it must also prove that the effects of the practice were harmful.

There have been four merger waves in the past 100 years, the last of which is still taking place.

Competitive Trends in the U.S. Economy

A recent study indicates that the U.S. economy is more competitive today than it was twenty or even forty years ago. This increased competitiveness has been attributed to growing competition from abroad, deregulation, and antitrust activity. Further, technological change has promoted increased competitiveness in some industries.

IV. LAGNIAPPE

A Riot in Ephesus

The text states that producer groups seeking favorable legislation usually claim that the legislation is to aid consumers or society. Such claims are not new. An interesting incident is recorded in the book of Acts in the Bible. A silversmith named Demetrius called other silversmiths together for a meeting. The city they lived in, Ephesus, was the site of a temple to the goddess Artemis (Diana), and the silversmiths made and sold silver shrines of Artemis. The Christian missionary Paul had been preaching in the area with such success that many were converting to Christianity. The converts no longer bought silver shrines of Artemis. The silversmiths were upset because of the loss of business and started a riot. When pressing their case before others, however, they argued that Artemis and the city of Ephesus were being discredited by Paul's preaching. (See Acts 19:23-41.)

Question to Think About: Can you think of groups today that use public-interest arguments when lobbying for special favors from the government?

Does Antitrust Legislation Protect Competition or Competitors?

Many economists claim that the antitrust laws have often reduced competition by protecting smaller competitors from their larger rivals. In 1911, the Standard Oil Company was found guilty of violating the Sherman Act because it competed unfairly. A few years later, U.S. Steel was found not guilty because competitors had not been harmed by the giant steel company. U.S. Steel had been charging a high price, which encouraged other steel companies to expand. All steel producers profited by U.S. Steel's actions, although consumers of steel paid higher prices than necessary. In

1945, the Aluminum Company of America (Alcoa) was found guilty of violating the Sherman Act because it sought to meet a growing demand with increased capacity and sought to take advantage of new opportunities. If Alcoa had merely charged a higher, monopoly price and allowed other firms to enter and grow, it might have been found not guilty. The result of these cases was to encourage large firms to charge high prices rather than to compete vigorously with rivals.

Question to Think About: Would you rather have been a customer of U.S. Steel or Standard Oil?

V. KEY TERMS

Market power
Social regulation
Economic regulation
Antitrust activity
Capture Theory of Regulation
Sherman Antitrust Act of 1890
Clayton Act of 1914
Federal Trade Commission Act of 1914
Cellar-Kefauver Merger Act
Tying contract

Exclusive dealing
Interlocking directorate
Horizontal mergers
Vertical mergers
Consent decree
Per se illegality
Rule of reason
Predatory pricing
Herfindahl index
Conglomerate merger

VI. QUESTIONS

A. Completion

1. A firm that possesses _____ is able to maintain price above the competitive level.

2. _____ regulation is concerned with health and safety.

3. _____ regulation is concerned with prices and output.

4. _____ tries to prohibit monopolization and collusion.

5. A _____ exists when the long-run average cost curve slopes downward over the entire range of market demand.

6. A public utility that is forced by regulation to set price equal to marginal cost will earn economic _____.

7. When a public utility is not subsidized, regulators often try to get the utility to set price equal to _____.

8. According to the _____ theory, regulation tends to benefit producers.

9. Airfares were set by the CAB but _____ competition was abundant.

10. A(n) _____ exists when the seller of one good requires buyers to purchase another good as well.

11. A(n) _____ exists when the same individual sits on the boards of directors of competing companies.

12. In antitrust cases, a _____ ruling simply requires evidence that a certain practice was carried on; in using a _____, a court requires additional evidence that the effects of the practice are harmful.

13. The U.S. Justice Department's merger guidelines use the _____ in determining whether to challenge a proposed merger.

14. A _____ merger involves two unrelated firms.

15. Joseph Schumpeter argued that competition should be thought of as a _____ process.

B. True/False

_____ 1. Market power exists when a firm can maintain price above the competitive level.

_____ 2. The Environmental Protection Agency is an example of economic regulation.

_____ 3. Regulation of electric utilities is an example of economic regulation.

_____ 4. The government seeks to control the price and output of an industry when it uses antitrust policy.

_____ 5. Under natural monopoly, the average costs of production are lower if one firm produces the good than if more than one firm produces the good.

_____ 6. If the government sets price equal to marginal cost for a natural monopoly, the monopoly most likely will go out of business in the long run unless it is subsidized.

_____ 7. Regulating agencies usually try to set the price that allocates resources \ efficiently.

_____ 8. According to the special-interest theory of regulation, consumers exert a lot of influence on regulatory agencies.

_____ 9. Legislation favoring producer groups usually is described as an advancement of consumer interests.

_____ 10. According to the capture theory of regulation, regulation is operated for the producers' benefits.

_____ 11. One consequence of deregulation in the airline industry is that airline pilots and other workers receive lower wages.

_____ 12. Deregulation of airlines has made air travel less safe.

13. Competing firms may want to form trusts to stabilize markets during turbulent economic times.

14. Price fixing is illegal per se in the United States.

15. A horizontal merger involves firms in the same market.

16. The Supreme Court has consistently used market conduct instead of market structure as the test of legality.

17. The merger wave in the 1950's and 1960's involved mostly horizontal mergers.

18. Since World War II, the largest U.S. firms have increased their share of the country's manufacturing assets.

19. The U.S. economy is less competitive today than it was at the start of World War II.

20. Where markets are open to foreign competition, antitrust enforcement that focuses on domestic production doesn't make good economic sense.

C. Multiple Choice

1. The term "market power" refers to the ability of a firm to
   a. force consumers to buy its product.
   b. make long-run profits.
   c. induce the government to grant special favors to the firm.
   d. maintain price above the competitive level.
   e. all of the above

2. Which of the following is an example of social regulation?
   a. Interstate Commerce Commision
   b. National Highway Traffic and Safety Administration
   c. Civil Aeronautics Board
   d. Federal Trade Commission
   e. all of the above

3. Economic regulation is usually carried out by regulatory bodies at the
   a. local government level.
   b. state government level.
   c. federal government level.
   d. all of the above
   e. b and c only

4. The fundamental dilemma in regulating public utilities is
   a. whether to subsidize a monopoly that is charging a price equal to its average cost.
   b. whether to subsidize a monopoly that is charging the socially optimal price or let the firm charge a higher price.
   c. that a firm can charge the socially optimal price only if it is a natural monopoly, which most are not.
   d. that the socially optimal price is higher than consumers ought to pay.
   e. none of the above.

5. Regulation of a natural monopoly can increase social welfare by
   a. bringing price closer to marginal cost.
   b. increasing consumer surplus.
   c. reducing economic profits of the monopoly.
   d. all of the above.
   e. a and b only.

6. Some argue that business regulations often favor producer interests over consumer interests because
   a. there are more producers than consumers.
   b. producers are richer than consumers.
   c. producers have more interest in matters that affect their income than consumers have in matters that affect the prices they pay.
   d. the regulations are needed to promote the public interest.
   e. a, b, and c

7. Which of the following is difficult to explain using the capture theory of regulation?
   a. Public-minded reformers sponsored the legislation establishing regulation.
   b. The firms that were to be regulated opposed regulation.
   c. Regulation appears to benefit producers more than consumers.
   d. all of the above
   e. none of the above

8. Which of the following statements is true?
   a. The capture theory says that consumer-interest groups usually influence regulators more than producer-interest groups.
   b. Interest groups have less influence today than 30 years ago.
   c. Legislation favoring producer groups is usually introduced under the guise of advancing consumer interests.
   d. all of the above.
   e. a and b only.

9. Which of the following was not a form of competition within the airline industry under CAB regulation?
   a. frequent flights
   b. roomy seats
   c. price
   d. advertising
   e. quality of meals

10. A factor that has restricted competition in the airline industry after deregulation has been
    a. safety regulation imposed by the FAA.
    b. high oil prices.
    c. bankruptcies of some airlines.
    d. the failure of airport capacity to increase.
    e. all of the above.

11. Developments that led to the passage of the Sherman Antitrust Act included
    a. an increase in the cost of transporting manufactured goods.
    b. growth of firms, leading to diseconomies of scale.
    c. technological change, leading to more extensive use of capital and greater economies of scale.
    d. business booms that led to rapidly increasing prices.
    e. all of the above.

12. The Clayton Act prohibits which of the following if it substantially lessens competition?
    a. price discrimination.
    b. tying contracts.
    c. interlocking directorates.
    d. exclusive dealing.
    d. all of the above.

13. The Clayton Act prohibits
    a. monopolization
    b. all price discrimination
    c. price discrimination that leads to monopoly.
    d. monopoly.
    e. all of the above

14. Mergers accomplished by acquiring assets of another company were restricted by
    a. the Clayton Act.
    b. the Robinson-Patman Act.
    c. the Sherman Act.
    d. the Wheeler-Lea Act.
    e. the Celler-Kefauver Act.

15. A firm found guilty of breaking the antitrust laws and of causing harm to another firm equal to $1 million will have to pay damages to that firm equal to
    a. zero. The officers of the firm will go to jail.
    b. $100,000.
    c. $1 million.
    d. $3 million.
    e. $10 million.

16. In 1920, the Supreme Court ruled that U.S. Steel
    a. had no monopoly power.
    b. possessed monopoly power.
    c. had not used its monopoly power in unreasonable ways.
    d. had engaged in predatory pricing.
    e. b and c

17. In the Alcoa case, the courts ruled
    a. in Alcoa's favor.
    b. that Alcoa was guilty because of its large share of the market.
    c. that Alcoa was guilty because the firm's actions were unreasonable.
    d. that Alcoa had to pay its rivals $15 million in damages.
    e. c and d

18. The merger guidelines used by the Justice Department
    a. no longer use the Herfindahl index.
    b. treat vertical mergers differently from all other types of mergers.
    c. treat horizontal mergers differently from all other types of mergers.
    d. allow all mergers to occur.
    e. a and b

19. The merger between Daimler Benz and Chrysler is an example of a
    a. horizontal merger.
    b. vertical merger.
    c. conglomerate merger.
    d. all of the above.
    e. none of the above because Daimler Benz is a foreign firm.

20. Foreign imports increase U.S. competitiveness by
    a. providing cheaply made, low-quality substitutes for U.S. products.
    b. penetrating domestic oligopolistic markets with lower-priced products.
    c. taking jobs from Americans.
    d. getting around tariff barriers, which keep prices high.
    e. none of the above.

D. Discussion Questions

1. Explain why answers a, b, and c are not correct in multiple choice question 1.

2. What is market power and what are its effects?

3. How does social regulation differ from economic regulation?

4. What options are available to the government for dealing with a natural monopoly? Which one tends to be used in the United States?

5. What dilemma faces regulators trying to regulate natural monopolies?

6. How does the public-interest theory of economic regulation differ from the special-interest theory? How are the capture theory and the special-interest theory alike and how are they different?

7. Why do economists argue that producer interests will be stronger than consumer interests when it comes to influencing regulators?

8. CAB regulations generated higher prices and revenues for producers, but producers did not receive all the profits. What happened to the profits the producers did not capture?

9. What hampered enforcement of the Sherman Act?

10. For the following practices, indicate what type of pricing practice is involved:
    a. Shoelaces included when buying shoes
    b. Levis requires a store to carry only Levi jeans and no other brands
    c. McDonalds requires its franchises to purchase their straws from McDonalds
    d. A person on Coca-Cola's Board of Directors also sits on Pepsi-Cola's Boards
    e. A member of GM's board and a member of Ford's board sit on Citibank's board

11. Why does the Clayton Act prohibit interlocking directorates?

12. Explain the difference between per se illegality and the rule of reason. Which would you prefer to use if you were prosecuting a case for the Justice Department?

13. "Tariffs are the friend of monopoly." Is this statement true or false? Explain.

14. Using the data in Exhibit 1, calculate the Herfindahl index.

Exhibit 1

Firm	Market Share (Percent)
A	20
B	20
C	15
D	15
E	10
F	6
G	5
H	4
I	3
J	2

15. In the above exhibit, if firms A and E merged, what would the Herfindahl index be?

16. According to William Shepherd, what factors have contributed to the increased competitiveness of the U.S. economy?

17. What difference would it make if the antitrust authorities focused more on activities that harmed consumers or on activities that harmed competitors?

18. Explain why True/False question #20 is true.

VII. ANSWERS

A. Completion

1. market power
2. Social
3. Economic
4. Antitrust activity
5. natural monopoly
6. losses
7. average cost
8. special interest

9. nonprice
10. tying contract
11. interlocking directorate
12. per se; rule of reason
13. Herfindahl index
14. conglomerate
15. dynamic

B. True/False

1. True
2. False
3. True
4. False.
   Controlling
   price and
   output is part
   of economic
   regulation.

5. True
6. True
7. False
8. False
9. True
10. True
11. True
12. False
13. True

14. True
15. True
16. False
17. False
18. True
19. False
20. True

C. Multiple Choice

1. d	6. c	11. c	16. e
2. b	7. e	12. e	17. b
3. d	8. c	13. c	18. c
4. b	9. c	14. e	19. a
5. e	10. d	15. d	20. b

D. Discussion Questions

1. Market power is the ability to raise price by restricting output. People can choose not to buy the good at all, so answer a is incorrect. It is possible that there is no price that will permit the firm to make economic profits, so answer b is incorrect. A firm can possess market power without being able to influence public policy, and firms (or other economic actors) without market power are able to influence public policy in some situations (e.g., farmers), so answer c is incorrect.

2. Market power is the ability to raise price and maintain it above the competitive level. Under perfect competition, price equals marginal cost. The effect of market power is to raise price above marginal cost, which causes inefficiency. Market power creates a misallocation of resources and a transfer of wealth from consumers to producers.

3. Social regulation is concerned with health and safety issues while economic regulation is concerned with price, output, entry of new firms, and quality of service in industries that have monopoly power.

4. The government can do nothing, or it can sell rights to monopoly, or it can own and operate the monopoly itself, or it can regulate the privately owned monopoly. The last option is usually taken, but there are situations in which one of the others is used.

5. The optimal policy from the point of view of economic efficiency is to set price equal to marginal cost. But if the firm is a natural monopoly, marginal cost will lie below average cost, so if price is set equal to marginal cost the firm will suffer economic losses and go out of business in the long run. The dilemma, then, is whether to seek the efficient price and subsidize the monopoly or to allow for a normal profit by setting price equal to average cost.

6. The public-interest theory is that economic regulation is designed to promote the public interest by controlling natural monopolies when production by one firm seems most efficient and encouraging competition in some industries when it is economically desirable. The special-interest theory says that regulation benefits special-interest groups—in particular producers. According to the latter theory, regulation prevents entry into the market or prevents competition among existing firms, enabling them to charge a price above the competitive level. Both the special-interest theory and the capture theory hold that producers benefit from regulation. They differ in that the special-interest theory says that regulation is designed to benefit producers; the capture theory says that the intent of the legislation may be to benefit consumers but that over time the producers exert more influence on the regulatory agency and "capture" it.

7. Producers are affected more by regulations that affect the price of the good than consumers are. Hence, producers have more at stake when regulators are considering policy. Producers can be expected to work harder to influence policy than consumers will work to generate lower prices.

8. Employees captured some of the profits in the form of higher wages. Consumers in smaller cities captured some, in that service was provided to these areas at prices below cost. Some of the profits were lost through nonprice competition.

9. The law prohibited the creation of trusts, restraint of trade, and monopolization, but didn't define what constituted these activities.

10. a. Tie-in sale (pun intended)
    b. Exclusive dealing
    c. Tying contract
    d. Interlocking directorates
    e. None—legally, this would not be considered an interlocking directorate.

11. Interlocking directorates occur when one person serves on the board of directors of competing firms. This would make collusion between the firms easier, so it is illegal.

12. If per se illegality applies, all a prosecutor must show is that a firm actually committed an illegal practice. The rule of reason requires that a prosecutor also show that the effects of the practice were harmful. Hence, a prosecutor would prefer to be able to use a per se approach than to have to satisfy the rule of reason.

13. True. Tariffs raise the prices of imported goods, which shields domestic firms from foreign competition and permits higher prices and profits.

14. The Herfindahl index is 400 + 400 + 225 + 225 + 100 + 36 + 25 + 16 + 9 + 4 = 1,440.

15. 900 + 400 + 225 + 225 + 36 + 25+16 + 9 + 4= 1,840

16. Increasing foreign competition, deregulation, and antitrust activity.

17. Consumer welfare is safeguarded when the antitrust authorities focus more on activities that harm consumers than on activities that harm competitors. In market competition, some firms are harmed, that is, they lose the competitive battle. But it is the competitive battle that provides consumers with better products and lower prices. Competitors aren't harmed under collusion, but consumers are harmed.

18. The answer turns on the issue of market definition. If the Antitrust Division computes a Herfindahl Index based on domestic market shares, it may find a specific market to be highly concentration. (Think about the U.S. automobile industry.) But it may be that foreign competitors have a significant share of that domestic market. (Again, think of automobiles.) In that case, the market may be much less concentrated than the Herfindahl Index suggests.

CHAPTER 16

Public Goods and Public Choice

I.   INTRODUCTION

This chapter examines the role of government more closely. Until now, the government has been treated as an economic agent that makes optimal decisions when it steps in to correct deficiencies in the marketplace. Now we examine problems with the decision-making process used in government as well as the distortions the government can introduce into the economy.

II.   OUTLINE

1.   Optional Provision of Public Goods

   1.1   Private Goods, Public Goods, and In Between
      a.   Public goods are nonrival in consumption.
      b.   Once a public good is produced it is impossible to exclude those who refuse to pay for it.
      c.   Because public goods are nonrival and nonexclusive, private firms cannot sell them profitably.
      d.   Some goods are nonrival but exclusive, and are called quasi-public goods.
      e.   Some goods are rival but nonexclusive, and are called open-access goods.

   1.2   Optimal Provision of Public Goods
      a.   The market demand curve for a public good is the vertical sum of each consumer's demand for the good.
      b.   The efficient level of a public good is where the market demand curve intersects the marginal cost curve.
      c.   The free-rider problem occurs because people try to benefit from the public good without paying for it.

2.   Public Choice in Representative Democracy

   2.1   Median Voter Model
      a.   Under certain conditions, majority rule delegates the choice to the person whose preference is the median of the group.
      b.   Only the median voter receives his or her most preferred amount of a good or most preferred policy decision.
      c.   Political candidates try to get elected by appealing to the median voter.

   2.2   Special Interest and Rational Ignorance.
      a.   Elected officials may try to maximize their political support.
      b.   Elected officials may cater to special interests rather than common interests because of the asymmetry between special interests and the common interest.
      c.   The individual voter or consumer is unlikely to have an effect on public choice.
      d.   The benefits to the individual voter or consumer of a change in public policy are likely to be small.

     e. Hence, the rational voter or consumer is unlikely to spend resources to acquire information concerning proposed changes in public policy.

2.3   Distribution of Costs and Benefits
    a. The costs and benefits of a policy change or legislative measure may be either widely or narrowly distributed.
    b. The more widely distributed the costs or benefits, the less incentive an individual has to try to influence the public choice.
    c. *Traditional public goods legislation* has widespread benefits and costs. National defense is one example of this.
    d. *Special-interest legislation* involves cases in which benefits are concentrated and costs are widely distributed. A tariff on imported textiles is one example of this.
    e. *Populist legislation* has widespread benefits but concentrated costs. A special tax levied on the rich would be an example of this.
    f. *Competing-interest legislation* involves cases in which both benefits and costs are concentrated. The legislation affecting bargaining between a union and firms in an industry is an example of this.

2.4   *CASE STUDY:* Farm Subsidies

2.5   Rent Seeking
    a. *Rent seeking* involves activities that interest groups undertake to elicit special favors from government.
    b. To the extent that special-interest groups engage in rent-seeking activities, resources are diverted from wealth-creating activities to activities that transfer wealth, which usually results in a reduction of wealth.

2.6   *CASE STUDY:* Campaign Finance Reform

2.7   The *underground economy* refers to market activity that goes unreported to the government in an attempt to avoid taxes. Tax avoidance is the legal attempt to arrange one's economic affairs so as to minimize taxes. Tax evasion involves fraudulent or illegal behavior.

3.   Bureaucracy and Representative Democracy. The task of implementing legislation passed by elected representatives is typically left to government bureaus.

3.1   Ownership and Funding of Bureaus
    a. Bureaus have different incentives than business firms.
    b. Ownership in a government jurisdiction does not include the right to transfer ownership to others in the way stockholders can.
    c. Bureaus are typically financed by a budget appropriation from the legislature rather than by the sale of output.

3.2   Ownership and Organizational Behavior
    a. Bureaus receive less information concerning the customers' desired quantity and quality of output.
    b. There is less incentive for workers in bureaus to respond to the wishes of consumers than is the case in business firms.
    c. Government bureaus tend to be less concerned with minimizing costs than private firms.

3.3 Bureaucratic Objectives
   a. One theory of bureaucratic behavior assumes that bureaus attempt to maximize their budgets.
   b. Budget maximization results in a larger budget than that desired by the median voter.

3.4 Private Versus Public Production. Governments sometimes contract with private firms to provide services to a community.

III. DISCUSSION

Optimal Provision of Public Goods

Public goods are characterized by nonrival consumption and nonexclusion. Nonrival consumption is when one person's consumption of a good doesn't reduce the amount available to others. Non-exclusion refers to when no one can be excluded from consuming a good once it is produced. Examples of public goods include national defense and flood control. A quasi-public good is a good characterized by nonrival consumption but exclusion is possible. Cable television is an example. A good that is rival but nonexclusive is an open-access good.

Recall that the market demand curve for a private good is found by summing horizontally the demand curves of the consumers. That is, the quantities demanded of each consumer are added at a price to determine the market quantity demanded at that price. The market demand curve for a public good is found by summing vertically the demand curves of the consumers. That is, for a given quantity, the price each consumer is willing to pay is summed for all consumers. The efficient level of provision of a public good is where the sum of the marginal valuations equals the marginal cost. Review Exhibit 2 in the textbook to ensure you understand this process.

Public Choice in Representative Democracy

Majority rule is often used to decide public choices. Often this means that the *median voter* actually chooses the public policy. Exhibit 1 illustrates how this happens. The line represents possible approaches to public funding of education. At point *a*, the policy is that no government funds are used to support education; at *e*, 100 percent of the spending on education comes from the government. Suppose one voter favors each point on the line. (Note that this means that there are 101 voters, since we are including 0 percent as a choice.) We assume that people prefer a point closer to their ideal than one that is further away. That is, a person who favors point *b* (10 percent of the cost of education to be provided by the government) would prefer point *a* (0 percent government funding) over point *d* (90 percent government funding) since *b* is closer to *a* than it is to *d*.

Exhibit 1

Based on the median voter model, we predict that point *c* will be chosen. Compare point *c* with any other point on the line. Any point to the left of *c* will generate fewer votes than *c* because all voters to the right of *c* will vote for *c*. So if the choice is between, say, 10 percent government funding of education (point *b*) and 50 percent funding (point *c*), *c* will garner at least 51 votes—that is, those who prefer more funding to less funding will vote for *c*. Obviously, the same is true for any point to the right of *c*: if the choice is between point *c* and point *d*, all voters to the left of the median voter will join with *c*. The preference of the median voter prevails even though 100 of the 101 voters have a different first choice.

It is very unusual for direct democracy to be used to make public decisions. Instead, representatives are usually elected to make the decisions. Representatives presumably make decisions on the basis of self-interest. Since they face reelection, they are interested in increasing their political support. Such support includes votes as well as campaign contributions.

Special-interest groups are often successful in obtaining favorable legislation that generates transfers of wealth to their members. This can occur even if, or perhaps because, the group is relatively small in number. Such a group may not provide a lot of votes to a representative but may contribute financially in a substantial way. As long as the transfer of wealth does not cause the larger group of taxpayers who pay for the transfer to vote against the representative, the representative gains by supporting the transfer. But why would the taxpayers not punish the legislator for the higher taxes? Because they might not be aware of the higher taxes or of the transfer. Since the taxes to pay for the transfer are spread out over a very large number of taxpayers, the additional tax paid by an individual taxpayer is not very large. Consequently, it is not worth the individual taxpayer's time to monitor all the activities of the legislator. Whenever the benefits of a change in policy are distributed over a relatively small group and the costs are borne by a relatively large group, there is a good chance that the special-interest group will be able to receive the transfer it seeks.

Recall that a resource owner receives economic rent whenever the payment received exceeds the opportunity cost of the resource. This is why monopoly profits are often called *monopoly rents*. Special-interest groups may try to obtain legislation that will allow them to earn rents. The activity undertaken to elicit such rents is called *rent seeking*. Generally, rent-seeking activity diverts resources from productive activities to unproductive activities. That is, the competition for rents is generally a negative-sum game.

Market activity often goes unreported to the government to avoid taxes or because the activity is illegal. One effect of a tax on an activity is the increasing use of the underground economy.

Bureaucracy and Representative Democracy

Although legislatures pass legislation, they seldom implement the legislation. Implementation is the responsibility of government *bureaus*. Just as some are concerned with whether managers of corporations act in the best interests of the shareholders, others express concern that bureaucrats may not always act in the best interests of the citizens or of the representatives who passed the legislation. The incentives that help keep corporate managers in line, such as stock options and fears of takeovers, are not applicable to government bureaucrats. Consequently, there is real concern over whether bureaucrats implement legislation in an optimal manner.

IV. LAGNIAPPE

Change at the New York Stock Exchange

For over 175 years, the New York Stock Exchange (NYSE) established fixed brokerage rates. The NYSE limits the number of members and regulates the business practices of its members. The Securities and Exchange Commission (SEC), which is the government agency established to regulate the exchanges, helped enforce the fixed prices established by the NYSE until 1975. In 1975, the SEC outlawed the fixed brokerage rates. Such a policy change does not seem to be consistent with the discussion in this chapter concerning the political power of special-interest groups. However, in the 1960s and 1970s, institutional buyers became a larger part of the total market. Institutional buyers include insurance companies and other financial institutions that handle large blocks of stock for pension funds, college endowments, and the like. As the institutional buyers became more numerous and important, they were able to exert influence on the SEC to get lower rates. In earlier years, the costs of the high fixed rates had been spread over a large group, but as institutions became more important, the costs were borne by a smaller group. Eventually, this smaller group was able to get the fixed rates eliminated, and brokerage rates fell by approximately 25 percent.

Question to Think About: Could forces similar to those that brought changes in brokerage rules have led to deregulation of airlines?

Rent-Seeking and the Line-Item Veto

Many Republican presidents have tried to get the line-item veto power as a way of lowering government spending. Finally, the Republican Congress passed a line-item veto bill, and President Clinton used it to eliminate some specific spending programs. However, the law was challenged in the courts and found to be unconstitutional.

An argument for the line item veto is that the President is less susceptible to the rent-seeking lobbying of special-interest groups than Congress is. If so, Congress is likely to pass specific programs to benefit specific special-interest groups, which a more independent president can excise from the budget with a line-item veto.

Question to Think About: Would a line-item veto actually lead to less spending for special interests than the status quo?

V. KEY TERMS

Quasi-public good
Open-access good
Free-rider problem
Median voter model
Rational ignorance
Special-interest legislation

Traditional Public Goods Legislation
Populist legislation
Competing-interest legislation
Underground economy
Bureaus

VI. QUESTIONS

A. Completion

1. If the amount of a good consumed by one individual is not available for others to consume, then the good is characterized by _____ consumption.

2. If a firm is unable to exclude those households who haven't paid for a good, then the good is characterized by _____ consumption.

3. Quasi-public goods are characterized by _____ and _____ consumption.

4. The whales in the ocean are an example of _____ goods.

5. The market demand curve for a public good is found by _____ summing the individual consumers' demand curves.

6. The government can solve the problems caused by non-exclusion by producing a public good and paying for it with_____

7. When a single issue is under consideration, the policy selected is likely to reflect the preferences of the _____

8. We assume that elected officials seek to _____ their political support.

9. Taxpayers may choose to remain _____ of a change in policy when the costs to an individual taxpayer are very low.

10. Political candidates who want to please the median voter take _____ positions.

11. _____ legislation involves concentrated benefits and concentrated costs.

12. Special-interest groups engage in _____ activity when they attempt to obtain special favors from the government.

13. The _____ consists of market activities that are not reported to the government in order to avoid taxation.

14. Tax _____ is illegal.

15. Niskanen argues that bureaus attempt to maximize their _____.

B. True/False

_____ 1. A good that is nonrival is a public good.

_____ 2. Government can solve the market failure associated with a public good by providing the good and paying for it through enforced taxation.

_____ 3. Once congestion sets in, quasi-public goods become actual public goods.

_____ 4. Private goods are usually provided by private firms.

_____ 5. In a society, everyone consumes the same amount of a public good.

_____ 6. The market demand curve for a public good is the horizontal summation of the individual consumers' demand curves for the good.

_____ 7. The median voter model says that the policy that is the first choice of most people will be selected.

_____ 8. There will be few differences among candidates if all the candidates attempt to appeal to the median voter.

_____ 9. There are likely to be many dissatisfied voters under majority rule.

_____ 10. There is a greater chance that representative democracy will represent the choice of special interests than is the case with direct democracy.

_____ 11. When the cost of acquiring and acting on the information needed to affect legislation exceeds the expected benefits, rational citizens ignore what is going on in Congress.

_____ 12. A public policy that transfers income from a small group to a very large group will probably pass Congress.

_____ 13. Competing-interest legislation often involves concentrated costs and concentrated benefits.

_____ 14. The total costs generally exceed the total benefits of legislation that caters to special interest groups.

_____ 15. Rent seeking is an important type of productive activity.

_____ 16. The underground economy would be much smaller if there were no taxes.

_____ 17. An important portion of the underground economy results from tax avoidance.

_____ 18. Managers of government bureaus face the same incentives as managers of private corporations.

_____ 19. Government bureaus tend to produce goods or services at higher cost than private firms.

_____ 20. All goods financed by the government are produced by government agencies.

1. Private goods are
   a. quasi-public goods produced by the government.
   b. always produced by private firms.
   c. rival but nonexclusive.
   d. exclusive but nonrival.
   e. both rival and exclusive.

2. Goods that are nonexclusive and rival are
   a. private goods.
   b. public goods.
   c. quasi-public goods.
   d. open-access goods.
   e. none of the above.

3. An example of a public good is
   a. cable TV.
   b. flood control.
   c. a crowded swimming pool.
   d. Yellowstone National Park.
   e. the fish in the ocean.

4. Fred values a specific quantity of national defense at $1,000, Sandy values it at $200, George values it at $500, Joan at -$200, Archie at $1,500, and Bill at zero. The social value of the national defense is
   a. $0.
   b. $500.
   c. $1,500.
   d. $3,000.
   e. can't tell without more information.

5. The decisions concerning what public goods should be produced, in what quantities, and who should pay are decided
   a. by consumer sovereignty.
   b. by equating the sum of the total valuations with the total cost of producing the public goods.
   c. optimally when each resident pays a tax equal to his or her marginal valuation.
   d. optimally when each resident can tell the government how much they value the public good.
   e. by public choice.

6. Public choices are those choices that are
   a. best.
   b. fair.
   c. made collectively by all voters directly.
   d. made collectively by representatives.
   e. both c and d.

7. Majority voting often amounts to delegating the choice to the
   a. mean voter.
   b. median voter.
   c. richest voter.
   d. most important special-interest group.
   e. most committed voter.

8. Under majority rule,
   a. there are usually many dissatisfied voters.
   b. there is always a clear choice.
   c. the first choice of the majority of people is chosen.
   d. all of the above
   e. none of the above

9. In a representative democracy, there is a good chance that public choice will serve special interests rather than the interests of the majority because
   a. representatives tend to be corrupt.
   b. the median voter tends to be a member of a special-interest group.
   c. special interests have more votes.
   d. there is an asymmetry between special interests and majority interests in terms of potential individual gains and losses.
   e. all of the above

10. Rational voters often remain ignorant of the costs and benefits of many proposals because
   a. the costs of acquiring and acting on the required information exceed the expected benefits.
   b. they take democracy for granted.
   c. they know that they cannot influence politicians.
   d. they trust their representatives.
   e. they know they are not intelligent enough to understand the policies.

11. Special-interest legislation involves issues in which
   a. both the benefits and the costs are widely dispersed.
   b. the benefits are concentrated and the costs are widely dispersed.
   c. the costs are concentrated and the benefits are widely dispersed.
   d. both the benefits and costs are concentrated.
   e. either b or d

Exhibit 2

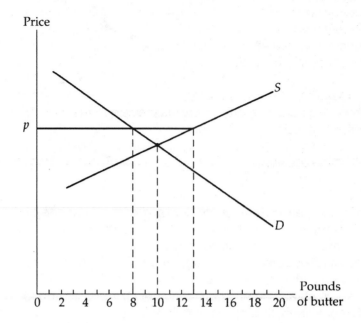

12. Exhibit 2 illustrates a system of price supports for butter. How many pounds of butter will the government buy?
    a. 0
    b. 2
    c. 3
    d. 5
    e. There is not enough information to be able to tell.

13. In Exhibit 2, the higher price for butter benefits
    a. all dairy farmers.
    b. dairy farmers who enter the industry after the subsidy is introduced.
    c. owners of resources specialized to dairy farming.
    d. consumers.
    e. The question cannot be answered without more information.

14. Which of the following is an example of rent seeking?
    a. steel companies seeking tariffs on steel
    b. dairy farmers trying to get an increase in price supports for milk
    c. accountants trying to make the CPA exam more difficult
    d. homeowners lobbying for zoning laws that restrict the number of new homes that can be built in a community
    e. all of the above

15. Resources employed in trying to get the government to redistribute income
    a. tend to create income.
    b. are used by people to help the poor.
    c. make society more productive.
    d. have little effect on government policy.
    e. generally make society less productive.

16. People use barter more when
    a. they do not have good jobs.
    b. they are unemployed.
    c. tax rates fall.
    d. tax rates increase.
    e. none of the above

17. Which of the following is **not** a part of the underground economy?
    a. A cab driver doesn't report all his income to the IRS.
    b. A drug dealer buys a large quantity of cocaine.
    c. A woman operates an unregulated taxi in New York City.
    d. A family buys a tax-exempt municipal bond to avoid taxes.
    e. All of the above are examples of underground economic activity.

18. The residual claimants of bureaus are
    a. the residents of the jurisdiction.
    b. the heads of the bureaus.
    c. the head of the executive branch of the government.
    d. the stockholders of the bureaus.
    e. none of the above. There are no residual claimants.

19. Which of the following is the source of differences between bureaus and business firms?
    a. Ownership in a firm is transferable, but ownership in a bureau is not.
    b. Firms have greater feedback from customers than bureaus do.
    c. Workers in bureaus are lazier than workers in business firms.
    d. both a and b
    e. a, b, and c

20. Legislatures often prefer dealing with bureaus to dealing with private firms because
    a. bureaus are always more efficient at spending taxpayers' money.
    b. firms tend to be too greedy.
    c. bureaus may provide legislators more opportunities to reward friends with jobs.
    d. contracts with firms are sometimes difficult to specify completely.
    e. both c and d

D. Discussion Questions

1. Distinguish among private goods, public goods, quasi-public goods, and open-access goods.

2. Police services generally are provided by government. Are police services a public good? Explain.

3. Local governments usually provide some or all of the following services. For each, indicate in which section in Exhibit 1 in the text the good or service fits.
    a. provision of parks
    b. education
    c. snow removal on streets
    d. garbage pickup
    e. street lighting

4. Is Yellowstone National Park a public good. Why or why not? Is Disneyland?

Exhibit 3
Marginal Valuation

Quantity	Alice	Bill	Cindy	Dave	Ernie	Linda
1	$10	$25	$50	$10	$12	$25
2	8	22	30	5	10	20
3	6	18	10	0	8	15
4	4	14	1	0	4	10
5	2	10	0	0	0	5
6	0	5	-50	0	0	0

5. Use Exhibit 3. If the good is a private good, what would be the quantity demanded at $10? What is the market demand schedule if the good is a public good?

6. If the good in Exhibit 3 is a public good, how much should be produced if the marginal cost of producing the good is always $95? When should zero units be produced?

7. Suppose seven people are trying to decide whether to get a pizza with pepperoni, a pizza with sausage and pepperoni, or a pizza with everything on it. Four people want everything, one wants pepperoni and sausage, and two want pepperoni only. Assume that each person prefers a pizza closer to his or her first choice to a pizza that is unlike the first choice. What is the preference of the median voter? Which pizza will be selected if the majority rules?

8. Suppose that three people favor pizza with everything, three favor pizza with pepperoni only, and one favors pizza with pepperoni and sausage. Assume that each person prefers a pizza closer to his or her first choice to a pizza that is unlike the first choice. What is the preference of the median voter? Which pizza will be selected if the majority rules?

9. Why are there likely to be many dissatisfied voters under majority rule?

10. How does representative democracy differ from direct democracy? What differences are there in the policies chosen under the different systems?

11. Explain why it is often rational for taxpayers to remain ignorant about the effects of some policies.

12. For each of the following, indicate whether the legislation is an example of traditional public-goods legislation, special interest legislation, competing interest legislation, or populist legislation.
    a. building the interstate highway system
    b. quota that limits the number of cars Japanese firms can export to the U.S.
    c. limitation of logging on government owned land in the West.
    d. Prevailing-wage legislation, which requires government agencies to pay union wages even when using non-union workers.
    e. Luxury tax on boats worth over $100,000
    f. Decision to build an army base in Louisiana instead of New Hampshire

13. What is the difference between special-interest legislation and competing-interest legislation?

14. What is rent seeking? How does rent seeking affect efficiency? Why do legislatures permit such activities?

15. Accountants who pass the CPA exam are considered to be of high quality and earn more than other accountants. Some believe that in order to keep the number of CPAs relatively low, the CPA exam is made more difficult than is necessary. Why would CPAs want to do this? Will someone who passes the exam earn rents? Explain.

16. How is the size of the underground economy related to tax rates?

17. Political corruption is relatively great in Russia today. What effect does this have on the Russian economy?

18. Distinguish between tax avoidance and tax evasion.

19. Each year, there are many wealthy people who pay very little in federal income taxes. Are they involved in tax evasion?

20. Compare and contrast bureaus and business firms.

VII. ANSWERS

A. Completion

1. rival
2. nonexclusive
3. nonrival; exclusive
4. open-access
5. vertically
6. taxes
7. median voter
8. maximize
9. rationally ignorant
10. similar
11. Competing-interest
12. rent-seeking
13. underground economy
14. evasion
15. budgets

B. True/False

1. False. Public good is also non exclusive.
2. True
3. False
4. True
5. True
6. False
7. False. The policy preferred by the median voter will be selected.
8. True
9. True
10. True
11. True
12. False
13. True
14. True
15. False
16. True
17. False. Tax avoidance is legal
18. False
19. True
20. False

C. Multiple Choice

1. e	6. e	11. b	16. d
2. d	7. b	12. d	17. d
3. b	8. a	13. c	18. a
4. d	9. d	14. e	19. d
5. e	10. a	15. e	20. e

D. Discussion Questions

1. Private goods are rival and exclusive, public goods are nonrival and nonexclusive, quasi-public goods are nonrival but exclusive, and open-access goods are rival but nonexclusive. Private goods usually are produced by private firms, and public goods by the government. Quasi-public goods can be produced by the private or the public sector. Open-access goods generally are regulated by government.

2. Police services are not a pure public good, but have some of the characteristics of a public good. To the extent the level of police services benefit everyone in a city, it is nonrival. But, the more police there are in one part of town the less police are available for another part of town. Further, there are private firms that provide police services to specific neighborhoods, so they can be considered exclusive. Probably it is best to consider police services a quasi-public good.

3. a. nonrival when not crowded and exclusive, so quasi-public good.
    b. rival and exclusive so private good (could be nonrival when the numbers are small)
    c. rival and exclusive so private good
    d. nonrival and nonexclusive so public good

4. Yellowstone and Disneyland are both examples of quasi-public goods. They are nonrivalrous when uncrowded, but they are also exclusive. The nonrival characteristic of Yellowstone is greater than Disneyland since the rides in Disneyland are rivalrous.

5. The quantity demanded at $10 is 1+5+3+1+2+4=16 units. If the good is a public good, the market demand schedule is:

Quantity	Sum of Marginal Variations
1	$132
2	95
3	57
4	33
5	17
6	-45

6. Marginal cost equals the sum of the marginal valuations at 2 units. Zero units should be produced when the marginal cost of producing the first unit exceeds $132.

7. The median voter will prefer a pizza with everything, since three people want some other kind of pizza and four want pizza with everything. The group will choose to get a pizza with everything on it.

8. The preference of the median voter is for pizza with pepperoni and sausage. This is the choice that will be made, even though only one person actually wants this kind of pizza. In each choice between two kinds of pizza, three people will join with the single individual because her preference is as close as they can get to their own preferences.

9. There will be many dissatisfied voters because only the median voters will get exactly what they most prefer.

10. In a direct democracy, people make choices by voting directly on every issue. The median voter often determines public choices in a direct democracy. In a representative democracy, people elect representatives to make public choices. Representatives must then try to respond to the various wishes of the people in their constituencies. Special-interest groups have more influence under representative democracy than under direct democracy because of the asymmetry between special interests and the common interest; individual voters concentrate on private choice rather than attempting to influence public choices.

11. The cost to a single taxpayer of a given policy is likely to be low. Further, the taxpayer is unlikely to have an effect on policy unless he or she organizes many other taxpayers. This will involve a lot of time and money. The expected benefit from getting involved is generally less than the cost of the policy that favors a special-interest group.

12. a. traditional public-good legislation with widespread benefits and costs
    b. special-interest legislation with widespread costs (car buyers), and narrow benefits (domestic auto makers)
    c. competing interests legislation with environmental groups competing with logging interests
    d. special-interest legislation with widespread costs (higher taxes and narrow benefits (union members)
    e. populist legislation with widespread benefits (lower taxes for most people) and narrow costs (the wealthy and those who produce the boats).
    f. Competing-interest legislation with residents of Louisiana competing with residents of New Hampshire

13. Special-interest legislation refers to legislation that generates concentrated benefits, but the costs are borne by many people. Competing-interest legislation involves concentrated costs and concentrated benefits. It is usually easier to get legislation through when the costs are widespread than when the costs are concentrated.

14. Rent seeking is activity undertaken by special-interest groups to persuade Congress to give them some special market advantage or transfer payments. Such activity shifts resources from the production of output to efforts to transfer income and thus tends to reduce the total output of society from what it would be if there were no rent seeking. Congress and state legislatures do not legislate against the activity because it provides political support and campaign funds to individual legislators.

15. Current CPAs want to make the tests hard so that fewer people can become CPAs. This keeps their salaries higher. Someone who passes the exam will earn rent, but the rent will not be as large as those of CPAs already in the profession. This is because people tend to invest in courses to help them pass the CPA exam. Such expenditures raise the costs of becoming a CPA. Further, the high income of CPAs may attract able people from other fields who would have earned high salaries in the other fields. That is, the opportunity cost of those who actually become CPAs may be relatively high, so their rents will not be as great as those of current CPAs.

16. Part of the underground economy exists to avoid taxes. The larger marginal tax rates are, the greater the incentive to hide income and participate in the underground economy.

17. The underground economy tends to expand when there is political corruption. One effect is   to reduce the taxes collected by the government. The size of the overall economy generally is smaller the greater the political corruption.

18. Tax avoidance is legal activity designed to reduce one's tax burden. Examples include giving to charities, buying tax-free municipal bonds, and investing in tax-deferred IRAs. Tax evasion is illegal and involves either failing to file a return or understating one's income or overstating one's deductions.

19. Not necessarily. They may own many tax-exempt municipal bonds, have capital gains losses in one year, or have paid substantial income taxes in other countries. They likely are engaged in tax avoidance, though.

20. Bureaus are government agencies designed to implement some legislation. Their revenues generally come from taxes allocated by the legislature. Residents in the jurisdiction are the residual claimants. Unlike stockholders, they cannot sell their ownership in the bureau if they are unhappy with the performance of the bureau. It is also more difficult for the customers of the bureau to provide the bureau with information concerning their level of satisfaction with the service the bureau provides than is the case with customers of business firms. Consequently, bureaucrats have less incentive to minimize costs or operate efficiently than do managers of business firms.

CHAPTER 17

Externalities and the Environment

I. INTRODUCTION

Our implicit assumption throughout most of the text has been that property rights are well defined and easily enforced. Under such conditions, we expect that market prices will allocate resources to their highest-valued use, and the economy will operate efficiently. There are many situations in which property rights are not well defined, however, and society ends up using a resource inefficiently. This chapter explores some of these situations.

II. OUTLINE

1. Externalities and the Common Pool Problem.

    1.1 Renewable Resources
       a. A resource is exhaustible if it is available in a finite amount and cannot be renewed.
       b. A resource is *renewable* if periodic use of it can continue indefinitely.
       c. Biological resources such as fish, timber, and grasslands are renewable resources if they are husbanded properly.
       d. Some renewable resources are *open-access resources*, which means that it is costly to exclude people from using the resource.
       e. Open-access resources are often subject to the common pool problem.
       f. *Negative externalities* arise when there are no enforceable property rights to commonly owned resources, and the market prices fail to reflect the cost to society of the externalities.
       g. Property rights allow individuals the right to control the use of certain resources.
       h. Not all resources are owned as private property because defining and enforcing property rights on some resources is very costly.
       i. Pollution arises because private property rights to some open-access resources are not practical.

    1.2 Resolving the Common-Pool Problem
       a. Open-access resources tend to be overused or overharvested.
       b. The common-pool problem can be reduced if some central authority imposes restrictions on resource use.
       c. Government regulations can improve allocative efficiency when imposing and enforcing private property rights would be too costly.

2. Optimal level of pollution

    2.1 External Costs with Fixed Technology
       a. When the only way to reduce a negative externality is to reduce output, the negative externality occurs with a fixed production technology.
       b. The marginal external cost of a negative externality is the extra cost to society that is not reflected in the market price of a good or service.

c. The marginal social cost includes both the marginal private cost and the marginal external cost.
d. Since market participants ignore the marginal external cost, equilibrium occurs at a greater rate of output than is optimal. The equilibrium generates a market failure.
e. The efficient rate of output occurs where the demand curve (reflecting marginal benefits) and the marginal social cost curve intersect.
f. A tax equal to marginal external cost would induce industry to generate the optimal rate of output.

2.2 External Costs with Variable Technology
a. In the long run, firms can change their resource mix to reduce negative externalities.
b. The marginal social cost curve of pollution abatement slopes upward; the marginal social benefit curve of pollution control slopes downward.
c. The optimal level of pollution abatement occurs where the marginal social cost of further abatement equals the marginal social benefit of that abatement.
d. Pollution should be abated only as long as the marginal benefit of additional abatement exceeds its marginal cost.

2.3 *CASE STUDY:* Destruction of the Tropical Rain Forests

2.4 The Coase Theorem
a. Ronald Coase points out that external costs can arise when the activities of two parties are incompatible.
b. The efficient solution to the problem of externalities depends on which party can avoid the problem at lower cost.
c. With a private property rights arrangement, the two parties could agree on the efficient outcome.
d. The *Coase theorem* states that an efficient solution to the problem of externalities will be achieved regardless of which party is assigned property rights as long as bargaining costs are small.

2.5 Markets for Pollution Rights
a. One solution to the problem of pollution is to sell the right to pollute.
b. The price per unit of discharge is often called an *effluent fee.*
c. Only those who value the pollution rights the most will buy the rights, so an efficient method of reducing pollution is achieved.
d. A problem is that legislation dealing with pollution suffers from rent-seeking activities as does other public policy questions in a representative democracy.
e. Prior to 1990, the government tended to use command-and-control environmental regulation.
f. The market for pollution rights utilize an economists efficiency approach.

3. Environmental Protection in the United States

3.1 Air Pollution
a. The Clean Air Act of 1970 set national standards for the amount of pollution that can be emitted.
b. Average pollution levels are down from the 1970s.
c. A tentative accord was reached in Kyoto, Japan in 1997 to improve air quality on a global scale.

3.3   Water Pollution
    a.   The major sources of water pollution are sewage and chemicals.
    b.   Most of the money of the Environmental Protection Agency has gone to constructing sewage treatment plants.
    c.   Most chemical pollution results from runoff of pesticides and fertilizers used in agriculture.

3.4   Hazardous Waste and the Superfund
    a.   The Comprehensive Environmental Response, Compensation, and Liability Act of 1980, or Superfund law, requires that anyone generating, storing, or transporting hazardous waste must pay to clean it up.
    b.   Superfund administrators have often reacted to political pressure in addressing pollution rather than tackling the most widespread or long-term problems first.

3.5   Solid Waste: "Paper or Plastic?"
    a.   The country is running out of landfills.
    b.   In the United States, only a small percentage of solid waste is recycled.
    c.   Recycling also imposes costs on the environment.

4.   Positive Externalities
    a.   The benefits of consuming some goods accrue to people other than the consumer.
    b.   Marginal social benefits include both the marginal private benefits and the positive externalities.
    c.   An individual consumer making decisions on the basis of marginal private benefits and marginal private costs will underconsume a good that generates positive externalities.
    d.   The government often encourages the consumption of goods with positive externalities by subsidizing consumption of the good.

III.   DISCUSSION

Externalities and the Common Pool Problem

A resource is renewable if periodic use of it can continue indefinitely. Most biological resources, such as fish, forests, and grasslands are renewable. A renewable resource that is also an open-access good is subject to the common-pool problem. Such goods tend to be overused or overharvested. With an open-access good, each person may make decisions concerning the use of the resource without taking into consideration the effects of this use on the other owners.

Suppose a community sets aside a pasture where all members can graze their cows. The land will accommodate only a certain number of cows, and any more than this number will lead to overgrazing and diminish the quality of the pasture. A person's marginal private benefit of placing a cow in the pasture is the value of the milk the person gets from the cow. The marginal cost is the price of keeping the cow and the cost of the deterioration in the pasture caused by an extra cow's grazing in it. This latter cost, though, is borne by the community as a whole, so each individual bears only a small portion of this cost. That is, the marginal social cost of the extra cow is greater than the marginal private cost of the extra cow. Consequently, an individual is likely to add an additional cow to the pasture even though the result may be overuse of the land. If everybody adds extra cows to the pasture, the collective result is a serious overuse of the land.

In such cases, rational decision making on the part of each individual leads to decisions that are harmful for the group as a whole.

The efficiency of markets is directly related to the existence of a system of *private property rights.* Resource owners with easily enforceable private property rights have an incentive to devote their resources to their highest-valued use because they maximize their own return by doing so. This is an example of Adam Smith's "invisible hand" at work-resources are used efficiently when people act in their own self-interest.

Negative externalities are unpriced by-products of consumption or production that impose costs on other consumer firms. Pollution is the best-known example of a negative externality, but it is certainly not the only example. A homeowner who fails to maintain his home or property imposes negative externalities on his neighbors; a teenager who plays a radio at high volume imposes negative externalities on those nearby; a diner with very bad table manners imposes negative externalities on other patrons of a restaurant. Pollution and other negative externalities arise when there are no practical enforceable private property right to open-access resources.

The *common pool problem* applies to many situations: air and water pollution, the hunting of whales today or buffalo in the nineteenth century, fishing for lobsters in New England or for redfish in Louisiana. Eventually, the overuse of a resource results in a change in property rights, government action, or depletion of the resource. One solution is to convert property held in common to private property. This solution has often been used and offers the best chance of the resource's being used efficiently. However, it is not possible to assign private property rights to some resources—the air or whales, for example. Another solution is for the government to take action and restrict the use of the resource. Hunting and fishing seasons and limits on takes, a ban on killing buffalo, and restrictions on air pollution are examples of this response. One difficulty with this approach is that there is not a world government that can enforce a ban in all nations. As a result, some common pool problems are difficult to solve. For example, the overharvesting of whales is not as easy to stop as was the overharvesting of buffalo.

Optimal level of pollution

Negative externalities generate *marginal social costs* that are greater than marginal private costs. The individual equates marginal private benefits and marginal private costs instead of equating marginal private benefits and marginal social costs. Since marginal social costs are greater than marginal private costs, the individual selects a rate of output that exceeds the optimal rate. (In this case, we are assuming that marginal private benefits and *marginal social benefits* are the same.)

Most people agree that the less pollution there is, the better. However, zero pollution is not optimal because there are substantial costs to reducing pollution. The level of pollution can be reduced only by increasing the costs of production that generate the pollution (e.g., by installing pollution abatement equipment in factories) or by reducing the production that generates the pollution. Thus, one consequence of reducing pollution is to reduce the quantity of consumer goods and services available. Of course, there are also benefits to reducing pollution, such as improved health and increased attractiveness of the environment. The total benefits of pollution abatement will increase with additional abatement, but the marginal benefits will decline; the marginal costs of pollution abatement will increase with additional abatement. The optimal quantity of abatement is determined at the point where marginal social benefits and marginal social costs are equal. Study Exhibit 2 in the text carefully to be sure that you understand this.

The Coase Analysis of Externalities

Ronald Coase offers a different way of treating the question of externalities. If a factory emits pollution that bothers the residents in its vicinity, it is creating a negative externality. But why does the externality exist? The traditional response is that the externality exists simply because the factory emits pollution. Coase argues that this is incorrect—the externality exists because the pollution from the factory disturbs the people living in the vicinity. If the factory is removed, the externality no longer is a problem; the same is true if the residents are removed. That is, an externality is not the fault of one party but is the result of the incompatible activities of both parties. It takes at least two to have an externality.

Coase also points out that people have an incentive to alter the situation when there is a negative externality. Suppose the factory could reduce the pollution for a cost of $1,000, and that the pollution is imposing costs on the local residents (in the form of health problems and lower property values) that total $2,000. In this situation, society is better off if the pollution is reduced, for the savings to the residents ($2,000) exceed the cost to the factory ($1,000). Will the pollution be curtailed? According to Coase, it will be if property rights are assigned and bargaining costs are low. The parties involved will negotiate an agreement that produces this result. Suppose that the law allows the residents to force the factory to spend the $1,000 to reduce the pollution. Then obviously they will force the factory to do so. But what if the factory has the legal right to pollute? It will still reduce its level of pollution because the residents will agree to pay the factory to do so. That is, the residents would be willing to pay the $1,000 to have the pollution reduced because the cost of the pollution is greater than the cost of reducing it. The negotiated solution will reduce the pollution. But what if the cost to the residents is only $500? In this case, the factory will continue to pollute. If the factory is liable for damages, it will pay the $500 in damages because this is less than the $1,000 it takes to clean up the pollution. If the factory is not liable, then the residents will be unable to pay the factory to reduce the pollution level because the most they will offer is $500. Hence, the efficient outcome is achieved via negotiations when property rights are assigned and negotiating costs are minimal.

What happens when negotiating is very costly? Then there is no reason to think that the outcome will be efficient. In this situation, the courts or the government may have to step in. Coase argues that if this happens, the liability should be determined on the basis of which party can avoid the costly interaction (the negative externality) at the lowest cost. In this way, the combined private and external costs of production are minimized.

The optimal level of pollution can be achieved in some situations by selling pollution rights. Under such a system, firms would pay for the right to pollute—for example, to dispose of a given level of effluents into a commonly owned resource, a river. The optimal level of pollution can be achieved by this method when polluters can be easily identified and monitored. The price per unit of discharge is called an effluent fee. A market for pollution rights is a more efficient way to reduce pollution than is a system of command-and-control regulations.

Environmental Protection

The federal government has attempted to reduce pollution by imposing environmental standards on industry. The Clean Air Act of 1970 established national standards for the amount of pollution that can be emitted into the atmosphere. The government has also established standards for water pollution. Two pollution problems that have not been addressed adequately as yet are solid waste and hazardous materials.

Positive Externalities

Positive externalities arise when the unpriced by-product of consumption or production benefits other consumers or firms. When positive externalities arise, people do not produce or consume as much of the good as is optimal from society's viewpoint. Education is an example of a good that generates positive externalities. If all schools were private, then individuals would face higher prices for education and would consume less education. Each person would calculate the expected marginal private benefits of additional units of education and purchase additional education until the marginal private benefit equaled the marginal private cost. However, education benefits not only the individual but also others. The educated person is less likely to commit crimes, to be on welfare, or to be a burden on other members of society. The marginal social benefit of education thus is greater than the marginal private benefit. Usually people do not take into account these benefits that spill over onto others when deciding how much education to purchase. If they took these external benefits into consideration, people would purchase more education. To encourage people to purchase more education, the government subsidizes education in this country.

IV. LAGNIAPPE

Exporting Pollution

Pollution abatement requirements imposed on industry by the federal government generate higher production costs for many products. This is especially true for products that generate serious pollution, such as steel. Since firms' costs increase because of the pollution abatement efforts, U.S. firms find it more difficult to compete with producers from other countries. Consequently, their production levels decrease and imports increase. The increase in imports increases production of these pollution-causing products by other countries. In a sense, the United States is exporting pollution to other countries that are producing more of the goods and selling them to the United States.

Question to Think About: Why do the governments of other countries allow the increased production of such products if it also causes increased pollution?

Rationality in Los Angeles

It is well known that Los Angeles has a smog problem, and that pollution from automobiles is a major source of the smog. Consequently, California has the strictest pollution-control requirements for autos of any state in the country. But the pollution abatement equipment on a car imposes costs on the car owner above and beyond the higher sticker price for the car. The equipment makes a car less fuel efficient and reduces the performance of the engine. These costs are borne by the individual car owner, and the owner can benefit by removing the pollution abatement equipment. However, if the owner removes the equipment, the amount of pollution in Los Angeles increases.

Why would a car owner remove the equipment? The owner realizes that the total amount of pollution in Los Angeles is not affected in any meaningful way if he or she removes the pollution abatement equipment on one car. That is, the extra costs to society are virtually zero, whereas the benefits to the car owner are positive. So a car owner who removes the pollution abatement equipment benefits, and nobody is really hurt. This is true for an individual. The problem is that when one million people reach the same conclusion and also remove pollution abatement equipment from their cars, the combined effects of the extra pollution are significant. Note that people who do not remove the pollution abatement equipment from their cars cannot bring about a noticeable improvement in air quality because it is true that the extra pollution from one more car is minuscule.

Question to Think About: Why would a person not remove the pollution abatement equipment from a car under these circumstances?

V. KEY TERMS

Exhaustible resource
Renewable resource
Private property rights
Common pool problem
Fixed-production technology
Marginal social cost
Market failure
Pollution tax

Variable technology
Marginal social benefit
Greenhouse effect
Coase theorem
Point pollution
Nonpoint pollution
Command-and-control environment regulations
Economic efficiency approach
Recycling

VI. QUESTIONS

A. Completion

1. _____ property rights allow individuals to control the use of certain resources now and in the future.

2. A resource is _____ if it is in a finite quantity and cannot be renewed.

3. A _____ resource is one that can be used at a certain rate indefinitely because the amount that is used can be replaced.

4. Open-access resources are often subject to _____ problems.

5. A resource that is owned in common tends to be _____.

6. If the only way to reduce pollution from the production of a good is to reduce the amount of the good produced, the technology used to produce the good is called a _____ technology.

7. The marginal social cost of production includes the marginal private cost of production and the marginal _____ cost of production.

8. _____ reduces the quality of air because there are fewer trees to convert carbon dioxide into oxygen.

9. The _____ states that the efficient solution to the problem of externalities will be achieved by bargaining if property rights are assigned and bargaining costs are low.

10. One way of keeping pollution to an optimal level is for government to sell _____.

11. _____ pollution refers to water pollution from factories; _____ pollution refers to water pollution from the runoff of pesticides and fertilizers from agricultural land.

12. Prior to 1970, control of pesticides was handled by the U.S. _____.

13. The _____ gives the federal government authority over hazardous waste sites.

14. Most solid waste in the United States is disposed of by using _____.

15. _____ is the process of converting waste products into reusable material.

B. True/False

_____ 1. A resource is renewable if you can take as much as you want every year and still have some in the future.

_____ 2. The common pool problem refers to the overuse of goods used by some large corporations.

_____ 3. Open access resources are often overused.

_____ 4. Negative externalities are more likely to arise when a resource is privately owned than if the resource is an open-access resource.

_____ 5. The way to establish ownership of a fish in the ocean is to catch it.

_____ 6. The government can use a tax to force competitive firms to use a resource at the optimal rate.

_____ 7. Private property rights are usually easy to establish on open-access resources.

_____ 8. An individual's demand curve for a good is the good's marginal social benefit curve.

_____ 9. Pollution arises because there are no enforceable property rights to some commonly owned resources.

_____ 10. With fixed technology, the only way to reduce pollution is to reduce output.

_____ 11. Unlike the production of other goods, the production of cleaner air is not subject to diminishing marginal returns.

_____ 12. The optimal level of pollution is zero.

_____ 13. The world's rain forests tend to be located in countries that are relatively poor.

_____ 14. According to Ronald Coase, it is always possible to find out who is at fault when there is an externality.

_____ 15. The efficient solution to an externality problem depends on which party can avoid the problem at the lowest cost.

_____ 16. Selling permits to pollute can reduce pollution, but it is an inefficient solution to the problem.

_____ 17. Positive externalities tend to be overproduced by competitive firms.

_____ 18. Over 80 percent of air pollution in the United States comes from industry.

_____ 19. The United States and Japan rely on incineration of solid waste to the same extent.

_____ 20. Most of the Superfund budget is spent on costs associated with litigation.

C.   Multiple Choice

1. Which of the following is an example of a renewable resource?
   a. oil
   b. agricultural soil
   c. silver
   d. bauxite
   e. none of the above

2. Resources that are not privately owned often are
   a. overused.
   b. exhaustible.
   c. nonappropriable.
   d. all of the above
   e. a and c only

3. Open-access resources tend to be
   a. used until the net marginal value of additional use is less than zero.
   b. used until the marginal private cost and marginal social cost are equalized.
   c. resources in abundant supply and thus have no price.
   d. overharvested, because everyone uses the resource until the net marginal value of additional use is zero.
   e. owned by the military.

4. Which of the following is an example of an open-access resource?
   a. air
   b. oceans
   c. a military base
   d. all of the above
   e. a and b

5. Private property differs from open-access property in that
   a. private property involves consumer goods and open-access property involves productive resources.
   b. private property refers to things owned by individuals and open-access property refers to things owned by governments.
   c. private property is owned by specific individuals whereas open-access property is owned by everyone.
   d. private property involves goods that are scarce and open-access property involves goods that are not scarce.
   e. private property is owned by individuals and open-access property is owned by corporations.

6. Pollution exists because
   a. people do not realize that their actions cause pollution.
   b. the government does not subsidize production of goods characterized by negative externalities to the optimal degree.
   c. people have bounded rationality and are not able to calculate their marginal private benefits and marginal private costs.
   d. people only care about consumer goods and not about the quality of the environment.
   e. there are no enforceable property rights in the case of commonly owned resources.

7. The efficient level of output of a good with negative externalities is where
   a. marginal private benefits equal marginal private costs.
   b. marginal private benefits equal marginal social costs.
   c. total private benefits equal total private costs.
   d. total private benefits equal total social costs.
   e. the pollution tax equals marginal private costs.

8. The marginal social benefit of pollution abatement
   a. increases at an increasing rate with the quantity of pollution abated.
   b. increases at a decreasing rate with the quantity of pollution abated.
   c. decreases in direct relation to the quantity of pollution abated.
   d. is constant as the quantity of pollution abated increases.
   e. can be increasing, decreasing, or constant relative to the quantity of pollution abated, depending upon the type of pollution under consideration.

9. An increase in the costs of pollution abatement would
   a. cause the optimal quantity of abatement to increase.
   b. cause the optimal quantity of abatement to decrease.
   c. have no effect on the optimal quantity of abatement.
   d. have no effect on the optimal quantity of abatement unless the benefits of abatement changed also.
   e. The question cannot be answered without more information.

10. Improving air quality benefits society as long as
    a. any air pollution exists.
    b. the marginal benefit of cleaner air is positive.
    c. the marginal cost of cleaner air is more than the marginal benefit of cleaner air.
    d. the marginal cost of cleaner air is less than the marginal benefit of cleaner air.
    e. there are any social costs to pollution.

11. Which of the following could reduce the effects of a negative externality to the socially optimal level?
    a. converting an open-access resource to a privately owned resource
    b. converting a privately owned resource to a government owned resource
    c. setting a tax equal to the marginal private cost of the externality
    d. prohibiting production of the good
    e. none of the above

12. Deforestation is the result of
    a. growing world demand for lumber.
    b. clearing of land for farming.
    c. lack of private property rights on most of the world's rain forests.
    d. all of the above.
    e. a and b only.

13. Coase argued that the efficient resolution of an externality problem will be achieved as long as
    a. the government assigns property rights to one of the parties and bargaining costs are low.
    b. the government imposes a tax on the party generating the negative externality.
    c. the government assigns property rights to the party that is able to avoid the problem at the lowest cost.
    d. the parties do not act selfishly.
    e. none of the above. He argued that an efficient outcome will not be achieved.

14. According to the Coase theorem, the solution to an externality problem is likely to be inefficient if
    a. transaction costs are very high.
    b. property rights are not assigned to one of the parties.
    c. it is difficult to determine who is at fault.
    d. all of the above
    e. a and b

15. Suppose the government has sold pollution permits that set a maximum total allowable level of pollution that can be discharged into a certain river. If a new firm wants to set up a factory along the river and wants to discharge effluents into the river,
    a. it will be unable to do so.
    b. it will be given a permit to pollute because it is new.
    c. it will buy a permit from another firm so long as it values the discharge rights more than the firm currently holding the permit.
    d. it will sue and receive another firm's permit if it can prove it values the permit more than the firm that currently holds the permit.
    e. none of the above

16. Which of the following is true of water pollution in the United States that is caused by chemicals?
    a. The majority of the pollution is point pollution which is pollution from factories.
    b. The majority of the pollution is nonpoint pollution which is pollution from factories.
    c. The majority of the pollution is nonpoint pollution which is runoff of pesticides and fertilizers from agriculture.
    d. The majority of the pollution is caused by sewage.
    e. The EPA has spent most of its money on cleaning up water that has been polluted by chemicals.

17. According to the Superfund law, the cleanup of hazardous waste is to be paid for by
    a. those who generate the waste.
    b. those who store the waste.
    c. those who transport the waste.
    d. all of the above.
    e. a and b.

18. In the absence of government intervention, a person who consumes a good that is characterized by positive externalities
    a. overconsumes the good because the good is usually commonly owned.
    b. underconsumes the good because he or she does not take into consideration the benefits of consumption that accrue to others.
    c. underconsumes the good because he or she does not realize how much private benefit the good really provides.
    d. overconsumes the good because he or she does not bear the full cost of the consumption.
    e. none of the above

Exhibit 1

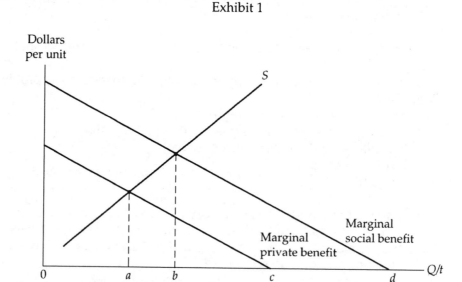

19. Exhibit 1 illustrates supply and demand for a good that generates a positive externality. In the absence of government intervention, the output that will be selected by an individual is _____; the optimal output is _____.
    a. c; d
    b. b; d
    c. a; c
    d. a; b
    e. b; a

20. The optimal amount of the good in Exhibit 1 can be achieved if the government
   a. imposes a tax on the good.
   b. provides a subsidy equal to the amount *a-b*.
   c. provides a subsidy equal to the amount *c-d*.
   d. provides a subsidy equal to the vertical distance between the marginal social benefit curve and the marginal private benefit curve.
   e. none of the above

D. Discussion Questions

1. Explain how property rights and negative externalities are related.

2. Why are open-access resources often overused?

3. If easily enforceable private property rights allow the most efficient use of resources, why are people not assigned property rights to all resources?

4. What is the difference between fixed production technology and variable technology when it comes to pollution reduction?

5. How can a tax be used to correct a problem of negative externalities?

6. Explain why the optimal level of pollution is not zero.

7. Suppose there are four factories along a river and each dumps the same amount of pollution into the river. The government determines that the amount of pollution should be cut in half. The only way the pollution can be reduced is if one or more of the firms closes down and moves elsewhere. The firms' costs of moving are as follows: firm 1, $5,000; firm 2, $10,000; firm 3, $4,000; and firm 4, $7,500. If the government sells two permits to pollute, which firms will buy them and how much will they pay? Which firms will move? Why is this solution optimal?

8. Explain how the deforestation of tropical rain forests is related to the greenhouse effect.

9. According to Coase, what causes a negative externality?

10. Suppose a factory is next door to a laundry, and the smoke emitted by the factory increases the costs of operating the laundry. The laundry's extra cost is $500; the cost of eliminating pollution by shutting down the factory is $600.
   a. If transaction costs are zero, what will happen if the laundry has the legal right to receive compensation for pollution damages? What will happen if the factory has the legal right to pollute?
   b. Suppose a scrubber that eliminates pollution can be installed at the factory for $550. Transaction costs are zero. What will be the result? What if the cost of the scrubber is $250?
   c. Suppose that the costs of negotiating and bargaining are very great, so no bargaining takes place. What will happen if the laundry has the legal right to operate free of pollution from the factory? if the factory has the legal right to generate pollution?

11. Suppose there are three firms along a river. Each discharges 1,000 units of effluent into the river. The government determines that 2,000 units of effluent is the maximum that should go into the river, and the government will sell two permits to the highest bidder. A device that eliminates the effluent can be installed by any firm. It would cost firm A $10,000, firm B $15,000, and firm C $20,000 to install the device. Which firms will buy the permits and at what price? If a fourth firm enters and the cleaning device costs it $25,000, what will happen?

12. According to an EPA study, the health hazards of Superfund sites have been greatly exaggerated and air pollution tends to be a bigger health hazard than toxic waste dumps. Why is more attention focused on toxic waste dumps than on air pollution?

13. Explain why the Japanese use landfills for disposal of solid waste much less than we do in the U.S. Why might the U. S. behave more like the Japanese in the future?

14. Suppose a freak of nature caused the Los Angeles area to be free of air pollution forever. How might this affect the residents of Los Angeles?

15. Explain why goods characterized by positive externalities tend to be consumed in quantities that are less than optimal.

16. Education is often used as an example of a positive externality. Are the external benefits greater for elementary, secondary, or college education? Explain.

VII.   ANSWERS

A.   Completion

1. Private
2. exhaustible
3. renewable
4. common pool
5. overutilized
6. fixed production
7. external
8. Deforestation
9. Coase theorem
10. pollution rights
11. Point; nonpoint
12. Department of Agriculture
13. Superfund law
14. landfills
15. Recycling

B.   True/False

1. False.
   only if it is allowed to replenish itself; you cannot take as much as you want each year because the resource will be used up faster than it can be replenished.
2. False
3. True
4. False
5. True
6. True
7. False
10. True
11. False
12. False. The optimal level occurs where the marginal social cost of abatement equals the marginal social benefit of abatement.
13. True
14. False
15. True
16. False
17. False
18. False

8.	False		19.	False
9.	True		20.	True

C. Multiple Choice

1.	b	6.	e	11.	a	16.	c
2.	e	7.	b	12.	d	17.	d
3.	d	8.	c	13.	a	18.	b
4.	e	9.	b	14.	e	19.	d
5.	c	10.	d	15.	c	20.	d

D. Discussion Questions

1. Negative externalities may arise when a resource is owned in common by the members of a community. Each individual has an incentive to use the resource more intensively than it would be used if it were owned privately. Everybody ignores the effects of their actions on the other members of the community. The combined actions of everyone in the community result in overuse of the resource.

2. Anyone can use an open-access resource, but the full costs of using the resource are not borne by the person using it. Hence, each uses the resource more than is optimal.

3. It is impossible to define and enforce private property rights for some resources; the air and the oceans are obvious examples.

4. The only way to reduce pollution associated with a good produced with fixed-production technology is to reduce production of the good. With variable technology, there are ways of reducing pollution without reducing output of the good.

5. When production of a good generates a negative externality, some costs associated with the production are borne by people other than the producers of the good. The producers only take into consideration their own marginal private costs of production. A tax is a way to make the producers bear the full cost of their actions; it induces them to produce less of the good that is generating the negative externality.

6. Cleaning up pollution is costly, both in terms of resources devoted to cleanup efforts and in terms of a reduction in the quantity of consumer goods available to society. The marginal social cost of cleanup will increase and the marginal social benefit of cleanup will fall as cleanup efforts increase. The optimum level of cleanup is the level at which the marginal benefit of cleanup equals the marginal cost of cleanup. As long as costs are positive, the optimal level of pollution will be greater than zero.

7. Firms 2 and 4 will buy the permits at a price of $7,500 each, since this is the most that firm 4 will pay for a permit. Neither of the other two firms would be willing to pay that much, since it is cheaper for them to move. This result is optimal because the problem is solved at the lowest cost: the pollution created by the two firms with the cheapest moving costs is eliminated; total pollution is cut in half.

8. The greenhouse effect results from an increase in carbon dioxide in the atmosphere. Forests convert carbon dioxide into oxygen, so the depletion of tropical rain forests retards the rate at which carbon dioxide is being converted to oxygen.

9. A negative externality is caused by incompatible activities of two parties. If bargaining costs are relatively high, the two parties will not necessarily negotiate an efficient solution.

10. a. If the laundry is entitled to compensation for pollution damages, the factory will pay the laundry $500 in damages and continue to emit pollution, since the cost of paying damages is less than the cost of eliminating pollution. If the factory has the legal right to pollute, it will continue to operate (and to pollute). That is, the factory continues to pollute in either case. However, when the factory has pollution rights, it does not pay the laundry $500.

    b. The scrubber will not be installed, regardless of the parties' compensation or pollution rights, because at $550 the cost of the scrubber is more than the cost of the pollution. If the scrubber costs $250, it will be installed. If the laundry has compensation rights, then the factory will install the scrubber, since the $250 for the scrubber is less than the $500 it would have to pay in damages. If the factory has pollution rights, then the laundry will pay the factory to install the scrubber.

    c. If the laundry has the right to operate free of pollution, the factory will be forced to stop polluting even if its costs of doing so are larger than the laundry's costs. If the factory has pollution rights, it will continue to produce and impose pollution costs on the laundry. The outcome depends on who is assigned the property rights.

11. Firms B and C will buy pollution permits for $10,000 each, since firm A will drop out of the bidding at that price. Firm A will buy the pollution control device. If the new firm entered, it would buy a pollution permit from firm B for a price between $15,000 and $20,000, and then firm B would buy a pollution control device.

12. Those who are near a toxic waste dump know it and exert political pressure to close it down; those who are affected by air pollution are less likely to be aware of the danger and are less likely to apply political pressure.

13. Land is much more abundant in the United States than it is in Japan, which makes it less costly in the United States to use land for landfills than it is in Japan. As U.S. landfills close down, however, and it becomes more costly to open new ones, the cost of using landfills for solid waste will rise. Consequently, Americans will probably use landfills less in the future and turn more to burning and recycling.

14. The effects of such an event on residents of Los Angeles would be many and varied. On the positive side, clean air would mean fewer health risks, greater ability to enjoy the beauty of the area, lower costs for washing cars and painting houses, and the like. There would also be some negative effects, however. The improved air quality would probably lead to an influx of people into the area, which would cause greater congestion, crime, water pollution, and so forth.

15. People make decisions on the basis of the marginal private benefits and marginal private costs they face. A positive externality implies that people other than the decision maker are receiving benefits from the consumption of the good. These benefits are not considered by the decision-maker, who only equates marginal private benefits and marginal private costs in determining what quantity to consume. Since the good is being undervalued from society's perspective, too little is being consumed.

16. The external benefits of education are associated with people being better citizens, able to calculate and pay their taxes and so on. Elementary education, where one learns to read and write and to do simple mathematics, offers the greatest external benefits.

CHAPTER 18

Income Distribution and Poverty

I. INTRODUCTION

A family's income is determined by the resources it owns and the prices of those resources. Families that own few resources or whose resources command a very low price will earn less than those that own more or more valuable resources. The result is that the distribution of income is not equal. Some families have very large incomes; others live in poverty. In this chapter, we will examine how the distribution of income is measured and determined and describe government programs designed to reduce the level of poverty in this country.

II. OUTLINE

1. The Distribution of Household Income

   1.1 Income Distribution by Quintiles
   a. The share of income going to the top quintile of households has increased and the share going to the bottom quintile has decreased slightly in recent years.
   b. An important reason for the growing share of income to the highest group is the growth of two earner households in the top group and single-parent households in the lowest group.

   1.2 The Lorenz Curve
   a. The Lorenz Curve shows the distribution of income graphically.
   b. The further the Lorenz curve is from the line of even distribution, the more regular the distribution of income is.

   1.3 A College Education Pays More.
   a. Between 1980 and 2000, the real median wage for those with only a high school education declined 6 percent, while the real median wage for college graduates increased 12 percent.
   b. More educated workers have done better because:
   (1) demand for knowledge workers has increased
   (2) industry deregulation, declining unionization, and greater international trade have reduced the demand for unskilled workers.
   (3) immigration has caused the supply of unskilled workers to increase.

   1.4 Problems with Distributional Benchmarks
   a. There is no objective standard for evaluating them.
   b. Accounting for taxes and transfer payments reduces income inequality.
   c. Households are of different sizes.
   d. Income distribution estimates include only reported income.
   e. Household expenditures are more evenly distributed than income.

1.5 Why Do Household Incomes Differ?
   a. The number of family members who work differs.
   b. There are differences in education, training, and ability.
   c. The age of the family head affects income.

2. Poverty and the Poor

2.1 Official Poverty Level
   a. To derive the official poverty level, the U.S. government estimates the cost of minimum food consumption for each family size.
   b. This number is multiplied by three to calculate the official poverty level for each family size.
   c. The number of people below the poverty line fell from 1959 to 1973 but has fluctuated since. The most recent rate was lower than the rate in 1973.

2.2 Programs to Help the Poor
   a. The U.S. social insurance system is designed to help those who have worked but are now retired, temporarily unemployed, or unable to work because of total disability.
   b. U.S. income assistance programs provide money and in-kind assistance to the poor even if they have not worked or contributed to the program.
      (1) Income assistance programs are *means tested*, i.e., the programs require that a household's income and/or assets fall below a certain level before the household members can qualify.
      (2) People who qualify are entitled to receive the benefits of the program, so these programs are also called *entitlement programs*.
   c. There are two primary cash transfer programs.
      (1) Aid to Families with Dependent Children provides cash to poor households with children.
      (2) Supplemental Security Income provides cash to the indigent elderly and the totally disabled.
   d. The federal government provides an earned-income credit to help the working poor.
   e. There are several in-kind transfer programs, including food stamps, Medicaid, and housing assistance programs.

3. Who Are the Poor?

3.1 Poverty and Age
   a. Poverty rates differ by age.
   b. The poverty rate for the elderly has fallen dramatically over the last forty years because of increases in Social Security and Medicare transfers.

3.2 Poverty and Public Choice. The elderly are a powerful interest group who have been successful in lobbying Congress for greater Social Security benefits.

3.3 The Feminization of Poverty
   a. Married couples have poverty rates only one-third that of female householders.
   b. Hispanic families have the highest poverty rates.
   c. The highest U.S. poverty rate is among Hispanic families headed by women.
   d. Households headed by women have become an increasingly large proportion of house-holds in poverty.
   e. The growth in the number of poor families since 1969 resulted primarily from the growth in the number of female householders.

3.4 Poverty and Discrimination
   a. Nonwhite workers earn less than white workers on average.
   b. When factors such as education, age, and job experience are considered, the gap between nonwhite and white workers narrows. Differences in education and job experience could themselves reflect past discrimination.

3.5 Affirmative Action
   a. The federal government requires firms that do business with the government to meet numerical hiring, training, and promotion goals for minorities.
   b. The constitutionality of some affirmative action plans has been questioned in recent years.
   c. The distribution of income among black families is more uneven than it is among the population as a whole.

4. Unintended Consequences of Income Assistance

4.1 Disincentives. Families that do earn income see transfers reduced sharply as a result, which discourages them from working.

4.2 Does Welfare Cause Dependency?
   a. Most recipients receive welfare benefits for only a short time.
   b. There is a correlation between people's income levels and the income levels of their parents.

5. Welfare Reform

5.1 Recent Reforms
   a. Many states require welfare recipients to seek work or participate in training programs.
   b. The Personal Responsibility and Work Reconciliation Act of 1996 was the biggest reform in the welfare system in the last 60 years.
      (1) The act replaced AFDC with Temporary Assistance for Needy Families (TANF)
      (2) TANF offers a block grant to states to run their welfare programs.
      (3) States are granted wide latitude to run their own welfare programs.
      (4) The act imposes a lifetime limit of five years a recipient can be on welfare
      (5) Benefits are limited for non-citizens and for teenage mothers not living at home.
      (6) The act tightens eligibility requirements for disabled children receiving Supplemental Security Income
   c. States have an incentive to constrain the growth of welfare rolls.

5.2 CASE STUDY: Is Welfare-to-Work Working?

5.3 CASE STUDY: Oregon's Program of "Tough Love"

III. DISCUSSION

The Distribution of Household Income

If all families earned the same income, there would be an equal distribution of income. This is not the case in the United States, which has an unequal distribution of income. There are many ways to measure the distribution of income. One way is to assign families to equal-sized groups so that the lowest-income families are grouped together. The next group consists of the next-lowest income families, and so on. Exhibit 1 shows two hypothetical distributions using five equal-sized groups, or quintiles, in each case. Income distribution B is more unequal than A.

Exhibit 1

Income Distribution

	Lowest Fifth	Second-Lowest Fifth	Middle Fifth	Second-Highest Fifth	Highest Fifth
A	15%	18%	20%	22%	25%
B	2%	8%	18%	22%	50%

Exhibit 1 in the textbook provides actual quintiles for the U.S. for 1970, 1980, 1990, and 2000. Exhibit 2 in the text presents the data for 1920 and in 2000 an alternative way—Lorenz Curves. The top quintile has increased slightly, the bottom three quintiles have decreased slightly, and the second highest quintile has been relatively unchanged. The poorest 20 percent of families receive less than 5 percent of aggregate household income, while the top richest 20 percent of households receive over 45 percent of aggregate household income. It appears the rich have gotten richer and the poor poorer. Is this accurate?

Yes and no. Other things in the economy have changed as well. Several factors contribute to the rising inequality. First, the premium paid college graduates has increased since 1980. The information age puts greater emphasis on education, while the demand for unskilled labor has fallen. Further, the supply of unskilled labor has increased. Household incomes differ because the number of household members who work differs. Differentiation incomes also reflect differences in age and work experience.

Poverty and the Poor

Poverty is a relative term, and what is considered poverty in one country or in one historic period may be considered a more-than-adequate living standard in another country or time. The U.S. federal government has been calculating an official poverty level since 1955. It is based on the cost of minimum food consumption for each family size. This figure is then multiplied by three, on the grounds that poor families spend one-third of their income on food. The percentage of the U.S. population below the official poverty line fell during the 1960s, fluctuated during the 1970s, rose slightly between 1979 and 1983, declined between 1983 and 1989, rose until 1993, and fell until 2000.

The two primary types of U.S. government programs to help the poor are social insurance programs and income assistance programs. The most important social insurance program is Social Security. The two most important income assistance cash transfer programs are Aid to Families with Dependent Children (AFDC) and Supplemental Security Income (SSI). In 1997, Temporary

Assistance for Needy Families replaced AFDC. There are also in-kind assistance programs, such as Medicaid and food stamps. Medicaid is by far the largest welfare program. Most of the government expenditures to these programs are for social insurance programs; welfare spending amounted to only about 4 percent of GDP in 1995.

Who Are the Poor?

Poverty in the United States is greater among families headed by relatively young people, among families headed by women, and among nonwhite families. The number of poor in households headed by women has increased significantly in the last thirty years, mostly because the number of households headed by women has increased as more children have been born to unwed mothers and divorce rates have risen. The growth in the number of poor families since 1969 resulted mainly from the growth in the number of female householders. Poverty among the elderly has fallen substantially—from 30 percent in 1959 to 9.7 percent in 2000. This is in part because the elderly have become a very effective lobbying force in Congress.

Because there is a greater incidence of poverty among nonwhites than among whites on average, it is appropriate to examine whether this situation is due to discrimination or to other factors. Income depends on the productivity of workers, which depends on such factors as age, experience, and education. Once these factors are controlled for, the difference between incomes of whites and nonwhites narrows. However, the fact that there are more nonwhites living in poverty could be accounted for by the fact that the unemployment rate of nonwhites is greater than that of whites, or by the fact that the percentage of nonwhites with college degrees is significantly smaller than the percentage of whites with college degrees. Such differences in education levels and experience may themselves be results of discrimination.

Unintended Consequences of Income Assistance

The goal of programs for the poor is to reduce the number of people living in poverty. The programs have other consequences that are not intended yet are often very important. First, welfare may create disincentives to work. Two things happen when a member of a household that is receiving welfare obtains a job. The first is that the income from the job is taxed (if it is high enough), so the after-tax income is less than the pretax income. (This applies to all income earners, whether they are on welfare or not.) The second thing that happens is that welfare payments decrease. The combination of the effects of these events is equivalent to increasing the tax rate on the income of the worker. If the welfare payment falls dollar for dollar, then the effective tax rate can be more than 100 percent. Unless the income from the job is significantly greater than the welfare payments, many people rationally choose not to work.

Some observers fear that a second unintended consequence of antipoverty programs is that welfare causes dependency on the welfare system. There is very little evidence to suggest that this is the case, but it is true that almost half of the young adults who grew up in the lowest income group are themselves in the lowest group when they form their own households.

To some extent, the pattern of poverty is a result of public choice. The bulk of government expenditures for the poor are for social insurance programs rather than for welfare. This means that most of the expenditures are directed to the elderly. As noted, in recent years the elderly have become a powerful interest group that has received a great deal of attention in Congress. Even though the poverty rate of the elderly is very low, the government has been more likely to reduce welfare benefits to the poor than to reduce Social Security benefits.

Welfare Reform

States have been trying to reform welfare programs to reduce their cost and increase their effectiveness. Many states now require a "work fare" component for welfare recipients. Federal welfare reform includes the Personal Responsibility and Work Reconciliation Act of 1996. This act replaced AFDC with TANF, provided block grants to states, and set limits on how long people can receive welfare.

IV. LAGNIAPPE

Private Charity

Historically, governments did not provide for the poor. Instead, the poor were the concern of private charity. An important source of income for the poor in such situations was begging. Beggars usually had a disability of one sort or another, although disabilities might be faked to generate increased sympathy and gifts. Arthur Conan Doyle wrote a story about a man who quit his job as a reporter because he made more money begging. (See "The Man with the Twisted Lip," in *The Complete Sherlock Holmes*. Garden City, NY: Doubleday & Company, Inc., 1960.)

Many societies established customs to help the poor. In ancient Israel, the Mosaic Law contained numerous instructions on the care of the poor. These included exhortations to be charitable, rules concerning gleaning, and even provisions for the return of land to the original owners every so often.

In the United States today we rely much more on government than on private charity. As society becomes more complex and urbanized, the poor become more anonymous; it is easy to forget their problems and even their existence. As both the group of potential recipients and the group of potential donors increase in size, the free rider problem increases—that is, people assume that someone else will deal with the problem—and per capita giving decreases. Note, too, that much of what are classified as charitable donations have little to do with helping the poor. Charitable donations to medical research may have important future benefits but do not help the poor today. Donations to churches are called charitable donations, but the money may be used for the operations of the church rather than to help the poor.

Question to Think About: Would people give more to help the poor if the government did not operate welfare programs?

Age and Earnings

We must be careful in comparing average earnings of various racial and ethnic groups because there can be variations that have nothing to do with discrimination. Blacks, Puerto Ricans, and Mexicans are groups that earn, on average, significantly less than the U.S. national average; Japanese, Chinese, and Jews earn significantly more than the U.S. national average. Since all six groups have been targets of discrimination in this country, the income differences among them may not be due to discrimination. An important difference is the average age of the groups. The average age of members of the first three groups is less than twenty years old, whereas the average age of members of the latter three groups is over thirty-five years old. Since thirty-five-year-olds generally earn more than twenty-year-olds, part of the difference in average incomes is due to differences in demographic characteristics.

Question to Think About: What other differences among the groups would help account for differences in average earnings?

V. KEY TERMS

Lorenz Curve
U.S. official poverty level
Social insurance
Social Security
Medicare
Income assistance programs
Means tested program

Temporary Assistance for Needy
 Families (TANF)
Supplemental Security Income (SSI)
Earned-income tax credit
Medicaid
Food Stamps

VI. QUESTIONS

A. Completion

1. The distribution of income in all societies is _____.

2. The _____ income is the middle income when incomes are ranked from lowest to highest.

3. The Census Bureau includes only _____ transfers in the definition of income.

4. Differences in earnings based on age and education reflect the _____ pattern of income.

5. The growth in the number of poor families since 1969 resulted from the growth in the number of _____ households.

6. Aid to Families with Dependent Children is an example of an _____ program.

7. A _____ program requires that a household's income and/or assets fall below a certain level before the family can qualify for benefits; those families that do qualify are _____ to the program.

8. Food stamps are an example of a(n) _____ program.

9. A problem with some welfare programs is that they create work _____.

10. Some states have implemented _____, which is a requirement that welfare recipients participate in training programs or search for work.

B. True/False

_____ 1. The share of total income received by 20 percent of families in the highest U.S. income group has decreased steadily since 1929.

_____ 2. One reason incomes differ across families is that the number of family members who are working varies.

_____ 3. The average income of all households is also known as the median income.

_____ 4. The cost of housing is the basis on which the U.S. official poverty level is calculated.

_____ 5. Benefits in most social insurance programs depend on a prior record of employment.

_____ 6. People must have worked and contributed to an entitlement program to be entitled to the benefits of the program.

_____ 7. Social insurance programs account for a larger share of total U.S. government expenditures than entitlement programs.

_____ 8. Poverty rates for U.S. families headed by someone under twenty-five are greater than the rates for all U.S. families.

_____ 9. The poverty rate for the elderly is lower than that of any other age group in the United States.

_____ 10. The black poverty rate in the United States is about three times the white poverty rate.

_____ 11. Any difference in average earnings between whites and nonwhites is due to discrimination.

_____ 12. The distribution of income among black families is more even than for the population as a whole.

_____ 13. Differences in earnings between blacks and whites that can be attributed to differences in experience and differences in quality of education cannot be due to racial discrimination.

_____ 14. Current welfare programs create work disincentives.

_____ 15. TANF is designed to limit federal welfare costs.

C. Multiple Choice

1. Since the end of World War II, the distribution of income in the United States has been
   a. increasingly more unequal.
   b. increasingly more equal.
   c. relatively stable.
   d. fluctuating considerably, becoming more unequal at times and more equal at other times.
   e. very different from the distribution of income in other industrialized countries.

2. Differences in family incomes arise from differences in
   a. the age of the head of the household.
   b. education.
   c. ability.
   d. the number of people in the household who are working.
   e. all of the above.

3. A high-income household usually consists of
   a. people who were in low-income households when children.
   b. well-educated couples who both are employed.
   c. female-headed households.
   d. single males who have no children.
   e. both a and b only.

4. The percentage of the U.S. population below the official poverty level
   a. has declined steadily since 1960.
   b. declined during the 1960s, fluctuated during the 1970s, increased from 1979 to 1983, and decreased since 1983.
   c. declined during the 1960s, rose during the 1970s, fluctuated in the early 1980s, and fell in the latter 1980s.
   d. has been unaffected by any government policies since 1960.
   e. declined steadily from 1960 to 1975 and has risen steadily since 1975.

5. Which of the following is not an example of a social insurance program?
   a. Social Security
   b. Medicare
   c. Worker's Compensation
   d. Unemployment Insurance
   e. Supplemental Security Income

6. Which of the following is not an example of an in-kind transfer program?
   a. school lunches
   b. low-income housing
   c. AFDC
   d. food stamps
   e. Medicaid

7. Which of the following has the greatest effect on reducing poverty?
   a. increased spending on social insurance programs
   b. a strong economy that creates a lot of new jobs
   c. excluding in-kind transfers from the definition of income
   d. raising the benefits associated with in-kind transfers
   e. All of the above reduce the number of citizens who are below the official poverty line.

8. The number of households below the poverty line that are headed by women has been increasing because
   a. female-headed households have become more common in the population as a whole.
   b. discrimination against women has increased.
   c. women have been moving out of the labor force.
   d. the service sector has been growing faster than the manufacturing sector.
   e. all of the above

9. For any given age group,
   a. nonwhite workers are likely to have less job experience than white workers.
   b. nonwhite workers earn a lower wage rate than white workers even after the data are adjusted for experience, education, marital status, and geographic location.
   c. nonwhite workers earn the same wage as white workers when experience, education, marital status, and geographic location are taken into consideration.
   d. a and b
   e. a and c

10. The work disincentives associated with welfare are due to
    a. the fact that welfare recipients are lazy.
    b. the requirement that welfare recipients not work.
    c. the fact that most welfare programs involve in-kind rather than cash transfers.
    d. the sharp decline in benefits received as earned income increases.
    e. all of the above.

11. A University of Michigan study found that most recipients
    a. receive welfare for less than one year
    b. receive welfare for 3-5 years.
    c. receive welfare for at least five years.
    d. receive welfare for their entire adult life.
    e. lived in families that received welfare when they were children.

12. One concern with recent welfare reform is that
    a. states may be tempted to offer relatively low levels of benefits.
    b. the costs to the federal government may skyrocket.
    c. the reforms may cause a recession.
    d. all of the above.
    e. none of the above.

D. Discussion Questions

1. Exhibit 4 contains data on four distributions of income. Which is the most equal distribution? Which is the most unequal? Explain.

Exhibit 4

Distribution	Lowest Fifth	Second-Lowest Fifth	Middle Fifth	Second-Highest Fifth	Highest Fifth
A	2%	5%	8%	15%	70%
B	12%	15%	20%	23%	30%
C	5%	10%	25%	26%	34%
D	10%	14%	16%	20%	40%

2. Why do family incomes differ?

3. How is the life-cycle pattern of income related to the measurement of income equality at a point in time?

4. Why is private charity not enough to care for the poor?

5. What are the differences between social insurance programs and income assistance programs?

6. What has caused the "feminization" of poverty?

7. Discuss the factors that cause the average income of nonwhites to be lower than the average income of whites.

8. Explain how differences in earnings between nonwhites and whites due to differences in education levels and work experience can be a result of racial discrimination.

9. Explain how welfare creates work disincentives.

10. Does welfare cause dependency?

11. What has caused the recent poverty rate among the elderly to be lower than that of any other group in the United States?

12. Explain the changes in welfare caused by the "Personal Responsibility and Work Reconciliation Act" of 1996.

VII. ANSWERS

A. Completion

1. unequal
2. median
3. money
4. life-cycle
5. female
6. entitlement (or income assistance)
7. means-tested; entitled
8. in-kind
9. disincentives
10. workfare

B. True/False

1. False
2. True
3. False
4. False. The official poverty level is based on the cost of food.
5. True
6. False
7. True
8. True
9. True
10. True
11. False
12. False
13. False
14. True
15. True

C. Multiple Choice

1.	c	4.	b	7.	b	10.	d
2.	e	5.	e	8.	a	11.	a
3.	b	6.	c	9.	a	12.	a

D. Discussion Questions

1. Distribution B is the most equal because the bottom quintile's share of household income is the greatest of the four distributions, and the top quintile's share of household income is the lowest of the four distributions. For opposite reasons, A is the least equal. It is difficult to compare distributions C and D since their middle quintiles differ.

2. Family incomes differ because of differences in the number of members who work; differences in education, ability, and training; and racial and gender discrimination.

3. People typically earn lower wages when they are young. As they obtain work experience, they become more productive and receive greater wages as they get older. A person could be in poverty while relatively young, but in a much higher income bracket when older.

4. Each person realizes that the plight of the poor will not be materially affected if he or she provides assistance, so the amount of help individuals provide is limited. Each person has little incentive to help and counts on others to do it instead. Consequently, private charity is likely to be insufficient to alleviate the problems of the poor.

5. Social insurance programs are designed for people who have worked and contributed to their own support. Income assistance programs are provided to people in need, whether they have ever worked or not.

6. The main reason is that the number of female householders has increased.

7. Discrimination is one factor that causes average incomes to differ between the two groups. Related factors include differences in education levels, differences in quality of education, and differences in job experience.

8. Differences in quality of education and job experience may be the result of discrimination, so any differences in income that are due to these factors are, by extension, caused by racial discrimination.

9. Welfare creates work disincentives because benefits are reduced if the recipient earns income. The extra income from a low-paying or part-time job may not be sufficient to over-come the loss of benefits. Consequently, there is less incentive to work.

10. The evidence is mixed. Most recipients of welfare receive it for less than one year. But there is a core of people who remain on welfare for years. Further, there is evidence that daughters raised in welfare families are more likely than daughters in other families to participate in the welfare system themselves.

11. The elderly have become a powerful interest group and have successfully lobbied Congress for increases in benefits, especially in Social Security benefits.

12. The act replaced AFDC with TANF, which provides block grants to states to run their welfare programs. States are given more latitude to run their own welfare programs. The act tries to limit welfare dependency by imposing a lifetime limit of 5 years a recipient can be on welfare. The act also tightens eligibility requirements for disabled children and limits benefits of non-citizens and teenage mothers who do not live at home.

CHAPTER 19

International Trade

I. INTRODUCTION

This chapter examines trade among nations. Given the growing importance of international trade, you should understand the forces that determine patterns of trade.

II. OUTLINE

1. The Gains from Trade

   1.1 A Profile of Imports and Exports
   - a. Countries' levels of involvement in international trade differ.
   - b. U.S. exports are about 12 percent of GDP.
   - c. The main exports of the United States are high-technology products, industrial supplies and materials, agricultural products, and entertainment products.
   - d. The main imports of the United States are manufactured consumer goods, capital goods, and oil.
   - e. U.S. imports are about 14 percent of GDP.

   1.2 Production Possibilities without Trade
   - a. In the absence of trade, a country's consumption possibilities are determined by its production possibilities.
   - b. A country's possible production combinations can be portrayed graphically.

   1.3 Consumption Possibilities Based on Comparative Advantage
   - a. Each country specializes in the product for which its opportunity cost is lowest relative to other countries.
   - b. Two countries can each consume more by trading than they could before trading when the terms of trade are based on the two countries' opportunity costs.
   - c. Total world production of each good increases if each country specializes in producing the good for which it has a comparative advantage.
   - d. The exchange of goods between two countries yields a surplus to both consumers and producers.

   1.4 Reasons for International Specialization
   - a. People expect to benefit when they engage in trade.
   - b. Exchange can benefit those involved when
     - (1) there are differences in resource endowments
     - (2) there are economies of scale
     - (3) there are differences in tastes

2. **Trade Restrictions**

   2.1 Tariffs
       a.   A *tariff* is a tax on imports or exports.
           (1) A *specific tariff* is a lump-sum tariff per unit of a good.
           (2) An *ad valorem tariff* is a percentage of the cost of the imports at the port of entry.
       b.   Tariffs generate higher prices for domestic producers of goods that compete with imports.
       c.   Consumers are harmed by tariffs; domestic producers whose products compete with imports benefit from tariffs.
       d.   The loss in consumer surplus from tariffs is greater than the increase in producer surplus and government revenue from tariffs.
       e.   Tariffs redistribute income from consumers to producers and government.

   2.2 Import Quotas
       a.   An *import quota* is a legal limit on the quantity of a particular commodity that can be imported per year.
       b.   Tariffs and effective quotas have similar effects.
       c.   An effective quota limits imports and raises domestic price.
       d.   If a tariff and an effective quota have the same effect on price, then they result in the same quantity demanded, the same loss in consumer surplus, and the same increase in producer surplus for domestic firms.

   2.3 Quotas in Practice
       a.   The quota system creates two groups that want to secure and maintain the quotas–domestic producers and foreign producers with the right to sell goods to the U.S.
       b.   An important difference between a quota and a tariff is that the government obtains revenue with tariffs, whereas those with the right to export gain revenues with quotas.

   2.4 Tariffs and Quotas Compared
       a.   The government receives revenue from a tariff, but not from a quota.
       b.   If the quota rights belong to foreigners, the domestic economy is worse off with a quota than with a tariff.

   2.5 Other Trade Restrictions
       a.   Free trade is restricted by government subsidies to export firms and low-interest loans to foreign buyers.
       b.   Other rules and regulations, such as domestic content requirements, can be used to discriminate against foreign producers.

   2.6 Freer Trade by Multilateral Agreement
       a.   The General Agreement on Tariffs and Trade (GATT) is an international treaty to reduce trade barriers.
       b.   Tariffs have fallen sharply since World War II due to GATT.

   2.7 World Trade Organization (WTO). The WTO provides a legal and institutional foundation for the international trading sphere.

   2.8 *CASE STUDY:* WTO and the "Battle in Seattle"

2.9 Common Markets.
  a. Some countries join together into common markets in order to take advantage of free trade with other countries.
  b. Examples include the European Union and NAFTA.

3. Arguments for Trade Restrictions

  3.1 National Defense Argument
    a. Certain industries are essential in wartime so they must be kept viable.
    b. Many industries try to use this argument even though their military application is often nebulous.
    c. Government subsidies to domestic producers would be more efficient than import restrictions.

  3.2 Infant Industry Argument
    a. Emerging domestic industries need temporary protection so they can compete with mature industries in other countries until they can exploit economies of scale.
    b. Among the problems with this rationale are the fact that it is difficult to identify industries with the potential to become competitive and the fact that it is possible that protection itself will foster inefficiencies so that protected industries will not mature.

  3.3 Antidumping Argument
    a. *Dumping* is the sale of a commodity abroad for less than its domestic price.
    b. Predatory dumping by foreign firms may deter domestic firms from entering an industry.

  3.4 Jobs and Income Argument
    a. Some foreign countries are able to compete because of low wages.
    b. The high wages in the United States reflect the greater productivity of U.S. labor.

  3.5 Declining Industries Argument
    a. Tariffs can be used to ease the transition of domestic industries that are in decline.
    b. If tariffs are imposed for this reason, care must be taken to ensure that the protection is not so great as to encourage new investment in the industry.
    c. Wage subsidies or special tax breaks can be used instead of import restrictions.

  3.6 Problems with Protection
    a. Protecting one industry often leads to protecting other industries because of the need to counteract the effects of higher prices in the protected industry on the other industries.
    b. Costs of rent seeking also are associated with protection.
    c. Policing protective arrangements can be costly.

  3.7 *CASE STUDY:* Enforcing Trade Restrictions

4. Conclusion. Trade allows people to use their scarce resources more efficiently. Yet, trade restrictions are common. Losers from trade restrictions include consumers, exporting industries, and businesses that use the same resources as the protected industries. Winners from trade restrictions include the domestic producers of goods that compete with imports and, in the case of quotas, those who have secured rights to import a good.

III. DISCUSSION

The Gains from Trade

People exchange goods with those in other nations for the same reasons they exchange goods with other people in their own nation—because they believe they will be better off as a result. Individuals gain by specializing in the production of one thing, selling their output for money, and using the money to buy the goods and services they want. Similarly, nations specialize in production and sell the goods they specialize in for goods in which they do not specialize. There is one difference between individuals who specialize and nations that specialize. Individuals often specialize completely and produce none of the goods they buy; nations often produce some of almost all goods but not enough to satisfy domestic demand for some goods.

Suppose a worker in the United States can produce either 10 units of wheat or 5 units of cloth per day, and a worker in Britain can produce either 5 units of wheat or 3 units of cloth per day. The U.S. worker is more productive than the British worker in either case, so the United States has an absolute advantage in producing both commodities. However, trade is based on comparative, not absolute, advantage. The opportunity cost of a unit of wheat in the United States is 1/2 unit of cloth, and the opportunity cost of a unit of cloth is 2 units of wheat. In Britain, the opportunity cost of a unit of wheat is 3/5 unit of cloth, and the opportunity cost of a unit of cloth is 5/3 units of wheat. Hence, the opportunity cost of wheat is lower in the United States than in Britain (1/2 < 3/5), and the opportunity cost of cloth is lower in Britain than in the United States (5/3 < 2). The United States has a comparative advantage in wheat and Britain has a comparative advantage in cloth.

The different opportunity costs in the two countries mean that world production of wheat and cloth can increase if each country specializes in the commodity that it can produce more cheaply. If the United States produces 1 less unit of cloth, it can produce 2 additional units of wheat. If Britain produces 1 less unit of wheat, it can produce 5/3 additional units of cloth. So the United States produces 1 less unit of cloth, Britain produces an additional 5/3 units of cloth, and, on net, there is 2/3 unit of cloth more than before. Similarly, Britain produces 1 less unit of wheat, but the United States has produced 2 additional units of wheat. On net, the world now has 1 additional unit of wheat and 2/3 additional unit of cloth.

Since world production is greater when each country specializes, it is possible for residents of each country to consume more with trade than without. Suppose each country has 100 workers (and consumers). Exhibit 1 presents the production possibilities schedule for each country, and Exhibit 2 illustrates the production possibilities frontier (PPF) of each. The PPF for the United States is line *AB*, with a slope equal to the opportunity cost of cloth in the United States, and the PPF for Britain is line *CD*, with a slope equal to the opportunity cost of cloth in Britain. The price of a unit of cloth in the United States is 2 units of wheat, but the price of cloth in England is 5/3 units of wheat. Trade is beneficial to both as long as they trade cloth at a price that is between the domestic prices without trade. That is, both can benefit if wheat can be exchanged for cloth at a rate that is more than 1. 67 (5/3) but less than 2.

Exhibit 1

Production Possibilities Schedules

United States

Wheat	1,000	800	600	400	200	0
Cloth	0	100	200	300	400	500

Britain

Wheat	500	400	300	200	100	0
Cloth	0	60	120	180	240	300

Exhibit 2

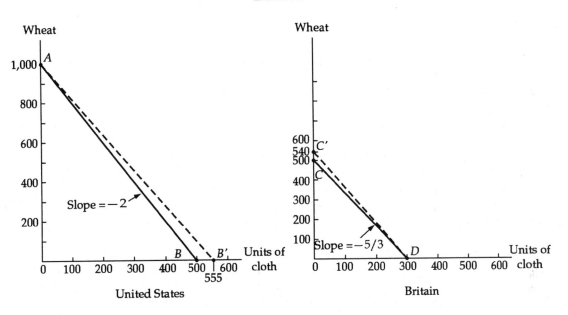

United States

Britain

Suppose the exchange ratio, or *terms of trade*, is 1.8 units of wheat per unit of cloth. Without trade, in the United States 2 units of wheat had to be given up to get a unit of cloth. Now the United States can completely specialize and produce 1,000 units of wheat, and exchange wheat for cloth at a rate of 1.8 instead of 2. Exhibit 3 presents the consumption possibilities schedules when the rate of exchange is 1.8 units of wheat for 1 unit of cloth and the United States produces wheat while Britain produces cloth. Exhibit 2 also shows the consumption possibilities frontiers: *AB′* in the United States and *C′D* in Britain. Each country is able to consume more of both commodities than it could when it did not trade.

Exhibit 3

Consumption Possibilities Schedules
(Terms of trade = 1.8 units of wheat for 1 unit of cloth)

United States

Wheat	1,000	800	600	400	200	0	
Cloth	0	111	222	333	444	555	

Britain

Wheat	540	450	360	270	180	90	0
Cloth	0	50	100	150	200	250	300

Exchange among nations can be beneficial when the nations involved differ in resource endowments. Resources are not equally distributed among countries. Some countries have more oil than others; other countries have more skilled labor. Countries with a relatively large supply of skilled labor have a comparative advantage in producing goods that require skilled labor. Exchange can also be beneficial if there are differences in tastes among nations. Further, exchange can occur if there are economies of scale so that specialization generates lower production costs.

Trade Restrictions

Even though the gains from trade exceed the losses from trade, restrictions on trade are ubiquitous. The two major types of trade restrictions are import *tariffs* and import *quotas*. Both have the effect of raising price in the domestic economy above the world price. A tariff raises price directly, since an import tariff is a tax on imports. Import quotas raise prices indirectly by restricting the quantity of imports. Their effects are almost identical to those of a tariff.

Exhibit 4 illustrates the effects on imports of tariffs and effective quotas. Domestic demand and supply of cloth are represented by D and S, respectively. The world price, $5.00, is below the domestic equilibrium price, so in the absence of trade restrictions the relevant supply curve is mnS_w. It intersects the demand curve at point v, so domestic quantity demanded is 6,000 units, and 2,000 units is the quantity supplied by U.S. cloth producers. The United States imports 4,0,00 units of cloth. A specific tariff adds $1.00 to the world price, so the new domestic price is $6.00, and the new supply curve is $mn'S'_w$. Quantity demanded falls to 5,000 units, the amount of cloth produced by domestic firms increases to 3,000 units, and imports fall to 2,000 units. Instead of a tariff, the government could have imposed a quota and achieved the same result. A quota equal to 2,000 units of cloth causes the supply curve to shift to $mnrS'$. In other words, the supply curve shifts out by the quota limit at the world price of $5.00. It intersects domestic demand at f, which implies a price of $6.00. Domestic production increases from 2,000 to 3,000 units, and domestic consumption falls from 6,000 to 5,000 units.

Exhibit 4

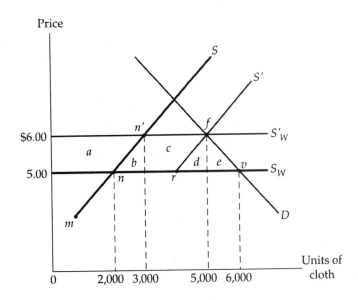

The increase in price due to the tariff (or quota) makes consumers worse off. Consumer surplus falls by areas *a*, *b*, *c*, *d*, and *e*. Some of the loss to consumers is transferred to other members of society, but the rest of the loss to consumers represents a deadweight loss to society. In Exhibit 5, area *a* represents a transfer of surplus from consumers to domestic producers and areas *c* and *d* represent revenue received by the government as the result of a tariff. (In the case of a quota, areas *c* and *d* represent a transfer from domestic consumers to those who obtain the right to import cloth.) The remaining areas, *b* and *e*, represent deadweight losses to society of the tariff (or quota). Clearly, the losses from the trade restrictions exceed the gains from the restrictions.

Arguments for Trade Restrictions

Arguments for trade restrictions are generally expressed in terms of national welfare. Proponents of trade restrictions justify them by using national defense, infant industry, and antidumping arguments. In recent years, proponents in the United States have argued that restrictions are needed to protect U.S. labor from cheap foreign labor. Wages in the United States are considerably higher than wages in many less developed nations, and those in favor of trade restrictions fear that U.S. labor cannot compete with the foreign labor. However, this argument ignores the reason for the higher U.S. wages: labor in the United States is more productive than labor in less developed nations. Thus, many goods can still be produced at lower cost in the United States.

IV. LAGNIAPPE

The Cost of Automobile Quotas

Robert Crandall attempted to estimate the cost to U.S. consumers of import quotas on Japanese autos. He calculated the difference between the average price of autos with the quotas and the average price without the quotas. He found that the quotas added approximately $235 to the price of a car in 1981 and 1982, and $829 in 1983. He also estimated the number of jobs saved in the U.S. auto industry because of quotas and concluded that the cost to consumers per job saved was nearly $160,000 per year.

(See Robert W. Crandall, "Import Quotas and the Automobile Industry: The Costs of Protection," *The Brookings Review*, Summer 1984: 8-16.)

Question to Think About: Can you think of ways to help auto workers that might be less expensive than using import quotas?

Economists, Tariffs, and Influence

George Stigler, a winner of the Nobel Prize in economics, has argued that the continued use of tariffs is proof that economists have no influence on policy. Since virtually all economists believe that free trade is preferable to protection, and since all countries decide to protect a large portion of their economies, politicians must not be paying attention to economists.

Given that tariffs and quotas do more harm than good, why do they continue to be used? Free trade does not benefit all members of society. In particular, it harms those who work in industries that compete with lower-priced foreign goods. The owners and workers in the industries that face considerable competition from abroad lobby their representatives for help. Those who are harmed tend to be harmed a great deal, even though the number of people harmed may not be large relative to the total population. Consumers are major beneficiaries of free trade. However, each individual consumer receives relatively small benefits from free trade in any particular industry. Consumers are unlikely to lobby their representatives concerning tariff legislation. Consequently, the industry groups lobby harder than consumers, and the tariff legislation passes.

Question to Think About: Are there groups that might lobby effectively against tariffs?

V. KEY TERMS

Autarky
Terms of trade
World price
General Agreement on Tariffs and
Trade (GATT)

Dumping
Uruguay round
World Trade Organization (WTO)
Import substitution
Export promotion

VI. QUESTIONS

A. Completion

1. The two main types of imports to the United States are _____ and _____.

2. In the absence of trade, a country's production possibilities schedule is also its _____ possibilities schedule.

3. National self-sufficiency is called _____.

4. Trade is based on _____ advantage rather than on _____ advantage because gains can be made from specialization and trade whenever relative production costs of two goods in two countries differ.

5. The _____ must lie between the no-trade equilibrium prices in two countries.

6. The only constraint on trade is that, for each good, total world _____ must equal total world _____.

7. Comparative advantage is determined by _____ costs.

8. Countries can benefit from trade when there are differences in _____ or differences in tastes.

9. Countries can gain from trade if production is subject to _____ so that the per-unit cost of production falls as a country specializes in a good.

10. A tariff on oil of $10 a barrel is a(n) _____ tariff.

11. A(n) _____ is a legal limit on the quantity of a commodity that can be imported into a country.

12. Tariff reductions granted to one country must be granted to all other trading members of GATT under the _____ clause.

13. Domestic firms may not find entry into an industry attractive if foreign producers are _____.

14. The _____ argument for trade restrictions views the restrictions as a temporary device for allowing domestic firms to achieve sufficient economies of scale.

15. The cost of protection includes the deadweight loss arising from the higher domestic prices and the cost of _____.

B. True/False

_____ 1. Foreign trade is more important to the United States than to most of the countries in western Europe.

_____ 2. The majority of U.S. imports are manufactured consumer goods.

_____ 3. Under autarky, each country can concentrate on producing those goods and services that involve the least opportunity costs.

_____ 4. A country can have a comparative advantage in all goods.

5. If wheat and cloth are the only goods under consideration and the production costs of wheat in terms of cloth are less in the United States than in mythical Izodia, then the production costs of cloth are less in Izodia than in the United States.

6. All countries can benefit if countries specialize in producing the goods for which they are the least-cost producers.

7. Market exchange usually benefits one country at the expense of the other country.

8. Differences in resource endowments generate differences in costs of production, which lead to trade.

9. A country will import a good for which the world price is above the domestic equilibrium price.

10. The gains from trade to an importing nation tend just to offset the losses from trade to an exporting nation, so the world is neither better nor worse off.

11. A tariff raises the price of the good to consumers, but a quota does not.

12. Tariff revenue represents a net loss to a society.

13. Each member of GATT has agreed to treat all other member nations equally with respect to trade.

14. The effect of an import quota is to redistribute income from consumers to producers and to impose losses on consumers that are not transferred to anyone.

15. Consumers who are also taxpayers do better if government imposes a tariff than if it imposes an equivalent quota.

16. Regional trading blocs like NAFTA and the EC are permitted by the rules of GATT.

17. The infant industry argument for tariffs is an argument for temporary tariffs.

18. The Trade Agreement Act of 1979 prohibits only predatory dumping.

19. Using tariffs to protect domestic jobs often reduces trade and the gains from trade.

20. A tariff on steel likely will lead to pressure for a tariff on autos.

C. Multiple Choice

1. The largest trading partner of the United States is
   a. Japan.
   b. Germany.
   c. Canada.
   d. Mexico.
   e. Great Britain.

Consider the following information in answering questions 2 through 7. A worker in the United States can produce either 8 computers or 6 motorcycles in a day; a worker in Japan can produce either 12 computers or 9 motorcycles in a day.

2. If there are 100 million workers in the United States, then the autarkic equilibrium will be
   a. 800 million computers and 600 million motorcycles produced and consumed.
   b. 400 million computers and 300 million motorcycles produced and consumed.
   c. 400 million computers and 600 million motorcycles produced and consumed.
   d. 800 million computers and 300 million motorcycles produced and consumed.
   e. The question cannot be answered without more information.

3. Which of the following is true?
   a. Japan has an absolute advantage in both goods and a comparative advantage in computers.
   b. Japan has an absolute advantage in both goods and a comparative advantage in neither good.
   c. Japan has an absolute advantage in both goods and a comparative advantage in motorcycles.
   d. Japan has an absolute and a comparative advantage in both goods.
   e. The United States has an absolute advantage in computers and a comparative advantage in motorcycles.

4. Which of the following is true?
   a. Japan will specialize in motorcycles because its opportunity cost of producing motorcycles is less than the opportunity cost of producing motorcycles in the United States.
   b. Japan will specialize in computers because its opportunity cost of computers is less than the opportunity cost of computers in the United States.
   c. The opportunity cost of computers is the same in both countries, so there will be no specialization in trade.
   d. Japan will specialize in both computers and motorcycles because the cost of each is less in Japan than in the United States.
   e. none of the above

5. Suppose the conditions change so that a worker in Japan can now produce 15 motorcycles in a day. Under these conditions,
   a. Japan has a comparative advantage in computers.
   b. the opportunity cost of motorcycles in Japan is less than the opportunity cost of motorcycles in the United States.
   c. the United States has a comparative advantage in motorcycles.
   d. the cost of a motorcycle in Japan is 1.25 computers.
   e. a, c, and d

6. Given the change described in question 5,
   a. Japan has an absolute advantage in motorcycles but a comparative advantage in computers.
   b. Japan will export motorcycles and import computers.
   c. Japan will export computers and import motorcycles.
   d. there will be no trade.
   e. The question cannot be answered without more information.

7. Given the information in question 5, suppose the terms of trade are 1 computer in exchange for 0.8 motorcycle. We know that
   a. Japan's consumption possibilities frontier shifts farther out from its production possibilities frontier than does that of the United States.
   b. The United States' consumption possibilities frontier shifts farther out from its production possibilities frontier than does that of Japan.
   c. the consumption possibilities frontiers shift out by the same amount in both countries.
   d. both countries share equally in the gains from trade.
   e. both c and d

8. If all countries had an equal endowment of all resources,
   a. there would be no trade.
   b. trade would arise only from differences in taste or economies of scale.
   c. trade would depend on absolute advantage rather than comparative advantage.
   d. trade flows would be larger than they currently are.
   e. none of the above

9. Moving from autarky to free trade will generate
   a. increases in consumer surplus for consumers of the imported good.
   b. decreases in consumer surplus for consumers of the exported good.
   c. increases in producer surplus for the producers of the exported good.
   d. decreases in producer surplus for the producers of the imported good.
   e. all of the above.

10. If the domestic equilibrium price of wheat in the United States is $4.00 a bushel, then
   a. the United States will export wheat at any world price below $4.00.
   b. the United States will export wheat at any world price above $4.00.
   c. there will be an excess demand for wheat at any world price above $4.00, and this excess demand will be met by imports.
   d. a and c
   e. none of the above. More information is necessary to answer the question.

Exhibit 5

11. The world price for wheat in Exhibit 5 is p_W and the price in the United States is p_D. The loss to domestic consumers if trade occurs in the wheat market is represented by area(s)
    a. *a.*
    b. *a* and *b.*
    c. *b.*
    d. *b* and *c.*
    e. *a*, *b*, and *c.*

12. The gain to domestic producers from trade is represented in Exhibit 5 by area(s)
    a. *c.*
    b. *d.*
    c. *c* and *d.*
    d. *a*, *b*, *c*, and *d.*
    e. *e.*

13. In Exhibit 5, if the United States imposes a tariff equal to $p_W - p_D$,
    a. trade will stop.
    b. domestic producers will be harmed and domestic consumers will benefit.
    c. domestic consumers will be harmed and domestic producers will benefit.
    d. a and b
    e. none of the above. The tariff will have no effect since the United States is exporting wheat.

14. In Exhibit 5, if the trading partner imposed a prohibitive tariff on wheat from the United States,
    a. the gain to U.S. consumers of wheat would be greater than the loss to U.S. producers of wheat.
    b. the gain to U.S. consumers of wheat would be less than the loss to U.S. producers of wheat.
    c. the gain to U.S. consumers of wheat would exactly offset the losses to U.S. producers of wheat.
    d. the gain to U.S. consumers of wheat would exactly offset the loss to U.S. consumers of whatever good had been imported from the trading partner.
    e. The question cannot be answered without more information.

15. The net social loss of a tariff is greater,
    a. the steeper the domestic supply curve.
    b. the flatter the domestic demand curve.
    c. the steeper the domestic demand curve.
    d. the larger the tariff revenue the government receives.
    e. all of the above except c

16. An import quota differs from a tariff in that
    a. a quota does not affect the domestic price of a commodity.
    b. a quota does not harm consumers the way a tariff does.
    c. a quota encourages increased domestic production more than a tariff does.
    d. a tariff generates revenue to the government but a quota does not.
    e. a tariff harms all consumers of the commodity; a quota harms only those who cannot obtain as much of the commodity as they would like.

17. Japanese auto producers would prefer
    a. a tariff on their cars rather than a quota because tariffs tend to be removed before quotas.
    b. a tariff on their cars rather than a quota because tariffs do not cost the exporter as much.
    c. a quota on their cars rather than a tariff because quotas generate extra profits for the exporter.
    d. a quota on their cars rather than a tariff because quotas tend to be reversed faster.
    e. none of the above.

18. Suppose it costs a U.S. steel company $20 a ton to produce steel, it costs a Japanese firm $15 a ton, the domestic price of steel in Japan is $18, and the domestic price in the United States is $22. Japanese firms would be dumping if they charged U.S. firms
    a. any price below $22.
    b. any price below $20.
    c. any price below $18.
    d. any price below $15.
    e. none of the above.

19. Low wages in developing countries indicate that
    a. U.S. workers cannot compete with workers in developing countries.
    b. the United States cannot have a comparative advantage in any product produced by developing countries.
    c. the standard of living of U.S. workers must fall in order for them to compete with workers from developing countries.
    d. all of the above
    e. none of the above

20. One problem with trade restrictions is that
    a. policing and enforcing restrictions is costly.
    b. they do not last long enough to have the beneficial effects they are designed to provide.
    c. they tend to be imposed in inefficient ways, i.e., tariffs tend to be used instead of more efficient quotas.
    d. the national defense argument is not used for some industries vital to the defense of the country.
    e. all of the above

D. Discussion Questions

1. What additional information is needed to answer multiple choice question 2?

2. How can two countries both be better off as a result of trade?

3. Explain why trade is based on comparative advantage and not absolute advantage.

4. Suppose that a worker in Brazil can produce 10 units of coffee and 6 units of cloth per day, and a worker in the United States can produce 5 units of coffee and 5 units of cloth. Brazil has 500 workers; the United States has 1,000 workers.
   a. What is the opportunity cost of cloth in Brazil? in the United States?
   b. What is the opportunity cost of coffee in Brazil? in the United States?
   c. Which country has a comparative advantage in producing coffee? in producing cloth?
   d. Draw production possibilities frontiers for both Brazil and the United States, with cloth on the horizontal axis. What is the slope of Brazil's production possibilities frontier? What is the slope of the production possibilities frontier for the United States?
   e. If the United States and Brazil trade, which country will export coffee and which will export cloth? At what rate will trade take place?
   f. Show on your graph the gains from trade for both countries for one set of prices that would lead to trade.

5. If the terms of trade in question 4 are 1.01 units of coffee for 1 unit of cloth, which country receives a larger share of the gains from trade? How do you know?

6. The U.S. both imports and exports autos. Which of the explanations for international specialization explains this?

7. Why do differences in resource endowments lead to trade?

8. "Everyone benefits from free trade." Do you agree or disagree? Why?

9. How does an ad valorem tariff differ from a specific tariff?

10. Suppose a $10 shirt is subject to a $1 specific tariff and a $10 blouse is subject to a 10-percent ad valorem tariff. If the prices of both goods double, what happens to the tariff on each good?

11. What is an import tariff? What are the effects of a tariff? Use a graph to illustrate your answers.

12. What is an import quota? What are the effects of an effective quota? Use the same graph you used for question 10 to illustrate your answers to this question.

13. How can tariffs protect U.S. jobs? Do tariffs lead to a net increase in jobs? Explain.

14. Explain why true/false question 16 is false.

15. American workers are more productive than workers in Mexico because American workers have more physical and human capital to work with. How can Mexican workers compete with the more productive workers?

16. What are some of the problems associated with trade restrictions?

17. Explain why true/false question 20 is true.

18. Who are the winners and losers from trade restrictions? Given that trade restrictions impose losses on an economy, why are trade restrictions so common?

VII. ANSWERS

A. Completion

1.	manufactured consumer goods; capital goods	8.	resource endowments
2.	consumption	9.	economies of scale
3.	autarky	10.	specific
4.	comparative; absolute	11.	import quota
5.	terms of trade	12.	most-favored-nation
6.	production; consumption	13.	dumping
7.	opportunity	14.	infant industry
		15.	rent seeking

B. True/False

1. False. Trade as a percent of GDP is less for the United States than for the western European countries.
2. True
3. False
4. False
5. True
6. True
7. False
8. True
9. False. The country will export goods whose world price exceeds the domestic equilibrium price.

10. False
11. False
12. False
13. True
14. True
15. True
16. False
17. True
18. False
19. True
20. True

C. Multiple Choice

1.	c	6.	b	11.	b	16.	d
2.	e	7.	a	12.	d	17.	c
3.	b	8.	b	13.	e	18.	c
4.	c	9.	e	14.	b	19.	e
5.	b	10.	b	15.	b	20.	a

D. Discussion Questions

1. Information concerning the tastes of the citizens is needed in order to determine which part of the production possibilities frontier the autarkic equilibrium will lie on.

2. Two countries can be better off as a result of trade if their opportunity costs of producing the goods being traded differ. Different opportunity costs imply that relative prices in the two countries are different, which means that each country can gain if it produces the good for which its opportunity cost is lowest and buys the other good from the other country.

3. Trade is based on relative differences and not on absolute differences. Opportunity costs--the production of an additional unit of a good always means giving up something else. Differences opportunity costs generate comparative advantages.

4.   a.   10/6, or $1^2/_3$, units of coffee; 1 unit of coffee
     b.   0. 6 unit of cloth; 1 unit of cloth
     c.   Brazil has a comparative advantage in producing coffee and the United States in producing cloth. That is, the opportunity cost of coffee is lower in Brazil than it is in the United States, and the opportunity cost of cloth is lower in the United States than it is in Brazil.
     d.   The slope of Brazil's PPF is −10/6 (or $^5/_3$) and the slope of the United States' PPF is −1. (See the exhibit.)

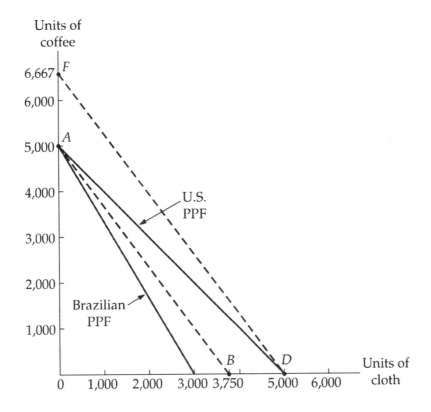

     e.   Brazil will export coffee and the United States will export cloth. The rate at which trade will take place lies between 1 and 10/6 units of coffee for 1 unit of cloth.
     f.   Refer again to the graph. At a rate of exchange of 4 units of coffee for 3 units of cloth, each country's consumption possibilities frontier is farther from the origin than

its PPF. (Brazil's consumption possibilities curve is line *AB* and the United States' is line *DF*, assuming Brazil specializes in the production of coffee and the United States specializes in the production of cloth.)

5. Brazil will receive larger gains from trade. The terms of trade imply a very large shift of Brazil's consumption possibilities frontier, whereas the consumption possibilities frontier for the United States lies very close to its production possibilities frontier.

6. A combination of economies of scale and different tastes help explain this. If most people in the U.S. want larger cars and most people in Japan want smaller cars, then it makes sense for U.S. auto firms to make large cars to satisfy their domestic market, and for Japanese firms to make small cars. Those Japanese who want large cars then can import them from the U.S.

7. Differences in endowments of resources lead to differences in opportunity costs of production, which lead to trade.

8. Disagree. Some people are harmed by free trade—some consumers pay higher prices, and some producers make less money. But, the gains from free trade are larger than the losses.

9. A specific tariff is an amount per unit of the good; an ad valorem tariff is a percent of the price.

10. At the initial prices, the tariffs are equivalent. If prices double, the ad valorem tariff doubles because it is based on the price of the good. The specific tariff remains $1, so the price of the shirt is now $21, whereas the price of the blouse is $22.

11. A tariff is a tax on imports. A tariff raises the domestic price of an imported good. The graph shows that 245 units of a good are purchased when the world price is p_W; of these, 30 are produced domestically. Hence, imports are 215 units. A tariff of *T* per unit raises the domestic price to $p_W + T$. At this price, quantity demanded drops to 200 units, domestic producers supply 85 of them, and imports fall to 115 units (200 – 85). Area *a* represents a transfer of surplus from consumers to producers, areas *c* plus *d* represent the revenue raised by the tariff, and areas *b* and *e* represent net social losses from the tariff.

12. An import quota is a limit on the number of units of a good that can enter a country. A quota of 115 units generates the same results as the tariff of *T*. The relevant supply curve is $S + 115$ (see the graph in answer 11). With a quota, price increases from p_W to $p_W + T$, and imports are at 115 units. The revenue shown by areas *c* plus *d* no longer flows to the government but instead is a transfer from consumers to firms that obtain the right to import the good.

13. In the graph in answer 11, the tariff was shown to increase domestic production of the good from 30 to 85 units. This increase in production creates jobs for people in the industry. However, the tariff does not necessarily create a net increase in jobs. If we buy fewer imports we usually sell fewer exports, so some people may lose their jobs in the export industries.

14. Trading blocs violate the GATT provision that requires all members of the GATT agreement to treat all the other members equally with respect to trade. Trade blocs require an exemption from the GATT rules.

15. Mexican workers compete by receiving lower wages. The lower wages are necessary to counteract the greater productivity of American workers.

16. Protecting one industry often requires protecting other industries. For example, protecting the textile industry raises the price of textiles for the clothing industry, which may in turn require protection because of its higher costs. Since protection creates higher profits for domestic firms, firms may lobby for protection; the resources expended on lobbying are also lost to the economy. Further, it is often difficult to police and enforce trade restrictions.

17. The higher price of steel raises costs to U.S. auto makers, which will lead to a higher price for domestic autos and more imports. This may lead the auto makers to lobby for a tariff or quota on autos.

18. The winners are the domestic producers of goods that compete with imports (and their employees), who receive higher prices as a result of trade restrictions. With an import quota, those to whom the quota is allocated are also winners. The losers are consumers, domestic producers who use imported intermediate goods, and producers (and their employees) in export industries, especially if other countries respond to tariffs by instituting tariffs of their own. Firms facing stiff competition from trade are obviously harmed a great deal by the competition, so they have a strong incentive to lobby Congress for protection. Consumers are harmed by protection, but no single consumer is harmed enough to make it worth his or her while to lobby against a tariff bill. Hence, Congress is likely to pass a given trade restriction bill.